Michigan
GARDENER'S
GUIDE

The What, Where, When, How & Why
Of Gardening In Michigan

Michigan
GARDENER'S
GUIDE

TIMOTHY BOLAND
LAURA E. COIT
MARTY HAIR

COOL
SPRINGS
PRESS

Hair, Marty.
   The Michigan Gardener's Guide by Timothy Boland, Laura E. Coit and Marty Hair.

   p.   cm.
   Includes bibliographical references and index.
   ISBN 1-888608-29-3
   1. Gardening, Michigan 2. Michigan, Gardening, Guidebooks.
   I. Boland, Timothy. II. Coit, Laura E. III. Title.
635.9--dc20
Bol/Coi/Hai

Cool Springs Press, Inc.
118 Fourth Avenue South
Franklin, Tennessee 37064

First printing 1997
Printed in the United States of America
10 9 8 7 6 5 4 3

On the cover (clockwise beginning upper left): Yellowwood, Pansy, Lilac, Common Tulip.

Cover design by Patterson and Graham

Photographs by Horticultural Printers

Map provided by Agricultural Research Service, USDA

Visit the Cool Springs Press website at:

   www.coolspringspress.com

ACKNOWLEDGEMENTS

WE ARE GRATEFUL TO THE MANY PEOPLE who generously shared their horticultural knowledge during the preparation of this book.

For their technical assistance and support, we especially thank Jim Adams, Doug Badgero, Bob Bricault, Andrew Bunting, William Carlson, Frederick Case, Carolyn Coit, Lowell Ewart, Tim Flint, Bruce Fox, Erica Glasener, Nancy Goulette, Susan Gruber, Ann Hancock, and George Hartley.

We also thank Judy Hollingworth, Don Juchartz, Scott Kunst, Greg Lyman, Cheryl Lyon-Jenness, Nancy McDonald, David Michener, Stuart Ouwinga, Paul Rieke, Miriam Rutz, Donna Schumann, Patty Shea, Jane Taylor, Lee Taylor, and Frank Telewski.

The publisher wishes to thank Andrew Bunting of the Scott Arboretum at Swarthmore College for serving as horticultural editor.

6

CONTENTS

The Pleasure of Michigan Gardening

WHY GARDEN IN MICHIGAN? Because it's a pleasure. The landscape stages its own theater, a natural drama in four acts. The plot unfolds with new life in spring that turns lush and green in summer, transforms to brilliant golds and reds in autumn, and lies serenely dormant in winter. Gardening heightens our awareness of the seasons and cycles of nature, bringing it right into our own backyards.

Michigan's motto—"If you seek a pleasant peninsula, look about you"—is as true of its gardens as of its sandy lakeshores, fields, and woods. The state's unique climate, geography, and natural features make it a special place to tend a plot of land.

This book is for people wondering which of the thousands of plants available will do best in Michigan gardens. We include profiles of 175 trees, shrubs, and flowering and foliage plants as well as lawn grasses selected because they will thrive here. We also explain how to plant and care for each of them.

Gardening is America's most popular hobby, and it is immensely popular in Michigan. The opportunity to be outside is certainly a good reason to garden, and studies suggest that tending plants or even just looking at them from a window offers rewards in improved physical and mental well-being.

Compared to residents of some other parts of the country, Michigan gardeners are lucky. Our climate offers enough warmth, sunlight, and natural moisture to support a richly diverse group of both native and cultivated plants. Snow cover, prevalent in most parts of the state, insulates plants in winter. Soils range from sandy to loamy to clay, but, for the most part, they are fertile enough to grow beautiful gardens.

Introduction

The climate may concern newcomers, especially those moving to Michigan from warmer climates. It's true that for several months of the year the weather here can be gray or snowy and cold. That doesn't mean, however, that gardens have to be boring in winter. Selecting woody plants with interesting bark and colorful fruits, incorporating ornamental grasses, and planning for good landscape design make for an attractive garden in every season. So while gardening in Michigan is full of challenges, it's just as full of rewards.

MICHIGAN'S GARDENING TRADITIONS

Michigan is a vast state—more than 400 miles from the Upper Peninsula's Copper Harbor on Lake Superior to Monroe near the state's southeastern border—and its climate is varied. Perhaps for these reasons, and because the population is spread over such a large area, there is no single style of gardening in Michigan or even a trademark plant that characterizes Michigan gardens.

Still, Michigan has a rich tradition of people who cared about gardening and horticulture. Native Americans who lived in the area used plants for food, medicine, and many other purposes. According to legend, they showed French explorers how to make a vitamin-rich tea from white cedar, and the grateful French nick-named the plant "tree of life" or arborvitae.

According to Miriam Rutz, a landscape historian at Michigan State University, the French explorer Cadillac brought a gardener to Detroit in the early 1700s to design gardens and orchards and southeastern Michigan was famous for its gardens for the next 150 years.

The earliest scientific explorer to visit the region was Thomas Nuttall, a botanist who visited the Great Lakes in 1810 to survey what was growing here. Nuttall found nearly two dozen plants that had never before been described including, at Mackinac Island, the dwarf lake iris, *Iris lacustris*. The only place in the world where this plant exists is along the northern Great Lakes shoreline, mainly in Michigan. It is on the state and federal lists of threatened plants.

Michigan became the first state west of the Alleghenies to form agricultural and horticultural societies, which were organized in the 1840s and 1850s, according to Miriam Rutz's research. What is now Michigan State University was founded in 1855 as the Agricultural College of the State of Michigan, and it has had a continuing impact on research and teaching about horticulture, gardening, and agriculture. An early professor was William J. Beal, a native of the Adrian area, who taught botany, horticulture, and forestry from 1870 to 1910.

One of Beal's experiments is still going on. In 1888, he buried many bottles containing weed seeds, with the idea of digging up a bottle every 5 years and then planting the seeds to see how long they would remain viable, or able to grow. Since Beal's death, others have continued this germination project, and the time between unearthing the bottles is now 20 years. Mullein seeds that are more than a century old continue to germinate! Beal was also instrumental in the establishment in 1873 of the W. J. Beal Botanic Garden, one of the oldest continuously operating botanical gardens in the country.

One of Beal's students was South Haven native Liberty Hyde Bailey, who became a horticulture professor in 1885 and chaired the first horticulture department in the nation at what is now Michigan State University. Bailey is recognized as the dean of American horticulture. He wrote nearly 200 books on horticulture and agriculture, and he led a national commission on country life, which resulted in the formation of the Cooperative Extension Service and its youth component, 4-H, around the country. Bailey, who later moved to Cornell University, raised the study of agriculture to a science.

Outside the universities, the mid- to late 19th Century was a time of tremendous interest in gardening and horticulture as well as agricultural expansion. Nurseries and seed merchants were opening, among them Dexter Ferry in Detroit. At one time, his company, later

Introduction

Ferry-Morse, was the world's largest producer and distributor of garden seeds.

Gardening and plant study were popular activities, and some residents scoured their regions collecting plants. Some collections are preserved at the University of Michigan, founded in 1817, and at Michigan State University.

As new residents arrived in Michigan from other countries, they brought with them their own traditions of gardening. German, Italian, Irish, Polish, and Scandinavian people, as well as others, located here. People from Holland settled in western Michigan, and their strong interest in gardening is reflected in the area's commercial horticulture industry, private and public gardens, and the annual Holland Tulip Festival, which now draws a million visitors and features more than 2 1/2 million tulips in flower.

In the later 1800s, people indulged in the Victorian gardening craze of carpet bedding, where annuals are arranged in colorful patterns. You can see an example of this style of gardening on the grounds of the state Capitol in Lansing.

As the 1800s ended and the 1900s began, women's clubs across Michigan were working on civic improvements, creating and landscaping parks and school yards, and planting trees. When Michigan's farm population peaked in 1912, membership in the Grange was 52,836. The Grange supported development of 4-H and sponsored fairs, as well as many other activities.

In 1920, Genevieve Gillette became the first woman to graduate from the landscape architecture curriculum at what is now Michigan State University. She worked on many projects, including a low-cost housing development where she incorporated "thrift gardens" so that each family could raise its own vegetables. Gillette also led campaigns for the formation of state and national parks in Michigan.

Introduction

Louisa Yeomans King gardened in Michigan, but her work and insights were recognized throughout the whole country in her day. King, who described gardening as "this art, this adorable occupation," moved to Alma with her husband, Francis King, in 1907. She created gardens around their home, Orchard House, and became a garden writer whose work was published in many national magazines and books. In 1912, King founded the Garden Club of Michigan, and she became one of the first vice-presidents of the Garden Club of America the following year. She was the inaugural president of the Woman's National Farm and Garden Association in 1914.

In the first decades of the 20th Century, Michigan's wealthy industrialists were intrigued by formal French and Italian landscapes, and their properties reflected that design influence. Meanwhile, both Henry Ford and Edsel Ford hired Chicago landscape architect Jens Jensen to map out more naturalistic landscapes using many native plants. The era of the estate gardens lasted until the Depression.

With progressive landscapes in public parks as well as private residences, Michigan had an active gardening culture through the 1920s. The southwestern part of the state was especially influenced by the prairie style of landscape design popular in Chicago, according to David Michener, assistant curator of the Matthaei Botanical Gardens in Ann Arbor.

Gardening and horticulture, both as hobbies and as businesses, got a boost as greenhouses became more common and provided a way to overwinter plant material, according to William Carlson, professor of horticulture at Michigan State University.

Commercial vegetable production thrived in Michigan in the 1920s and 1930s. After World War II, some of that work shifted to California, and the smaller growers who remained in Michigan turned to selling flats of annuals at local markets to supplement

Introduction

their incomes. The bedding plant industry has continued to grow, and Michigan now ranks third in the nation. The state's wholesale floriculture industry—including indoor plants, bedding plants, cut flowers, and foliage plants—generates nearly $300 million a year.

In both World Wars I and II, Michigan gardeners put their patriotism in the soil when their government asked them to plant first Liberty Gardens and then Victory Gardens. There were 800,000 Victory Gardens statewide in 1943.

The interest in gardening seems to be stronger than ever and gardeners are growing more sophisticated all the time. For one thing, more information is available. Magazines, books, and cable TV channels make it possible to learn about gardening any hour, day or night. Plant catalogs are carried on the Internet.

People who want to join gardening groups have many to choose from, among them hosta, bonsai, cacti and succulent, and rose societies. There are also active garden clubs including chapters of the Federated Garden Clubs of Michigan, the National Woman's Farm and Garden Club, and the Garden Club of Michigan, in addition to men's gardening groups. They hold meetings, set up educational programs, and organize civic improvements; many also sponsor summer garden tours that are open to the public. More than 10,000 state residents have attended classes and satisfied the volunteer requirements that qualify them as Michigan Master Gardeners in a program administered through the Michigan State University Extension.

KNOW YOUR ZONE

During the summer, people often discuss the heat and its effects on plants. But the degree of cold in the winter is also important in determining which plants will survive.

The U.S. Department of Agriculture (USDA) has divided a map of the country into layers called hardiness zones based on their average minimum winter temperatures. Michigan's coldest areas, in the interior northern Lower as well as the central and western Upper Peninsula, are classified as Zone 3, with average winter lows from -30 to -40 degrees Fahrenheit. A few spots of southern Michigan are in the relatively balmy Zone 6, with an average minimum expected temperature of zero to -10 degrees Fahrenheit.

This book includes a map of Michigan showing the USDA hardiness zones (see page 19), and each plant profile lists the zones for which the plant is recommended. Being aware of zones is especially important when ordering plants from mail-order catalogs.

Even within a zone, there are often significant variations. Soil, rainfall, exposure, and humidity can all affect plant hardiness. Valleys or low areas frequently have late frosts. Areas near large lakes will have longer growing seasons than areas far inland. City dwellers find their average temperatures warmer than those in surrounding rural areas because the concentration of buildings, cement, asphalt, and pollution means more heat is retained.

Michigan's growing season, measured from the last frost in the spring to the first frost in the fall, varies from about 70 to 170 days in different parts of the state. The last frost date in spring is especially important in determining when it is safe to plant annuals and vegetables outdoors. If you don't know your local frost dates, call the county office of the MSU Extension.

The Great Lakes that nearly surround Michigan act as a cushion, keeping the temperature lower in summer and warmer in winter than in surrounding states. The lake effect brings moisture—and, yes, more clouds—but Michigan gardeners are most interested in the resulting moderate temperatures and abundant water. This moderating effect is also a reason for the state's commercial success in growing fruit. Michigan ranks fifth nationally in value of fruit production, with many growers concentrated along the Lake Michigan shoreline.

Introduction

PLANT FOR YOUR SITE

Just as in choosing real estate, the three most important things to consider when selecting a plant are location, location, and location. Analyze the site and the amount of sun it gets, the kind of soil, and its hardiness zone. Match the plant to the site. That gives the plants a good chance at staying healthy, which is the best way for them to resist pests and disease.

Soil has several components. There are tiny fragments of rock and minerals. The decomposing bits of plants and animals make up the soil's organic material. Soil also contains air, water, and small organisms.

Its texture depends on how much sand, silt, or clay the soil contains. Sand is grainy and has the largest-sized particles. A handful of sand will fall apart when released. Silt has a texture often described as floury or smooth. Wet clay feels slippery and remains in a ball when squeezed.

The ideal garden soil in general is sandy loam, which contains sand, clay, and silt and has a porous structure. If that's not what is in your garden, don't despair. You can improve your soil by adding organic material such as well-rotted compost, shredded leaves, or aged manure. This improves the drainage and porosity of heavy clay soils. It also helps sandy soils by making them better able to retain moisture. In the soil, worms, bacteria, and other microorganisms feed on the organic material and break it down, making more nutrients available for the plants.

For a free source of organic material, start a compost pile. Add leaves, healthy plant material, soil, vegetable scraps from the kitchen, and moisten the pile regularly. The material will break down into what gardeners call "black gold." For more on how to start a compost pile, consult your local extension office or a book on the subject.

Introduction

Plants need a number of nutrients for growth—including nitrogen, phosphorus, potassium, and others that may be found in the soil—in addition to hydrogen, oxygen, and carbon. To determine if necessary nutrients are lacking in your soil, call your county office of the MSU Extension and get instructions on how to take a soil test for analysis at Michigan State University. The soil test results will also tell you the soil pH, or whether the soil is acidic or on the alkaline side. This is important because the soil's pH determines what nutrients are available to plants.

A soil that is rich in organic material will provide adequate nutrients for many garden plants. The plants selected for this book do not require much—or, sometimes, any—additional fertilization. See specific chapters and entries for recommendations.

The biggest challenge for gardeners in many parts of Michigan is the growing population of foraging deer. Some gardeners use electric fences to keep the deer out. Check with your county extension office for other possible ways to deter deer.

LIGHT REQUIREMENTS

For best growing results, plants need to be placed where they will receive the proper amount of light. The light requirements are indicated in each plant profile. The following symbols indicate full sun, partial sun, and shade:

Full Sun   Partial   Shade
             Sun

PLANTS AND NAMES

This book uses both common and botanical names for plants. If you rely on common names, you may be disappointed, especially if you're ordering from a catalog and the plant you receive turns out

Introduction

to be different from the one you wanted. In contrast, the botanical name is unique to each plant and identifies exactly which one you have in mind.

Botanical names follow a system called binomial nomenclature. The first Latin word identifies the genus while the second word is the species. For instance, *Stachys byzantina* 'Silver Carpet' is an especially desirable lamb's ear that rarely flowers. *Stachys* is the genus name, *byzantina* is the species, and 'Silver Carpet' is the name of the cultivar (cultivated variety).

Don't be intimidated by botanical names. The more you use them, the easier they become. A wise gardener, discussing the use of Latin names, once said, "Say it with authority and no one will doubt you."

HOW TO USE THIS BOOK
The plants are divided into chapters—annuals, groundcovers, hardy bulbs, lawns, ornamental grasses, perennials, roses, shrubs, trees, and woodland flowers and ferns. Each plant profile includes specific information as well as suggestions on how to incorporate the plant into your landscape. The ones we include are generally easy to grow and relatively free of pests and diseases. We had to make choices and in some cases excluded favorite garden plants because they didn't meet the easy-to-grow, trouble-free criteria.

We also omitted plants that can outcompete native plants. Both ivy and vinca, two of the most popular and widely used groundcovers, will choke out native plants if they escape from gardens and grow into natural areas; so will most types of the popular perennial purple loosestrife (*Lythrum* sp.). This concern is particularly relevant for people whose property borders wetlands, water, or woods because seeds can be carried a distance by wind, water, and birds.

Other plants to avoid because of these tendencies are autumn olive (*Elaeagnus umbellata*), common and tallhedge buckthorn

Introduction

(*Rhamnus catharticus* and *R. frangula*), crown vetch (*Coronilla varia*), several species of honeysuckle (*Lonicera*), Norway maple (*Acer platanoides*), and Oriental or round-leaved bittersweet (*Celastrus orbiculatus*).

The MSU Extension offers many publications about home horticulture, most either free or very inexpensive. For a free copy of the publications catalog, write to the Michigan State University Bulletin Office, 10-B Agriculture Hall, Michigan State University, East Lansing, MI 48824-1039.

ENJOY GARDENING IN MICHIGAN

Michigan offers a unique gardening experience. Capitalize on it by creating a distinctly Michigan garden. Use native plants to their best advantage. Play up the changing seasons. Strive to choose the right plant for the site, and allow plenty of time to enjoy what you create.

Have fun, and know that there are no hard-and-fast rules in gardening. Don't be a slave to advice. Instead, experiment to learn what works best for you. Take time to teach youngsters about the pleasures of gardening, and let them experiment, too. You'll be enjoying quality family time and making sure that a new generation will continue Michigan's long gardening tradition.

"Resolved: to have a garden. If this wish is sincere, the garden will materialize. If ground is unpromising, it can be made good. If the size of lot is small, then ingenuity and imagination must be specially brought to bear upon it. With these, and taste, the smallest garden will be far more lovely than the largest without them."

—Louisa Yeomans King, *The Flower Garden Day by Day*, 1927

USDA HARDINESS ZONE MAP

Michigan

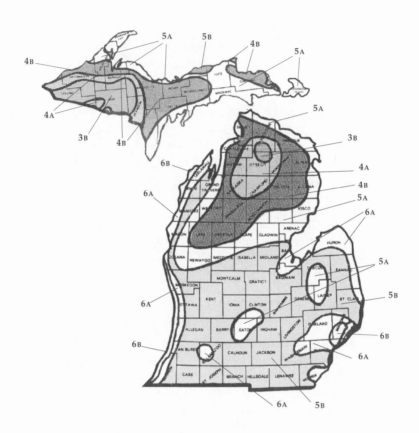

AVERAGE ANNUAL MINIMUM TEMPERATURE

3B	-30° F TO -35° F
4A	-25° F TO -30° F
4B	-20° F TO -25° F
5A	-15° F TO -20° F
5B	-10° F TO -15° F
6A	-5° F TO -10° F
6B	0° F TO -5° F

Annuals

*E*VERY YEAR IN MAY, WORKERS AT GARDEN CENTERS, NURSERIES, and farmers' markets all over Michigan set out colorful flats of annuals. Gardeners respond happily, buying their favorite flowers to plant outdoors as warm weather approaches.

This rite of spring celebrates the group of flowering plants called annuals. Annuals are plants that grow from seed, bloom, and set seed in one growing season, dying by the time winter arrives.

Michigan is a national leader in annual bedding plant production. Our selection of annuals is vast, and these flowers are fun and easy to grow. Annuals make it possible to fill a bed, border, container, or hanging basket with color that lasts from late spring until frost, all at a relatively low cost. Want something different next year? With annuals, the gardener has a clean slate every spring.

Many of us are introduced to annuals as youngsters, perhaps raising a few marigold seeds in a cup for an elementary school project or cultivating a small plot of cosmos in the backyard. Years later, grownup beginning gardeners usually start out with annuals. They are vibrantly colored, forgiving of less-than-perfect care or conditions, and highly productive—the perfect plants to boost a neophyte's confidence by yielding beautiful results.

Annuals also deserve a spot in the more experienced gardener's collection. Even sophisticates who scoff at a brash stand of screaming scarlet salvia or some other extremely bold display still rely on annuals for cut flowers and for summer color in flower beds.

There are many reasons to grow annuals. Most important is their long season of bloom. Annuals are blanketed with blossoms from June and July through the first fall frosts. Even a long-blooming perennial such as *Coreopsis verticillata* 'Moonbeam' can't top that!

Chapter One

Annuals begin to flower soon after they are planted, taking the garden from plain to drop-dead gorgeous in a relatively short time. Annuals, which generally grow in the top 8 inches of soil, are less demanding about elaborate soil preparation than are longer-lived plants.

Some annuals are well suited to the casual cottage style of gardening with its wide array of hues, heights, and textures. Others are bred to stay compact. These are used extensively in commercial beddings as well as home landscapes.

Our grandparents and even their grandparents grew many of the same annuals we grow today. Victorians loved to create patterns by carefully arranging annuals in carpet beds. These low-growing formal displays could be intricate and artistic or brazen and gaudy, depending on the designer and colors used. Either way, they certainly drew attention.

Hybridizers are constantly developing new varieties of annuals, many with disease resistance and other important characteristics that were unavailable a generation ago. In addition, many heirloom varieties are being rediscovered for their quaint charm and more natural habits.

Planting and Caring for Your Annuals

Many popular annuals are available two ways—as seed to start indoors under lights well before the last expected frost in spring, or as young plants in multiple containers called cell-packs that can be purchased at garden centers and nurseries in April, May, and June. Some may be sown directly in the garden in late spring. Some will self-sow, resulting in new plants growing from seed the following year.

It is usually suggested that the beginning gardener buy transplants rather than start seed indoors. Transplants are readily available. Growing plants from seed can take as long as 12 weeks and requires special lighting, considerable skill, and patience. Starting seed does appeal to more advanced gardeners because they can then grow more unusual varieties that are not available locally.

Chapter One

When to plant annuals depends on the date of the last expected frost in your area. If you are not sure of that date, call your county's MSU Extension office to find out.

Look for healthy transplants that are a rich green color and have sturdy stems. The choicest will have few if any flowers at time of purchase. Plants without flowers are more likely to have better root systems.

Plants started inside or those straight from a commercial green-house should be "hardened off"—gradually acclimated to outdoor conditions—for several days before planting in the garden. Move the pots or trays outside to a place sheltered from direct sun and wind for a few hours. Take them back inside at night. Every day, give the plants a bit more time outside, returning them to the house at night. After 5 to 7 days, the plants should be tough enough to tolerate the great outdoors.

Before planting annuals, check out the area where they will be planted and amend the soil as needed. The soil should be of at least average fertility and well drained. Adding generous amounts of well-rotted compost, decomposed leaves or leaf mold, or aged manure will improve both heavy clay and sandy soils. Don't econo-mize on this step! Investing in plants without first correcting soil or drainage problems is a waste of time and money.

Loosen the soil in the bed to a depth of at least 8 to 12 inches. Remove weeds and debris. For a mass planting, you can use a bulb planter to make planting holes quickly.

Pop the young plants from their cell-packs by squeezing the bottoms and pushing up. This is far kinder to the plant than grab-bing it by the leaves or stem and yanking. If the roots are compacted and intertwined into a tight ball, loosen the roots slightly with your fingers so they will spread readily once they make contact with the soil.

Annuals are generally planted at the same depth in the soil that they were growing in the container. Pinch off any flowers or buds at planting time to direct the plant's energy to getting established.

Chapter One

After planting, firm the soil around the plant and water well. Then give the transplants a boost of starter fertilizer such as 3-10-3. Some gardeners prefer to mix a slow-release fertilizer with the soil at planting time. This will last the entire growing season. Water the annuals and they'll soon start performing.

If you did not use slow-release fertilizer, feed annuals every few weeks or every month, depending on the plant and your garden's soil fertility. The annuals selected for this book are generally resistant to serious pests and diseases.

As the season progresses, provide water during dry periods. Water wands, or long metal arms with rain nozzles that may be attached to the hose, make it possible to apply moisture to the soil without drenching the plant's foliage. Wet leaves make the plant more disease-prone.

Keep the soil around the annuals weed-free so they won't have to compete for moisture or nutrients. Mulching around the annuals with a 2- to 3-inch layer of finely shredded bark, cocoa hulls, or other organic material helps prevent moisture in the soil from evaporating and discourages weeds. Maintain a mulch-free zone of several inches around the base of the plant so air can circulate.

Many annuals will continue blooming most of the season if they are deadheaded regularly. To deadhead, pinch off the faded flowers before they go to seed. Deadheading also keeps the plants looking neat and attractive.

Some annuals, such as impatiens and coleus, are easy to dig up and pot at summer's end to be brought indoors. They will provide welcome flower and foliage color in winter, and they may be cut back in early spring, yielding more stems to root and plant outside.

Brazilian Verbena

Verbena bonariensis

Height: 3 to 4 ft.
Flowers: Red-violet
Bloom Period: Early summer to frost
Zones: 4, 5, 6
Light Requirement:

Verbena bonariensis, in cultivation since the middle of the 18th Century, has recently become trendy in the United States. Tall, often reaching 4 ft., Brazilian verbena adds height and color to annual beds and perennial borders from July until frost. The square stems are tall and lanky. Group plants for the best effect or grow them up through lower-growing perennials. A single plant with its stiff, bare stems has a sculptural quality that is interesting in a front location. Each erect, virtually naked stem (very little foliage is produced) is topped with clustered heads of deep lavender-violet flowers. Flowers are produced freely in full sun. Well-grown plants create an airy cloud of luminous purple. No annual, except perhaps the cosmos, has a similar combination of height and grace that makes Brazilian verbena a perfect accent for perennial beds. It is particularly useful to add interest to newly established areas, where tall perennials have not yet reached their mature size. In the fall, *Verbena bonariensis* combines attractively with the white aster-like flowers of boltonia and the early orange-red autumn color of flame grass. Fill an informal large annual bed with Brazilian verbena, orange zinnias, and the acid yellow flowers and feathery foliage of dill. In full flower, this combination will attract a crowd of butterflies. The stiff, straight stems make Brazilian verbena a favorite with flower arrangers. The small flowers continue to open in a vase for more than a week. Brazilian verbena is a self-sower. Unless the flowers are deadheaded, scads of seedlings will appear the following year.

WHEN TO PLANT
Plant in the garden in spring after the danger of frost is past. Seed may be germinated inside and transplanted into the garden.

WHERE TO PLANT
Brazilian verbena is tolerant of a wide range of soils, from heavy moist soil to sandy, dry soil. Full sun is necessary for best growth. Plant in perennial beds, mixed beds, meadow-type plantings, and in cutflower gardens. Consider using this verbena as a tall accent in a

large planter. Self-sown plants will often surprise the gardener by finding their own best location.

How to Plant

Plants are increasingly available in cell-packs but they look like lanky stalks with few leaves when offered for sale in the spring. Don't be discouraged. Remove the young plants from the cell-pack and plant in the garden at the same level they were growing in the pack. Pinch back to 3 sets of leaves to create stocky, well-branched plants. Firm the soil around the transplants and then water. Seeds can also be sown in the garden. Follow the directions on the packet. Direct-sown plants will bloom later. Spacing closely (8 to 10 in.) will produce an airy mass of tangled stems.

Advice for Care

Mulch to discourage volunteers if you are concerned about self-sown seedlings. Removing spent flowers before the seed scatters will also help.

Additional Information

Seed of Brazilian verbena is easy to collect and save for spring sowing or to share with friends. The flat-topped clusters attract butterflies.

Additional Species, Cultivars, or Varieties

Most gardeners are familiar with the common garden verbena, *Verbena × hybrida* (8 to 12 in.), an excellent trailing annual for heat tolerance and summer flowers. Typically red, purple, magenta, or white, the selection 'Peaches and Cream' has beautiful elegant pale peach- and salmon-colored flowers. *Verbena tenuisecta* 'Imagination' (10 to 12 in.) is similar in habit to the garden verbena, but the foliage is lacy and the small flowers in 2-in. umbels are purple. Heat- and drought-tolerant, 'Imagination' can tumble out of a container, edge a walk, or fill in the front of a well-drained perennial bed. Space at 12 to 14 in. for an annual groundcover. In full sun, 'Imagination' verbena adds color from summer until frost to a perennial planting of mother-of-thyme and lamb's ears. Both 'Peaches and Cream' and 'Imagination' are All-America Selection award-winners.

Cleome

Cleome hasslerana

Other Name: Spider Flower
Height: 4 to 5 ft.
Flowers: Pink, lavender,
purple, rose, white
Bloom Period: Midsummer
to frost
Zones: 4, 5, 6
Light Requirement:

For informal, sunny gardens, cleome or spider flower is an outstanding annual. It's tough, yet airy and tall with a breezy, casual look. Cleome is perfect for planting behind other plants in a border or in a bed all its own, although it is more attractive with shorter plants in front to mask its somewhat rangy stems. From seed or purchased transplants, cleome quickly leaps to 4 ft. or even taller and spreads about 2 ft. wide. Its globe-shaped blooms begin in midsummer and are not only colorful, they're downright interesting. The flowers have curving stamens and are followed by intriguing seedpods. Cleome blooms through the fall with little care. Like most good things, cleome has a downside. Its leaves are sticky and the stem is thorny. It self-seeds freely, a characteristic that won't appeal to fastidious gardeners or to those with formal landscapes. Many people choose to remove the volunteer cleome plants. Some people find cleome unpleasantly fragrant, although others don't notice much of a scent. All in all, cleome's advantages outweigh its drawbacks. It is a strong performer, creating a colorful presence, towering over nearby plants. It was a favorite of Victorian gardeners, who often featured cleome as the tall central component of a circular bedding scheme. Gardeners who desire an airy, colorful, and freely flowering annual will appreciate cleome.

WHEN TO PLANT
Sow seed indoors 3 to 4 weeks before last frost and harden-off young plants before setting into the garden. Cleome may also be sown directly outdoors in late spring, or purchased as young plants to set out in late spring. It may be difficult to find at garden centers, since spider flower or cleome won't be in bloom in cell-packs.

WHERE TO PLANT

Plant cleome in a sunny, well-drained spot—the more sun, the better. Space plants 2 ft. apart. Keep this tall annual at the rear of the border. It makes a fine display behind perennials or in a mixed cottage garden with white, blue, pink, and purple flowers.

HOW TO PLANT

Sow seeds at the depth recommended on the seed packet. When transplanting, gently squeeze the bottom of the flexible container and push up the plant to avoid pulling it by the leaves. Plant at the same depth it was growing in the container. After planting, feed with a transplant fertilizer such as 3-10-3.

ADVICE FOR CARE

Cleome, which is native to South America, excels in hot weather. It also tolerates dry soil. In poor soils, the application of a balanced fertilizer such as 10-10-10 a few times during the growing season may be beneficial. Leave mature flowers on the plant so they will form attractive seedpods, or deadhead to encourage additional blooms and to eliminate self-sowing.

ADDITIONAL INFORMATION

Cleome is usually free of serious pests or diseases. Some gardeners stake tall varieties early in the summer to help cleome stand up to summer wind and rain storms. It can get topheavy and somewhat floppy as the season progresses. Use cleome as an annual screen or grow it against a wall or fence. A single cleome plant makes a more restrained statement, but it is still boldly vertical. Cleome is a fine cut flower as long as the fragrance, which is quite variable depending on the plant and the person sniffing it, isn't deemed unpleasant.

ADDITIONAL SPECIES, CULTIVARS, OR VARIETIES

'Helen Campbell' is a favorite with white flowers. Cleomes in the 'Queen' series, such as 'Pink Queen', are widely available in shades of pink, violet, and white.

Coleus

Coleus × hybridus

Height: 1 to 2 ft.
Flowers: Coleus is grown for its colorful foliage
Zones: 3, 4, 5, 6
Light Requirement:

There's nothing shy about coleus. This is a shade plant with a cutting-edge attitude. Its bright, improbable, even gaudy colors—neon green, pink, bronze, white, maroon, chartreuse—add irreverent zip to a shady spot. The result is an exuberant and almost tropical mood. A member of the mint family, coleus has flowering spikes, but they're quite forgettable when compared with its spectacular leaves. In fact, it's best to pinch off the flower spikes as they appear to encourage foliar growth. There are scores of varieties and color combinations to choose from, some with frilled leaf edges. Coleus is easy to grow from seed and equally easy to root from cuttings in water, making it a favorite plant for student observation in plant science and botany classes. In the classroom of the outdoor garden, coleus is a wake-up call in dark and shady corners. Its surprising colors are intensified in the shade. Coleus grows in leafy, erect mounds about 1 to 2 ft. high and wide and thrives in a location where there is plenty of moisture. This plant is eager to please. If it gets too tall or spindly, simply pinch it back to encourage bushier growth.

WHEN TO PLANT

Purchase young plants to set outdoors after the weather warms. Coleus is sensitive to frost, so it's better to wait than to rush to plant outdoors. After planting, feed with a transplant fertilizer such as 3-10-3.

WHERE TO PLANT

Coleus grows best in well-drained soil and light filtered shade to full shade. In areas with more light, it should be protected from direct afternoon exposure and may wilt without enough moisture. A mulch is recommended. Even in the shade, coleus may require frequent watering, but it is not fussy about soil fertility. It is appropriate for beds, borders, windowboxes, or containers, or to grow in pots as a houseplant. Use it in a shady area to plant over and hide dying daffodil leaves.

How to Plant

Space plants 8 to 12 in. apart. Plants may be pinched back at transplanting time to encourage branching, although some newer selections are bushier and don't need pinching back.

Advice for Care

Do not allow coleus to dry out. Feed with a general fertilizer such as 10-10-10 every 3 weeks if desired. Stems of coleus may be cut in late summer or early fall to bring indoors. Root in water or sand and then pot. Keep the plants where they will receive bright light and cool room temperatures. Take more cuttings in spring to plant outdoors.

Additional Information

With so many colors of coleus available, it's best to limit a planting to one or two main colors to make a strong, clear statement. Coleus calls attention to shady areas, where it teams beautifully with hostas, ferns, and astilbes, especially white ones such as 'Bridal Veil'. Use several coleus plants alone in a container for a stunning effect, or combine them with other plants. The ones with darker foliage set off other plants especially well. Choose dwarf varieties for windowboxes and pots, and pinch back the plants to prevent them from getting too tall. The festive foliage of coleus adds zip to the usual cast of shady characters, including impatiens, begonias, hostas, and astilbes.

Additional Species, Cultivars, or Varieties

The 'Carefree' series remains short. 'Figi' coleus has frilled leaves. Coleus in the 'Wizard' series are fairly compact at 10 to 12 in. tall with large leaves.

Cosmos

Cosmos bipinnatus

Height: 12 in. to 5 ft.
Flowers: Pink, white, light-
purple
Bloom Period: Midsummer
to frost
Zones: 3, 4, 5, 6
Light Requirement:

The tall, waving stems and daisy-like flowers of cosmos are perfect for rustic cottage gardens or beds where the goal is a loose, relaxed effect. Cosmos is easy to start from seed sown directly in the garden in late spring, making it a wonderful annual for children to grow. It is reliable and grows quickly to several feet tall, sometimes even taller than the young gardeners who cultivate it. Flower petals, which are actually separate ray flowers, have notched edges as though they'd been trimmed with pinking shears, and are available in several colors as well as singles and doubles. The bright yellow centers of cosmos are really its disk flowers. Excellent for cutting and use in arrangements, cosmos blooms from July until frost. These plants almost thrive on neglect, requiring little in the way of care when grown in full sun. Give them an occasional drink of water during dry periods. They are native from Mexico to Brazil and do best during warm weather. Cosmos is lovely in available spots in perennial beds or an informal meadow-type planting. Its ferny leaves, branching form, and substantial height create a painterly, romantic effect. It is particularly charming behind a white picket fence or against a dark stone wall. Give it plenty of room to sprawl and spread, then sit back and enjoy the show.

WHEN TO PLANT

Start cosmos seeds indoors under lights about 4 weeks before the last spring frost or buy transplants. Cosmos is easy to transplant and usually establishes quickly once the soil warms. Or sow directly in the garden in late spring.

WHERE TO PLANT

Give cosmos a location in full sun. Well-drained soil is a must. Cosmos tolerates soils of poor to average fertility. Too rich a soil or too much fertilizer makes for lush leaves and few flowers. Plant cosmos behind other annuals and perennials, where its graceful stems will wave in the breeze. It may be planted in a bed all its own or in a cutting garden. Shorter varieties are a good choice for containers.

How to Plant

Accept its rambling form and allow cosmos plenty of space between plants—at least 1 to 2 ft. Pinch back young plants to encourage bushier growth and branching.

Advice for Care

Cosmos grows best in warmer weather. It blooms better with no or minimal fertilizer. Water during dry periods. Taller varieties may be staked or supported by inserting twigs in the soil at the time seeds are planted. As the cosmos grows, it will obscure the twigs and benefit from the support. Cosmos may self-sow.

Additional Information

Cosmos is usually free of serious pests and diseases, although plants may be plagued by mildew late in the season. Space the plants so there is good air circulation between them and avoid wetting the foliage when watering. Sometimes cankers will girdle the stems of cosmos or the plants may be plagued by borers. Remove and destroy affected plants.

Cosmos is especially valuable in hot, sunny locations that might stress more heat-sensitive annuals. Dwarf varieties have a compact, mounded form.

Additional Species, Cultivars, or Varieties

'Sonata' is a favorite because it has 3-in. flowers on relatively small plants, about 24 to 30 in. 'Sensation' cosmos can reach 3$1/2$ ft. with 3-in. flowers. The 'Versailles' series is sturdy and can grow to 4 ft. tall. For hotter colors, look for *Cosmos sulphureus* or yellow cosmos. It has bright yellow to orange-red flowers with yellow centers and grows about 18 to 36 in. Its foliage is not as finely cut as *Cosmos bipinnatus*. Growth requirements are the same. The cultivar 'Diablo' has semi-double flowers in a burnt orange color. 'Sunny Red' grows up 14 in. with red single flowers.

Dusty Miller

Senecio cineraria

Height: 8 to 15 in.
Flowers: Grown for its silver
  leaves
Zones: 3, 4, 5, 6
Light Requirement:

When color in the garden gets a little too hot and heavy, bring in dusty miller. Its silvery foliage brings a visual cool to the reds, oranges, and yellows of many annuals and perennials. A close look at this plant's stems and leaves reveals that they are covered with a thick mat of whitish hairs. Dusty miller's botanical name, *Senecio*, comes from the Latin for "old man." Dusty miller grows in sun to partial sun. Keep it compact and within bounds with one or two prunings during the summer. Plants that are growing in windowboxes are more attractive when kept to a smaller size, perhaps 8 to 9 in. tall. Use dusty miller with red or pink geraniums in a box or containers for a dreamy combination. Many plants grown for foliage prefer the shade, but dusty miller loves the sunny garden, where its cool green-gray leaves provide relief among the annuals and perennials that are revved up in summer's heat.

WHEN TO PLANT
Buy young plants in late spring to set into the garden.

WHERE TO PLANT
Dusty miller may be used in full sun, part sun, or filtered sun, but it performs better in more sunlight. It is equally suited to border, bed, container, or windowbox as long as it has well-drained soil of average fertility. It is excellent for edging, formal bedding, and for creating patterns.

HOW TO PLANT
Space dusty miller about 10 in. apart. Plants in containers may be set closer together. After planting, feed with a transplant fertilizer such as 3-10-3.

ADVICE FOR CARE

To encourage leaf growth, pinch back flowers as they appear. Plants may be fed occasionally with a balanced fertilizer such as 10-10-10. Water when soil is dry. Prune back once or twice a summer to maintain a rounded, compact form. Plants will continue to be attractive into fall, often even after a frost.

ADDITIONAL INFORMATION

Dusty miller—like artemisias, Russian sage, and other plants with silvery green leaves—is invaluable for adding contrast and an almost icy element to the garden palette. Its leaves cool down the bright reds and oranges of hot-colored geraniums, marigolds, and zinnias. It is also lovely among the pinks, purples, and blues of cooler-colored geraniums, impatiens, and lobelia. Some cultivars have leaves that are more finely lobed than others. Dusty miller's silvery color is most pronounced when its leaves are dry.

ADDITIONAL SPECIES, CULTIVARS, OR VARIETIES

'Cirrus' is about 8 in. tall. 'Silver Dust' is the same height, but its leaves are more finely cut. The foliage of 'New Look' is close to white. A different plant with finely cut gray foliage, *Tanacetum ptarmiciflorum* 'Silver Lace', is sometimes sold under the common name of dusty miller.

Flowering Tobacco

Nicotiana alata

Height: 10 to 16 in.
Flowers: White, deep red, pale pink, bright pink, green
Bloom Period: Early summer to frost
Zones: 3, 4, 5, 6
Light Requirement:

Charming flowers on graceful stems, light fragrance, ease of cultivation—finally, a tobacco you can feel good about! Flowering tobacco, *Nicotiana alata*, with its dangling star-shaped trumpets, grows easily in sun or partial shade in Michigan gardens. The light natural appearance of flowering tobacco contrasts well with a wide range of annuals and perennials. A popular annual for nighttime fragrance, the original plant opened its white flowers on lanky stems in the evening and closed in the morning sun. Plant breeders have produced a range of selections. Shorter, more floriferous plants—each plant resembling a bouquet of bloom—are available in a range of colors from white, crimson-red, and shades of pink to a surprisingly refreshing green. Unfortunately, only a trace of the original fragrance remains in the newer plants. Flowering tobacco combines well with perennials and can mask the yellowing foliage of bulbs or add color to newly planted perennial beds. The 'Merlin' (8 to 10 in.), 'Domino' (10 to 14 in.), 'Havana' (12 to 14 in.), and 'Nicki' (18 in.) series all have excellent flower production and extended blooming periods, and have performed well in Michigan. Masses or drifts of a single hue allow you to create planned combinations, while the mixes offer a cheerful, informal abundance of color. Rare among annuals, some selections of flowering tobacco are available with green flowers. Sold as "lime," they are milky green, the color of key lime pie. This easygoing chartreuse mixes well with almost any other flower color, including orange, purple, or magenta! Green-flowered tobaccos can be planted in perennial beds without any worry of a garish clash.

WHEN TO PLANT

Like its kin, the petunias, flowering tobacco is cold-tolerant and may be planted in the garden earlier than more tender annuals. But cautious gardeners wait until the danger of frost is past. When choosing plants, look for healthy rosettes of foliage. Flowering tobacco seldom comes into flower in the cell-pack, which could explain why it's not more common in garden centers. It is possible to sow seed inside for later transplanting to the garden, but this is tricky without a home greenhouse or sunroom.

WHERE TO PLANT
Nicotiana likes moderately rich, well-drained garden soil. Plant in full sun or in locations that receive partial sun. Afternoon shade is particularly beneficial. The white, light pink, and green flowers brighten lightly shaded locations and are attractive with coleus. Flowering tobacco is also nice in planters.

HOW TO PLANT
Gently remove plants from containers or cell-packs—squeeze the sides, don't pull on the stems—and plant in the garden. Make sure the plant is growing at the same soil level in the garden as it was in the container. Firm the soil around the transplant and water. Plant-starter fertilizer, such as 3-10-3, can be applied at this time to encourage root growth. Space plants about 8 in. apart.

ADVICE FOR CARE
Water during hot, dry weather. After the first flush of flowers, plants may need to be deadheaded. Rebloom will occur in a few weeks. Many new varieties bloom almost continuously until frost.

ADDITIONAL INFORMATION
Flowering tobacco can and probably will self-sow. These seedlings will not be the same as the original plants. You can experiment and let them grow, but if you want to retain the original color, weed them out and replant every year. The unadulterated white-flowered species, sometimes called jasmine tobacco, is still commercially available for gardeners who wish to experience its sweet evening fragrance. It is also a self-sower and will "volunteer" for years to come.

ADDITIONAL SPECIES, CULTIVARS, OR VARIETIES
Nicotiana langsdorfii (3 ft.), a charming self-sower, has fresh green flowers that dangle like small tubular bells. A filler plant that blends with almost anything, it complements perennial borders, mixed borders of annuals and perennials (placed from the back to the middle of beds), and flower arrangements. At 4 to 5 ft., *Nicotiana sylvestris* always attracts attention in the garden. Large lyre-shaped foliage and bursts of 4-in.-long pendulous white flowers on tall stems make this flowering tobacco an architectural accent plant for borders. Plant 12 to 18 in. apart.

Geranium

Pelargonium × *hortorum*

Height: 1 to 2 ft.
Flowers: Many colors, solid and bicolors
Bloom Period: Early summer to frost
Zones: 3, 4, 5, 6
Light Requirement:

Although its botanical name is *Pelargonium*, this is the common geranium, among the most popular annuals for containers and beds. Its bright globes of clustered flowers start blooming in early summer and stage a continuous show until frost. Sturdy and erect with stems that can be woody by summer's end, geraniums are equally appropriate for an informal cottage garden and in formal urns outside the door of a stately mansion. Their habit is controlled but relentlessly cheerful. Regular deadheading keeps them attractive. Most geraniums reach about 14 in. in height and width. Geraniums with darker markings around the leaves are called zonal geraniums. These used to be propagated only by cuttings; now there are commercially produced zonal geraniums with and without the zoned foliage. Seed-grown geraniums tend to be sold in flats for bedding. They usually have single flowers, may or not have zoned foliage, and are excellent for large massed plantings. Geraniums grown from cuttings are often larger, more expensive, and better suited for container use. Geraniums were popular during the carpet bedding craze of the 1800s, when annuals were planted to create vast patterns designed to be viewed from high windows. Victorians particularly valued variations in leaf color and markings—so much that, according to David Stuart and James Sutherland in their book *Plants from the Past*, they often cut off the geranium flowers so they would not steal attention from the leaves.

WHEN TO PLANT
Purchase plants of blooming size in late spring to set into the garden or use in containers. Geraniums may also be overwintered indoors and propagated in early spring from stem cuttings.

WHERE TO PLANT
Geraniums prefer a mostly to completely sunny area with well-drained and fertile soil. Use geraniums in beds, as accent plants, and in containers and windowboxes.

How to Plant

Set into the garden at the same depth they were growing in containers. Remove flower buds at the time of transplanting to direct the plant's energy into root establishment. Plant about 12 in. apart. After planting, feed with a transplant fertilizer such as 3-10-3.

Advice for Care

Fertilize geraniums every 2 to 3 weeks with a general fertilizer such as 5-10-10 at the rate specified on the label. Water when the soil is dry. Avoid watering late in the day or evening. Flower clusters that stay wet are more susceptible to fungus problems. Yellow leaves may indicate too much water. Avoid overhead sprinklers. If the plant is getting leggy or spindly or is not blooming, it probably needs more sun. Regularly remove faded flowers, or deadhead, to encourage more blooms. Pinch back stems to encourage bushier growth. With proper growing conditions, geraniums are usually trouble-free. Avoid overcrowding the plants. Pick off and destroy any leaves that develop brown, sunken spots.

Additional Information

Geraniums grow best where days are sunny and warm and nights are cool and dry. When using these annuals in containers, combine them with low-growing flowers such as white sweet alyssum.

Additional Species, Cultivars, or Varieties

Plant scented geraniums where you and your visitors will brush against the leaves, releasing the fragrance. Rose, nutmeg, apple, peppermint, and lemon are among the tempting possibilities. *Pelargonium × domesticum*, the Martha Washington geranium, needs cool temperatures to bloom. It is usually grown as a florist's plant in spring. The ivy geranium, *Pelargonium peltatum*, is the ideal plant for windowboxes and hanging baskets. Its trailing stems can reach several feet long. Ivy geraniums spill over windowboxes in the Swiss Alps, their jubilant red and pink flowers creating a memorable contrast to the dark stained wood of the homes.

Globe Amaranth

Gomphrena globosa

Height: 8 to 24 in.
Flowers: Red-violet, magenta, pink, orange-red, white
Bloom Period: Early summer to frost
Zones: 3, 4, 5, 6
Light Requirement:

In full sun and well-drained soil, the brilliant blooms of globe amaranth shimmer in the summer sun in shades of pink, white, and electric magenta. The clover-like flowers (actually papery bracts that hold the tiny true flowers) seem to last forever—all summer in the garden and all winter in a vase. These sturdy ball-shaped flowers, resembling little pom-poms, are fun for children to grow and harvest. Use globe amaranth in annual beds, cutting gardens, or mixed plantings. Three or five well-grown plants will generously fill a large container. Several shorter compact selections have been bred for landscape and garden use but the taller ones are best for producing cut and dried flowers. Use the dwarf types for a mini-hedge or edging. Although mixed color plantings of annuals can be jarring, the standard globe amaranth mix of magenta, pink, and white flowers (sold as 'Mix' or 'Mixed Colors') is an exception. The paler colors temper the magenta and the whole group mingles pleasantly together. Take advantage of gomphrena's heat and drought tolerance by combining it with other sun-loving plants. The white- and pink-flowered forms have a silvery sheen and flatter other plants with silver foliage such as dusty miller. In a dry sunny site, combine dwarf white gomphrena with lamb's ears, wooly thyme, and pastel 'Jean Davis' lavender. Add a purple note to the composition with the purple, cream, and pink variegated foliage of 'Tricolor' sage and the dusky plum 'Vera Jameson' stonecrop. Or shake up your garden with one of the new scarlet-flowered globe amaranths. Combine 'Woodcreek Red' or 'Strawberry Fields' globe amaranth with bright gold gloriosa daisies, rich purple heliotrope, and tall lavender-purple Brazilian verbena for a flamboyant south-of-the-border color combination that will provide plenty of cut flowers.

WHEN TO PLANT

Plant in the spring after the danger of frost is past. Seed can be sown in the garden.

WHERE TO PLANT

A sunny location with well-drained soil is best. Globe amaranth tolerates poor and sandy soils. Try it in hot spots and for color in low-maintenance areas.

HOW TO PLANT

Gently remove plants from containers or cell-packs—squeeze the sides, don't pull on the stem—and plant in the garden 8 to 12 in. apart. Position so the plants are growing at the same soil level that they were in the container. Firm the soil around the transplant and water. Plant-starter fertilizer, such as 3-10-3, could be applied at this time to encourage root growth.

ADVICE FOR CARE

Globe amaranth is easy to grow and pest- and disease-free. Tolerant of heat and dry conditions, gomphrena resents being over-watered but will need irrigation during prolonged dry spells. In soils of normal fertility, no additional fertilizing is necessary.

ADDITIONAL INFORMATION

In late summer, large bunches of globe amaranth are often seen for sale in Michigan farmers' markets, but it's easy to produce your own. Pick flowers throughout the growing season or wait and harvest the entire plant before heavy frost. Flowers will elongate and lose their rounded shape as they mature. Strip the leaves and hang the plants upside down in a well-ventilated location to dry. Place the dried flowers in a vase for a colorful winter bouquet, or create a spectacular wreath with pink and magenta flowers of globe amaranth, 'Silver King' artemisia and the blue spires of mealy-cup sage.

ADDITIONAL SPECIES, CULTIVARS, OR VARIETIES

'Buddy' (10 to 12 in.) and 'Gnome' (8 to 10 in.) are tidy and compact, suitable for potting, massing in beds, or edging areas subject to heat and drought. 'Strawberry Fields' (18 to 24 in.) has longer stems and larger, scarlet-red flowers that hold the vibrant color as they dry. A similar selection, 'Woodcreek Red' (24 in.), has performed well in Michigan gardens. 'Lavender Queen' (24 in.) has a unique pale purple-pink flower. These taller selections are ideal for fresh or dried arrangements.

Gloriosa Daisy

Rudbeckia hirta

Height: to 36 in.
Flowers: Yellow with brown centers
Bloom Period: Early summer to frost
Zones: 3, 4, 5, 6
Light Requirement:

Hot, dry locations that intimidate other garden plants don't bother gloriosa daisies for a minute. This improvement on the familiar roadside native black-eyed Susan is a tough, resilient plant that's perfect for spots with full sun, even those on the dry side. Like other members of the daisy or composite family, the gloriosa daisy really has 2 types of flowers. The outer ones are ray flowers in yellow, orange, or bronze. The center is a cluster of rich brown disk flowers, suggesting this plant's nickname, "brown-eyed Susan." The stems are covered with stiff hairs. Tall and spreading about 18 in. wide, the gloriosa daisy makes a bold statement from early summer to frost toward the rear of a bed or mixed with other annuals and perennials. It is ideal to combine with Russian sage, purple coneflower, sedum 'Autumn Joy', and orange or yellow zinnias. In size and overall feel, the gloriosa daisy blends well into the perennial garden. Use it in natural meadow-type plantings with switch grass, blazing star, and butterflyweed. One of the nicest is the cultivar 'Indian Summer', which was an All-America Selection in 1995. Gloriosa daisies are short-lived perennials grown as annuals; they flower the first year they are planted. They are spectacular as cut flowers.

WHEN TO PLANT

Gloriosa daisies are fairly easy to transplant and establish outdoors in May, before planting more tender annuals. Sow seed outside in the garden after the last frost date or buy gloriosa daisies as transplants in the spring.

WHERE TO PLANT

Select a site in full sun and ordinary to fertile, well-drained soil. All varieties are good for beds, low-maintenance meadows, and cutting gardens. Use the smaller types for containers and windowboxes. The bright colors are eye-catching to say the least. These plants can be used for color in a perennial bed that peaked in June. Or combine with sunflowers in a daisy cutting garden.

How to Plant

Space 14 to 24 in. apart. Crowding plants reduces air circulation and encourages powdery mildew. After planting, feed with a transplant fertilizer such as 3-10-3.

Advice for Care

Gloriosa daisy is drought resistant, usually problem-free, and thrives in hot weather, but water during extended dry periods. Cutting to use the flowers in arrangements actually stimulates new growth on the plant. Taller varieties may profit from staking.

Additional Information

The dwarf types are great plants for containers because they are not fussy about heat or dry soil. Gloriosas make a brash and brilliant statement, but since plants may be bare of leaves toward the bottom, surround them with low-growing annuals such as dwarf French or signet marigolds. Gloriosa daisies may self-sow.

Additional Species, Cultivars, or Varieties

The compact variety called 'Becky Mix' is 8 to 14 in. tall with large yellow and orange flowers. It is useful for massing and bedding but not cutting. 'Indian Summer', a recent award-winner with large flowers, has performed well in Michigan, providing much color on sturdy stems well into the fall. 'Rustic Colors' is 18 to 22 in. in a range of rich shades. The perennial *Rudbeckia fulgida* var. *sullivantii* includes the popular black-eyed Susan 'Goldsturm'.

Heliotrope

Heliotropium arborescens

Other Name: Cherry-pie
Height: 14 to 18 in.
Flowers: Deep purple, lilac
Bloom Period: Early summer
to frost
Zones: 4, 5, 6
Light Requirement:

Heliotrope offers velvety purple flowers, sweet rich fragrance, and dark green, deeply veined leaves. The handsome, purple-tinged textured foliage, as big an asset as the flowers, flatters a wide range of other garden plants. This charming old-fashioned annual performs well year after year, flowering from July until frost, in the annual trials at Michigan State University in East Lansing. Cherry-pie, a common name, attempts to describe the sweet, fruity fragrance of the flowers, although it doesn't really get it right. The original fragrance that inspired the name has been bred out of the modern seed-grown selections, although a delightfully sweet vanilla scent remains. Popular in Victorian times for bedding plants, cut flowers, and conservatory plants, heliotrope's 1/4-in. flowers are born in large (6- to 8-in.) arching trusses on well-branched plants. There aren't scores of cultivars of heliotrope anymore, but this plant's rich color, interesting foliage, and pleasing fragrance merit a place in Michigan gardens. Use heliotrope in annual displays, cottage gardens, perennial beds, and in containers. Plant heliotrope with tangerine pot marigold, *Calendula officinalis*, and bright yellow melampodium; a small clump of variegated silver grass (*Miscanthus sinensis* 'Variegatus') would be the perfect vertical accent. Heliotrope will also work well in a mixed planting of annuals, perennials, and roses, cottage-garden style. Combine it with candy pink multiflora petunias, lime-green flowering tobacco, hazy lavender-blue Russian sage, and the pink-flowered hybrid rugosa rose 'Frau Dagmar Hastrup' for an unforgettable and fragrant garden picture.

WHEN TO PLANT

Plant transplants from cell-packs in the spring, one week or so after the frost-free date. You can grow heliotrope from seed but this is not a plant likely to germinate and grow well on a windowsill. It takes almost 3 months to grow plants large enough to set outside.

WHERE TO PLANT

Heliotrope likes warmth, sun, and moist but well-drained soil.
Don't allow it to dry out or the plants will suffer. Cherry-pie does
beautifully in containers where it contributes rich color, texture,
and fragrance.

HOW TO PLANT

Gently remove plants from containers or cell-packs by squeezing
the sides rather than pulling on the stem. Make sure they are
planted at the same depth in the garden as the plants were growing
in the container. Firm the soil around the transplant and water. You
could apply plant-starter fertilizer, such as 3-10-3, to encourage root
growth. Space heliotrope at least 1 ft. apart to allow plants room to
grow stocky and strong instead of tall and spindly.

ADVICE FOR CARE

Keep heliotrope well watered during dry spells. Mulch will help to
conserve moisture. Deadhead (remove faded flowers) as the blooms
turn from purple to brown. In a soil of average fertility, fertilize several times during the summer with liquid feed, such as 10-10-10, at
the rate recommended on the package.

ADDITIONAL INFORMATION

Plants are generally pest- and disease-free. Bring heliotrope inside
to enjoy over the winter if you can provide a cool sunny location.
Heliotrope roots easily from cuttings.

ADDITIONAL SPECIES, CULTIVARS, OR VARIETIES

Heliotropium 'Marine' (to 18 in.) has consistently grown well in
mid-Michigan. 'Marine' has large, deep purple flowers, a pleasing
fragrance, and attractive foliage. A new cultivar, 'Mini Marine'
(to 10 in.), is shorter and more compact. Try it in a sunny windowbox or patio container. A recent introduction called 'Midnight' has
a short habit and is a hybrid. Fragrant heirloom types, propagated
by cuttings, are available from specialty greenhouses.

Hyacinth Bean

Lablab purpureus

Height: 10 to 20 ft.
Flowers: White, pink-lavender
Zones: 5, 6; may not flower in colder zones
Light Requirement:

For a show-stopping vine, send hyacinth beans scampering up a fence or post. Soon you'll see the slightly furry oval leaflets, purple stems, and, later, the clusters of pea-like flowers. The blooms are followed by shiny mahogany seedpods that hang as curious ornaments among the dark green leaves, which also have a purplish cast. For foliage, flower, and seedpod, hyacinth bean is one of the most attractive annual vines around. When it's hot and sunny, this tropical vine practically erupts with rapid growth. It is perennial in warmer climates and is native to Egypt. In Michigan, it is grown as an annual vine from seeds started indoors in spring or outside after the soil warms and nighttime temperatures stay above 60 degrees Fahrenheit. Hyacinth bean requires a long growing season to reach flowering size, so starting seed indoors gives the plants a jump over those sown outside. Note, however, that this requires special care, since hyacinth bean can be difficult to transplant. Dramatic and unusual, these handsome annual vines will attract curious stares from those unfamiliar with their charms. They are definitely worth growing in warmer regions.

WHEN TO PLANT

Hyacinth bean loves heat, so there's no point in starting the seeds too early. Indoors, begin about 4 weeks before the last frost. Sow the seed in 3-in. peat pots. Later, when outdoor weather has warmed up to summery conditions, plant the peat pots directly in the garden. This will lessen transplant shock. Hyacinth bean may also be sown outdoors after all danger of frost, but may not begin flowering until late summer, putting the plant in peril if there is an early frost. In colder zones the growing season may not be long enough for hyacinth bean to reach blooming stage. Still, even without flowers, this is a decorative foliage vine.

WHERE TO PLANT

Plant hyacinth beans for a fast annual screen or a cover on a fence, trellis, or post, or let it scramble over the ground and among shrubs and perennials. It does best in full sun, warm growing conditions, and well-drained soil.

HOW TO PLANT

Space the seeds or plants about 12 in. apart and make sure the vine has something to climb on. If no permanent support, such as a fence or trellis, is available, let hyacinth bean climb up lengths of vertical twine to a wire or rope installed at the desired height. After planting, feed with a transplant fertilizer such as 3-10-3.

ADVICE FOR CARE

Water when the soil is dry. If desired, use a balanced fertilizer every 3 weeks.

ADDITIONAL INFORMATION

Hyacinth bean, which formerly had the botanical name *Dolichos lablab*, is extremely ornamental and deserves to be grown in more gardens. It is one of the finest annual vines for quickly screening a view, covering a fence, and bringing interest and color with its leaves, blossoms, and seedpods. Save the seedpods for next year for your own garden and to share with admiring neighborhoods. The pods are also attractive in fall arrangements.

ADDITIONAL SPECIES, CULTIVARS, OR VARIETIES

'Giganteus' is a larger hybrid. A cultivar called 'Ruby Moon' has bicolored flowers in light and darker pink.

Impatiens

Impatiens wallerana

Other Name: Busy Lizzie
Height: 6 to 18 in.
Flowers: Many colors, solid and variegated
Zones: 3, 4, 5, 6
Light Requirement:

Drive around established shady residential areas in the summer and you'll see impatiens in nearly every yard. These brightly colored annuals dress up the front of foundation plantings, beautify the base of lofty shade trees, and spill over the sides of baskets, windowboxes, and containers. In the last few decades, impatiens have outsold petunias to become the nation's most popular bedding plant. It is easy to grow in shade, and newer varieties also tolerate sun. A single plant, with proper water and fertilizer, can grow into a flower-covered mound up to 18 in. high and wide. It will bloom all summer and into September and October, or until hit by frost, when it will quickly wilt and die. Double impatiens, which are increasingly available as transplants, have flowers resembling fluffy miniature roses. Some homeowners stick with a pristine white or other one-color impatiens planting scheme. White and blush pink are especially effective in deep shade, where they almost glow. Other gardeners experiment with various color combinations, which range from pale and serene to hot and rambunctious. A planting of lavender and soft pink impatiens falls into the first category; a bed with hot pink, coral, and purple impatiens is clearly in the latter. In the fall, the seedpods of this plant spring open with the slightest pressure. Put one in a child's palm and the youngster will squeal with delight as the light green pod splits open and launches its tiny seeds. For windowboxes and containers in shade, try a combination of impatiens, ivy, and fuchsia for texture, color, and interest.

WHEN TO PLANT

Buy transplants to set into the garden in late May or early June. Impatiens, which are native to Africa, grow best after the soil has warmed. Plants set out in cool, wet spring weather won't start to take off until conditions improve.

WHERE TO PLANT

Impatiens are ideal in beds, in the shade of trees, and in containers and windowboxes. They make a lovely display on their own or combined with other shade-loving plants such as ferns, hosta, and pulmonaria or lungwort. Use them in part sun to shade. They flower more effectively where they receive at least some sun, and many varieties can tolerate considerable amounts of sun if they receive adequate moisture. Impatiens do best in rich well-drained soil. In heavy clay or sandy soils, dig in compost or other soil amendments before planting for best results.

How to Plant
Space impatiens about 8 to 12 in. apart. Plant them so they are growing in the garden at the same depth that they were in their containers. After planting, feed with a transplant fertilizer such as 3-10-3.

Advice for Care
The more sun they get, the more water impatiens need. Wilting foliage is a sign that the plants are desperate for moisture. Mulch to conserve water. Feed impatiens with a general fertilizer such as 10-10-10 every 3 to 4 weeks if desired. Too much nitrogen may result in lush foliage but scarce flowers. Impatiens are usually free of serious pest and disease problems.

Additional Information
Plant impatiens around spring wildflowers and smaller bulbs. The growing impatiens will disguise the other plants' ripening foliage. Use paler colored impatiens in shady areas and brighter colors where there is more sun. They may self-sow. Impatiens are easy to overwinter indoors. Take cuttings from the stems in late August, root them in water, and place them in potting soil or a soilless mix. Plants may be cut back in spring and those trimmings also rooted. Impatiens will flower indoors for most of the winter if located in a cool area with bright light.

Additional Species, Cultivars, or Varieties
There are many cultivars to choose from. 'Super Elfin' and 'Dazzler' impatiens are 8 to 10 in., a good size for containers and window-boxes. Other choice cultivars are 'Accent' and 'Tempo', an especially good choice for a mass planting. New Guinea impatiens, which have variegated leaves and larger flowers, can tolerate more heat, although plants may wilt if exposed to high wind or direct afternoon sun. During hot, dry periods, New Guinea impatiens growing in sun require daily watering. Garden balsam, *Impatiens balsamina*, is an old-fashioned garden favorite. It is a tall upright grower with double flowers in yellow, pink, or salmon. Its common name, touch-me-not, comes from the way the ripe seedpods erupt with pressure. It commonly self-sows.

Love-in-a-Mist

Nigella damascena

Height: 12 to 18 in.
Flowers: Blue, rose, white
Bloom Period: Early summer
to frost
Zones: 3, 4, 5, 6
Light Requirement:

The exquisite flowers of love-in-a-mist are worthy of close examination, but the culture is a quick study— good drainage, sun to partial shade, and a packet of seeds is all you need! The romantic common name, love-in-a-mist, describes the delicate flowers enveloped by a ferny web of soft green thread-like foliage. In stark contrast, devil-in-a-bush, another common name, refers to the horned seedpods. The most beautiful forms of this easily grown but short-lived annual are those with clear sky blue or delphinium blue blossoms, an uncommon color for flowers. Nigella is a delicate plant in appearance and stature. It's not suitable for massing in bedding displays or for providing all-season, bright color with plants such as marigolds and zinnias. It may languish when summer heat reaches the mid-80s. It's best used as a filler in perennial beds, cottage gardens, herb gardens, and, of course, in the cutflower garden, where it is grown both for its dainty flowers and its distinctive seedpods. The horned inflated seedpods striped with maroon are useful in arrangements, both fresh and dried, and in herbal wreaths. Each pod contains many black seeds, which can be saved, shared with other gardeners or left to scatter on their own. Love-in-a-mist is a determined self-sower and the small ferny seedlings are a welcome sight in the spring garden. Often they find the best place to grow and flower, the one you didn't think of and hope to remember for next year. Love-in-a-mist's slender stems come up easily between perennials at their existing spacing; there is no need to make special room unless you want a mass display. Try blue nigella with 'Silver King' artemisia, pale pink hardy geraniums and white peach-leaved bellflower in a perennial bed or cottage garden.

WHEN TO PLANT

Sow seed 1/4-inch deep in spring as soon as soil is workable. Germination generally takes about 2 weeks.

WHERE TO PLANT

Plant in normal garden soil with good drainage in full sun or partial shade. Use in perennial beds or let nigella self-sow in herb and vegetable areas.

HOW TO PLANT

Nigella has a taproot and doesn't like to be transplanted; sow directly in the garden for best results. Although seed packets often recommend waiting until after the danger of frost, love-in-a-mist tolerates cool temperatures and can be sown earlier. Thin seedlings to 6 to 8 in. apart. When transplanting from cell-packs, use extreme care. Disturb the roots as little as possible.

ADVICE FOR CARE

Plant seed early to obtain the greatest show before the hot temperatures of summer arrive. When love-in-a-mist reaches maturity (in about 6 weeks), blooming ceases; successive sowings from early spring through early summer can be made to ensure a long period of bloom. In average garden soil, extra fertilization isn't necessary.

ADDITIONAL INFORMATION

To harvest the pods for their ornamental value, pick them after the maroon coloration has begun to develop. If you wait too long, they will become brown and not be as attractive. Leave a few pods for seed to scatter for next year's crop. Let love-in-a-mist find a home in unusual places; for example, sow seed in a rose bed. The delicate plants set off the sturdy roses and don't significantly compete for water or nutrients.

ADDITIONAL SPECIES, CULTIVARS, OR VARIETIES

Mixed colors are widely available in garden centers. 'Persian Jewels' contains pink, white, and lavender-blue double flowers and produces the characteristic seedpods. The single color selections, which are best for planned color combinations, may need to be ordered from seed catalogs. 'Oxford Blue' (to 30 in.), a tall double-flowered form, brings a unique deep blue color and delicate grace to perennial borders. The shorter 'Miss Jekyll' (to 18 in.), also blue, was selected by and named for the famous British gardener, Gertrude Jekyll. 'Mulberry Rose' (15 in.) is a single pink. Other species with unusual pods are available. *N. orientalis* 'Transformer' has interesting seedpods that flatten to form a flower shape.

Marigold

Tagetes species

Height: 6 to 36 in.
Flowers: Yellow, lemon, orange, white
Bloom Period: Early summer to frost
Zones: 3, 4, 5, 6
Light Requirement:

The pungent, distinctive aroma of marigolds captures the essence of summer. These nearly carefree annuals offer a riot of yellow, orange, mahogany, and white in rounded full flowers that resemble small carnations or chrysanthemums. The hues are especially vibrant in fall when the plants end the season with a burst of vigor. Marigolds appeal to both beginning and experienced gardeners who seek a range of sizes and reliable color beginning in early summer. These plants grow from just a few inches tall to 3 ft. French marigolds (*Tagetes patula*) grow 6 to 18 in. and have fernlike leaves. Their flowers can be single or double or crested. The 'Bonanza', 'Gate', 'Hero', and 'Safari' series are recommended. The single French types, which have a more natural appearance than the doubles, are becoming very popular again, with some heirloom selections available. One favorite single is the 'Disco' series (12 in.). African marigolds (*Tagetes erecta*), sometimes called American marigolds, grow as tall as 36 in. With their huge flowers, they may be awkward when combined with other plants in borders. They are best massed on their own. The 'Lady', 'Marvel', and 'Discovery' series are popular. Hybrids combine characteristics of French and American or African marigolds, creating a vast array of sizes and colors. Showcase marigolds in a mass, or mix them with other sun-loving annuals and perennials, such as ageratum, cosmos, cleome, daisies, and coneflowers. Their large seeds are easy to handle, and the plants grow readily from seed planted indoors in spring or directly outside in late May or June. Many children are introduced to gardening in school when they start marigold seeds in paper cups, often as gifts for Mother's Day.

WHEN TO PLANT

Sow seed indoors 4 to 6 weeks before the last frost date or outdoors in late May to early June. Plants grown from seed started indoors or purchased transplants will bloom sooner than seed sown directly in the garden. In Michigan, African marigolds take too long to start from seed sown outdoors. Buy transplants instead.

WHERE TO PLANT

Choose a location in full to part sun and well-drained soil of poor
to average fertility. These plants' compact form makes them superb
for edging or massing in areas with poor soil such as under a fence,
and they do well as container plants.

HOW TO PLANT

Space marigolds 6 in. to as much as 15 in. apart, depending on type.
Plant them slightly deeper than they were growing in containers.
After planting, feed with a transplant fertilizer such as 3-10-3. Plant
seed of French marigolds in the garden according to directions on
the seed packet. The seed germinates quickly, usually in 5 to 7 days.

ADVICE FOR CARE

Avoid planting marigolds too early in spring. They grow best in
warmer weather. Soil that is rich may stimulate lush foliage but
few flowers. The same is true of frequent fertilizer applications.
Water when soil is dry. Marigolds will tolerate drought but prefer
more regular moisture. Flowering is reduced in partial shade.
Deadhead or remove faded flowers often to prevent plant from setting seed and to improve appearance. Marigolds are sometimes
troubled by a condition that turns their tips yellow. Plants with this
problem should be removed and destroyed.

ADDITIONAL INFORMATION

Marigolds are long-lived cut flowers. For a beautiful display, use
marigolds with chocolate cosmos and coreopsis. Many gardeners
ring their vegetable beds, especially tomatoes, with marigolds in
the belief that these annual flowers will repel pests.

ADDITIONAL SPECIES, CULTIVARS, OR VARIETIES

There are many interesting cultivars. The single French marigolds
such as 'Disco' (7 to 10 in.) are experiencing a resurgence of popularity. 'Gypsy Sunshine' is 6 to 8 in. with warm yellow flowers. Some
African marigolds have quilled or rolled petals, which are actually
ray flowers. Among them are 'Inca' (14 to 16 in.) and 'Discovery' (12
to 14 in.). Signet marigolds (*Tagetes tenuifolia*) have attractive ferny
leaves, small single flowers, and a natural habit as well as small size
(6 to 8 in.). They are useful for containers, windowboxes, and edging. 'Lemon Gem' and 'Paprika' are two favorites.

ANNUALS

Mealy-cup Sage

Salvia farinacea

Other Name: Blue Sage
Height: 16 to 20 in.
Flowers: Violet-blue, white
Bloom Period: Early summer
to frost
Zones: 3, 4, 5, 6
Light Requirement:

The mealy-cup sage, in contrast to the bright red flowers of its flashier cousin the scarlet sage (*Salvia splendens*), has a subtle combination of violet-blue flowers on bluish stems and somewhat grayish green foliage. White selections, subtle and refined, have pure white flowers emerging from woolly silver stems. Mealy-cup sage is a tireless performer, providing vertical form, fresh foliage, and violet-blue spikes with little effort. The unenticing common name refers to the covering of the stems and buds with a soft whitish powder or meal. Mealy-cup sage, sometimes called blue sage, is at home in perennial beds, annual displays, containers, and cutting gardens, where it blooms from late June until frost on upright, bushy plants. Mealy-cup sage is not a scene-stealer. It sets off other plants in borders and is a steady, understated presence in annual bedding combinations. Try 'Victoria' mealy-cup sage with 'Rose Queen' spider flower and magenta or pink bedding geraniums. Or, for an elegant look, plant the white-flowered cultivar 'Silver White' (18 in.) with white 'Sonata' cosmos, white or pale pink petunias, and silvery dusty miller. *Salvia farinacea* also works well in drifts and masses in perennial beds, where it can be planted over the yellowing foliage of bulbs. The violet-blue color complements the primrose yellow of 'Moonbeam' coreopsis or 'Moonshine' yarrow. It can also temper the bright magenta of purple coneflower or hardy geraniums. The flowers are excellent for cutting and for use as an everlasting. The stems and flowers dry to a deep blue, unusual among dried flowers. The vertical spikes and blue color of mealy-cup sage add a special note to late summer bouquets of zinnias.

WHEN TO PLANT
Plant blue sage in spring after the frost-free date for your area.

WHERE TO PLANT

Plant in full sun in well-drained soil. It will tolerate partial shade. Use in drifts and masses in perennial beds and annual displays.

HOW TO PLANT

Gently remove plants from containers or cell-packs—squeeze the sides, don't pull on the stem—and plant 8 to 12 in. apart in a prepared garden bed. Make sure the plant remains at the same level it was in the container or cell-pack. Firm the soil around the transplant, then water. Plant-starter fertilizer, such as 3-10-3, could be applied at this time to encourage root growth.

ADVICE FOR CARE

Water plants during drought. There are no serious pest and disease problems.

ADDITIONAL INFORMATION

To dry mealy-cup sage for use as an everlasting, harvest the flower spikes when they are almost but not quite fully open. Fasten small bunches with rubber bands, and hang them upside down in a well-ventilated location out of direct sun. Mealy-cup sage, although grown as an annual, is a native perennial in Texas and New Mexico.

ADDITIONAL SPECIES, CULTIVARS, OR VARIETIES

Violet-blue 'Victoria' (18 to 20 in.) has performed well in Michigan, as has 'Rhea Blue' (16 to 18 in.), a slightly more compact selection. 'Strata', a 1995 All-America Selection winner, has a unusual combination of blue flowers on silver spikes. Many white-flowered cultivars are available, including 'Cirrus' (16 to 18 in.) and 'Silver White' (18 in.). Red *Salvia splendens*, the scarlet sage, with cultivar names like 'Hot Stuff', 'Blaze of Fire', and 'Rambo', comes on strong and bright in the garden. Often seen in public bedding displays, this widely grown annual is difficult to integrate into home gardens. New color choices are now available in shades of purple, rose, and salmon that are easier on the eyes, although they all retain a clumsy, top-heavy quality. If you like red salvia, try *Salvia coccinea*, the Texas sage. This adaptable and long-blooming annual has a graceful growing habit and loose spikes of beautiful red flowers attractive to hummingbirds. The selection 'Lady in Red' is an All-America Selection winner and has done well in Michigan. 'Coral Nymph', another selection of *Salvia coccinea*, has coral-pink flowers.

Melampodium

Melampodium paludosum

Height: 15 to 25 in.
Flowers: Golden yellow
Bloom Period: Early summer
to frost
Zones: 4, 5, 6
Light Requirement:

A little known but easy annual, melampodium flowers all summer long, producing hundreds of inch-wide yellow daisies on bushy plants with medium green foliage. Melampodium has no easy common name or wide range of colors; however, its beauty and toughness have much to recommend it to Michigan gardeners. Its tiny little sunflowers are produced almost as soon as the plants are set out and continue blooming until a killing frost. An abundance of light green foliage and a loose habit give melampodium a natural appearance, more like a perennial than many of the flashy annuals that produce large, colorful flowers at the expense of looking genuine. It grows well in the heat of summer and with sun and well-drained soil. Melampodium is tough and needs no special coddling, deadheading, or fertilizing. Relatively new to cultivation, melampodium may not always be available at local garden centers. Ask for it and create a demand. Seed, however, is easily obtained from mail-order catalogs. Use melampodium in beds, borders, pots, planters, and windowboxes. The small, sunny daisies combine brilliantly with red, orange, and yellow flowers. For another look, combine with the deep blue spikes of mealy-cup sage for that favorite Michigan color combination, maize and blue. Melampodium is growing in popularity as gardeners discover its floriferous, sunny nature and adaptability.

WHEN TO PLANT

Plant melampodium from cell-packs or containers after the danger of frost is past. Seed may also be directly sown in the garden after the frost-free date.

WHERE TO PLANT

Melampodium likes heat and full sun. Plant in sunny annual, perennial, or mixed beds, by walkways, or in containers. Use it to plant over bulbs and disguise the yellowing foliage of daffodils or tulips.

How to Plant

For nursery-grown transplants, gently remove plants from containers or cell-packs—squeeze the sides, don't pull on the stem—and plant 7 to 10 in. apart in a prepared garden bed. Make sure the plant remains at the same level it was growing in the container or cell-pack. Firm the soil around the transplant and then water. A water-soluble plant-starter fertilizer, such as 3-10-3, could be applied at this time to encourage root growth. Melampodium's root system grows quickly. If it has become potbound in the container, tease out roots to encourage growth into the soil. Water until established. To direct sow outside, follow the directions on the seed packet. Flowering will be later than for purchased transplants.

Advice for Care

Melampodium doesn't need any special care and has no insect and disease problems. It is fairly tolerant of dry conditions, but water during severe drought or if plants look water stressed.

Additional Information

The cheerful yellow flowers of melampodium mix well with other hot colors. At the DeLapa Perennial Garden at Michigan State University, melampodium tied together the bright scarlet red of 'Lucifer' crocosmia, the similar but larger yellow-orange daisies of sunflower heliopsis, clear yellow of 'Golden Showers' coreopsis, and the orange of butterflyweed. Self-sown "volunteers" returned the next year for a repeat performance. To create a similar color scheme with annuals, plant golden marigolds, orange zinnias, and gloriosa daisies with melampodium. The tall stems and purple flowers of Brazilian verbena would be a sensational accent.

Additional Species, Cultivars, or Varieties

There are only a few cultivars. 'Medallion' (20 to 22 in.) is a compact and floriferous selection. 'Showstar' (24 in.) is another. 'Million Gold' (16 to 18 in.) is probably the shortest.

Moss Rose

Portulaca grandiflora

Height: 6 to 9 in.
Flowers: White, pink, orange, yellow, red
Bloom Period: Early summer to frost
Zones: 3, 4, 5, 6
Light Requirement:

Portulaca or moss rose is an annual for harsh places, but there is nothing harsh about its flowers. Their bright, glowing colors and satiny texture cover these low-growing plants, which tolerate hot, dry areas and infertile soils. Blooming from early summer to fall, moss rose is useful for edging paths or beds, growing in exposed locations such as between paving stones, or surrounding bricks in full sun—conditions that would bake other plants. They are excellent grouped in the front of a perennial bed or in containers. In the past, moss rose flowers closed when the sun went behind a cloud or by the midafternoon. Many modern selections, however, remain open most of the day, even when it is overcast. The 1- to 2-in. frilly blooms, available as singles or doubles, have bright yellow-orange centers. Moss roses can spread 12 to 15 in., creating a sprawling, trailing habit that is valuable in the garden as well as windowboxes and pots. With their succulent pointed leaves, moss roses are attractive and dependable for a hot, sunny spot. Plant moss roses once, and they're apt to self-sow and return the following year. Though still attractive, the second year's flowers may not be quite as vigorous or lovely as the originals. If the area gets close scrutiny, pull out the volunteers and replant with new ones. But if the self-sown crop is in a more casual bed, a crop of volunteer moss roses can put on a free, no-work, and quite enjoyable display.

WHEN TO PLANT

Young plants may be purchased and set out in the garden after danger of frost has passed and soil has warmed.

WHERE TO PLANT

Locate moss roses in full sun. They tolerate infertile soil, but the site must be well drained. They will not tolerate sites that remain wet. Plant them 6 to 8 in. apart.

How to Plant

After planting, feed with a transplant fertilizer such as 3-10-3, then stop fertilizing. Water the plants in well at planting.

Advice for Care

After they start showing new growth, little additional water is needed. Portulaca can withstand drought. It has no serious pest or disease problems and thrives with almost no care.

Additional Information

Moss roses are wonderful for rock gardens. The fleshy leaves help the plant retain water even in dry, exposed locations. Selections with mixed colors are especially fine as a pot plant. Or intensify the color punch by teaming moss roses with a contrasting color, such as the deep purple of *Verbena* 'Imagination'. It is also attractive with plants having softer or felty leaves, such as petunias.

Additional Species, Cultivars, or Varieties

There are many moss roses to choose from. The 'Sundial' series has performed well in trials in Michigan. It has double flowers and is available in 10 colors.

Pansy

Viola × *wittrockiana*

Height: 6 to 9 in.
Flowers: Blue, violet, white, mahogany, orange, yellow; sometimes multicolored
Bloom Period: Spring and fall
Zones: 3, 4, 5, 6
Light Requirement:

It's easy to be sentimental about pansies. With their cheery colors and markings like tiny faces, pansies are an old-fashioned favorite with continued appeal for gardeners today. Their bright yellow and purple colors are often the first annuals seen at garden centers in the spring, and they shine in the garden or containers for weeks during the cooler spring and early summer weather. Gardeners in the Southern states also grow pansies planted in the fall to enjoy in their mild winters and early spring. Fall planting is becoming popular among Northerners, including Michigan residents. These plants are sown in commercial greenhouses in July for sale in September. They may be planted by themselves to replace exhausted annuals or to cover an area recently planted with daffodils and tulip bulbs. The fall-planted pansies flower on warmer days into November and December—well beyond the early frosts—and revive, if mulched, at the first hint of spring. Pansies thrive with rich soil, frequent moisture, and cool weather—the typical conditions of spring and fall, although newer types better tolerate warmth. Regularly removing the faded flowers prolongs the bloom. Pansies grow 6 to 9 in. tall and wide. Enjoy their brilliant colors both early and late in the season when few other annuals are in fine form.

WHEN TO PLANT

For earliest spring bloom, buy plants to set out in the garden or containers about 2 to 3 weeks before the last frost. Gardeners in Zones 5 and 6 may purchase plants in September for flowers in the fall and the following spring. Mulch fall-planted pansies with evergreen boughs after the ground freezes.

WHERE TO PLANT

Place pansies in sun to light shade. Avoid a site with exposure to afternoon sun. Pansies need excellent drainage and rich soil; amend with compost or shredded leaves if necessary. When planting pansies in the fall, avoid areas that stay wet all winter. Use in beds and containers. In fall, use pansies over newly planted bulb beds. The pansies will bloom into early winter and return in the spring to flower at the base of daffodils, tulips, and other bulbs. They are particularly effective combined with yellows and reds.

How to Plant
Space plants about 4 to 6 in. apart. After planting, feed with a transplant fertilizer such as 3-10-3.

Advice for Care
Pinching off faded flowers encourages more bloom. Mulch to keep the soil cool. Pansies need moist conditions to thrive and do not tolerate drought. In early summer, warmer weather will cause some pansies to stall, and they may be replaced with more heat-tolerant annuals or cut back in July to encourage reblooming in fall. Feed pansies with a general fertilizer such as 10-10-10 about every 3 weeks while they are growing actively.

Additional Information
Rabbits love these annuals; protect the flowers with wire fencing. If slugs are a problem, surround the plants with a ring of diatomaceous earth.

Additional Species, Cultivars, or Varieties
The most cold-tolerant pansies have small to mid-sized blooms. Among the hardiest are the series named 'Crystal Bowl', 'Universal', and 'Maxim'. They make darling cut flowers, perfect for small vases or with grape hyacinths in May baskets. 'Maxim Marina' is an award winner. It is heat tolerant and has light blue flowers. Violas are similar to pansies but a little shorter, with smaller blooms; ones in the 'Jewel' series are especially hardy. *Viola tricolor* is the Johnny-jump-up, which is about 12 in. tall and has purple, white, and yellow flowers. It self-sows in cool, filtered shade.

Petunia

Petunia × hybrida

Height: 8 to 18 in.
Flowers: White, pink, red, purple, lavender, rose, light blue, yellow; may be patterned
Zones: 3, 4, 5, 6
Light Requirement:

Petunias are prized in the annual world for their wide ranges of hues and their long season of bloom, providing arresting color from late spring through first frost. They take heat and sun in stride. Newer hybrids offer additional advantages compared to older varieties of petunias, which for years were the country's most popular bedding plant. (Impatiens now hold that title.)

Multiflora petunias are covered with smaller, more delicately sized blooms all season and often don't require cutting back in early July the way older types of petunias did. Smaller flowered petunias are also better able to withstand wind and rain without permanent damage. Their spread is 10 to 18 in. depending on the cultivar. Multifloras are excellent for many uses in the garden, including bedding, edging, and additions to perennial beds. Beautiful lavender, blue, paler pinks, and deep purples are available, some with deeper veining. 'Primetime', 'Carpet', 'Celebrity', and 'Madness' are a few of these multiflora series. Grandiflora petunias have larger flowers but not as many flowers at any one time. 'Dream' and 'Ultra' are some of the grandiflora series. To cover a large area, consider recent introductions in the 'Wave' series, available in red-violet and now pink flowers. These are suitable to use as groundcovers, even on a steep bank in full sun. A single plant can cover an area as large as 4 sq. ft. Petunias come in a wide range of colors, some veined or striped, ruffled, single or double. The name *petunia* comes from the South American word for tobacco, to which it is related. Petunias are native to South America. With their velvety texture, funnel-shaped flowers, and distinctive fragrance, petunias are a natural for garden beds as well as hanging baskets and containers, where they quickly become a cascade of color.

WHEN TO PLANT

Buy transplants to set into the garden after chance of frost. Pinch back young plants to encourage more compact growth. Petunias are more cold tolerant than many annuals so may be set out a few weeks earlier.

WHERE TO PLANT

Petunias prefer sunny to mostly sunny locations with at least 6 hours of sun a day. Well-drained soil is a must; petunias grown in heavy clay will not thrive. Improve the site with soil amendments such as compost or leaf mold if necessary.

HOW TO PLANT

Space petunias 6 to 12 in. apart depending on the size of the cultivar. After planting, feed with a transplant fertilizer such as 3-10-3.

ADVICE FOR CARE

Remove faded blooms to encourage new growth. Both the flower and the seedpod must be removed to redirect the plant's energy into more flowers. Fertilize about once a month with a general fertilizer such as 10-10-10 at the rate recommended on the product. In dry periods, provide water. Some cultivars—and any petunia that's getting tired or scraggly—may be sheared in early July. Cut the plants back in half and then fertilize. Some people do this chore just before they leave for summer vacation. By the time they return in a few weeks, the petunias will be blooming again. Avoid watering late in the day. Plants that stay wet overnight are more prone to disease. Petunias are resistant to most pests and diseases, although occasionally leafhoppers may spread a disease that causes leaf tips to turn yellow. Remove infected plants.

ADDITIONAL INFORMATION

Petunias are beautiful in containers, especially pots with unusual textures or a grayish cast. Try them with white cosmos or spider flowers for an interesting effect. When using petunias in pots or boxes, plant them closer together than recommended for the garden. This slight overcrowding will force them to grow taller and to spill over the edges of the container rather than ramble along on the soil surface. White petunias are well suited to a sunny bed of white flowers, such as sweet alyssum and plants with silvery foliage such as artemisia 'Silver Mound', dusty miller, and lamb's ears.

ADDITIONAL SPECIES, CULTIVARS, OR VARIETIES

Single or double multiflora petunias have flowers about 2 in. wide. Multifloras are the most resistant to disease, heat, and drought. The flowers on single and double grandiflora petunias are 3 in. wide or larger, and the colors are beautiful. The low-growing 'Purple Wave' and 'Pink Wave' petunias are especially useful to cover large areas as well as to plant in hanging baskets for a dramatic, trailing display. 'Supertunias' are also recommended for containers.

Pot Marigold

Calendula officinalis

Height: 1 to 2 ft.
Flowers: Orange, yellow, cream
Bloom Period: Early summer to frost
Zones: 4, 5, 6
Light Requirement:

Pot marigold, that orange-flowered stalwart of British cottage gardens, now comes in a range of colors—apricot, tangerine, lemon, cream—so luscious that it will make your mouth water. Fortunately, you can indulge. The flowers have been consumed since medieval times for culinary, cosmetic, and medicinal purposes. A contemporary reason to grow pot marigold is for the beautiful large, silky-petaled flowers, blooming from early summer to late fall. Nonetheless, the petals still make a colorful garnish for a salad!

The flat, many-petaled flowers and simple butterknife-shaped leaves, resembling a child's first drawing of a flower, give pot marigold a likable quality. It helps that it's easy to grow, and the blossoms make wonderful cut flowers, lasting up to 2 weeks in a vase. Flower types include single, semidouble to fully double, some with a contrasting maroon-brown center. The petals have a silky sheen and are soft to the touch. Plant pot marigold in annual beds, cottage gardens, herb gardens, and containers. Sow a row in the vegetable garden to bring inside. The bright yellow and tangerine flowers blend easily with other hot colors but are particularly brilliant when combined with blue or purple flowers. In a cutting garden, sow seed of blue larkspur at the same time as *Calendula* for a dazzling blue-and-orange combination seldom seen in gardens. In the cottage or herb garden, combine pot marigold with the true blue starry flowers of borage, another edible flower, and 'Dark Opal' basil. Sow seed of sky blue love-in-a-mist and orange and yellow nasturtiums to carry the scheme even farther; 'Alaska' nasturtium, with its cream-splashed foliage, would be extra special. Pot marigold prefers the cooler temperatures of spring and fall and will flower until hard frost.

When to Plant

Plant small transplants in the spring after the danger of hard frost. Seed can be sown directly in the garden. *Calendula* is tolerant of cool temperatures and can be sown in spring before the frost-free date.

Where to Plant

Pot marigold prefers sun—it will tolerate a bit of shade—and moist, well-drained soil. Plant in beds, cutting gardens, herb gardens, and containers.

How to Plant

Gently remove young plants from containers or cell-packs, and plant 8 to 12 in. apart in a prepared garden bed. Make sure the plant remains growing at the same level it was in the container or cell-pack. Firm the soil around the transplant and then water. Seed may be sown directly in the garden. Germination will take 1 to 2 weeks.

Advice for Care

Deadhead (remove the faded flowers) of pot marigold to encourage rebloom. It is not particularly drought tolerant and should be watered during dry spells. In Michigan's relatively cool summers, pot marigold blooms throughout the summer. If plants begin to languish in a heat wave, remove the flowering stems and wait for cooler temperatures to restore vigor.

Additional Information

Pot marigold is quite cold tolerant. It flowers late into the fall and doesn't go black at the first touch of frost. It does self-sow, producing volunteers. *Calendula* is striking with purple flowers. Experiment with bright orange and yellow pot marigold, purple heliotrope, violet-blue 'Imagination' verbena, and small border-sized sunflowers; temper the mix with the smoky foliage of purple fennel. Pot marigold can also be used in perennial and mixed borders, but place the orange flowers carefully to avoid an unintended startling contrast.

Additional Species, Cultivars, or Varieties

Recently, many new types have been selected. Since they are so easy to grow from seed, try some of these: 'Pacific Beauty' (18 in.) for long-stemmed double flowers and heat tolerance; 'Bon Bon' (12 to 15 in.), a dwarf for bedding and pot culture; 'Touch of Red' (14 in.), with petals edged in dark red; or 'Kablouna', with an unusual crested center. An excellent older variety, 'Radio' (24 in.), has a luminous orange color and large dahlia-like flowers.

Purple Fennel

Foeniculum vulgare var. *purpureum*

Other Names: Bronze Fennel, Copper Fennel
Height: 3 to 6 ft.
Flowers: Yellow; plant actually grown for its purple foliage
Zones: 4, 5, 6
Light Requirement:

Fennel, often confined to the herb or vegetable garden, deserves to escape its culinary confines and mingle with the garden flowers. The purple-foliaged form called bronze, copper, or purple fennel commands the ornamental gardener's attention. The soft, ferny, thread-like foliage forms a shimmering smoky purple-bronze cloud that dramatically sets off annuals, perennials, and summer-flowering bulbs. Young plants have the deepest purple coloration, which later changes to a purplish bronze. Undemanding, fennel is best grown from seed in average garden soil and full sun. Purple fennel is actually a perennial that is grown as an annual. It may occasionally overwinter in Zone 5, but grow new plants for the best results. A prolific self-sower if allowed to form seed, fennel will produce plenty of seedlings for next year's garden. Both the seeds and the foliage of fennel can be used in cooking for the distinctive anise flavor, but the beautiful lacy contrast that purple fennel provides in the garden is its greatest asset. While purple fennel clearly belongs in the herb and kitchen gardens, it is beyond comparison as a foil for perennials and bulbs. Fennel's delicate purple-smoke color combines with almost any hue, setting off bright orange and yellow but equally flattering to white and pastel lavender, pink and pale blue. You can allow purple fennel to self-sow and let it form drifts in perennial beds, pruning it back or pulling it where it doesn't suit you. Or deliberately place a group of 3 where there is plenty of room, and let it form a large mass. Purple fennel provides a sublime backdrop for large showy flowers such as the blazing orange-red of 'Fire King' daylily or the remarkable salmon peach spotted flowers of lily 'Tiger Babies'. For another look, front purple fennel's dark haze with lavender and the silvery foliage of 'Valerie Finnis' artemisia, and use summer-flowering bulbs for an accent. Try the lilac-purple balls of ornamental onion, *Allium aflatunense*, coming up through the artemisia and later the white trumpets of regal lilies, the purple-maroon reverse of each petal echoing the smoky backdrop. Experiment with purple fennel's ability to calm bright combinations. In an annual bed, mix purple fennel with red zinnias, 'Lady in Red' Texas sage, lavender-purple Brazilian verbena, and tall 'Blue Horizon' ageratum. The ferny foliage of purple fennel adds the same unifying effect to indoor flower arrangements. Keep some on the kitchen windowsill, and don't forget to add the tasty leaves to salads.

WHEN TO PLANT

Plant nursery-grown seedlings after the danger of hard frost. Seed may be sown earlier.

WHERE TO PLANT

Fennel does well in ordinary, well-drained soils and a sunny site. Plant in herb gardens, cut flower gardens, perennial beds, and annual displays.

HOW TO PLANT

Seed of purple fennel can be planted directly in prepared beds as soon as the soil is workable. Seed will germinate in approximately 2 weeks. Transplants can also be purchased in cell-packs; these won't grow as well as plants directly sown in the spring garden. Look for healthy plants without exposed roots, and try to disturb the roots as little as possible when planting. Space fennel at 8 to 12 in. apart.

ADVICE FOR CARE

Fennel's yellow Queen Anne's lace-type flower begins forming in late summer. Plants are at their best earlier in the season and may lose some appeal when in flower. Removing the flowers as they appear will preserve the foliage effect for a while. To take advantage of self-sowing, be sure to let some of the flowers set seed. In the spring, weed out unwanted seedlings.

ADDITIONAL INFORMATION

The exotic-looking striped caterpillar of the swallowtail butterfly may appear and munch on the foliage as it does in the herb garden on fennel's relatives, parsley and dill. Usually, there are not enough caterpillars to be a nuisance. The arrival of the beautiful butterflies later in the season more than makes up for any lost foliage.

ADDITIONAL SPECIES, CULTIVARS, OR VARIETIES

The purple form of fennel is sometimes offered as *Foeniculum vulgare* 'Purpurea', or it will appear as "fennel, bronze form" on seed packets or nursery tags. The named selections 'Smokey' and 'Giant Bronze' are available. The green form of fennel is attractive as well.

Snapdragon

Antirrhinum majus

Height: 6 to 36 in.
Flowers: Pink, yellow, peach, purple, mahogany; some bi- and tricolored
Bloom Period: Early summer to frost
Zones: 3, 4, 5, 6
Light Requirement:

Plants that do tricks fascinate youngsters—and grownups as well when they think no one is looking. Snapdragon's "trick" is an all-time favorite: Pinch the sides of the bloom together to see the dragon's mouth snap open and closed. In addition to tricks, snapdragons offer many treats. This old-fashioned garden staple presents spikes loaded with flowers in pastel pinks, peaches, and purples. A cluster of pure white snapdragons adds formal grace to the perennial border. Snapdragons are useful for edging and bedding and, of course, in the cutting garden. Heights range from under 12 in. to several feet tall and some cultivars have ruffled flowers. Position smaller snapdragons at the front of beds, and use the taller ones toward the middle to back of the border. The dwarf and intermediate varieties do not require staking. Popular in the 1800s, snapdragons remain in vogue with gardeners a century later because they perform well in sunny locations. Newer cultivars retain their petals longer than their forebears. For container growing, try the dwarfs such as 'Floral Carpet' and 'Tahiti' for low-growing masses of color.

WHEN TO PLANT

Purchase plants to set out in spring. Snapdragons can tolerate cooler conditions than some annuals, so they may be planted a few weeks before the last frost date. Choose selections that resist rust.

WHERE TO PLANT

Plant snapdragons in full sun. Soil should be light, rich (amend if necessary with compost or leaf mold), and well drained. Avoid planting in heavy clay.

HOW TO PLANT

Space plants 8 to 15 in., depending on the plant's ultimate size. They should be pinched back for more compact, bushier form. After planting, feed with a transplant fertilizer such as 3-10-3.

ADVICE FOR CARE

Generally, snapdragons have a flush of bloom during the summer and then reflower later. They are especially suited to cottage gardens, old-fashioned gardens, and perennial beds but not for mass bedding. They can be tricky to grow. Snapdragons dislike conditions that are too wet or too dry, and it takes a period of trial and error to find the right balance. Fertilize the plants with a balanced food such as 10-10-10 as they near their expected size to stimulate flowering. After that, do not feed again until the snapdragons finish blooming. At that time, they may be cut back and fed again. Taller types may be staked at planting. Use plant supports or insert bushy twigs among the plants, which will hide the sticks as they grow. Deadhead regularly to improve appearance and redirect the plant's energy to new growth. Cutting for use in arrangements provides beautiful flowers for indoor decorations and also helps the plants stay vigorous.

ADDITIONAL INFORMATION

Snapdragons often continue blooming well into fall, staying active even after the first few frosts. They may self sow. Rust, the bane of older types of snapdragons, appears as small brown powder-filled dots on the underside of leaves. It is a fungus. Plant only snapdragons that are resistant to rust. Improve air circulation around plants through adequate spacing. This will help the plants stay healthy.

ADDITIONAL SPECIES, CULTIVARS, OR VARIETIES

You have many to choose from. The 'Liberty' series (18 to 28 in.) has done well in trials in Michigan. These are quick to reflower on long, sturdy stems and are available in a wide range of colors. The 'Sonnet' (24 to 28 in.) series has also been a good intermediate.

Sunflower

Helianthus annuus

Height: 3 to 12 ft.
Flowers: Yellow, gold, bronze, creamy white, chocolate
Bloom Period: Late summer
Zones: 4, 5, 6
Light Requirement:

A trip to the lake, red ripe tomatoes, and big bouquets of sunflowers are all part of late summer in Michigan. Currently, sunflowers are riding a tide of popularity, appearing on posters, fabric, and breakfast cereal boxes and in advertisements. And it's no wonder. Their cheerful countenance and sunny flowers are irresistible. The huge seed-producing types such as 'Mammoth', used for sunflower seed and oil, are too ungainly for most gardens, but dozens of smaller, more ornamental types are now available, including plants for cut flowers and dwarf selections suitable for bedding. Sunflowers, given sun and average soil, are easy to grow from seed and trouble free. They are well suited to our summers, and their golden yellow flowers often appear in meadows and old fields and along fences. The cutting types are available in yellow, gold, and a range of rich autumnal colors. The outer petals (actually ray flowers) typically surround a large purple-brown center, creating the classic sunflower shape, but breeders have produced bicolor, double, and semi-double flowers. It can be difficult to find the perfect place to plant sunflowers. Most are large, coarsely textured, and rarely refined. Plant them in large borders or cut flower beds, or consider the vegetable garden. The recent smaller selections are suitable for beds, borders, or even large containers. The seeds of sunflowers are attractive to birds, especially goldfinches, and also to squirrels and chipmunks. A large arrangement of sunflowers, immortalized in van Gogh's million-dollar painting, can be yours for the price of a seed packet. Cut flowers last 7 to 10 days in a vase.

WHEN TO PLANT

Sow seed in the spring after the danger of frost is past. Seed germinates quickly, often within a week.

WHERE TO PLANT

The giant seed-producing types are best confined to vegetable gardens or country fence lines, but many of the cutting types are suitable for the back of the annual border or mixed plantings. In a residential landscape, just one row at the edge of a small vegetable or herb plot will provide armfuls of flowers for cutting and plenty of seed for birds. Full sun is necessary.

How to Plant

Plant seed at the depth recommended on the seed packet, typically 1/4- to 1/2-in. deep. For the easiest and quickest method of spacing plants, sow 3 seeds together at the desired spacing, usually 1 to 3 ft. When the seedlings reach about 6 in., leave one and cut the extra seedlings down at soil level. Don't pull or the roots may be disturbed.

Advice for Care

Easy to grow, sunflowers will prosper in soil of average fertility. Although they are somewhat drought tolerant, regularly watering when rain is scarce will promote good health. Large plants may need to be tied to a stout stake to keep them upright, particularly in windy locations. A double row can be self-supporting. Keep flowers cut regularly to promote flower production. Squirrels can be a nuisance, breaking stems in their quest for seeds.

Additional Information

Children love growing sunflowers. The seeds are easy to plant, they grow quickly, and the results are dramatic. Youngsters will enjoy a sunflower house. Sow seed of a tall variety of sunflower in a rectangle or circle large enough to provide a hiding place for a child. Thin plants to 1 ft. apart, and leave a 2-ft. opening for the door. By late summer, the seeds will have grown to create a magical room!

Additional Species, Cultivars, or Varieties

The vast array of sunflower seeds available in any garden center attests to their current popularity. Check the ultimate size and spacing to be sure you have enough space to accommodate your selection. Here are a few favorites: 'Autumn Beauty' (5 to 6 ft.) is a blend of yellow, bronze, red, and mahogany including bicolors. It's excellent for cutflower use but too large for the border. 'Italian White' (4 to 5 ft.) has creamy white flowers with chocolate centers on more graceful stems and is suitable as a tall accent for garden beds. 'Teddy Bear' (2 to 3 ft.) has fully double flowers, creating a golden orb 6 in. across. 'Sunrich Orange' (4 to 6 ft.) has golden orange petals surrounding a dark center. It's pollenless so it doesn't create a mess when cut and brought inside. Another nice short cultivar is 'Pacino' (24 in.).

Wax Begonia

Begonia "Semperflorens Hybrids"

Other Name: Fibrous-rooted
Begonia
Height: 6 in. to 2 ft.
Flowers: Red, white, rose,
pink, coral, or bicolor,
with green, bronze, or
variegated leaves
Zones: 3, 4, 5, 6
Light Requirement:

Lining a red brick pathway or planted in a lightly shaded area, wax begonias bring a festive look to the garden. These dependable, minimal-care annuals are deservedly popular for their crisp effect and vibrant colors. Silky yellow-centered flowers of white, pink, or red dot the mounds of green or bronze leaves, which are slightly cupped, fleshy, and succulent. Wax begonias are tidy, long-flowering plants that quickly reach 6 to 14 in. tall (some new landscape varieties grow to 2 ft.) and 6 to 8 in. wide. They do not require dead-heading, and they bloom continuously from early summer until frost. These low-maintenance annuals are often used for landscaping and commercial bedding. Play up their neat, compact shapes by using them as miniature hedges along a path or as bedding plants for color and interest from both the blooms and the foliage. They make a stunning contrast grown with dusty miller or other plants with silvery foliage. Even alone, wax begonias provide enough variation of leaf and flower color to be an interesting study. Once considered a plant for shady spots, newer wax begonias tolerate and even thrive in sun as long as temperatures stay below 90 degrees Fahrenheit and the roots are kept cool with mulch. Plants grown in full sun may require more frequent watering than those growing in light shade. Since there are many choices among annuals for full sun, however, play up the wax begonia's strengths by displaying it in filtered light, part shade, or shade, perhaps with coleus. The brightly colored begonia flowers will echo the shades in the coleus leaves.

WHEN TO PLANT
Buy young plants in late spring to set out when the soil warms and nighttime temperatures stay above 50 degrees Fahrenheit. If the weather is cool and wet after transplanting, wax begonias may be slow to establish.

WHERE TO PLANT

Wax begonias are best in partial shade but will tolerate sun with adequate moisture. They prefer well-drained soil of average or better fertility.

HOW TO PLANT

Space wax begonias 6 to 10 in. apart, depending on the height of the variety selected. The seed packet or transplant tag will have specific spacing instructions. After planting, feed with a transplant fertilizer such as 3-10-3.

ADVICE FOR CARE

Wax begonias are easy to maintain. They require regular water, especially plants growing in sun. Those in sun should be mulched to conserve moisture and help keep the soil and roots cool. Use a slow-release fertilizer or feed with a balanced fertilizer such as 10-10-10 every 3 weeks or as desired. Usually, wax begonias are not troubled by pests or disease.

ADDITIONAL INFORMATION

Wax begonias are also known as fibrous-rooted begonias. There are many hybrids to choose from in a range of colors and heights. Begonias may be dug up and potted in late summer, then brought indoors for the winter as houseplants. Start cuttings from those plants in early spring, then plant outside when the weather warms.

ADDITIONAL SPECIES, CULTIVARS, OR VARIETIES

Dwarf cultivars such as 'Rose Perfection', which has green leaves, reach just 6 to 8 in. Other types grow to 14 in. Certain hybrids such as ones in the 'Party' line have larger flowers and have done well in Michigan trials. Hybrid tuberous begonias (*Begonia* "Tuberhybrida Hybrids") grow from tender tubers. To keep them for another year, dig the tubers in fall, and store them until spring. They are available in yellow, peach, orange, red, and white, with larger flowers and leaves than wax begonias. Tuberous begonias are choice plants for containers, hanging baskets, and windowboxes in protected shade. Too much water can cause the stems to rot at soil level. Keep them well drained and on the dry side.

ANNUALS

Zinnia

Zinnia angustifolia

Other Names: Classic Zinnia; Narrow-leaf Zinnia
Height: 12 in.
Flowers: White, yellow, orange
Bloom Period: Early summer to frost
Zones: 4, 5, 6
Light Requirement:

Centuries ago, the Aztecs grew classic zinnia, *Zinnia angustifolia*, as an ornamental plant, but this eager-to-please annual is unknown to many Northern gardeners. Not for long. *Zinnia angustifolia* 'Crystal White' won the All-America Selection award for 1997, a designation akin to the hiring of a press agent. You're going to be hearing more about this plant, and 'Crystal White' deserves the notoriety. These adaptable free-flowering zinnias have been getting top marks in the Michigan State University annual trial garden for years. Classic zinnia is heat and drought tolerant and flowers like crazy until frost. Narrow dark green foliage supports a multitude of small daisies (about 2 in. across) with orange centers. In addition to white, the flowers come in hot summer shades of brilliant orange and golden yellow. A slightly lighter stripe down the center of each petal gives the flowers a luminous glow. Use classic zinnia for edging, sunny patios, and annual and perennial beds. 'Crystal White' and the other white selections are easy to use in the garden, mixing effortlessly with other colors. Try them with bright pink portulaca and purple verbena in a hot site. In a perennial bed, white classic zinnia complements lavender-blue catmint and 'Moonshine' yarrow. It would be impossible to discuss narrow-leaf zinnia and exclude the common zinnia, *Zinnia elegans*, a well-loved and easy-to-grow but sometimes disease-prone summer beauty. This is the definitive cut-and-come-again annual; the more flowers you pick, the more flowers are produced. A bouquet of zinnias is one of summer's delights. A wide range of sturdy, disease-resistant, and colorful selections is available, ranging in height from 6 to 36 in. Many are appropriate for garden use. Both classic and common zinnias are simple to grow from seed.

WHEN TO PLANT

Zinnias are not frost tolerant, and seed won't germinate—it may even rot—in cold soil. Wait until a week or so after the frost-free date to sow seed or set out transplants.

WHERE TO PLANT

Zinnias prefer fertile, well-drained soil. Classic zinnia is more tolerant of poor, dry soils than common zinnia. Both types work well in garden beds and borders. Common zinnia should also be planted in vegetable gardens for cut flowers.

HOW TO PLANT

Gently remove young plants from containers or cell-packs—squeeze the sides, don't pull on the stem—and plant in a prepared garden bed. Plant transplants so that the soil around the seedling is even with the garden soil. Firm the soil around the transplant and then water. Keep zinnia transplants well watered to lessen transplant shock. Seed can be directly sown in the garden after the ground has warmed. Germination will take 5 to 7 days. Space plants of classic zinnia 6 to 10 in. apart and common zinnia 8 to 18 in. apart, depending on the mature height and your intended effect.

ADVICE FOR CARE

Plants of the common zinnia, especially the tall cutting types, should be pinched to promote bushy, well-branched plants. Taller types may need staking. Remove flowers as they fade. All zinnias are susceptible to foliar diseases. Avoid sprinklers and water at ground level to keep the leaves dry. Zinnias flourish in hot, dry summers, but water regularly during dry spells. Classic zinnia is more drought tolerant than common zinnia. A liquid fertilizer applied every 3 to 4 weeks at the rate recommended on the package will promote healthy, strong growth.

ADDITIONAL INFORMATION

Classic zinnia is pest- and disease-free and never needs deadheading or support. Common zinnia needs deadheading and taller types of common zinnia may need staking.

ADDITIONAL SPECIES, CULTIVARS, OR VARIETIES

Several selections of classic zinnia are available, and, except for flower color, they are quite similar. 'Crystal White' has larger flowers. Sometimes plants are offered as *Zinnia linearis*. Numerous selections of common zinnia are available. Choose those that are touted as being disease resistant to avoid problems. 'Scarlet Splendor', another All-America Selection winner, boasts 4- to 5-in. red flowers. It has performed well in Michigan. The 'Dreamland' and 'Border Beauty' series have also done well and come in a wide range of colors.

CHAPTER TWO

Groundcovers

*G*ROUNDCOVERS ARE OFTEN CALLED CARPET-LIKE, AND FOR GOOD REASON. They spread out over a large area, forming a dense mat. And just as there are many kinds of carpets—broadlooms, Berbers, and Orientals, to name a few—there are many different groundcovers for the garden.

Turfgrass is by far the most popular way to cover the soil "wall to wall." But there are scores of attractive groundcover options that offer patterned textures of overlapping leaves. These can bring life to the garden in much the same way a well-placed Oriental rug can bring interest to a living room.

Some groundcovers are just a few inches tall, but they will run quickly over the soil surface. *Ajuga*, for example, grows low, with its leaves so tightly packed together that it creates the effect of a rippling sea of bronze and green. Other plants used as groundcovers may be taller and form spreading clumps. The dwarf Chinese astilbe is 12 in. tall and has a fern-like texture and an overall delicate effect.

Some groundcovers are a deep green color all year; others are variegated, purple or maroon, and deciduous or semi-evergreen. Some have tiny insignificant flowers, while others have beautiful blooms.

Many plants beyond the Big Three—pachysandra, ivy, and myrtle—can be used as groundcovers if planted in a mass. Groundcovers are often under one foot in height, but they can be taller.

Groundcovers have a unifying effect, tying together the elements of the garden. Their rich colors and textures form a strong horizontal layer that sets the stage for trees, shrubs, and other plants. But unity doesn't have to mean boring—groundcovers can be used with creativity for unusual effects. They can border a lawn, spread under

Chapter Two

trees, and meander into woodland gardens. Although probably most widely used in full to partial shade, there are groundcovers for sunny areas, too.

The groundcovers selected for this book are easy to grow, and, once established in a favorable site, they require little care. Groundcovers sometimes grow where turfgrasses struggle or maintenance is difficult, such as in deep shade or on a hard-to-mow slope. They can be a viable low-maintenance and environmentally sound alternative to a lawn.

Groundcovers perform other tricks, too. Their leaves disguise the ripening foliage of daffodils and other spring bulbs. They often grow so densely that they are weed-free, which is good news for gardeners who want to maintain an attractive area with a minimum of maintenance. Evergreen groundcovers give the pleasure of green, full-of-life color even in dreary January and February.

If the only groundcovers you've met so far are pachysandra, ivy, and myrtle, read on. You're about to make the acquaintance of some new and useful plants.

CHOOSING A GROUNDCOVER

Look at how groundcovers are used in your area, both in private gardens and in public displays. Make note of each groundcover's color, height, texture, and overall effect.

Consider how much groundcover you'll need and where you can obtain it. Due to their spreading nature, most herbaceous groundcovers are easy to propagate by division in spring. They are also available at garden centers or through mail-order catalogs.

Find a groundcover that will be appropriate for your soil and exposure. Plants selected specifically for a site will have the best chance of being healthy, growing vigorously, and creating dense mats.

Beware of certain fast-spreading groundcovers such as goutweed or others described as aggressive. These can turn into invasive garden thugs. Even traditional groundcovers such as vinca and English ivy may spread into nearby natural areas, choking out the native plants.

PLANTING A GROUNDCOVER

Soil preparation for groundcovers is just as important as for a new lawn or perennial bed. Mark the outline of the area to be planted and remove turf and weeds. A soil test will determine if any nutrients are required. Unless the area is immediately surrounding a mature shade tree, loosen the soil to a depth of 6 to 12 in., depending on the type of groundcover being planted. Correct drainage problems and work in well-rotted compost, aged manure, leaf mold, or other organic material to improve heavy clay or sandy soils.

It's risky to plant a groundcover right around the base of a large shade tree. The tree's feeder roots are close to the soil surface and extensive digging can damage them. Rather than turning the soil over the whole area, dig only small pockets, amend with organic material, and plant the groundcover into these holes.

For larger plantings that are not under mature trees, prepare the bed, cover it with a 2- to 3-in. layer of mulch, then set out the groundcover containers. Spacing depends on each groundcover's growth rate and how fast you want the plants to completely cover the soil. Closer spacing will result in rapid cover. Planting farther apart is more economical, but it will take several years to cover the area. See individual entries for more on spacing.

Start planting at the rear of the bed. Remove the groundcover gently from its container and plant, pulling the mulch away from the area surrounding the crown. The groundcovers should be positioned so they are at the same level as they were in their containers.

Chapter Two

Water after planting and during dry periods until the ground-cover is well established. Weeding is crucial until the plants fill in. After that happens, maintenance chores are few.

In addition to the entries in this chapter, other plants in this book can be used for groundcovers. You'll find mention of these in the chapters on perennials, woodland plants and ferns, and shrubs.

Combine plants that cover the ground for a tapestry effect. Intermingle drifts of plants with similar cultural requirements. Add bulbs for spring interest and the distinction between groundcover planting and the rest of the garden becomes delightfully blurred.

Barrenwort

Epimedium × versicolor 'Sulphureum'

Other Name: Bishop's Hat
Height: 8 to 12 in.
Flowers: Yellow
Bloom Period: Mid-spring
Zones: 5, 6
Light Requirement:

The glossy heart-shaped leaflets of barrenwort, more often called epimedium, form a beautiful carpet under trees and shrubs. In addition, spring and fall bring special interest. In mid-spring, delicate sprays of little spurred flowers arise from the ground on thin stems. The foliage, suffused with bronzy red as it emerges, ripens to green and then in fall changes to a coppery hue. *Epimedium × versicolor* 'Sulphureum' is the toughest of the barrenworts, tolerating difficult dry shade and spreading to form a groundcover. In mid-Michigan it has prospered under the dense shade and root competition of a Colorado blue spruce. Although initially slow, once established the rhizomatous roots of barrenwort spread underground to form a weed-free carpet. Excellent as a groundcover, barrenwort also makes a delightful addition to a shade or woodland garden. The flowers of *Epimedium × versicolor* 'Sulphureum' don't jump out at you in May when there is so much else to look at, but they're worthy of close examination. Each dainty spray produces 10 to 20 spurred flowers in 2 shades of yellow, pale and bright. The foliage, divided into heart-shaped leaflets, arises from the ground on wiry stems. Delicate in appearance, the foliage is resilient, taking abuse and yet remaining attractive far into the fall. In warmer climates the foliage is semi-evergreen, but in Michigan it turns a coppery brown, providing some winter interest. Combine epimedium with the bigroot geranium, *Geranium macrorrhizum*, and wild oats, *Chasmanthium latifolium*, for an appealing contrast of color and texture and year-round interest in the shade.

WHEN TO PLANT
Container-grown plants can be planted in spring and September.

WHERE TO PLANT
Native to the moist woods of Asia, barrenwort prefers partial shade and moist soils that are high in organic matter. Many epimediums will tolerate dry, shady conditions, and *Epimedium × versicolor*

'Sulphureum' is the most adaptable. Plant in the shade garden, as a shady foundation planting, in a woodland garden, and as a groundcover under trees and shrubs. Barrenwort makes an elegant underplanting for winter hazel or fringe-tree.

HOW TO PLANT

Plant barrenwort in the garden 12 to 14 in. apart. Dig holes and position the plant so that the soil level is the same as it was in the pot. Water thoroughly. Mulch will help the plants stay moist.

ADVICE FOR CARE

If you leave the foliage for winter interest, cut it back in early spring to make way for the flowers. To increase your planting, divide clumps in the spring when new growth is just emerging. Lift plants to be divided, and pull apart the shallow fibrous roots into clumps. Replant in the garden at the same depth. Keep moist until established. Mulch to conserve moisture.

ADDITIONAL INFORMATION

Both the flowers and the foliage of barrenwort are excellent for cutting. The flowers, although small, are precious in small vases where you can appreciate them close up. Another common name, bishop's hat, describes their unusual shape. The glossy foliage is an attractive addition to arrangements from late spring until fall. These plants are pest- and disease-free.

ADDITIONAL SPECIES, CULTIVARS, OR VARIETIES

A range of species and cultivars of barrenwort exists. All are excellent for partial shade. *E. × versicolor* 'Sulphureum' is the most vigorous for use as a groundcover. It is a hybrid of *E. grandiflorum* and *E. pinnatum* subsp. *colchicum*. Other types may be used as a groundcover or as a shade perennial. The red barrenwort, *E. × rubrum* (8 to 12 in.), reportedly hardy to Zone 4, forms spreading clumps. A good groundcover choice, it has crimson flowers, foliage stained with garnet red in the spring, and reddish fall color. The longspur barrenwort, *E. grandiflorum* (12 in.), a clump former, has large flowers with delicate spurs. The best selections are 'Rose Queen' with dark purple-pink flowers and 'White Queen' with long-spurred white flowers. Both have bronzy leaves in early spring.

Bigroot Geranium

Geranium macrorrhizum

Height: 12 to 15 in.
Flowers: Magenta-pink, pink, white
Bloom Period: Summer
Zones: 3, 4, 5, 6
Light Requirement:

Geranium macrorrhizum earns its place among the hardy geraniums. Hardy in every sense of the word, bigroot geranium is rugged and vigorous with the ability to withstand adversity. Add beautiful and easy to grow to its list of attributes, and you've got a perennial groundcover with a place in almost any Michigan garden. The common name, bigroot geranium, describes its thick, fleshy roots, which give it the ability to overcome dry shade, root competition, and drought to form a dense groundcover. Its lobed leaves, with a scalloped edge, are softly hairy, creating a beautiful texture over the surface of the soil. Rising above the foliage, the rosy to light pink flowers have protruding floral parts, creating a delicate, wispy appearance. Bigroot geranium contributes extra interest in autumn when the older foliage turns scarlet and bronze. The younger foliage remains semievergreen, providing a green reminder of spring in the winter garden. Use this hardy geranium as a complement to shrub roses and spring bulbs. Ideal with daffodils, the geranium's foliage expands to mask the bulb's dying foliage. *Geranium macrorrhizum*, a superb groundcover for partial shade, has so much to offer that you'll want to plant it in your perennial beds as well.

WHEN TO PLANT

Plant container-grown bigroot geranium in spring or September. With adequate moisture, it may also be planted in summer.

WHERE TO PLANT

Geranium macrorrhizum prefers partial shade and well-drained soil. It will grow in full sun if provided with a moisture-retentive soil and a layer of mulch. Bigroot geranium tolerates a range of growing conditions, including dry shade, but it isn't for hot, dry locations. Use this hardy geranium as a groundcover under woody plants, in shady beds by the house, as an overplanting for bulbs, or in a perennial border.

How to Plant

Plant bigroot geranium 12 to 15 in. apart. Dig holes and position the plant so that the soil level is the same as it was in the pot. Keep moist until established.

Advice for Care

Although tolerant of dry conditions, bigroot geranium should be watered during drought for the best performance. Plants in full sun may need extra irrigation. In soils of low fertility, fertilize in the spring with a light application of balanced fertilizer such as 10-10-10. For propagation or rejuvenation, divide plants in the spring. Dig clumps and break apart. Replant pieces, each with a portion of thick stem and root. The rosettes of foliage on rhizome-like stems produce roots, and you can plant a section with few or no roots and still have success. Firm the soil around the new divisions, and keep moist until established. A layer of mulch is beneficial.

Additional Information

Bigroot geranium may self-sow, which is a useful trait in a ground-cover. Some of the cultivars don't produce seedlings. The foliage has a unique feature—fragrance, which separates *Geranium macrorrhizum* from any other. The crushed leaves emit a distinctive odor sometimes described as apple but really more of a "piney fresh" clean scent.

Additional Species, Cultivars, or Varieties

Several good cultivars of bigroot geranium are available. 'Album' (10 to 12 in.) is a notable selection with white flowers and pinkish-red calyces. 'Ingwersen's Variety' (12 in.) has pale pink flowers and glossy foliage. Many other hardy geraniums are useful as ground-covers. Dalmatian cranesbill, *Geranium dalmaticum* (4 to 6 in.), a lower carpeting plant, has small light pink flowers and fall color. We highly recommend *Geranium × cantabrigiense* (8 to 9 in.), a naturally occurring hybrid between bigroot geranium and Dalmatian cranes-bill. It has a low, ground-hugging habit and a multitude of flowers. It tolerates the dry shade under trees as well as sunnier locations. 'Biokova' has pink-flushed white flowers and a slightly less dense habit. In mid-Michigan, 'Biokova' has bloomed for more than 2 months, starting in June. A few cultivars and hybrids of *Geranium endressii* are also worth considering. *Geranium* 'Claridge Druce' (20 to 24 in.) and 'Wargrave Pink' (24 in.) are delicate pink-flowered plants, blooming over an extended period. Many other geraniums make superior groundcovers. (See the entry for bloody cranesbill in the chapter on perennials.)

Bugleweed

Ajuga reptans

Other Name: Carpet
Bugleweed
Height: 3 to 4 in.
Flowers: Blue
Bloom Period: Late spring
Zones: 4, 5, 6
Light Requirement:

Ajuga or bugleweed really deserves the label "groundcover." Its glossy, deeply veined leaves spread quickly to form a rippled carpet of green, purple, bronze, or variegated colors over the soil surface. The spikes of flowers, usually blue, appear above the low-growing leaves in May and early June, creating drifts of color that complement spring-blooming shrubs. The leaves remain a selling point all season. Plant bugleweed in shady banks, under flowering shrubs, along driveways and patios, or beneath hedges. The best place is where it will meet a hard surface such as pavement or brick. *Ajuga* is an aggressive spreader and will quickly invade a lawn, so select another groundcover if you need one to plant bordering grass. Bugleweed makes a fine, if somewhat assertive, groundcover in a woodland garden with ferns, hostas, astilbes, and other perennials in a lightly shaded corner. *Ajuga* is appropriate for many areas where a vigorous, weed-free groundcover is desired—so long as the site does not stay hot and dry, and it is not frequently traveled. *Ajuga* does not stand up to foot traffic.

WHEN TO PLANT

Container-grown *Ajuga* may be planted from spring to early fall. Keep new transplants watered during hot weather.

WHERE TO PLANT

Bugleweed prefers partial shade and moist, humus-rich soil. Plant it in a well-drained area to avoid disease such as crown rot. If the soil is heavy or infertile, amend before planting. Use *Ajuga* where you want a dense mat covering the soil surface. Bugleweed is one of the fastest growing groundcovers and is useful for small- to medium-sized areas. Its foliage and low habit make it a useful contrast to landscape plants, particularly shrubs, hostas, and daylilies. Use it to border a path or as a strip along the edge of a patio where it is contained by hard surfaces. Because it stays low to the ground and has a multitude of leaves that stick up at angles, *Ajuga* makes a beautifully textured surface.

How to Plant
Space plants 8 to 12 in. apart. Water after planting and during dry periods until the plants are established. Mulch to conserve moisture.

Advice for Care
Bugleweed requires no special care other than occasional watering during dry weather. Plants in sun, however, require additional water. Plantings should continue to perform well for many years. A general fertilizer such as 10-10-10 may be applied in the spring. The plants may be sheared after flowering to encourage new foliage and improve the appearance. Take divisions by separating the leaf rosettes that form at the end of the creeping above-ground stems called stolons, or lift clumps and split apart.

Additional Information
The foliage of *Ajuga* turns purple-bronze in fall. Markings of the variegated types are most brilliant in part shade. Occasionally, the variegated form will revert back to green. Remove the green-leaved pieces as soon as you notice them to maintain the true coloration. Bugleweed is susceptible to aphid infestations that cause the leaves to curl.

Additional Species, Cultivars, or Varieties
Interesting cultivars include 'Bronze Beauty', which has metallic bronze foliage and deep-blue flowers (6 in.), and 'Catlin's Giant', with purple-green foliage (10 in.). 'Burgundy Glow' (4 in.) is white, pink, rose, and green for a bright, multicolored effect. *Ajuga reptans* 'Atropurpurea' has bronze-purple leaves.

Creeping Juniper

Juniperus horizontalis

Height: 1 to 4 ft.
Foliage: Bluish-green, steel blue
Zones: 3, 4, 5, 6
Light Requirement:

One doesn't have to travel far from the beaches of Lake Michigan to find incredible juniper plants spread low and wide in the hottest, driest sandy soils imaginable. Their performance in nature is a sure sign that these plants can also be a valuable addition to our cultivated landscapes. Spreading to form an impenetrable weed barrier, *Juniperus horizontalis* offers steel blue or bluish-gray needles, attractive blue berries, and a striking purplish hue over the winter. The many selections of this evergreen native are a testament to its beauty and adaptability. Creeping juniper's toughness has led to extensive use in commercial landscapes, but its public persona shouldn't challenge its appeal. With a little imagination, the Michigan gardener can find a range of creative uses for this stalwart, ground-covering shrub. Creeping junipers can be used in many of the most difficult situations of the garden, from sandy, dry soils to heavy clay. They are easy to grow and adaptable to slightly acidic and alkaline soils. Use juniper to cover a steep slope, to fill in a rough spot or anywhere you need winter color. The low horizontal growth is perfect for foundation plantings, and its salt tolerance makes it useful along walks and driveways where deicing salts are commonly used. For a spring surprise, grow bulbs such as Dutch crocus through its low horizontal branches.

WHEN TO PLANT
Plant in spring or early fall.

WHERE TO PLANT
Creeping juniper prefers full sun for best performance, but it will tolerate light shade. Don't plant in deep shade. For use as a ground-cover, space plants at least 3 to 4 ft. apart because they spread over time. The colorful evergreen foliage of creeping juniper sets off shrubs with attractive bark and stems. Juniper's persistent foliage and winter color provide structure in a sunny perennial bed and are superb in a rock garden or on top of a stone wall.

How to Plant

Plant as a container-grown or balled-and-burlapped shrub. See the shrub chapter introduction for details on planting.

Advice for Care

Plant in full sun for strong, dense growth. Those in shade will become leggy and open with age and will not make effective groundcovers. Twig blight, *Phomopsis juniperovora*, is a common ailment of junipers that develops in the early spring, particularly in wet weather. The tips of the branches become a reddish brown, eventually turning an ash gray as needles die. Remove infected branches by pruning back to healthy growth. To avoid infection altogether, plant in open, dry areas and provide good drainage. Do not use overhead irrigation on your juniper plantings; this provides the moist conditions that favor disease development.

Additional Information

Use juniper for more than just a mass planting. Combine several cultivars for an attractive tapestry of textures and colors that may be more noticeable in winter. Plant it under the bright red stems of red-twig dogwood or the exfoliating bark of oakleaf hydrangea. Add perennials such as hellebores or 'Palace Purple' alumroot. Creeping juniper makes an excellent evergreen foil and winter interest plant for perennial plantings. Plant it on a sunny slope with blue oat grass, lavender, stonecrop, and other sun lovers. Add daffodils, botanical tulips, or ornamental onions for extra interest.

Additional Species, Cultivars, or Varieties

'Blue Chip' (8 to 10 in.) has excellent blue needle color, purplish winter color, and a low spreading habit. It may even reach 8 to 10 ft. wide. 'Wiltonii' or 'Blue Rug' is an extremely low-growing form, topping out at 4 to 6 in. and a width of 6 to 8 ft. The foliage is silvery blue, turning light purple in the winter months. A wide range of cultivars exists with different heights, textures, foliage color, and winter color.

Dwarf Chinese Astilbe

Astilbe chinensis var. *pumila*

Height: 8 to 12 in.
Flowers: Rose-purple
Bloom Period: Midsummer
   to early fall
Zones: 4, 5, 6
Light Requirement:

Astilbes require dappled shade and rich, moist soil, but this dwarf form of Chinese astilbe bends the rules. It endures sun or dry shade and less-than-rich soil. It also is spreading. An excellent groundcover, dwarf Chinese astilbe grows at a moderate pace and never becomes invasive. The rose-purple flowers borne on stiff spikes bloom from late July through September. They aren't as spectacular as the feathery plumes of the more familiar hybrid astilbe, but they prolong the astilbe season, adding interest to shade gardens when not much else is in bloom. Later, the flowering stalks provide interest in the winter garden. The medium-textured, ferny foliage, bronzy when new, hugs the ground. Not a clump-former like most astilbes, this carpeting perennial spreads by underground stems to form a weed-proof carpet. Of course, it prefers rich soil and partial shade, but it prospers in sun in moisture-retentive soil. Dwarf Chinese astilbe is easy to divide and can be spread to form large sweeps. In the shade garden, the foliage contrasts with the larger leaves of hosta, Siberian bugloss, and Solomon's seal. Try it with lady's mantle to edge a brick walk in filtered shade. Or in moist sun, combine the rosy-purple flowers with lavender-blue asters and the gray foliage and milky flowers of pearly everlasting, *Anaphalis triplinervis*. Use it as a groundcover under trees and shrubs and in smaller drifts with other herbaceous perennials.

WHEN TO PLANT
Plant container-grown plants in the spring or September.

WHERE TO PLANT
Dwarf Chinese astilbe prefers partial shade and moist, well-drained soil that is high in organic matter. It has proven to be tougher than other astilbes, tolerating sun in heavy, moist soil and dry soil in shade. Plant it in partial shade as a groundcover under trees and shrubs, in a shade garden, or in moist, sunny perennial beds.

HOW TO PLANT

Plant container-grown plants at the same depth that they were growing in their pots. Space at approximately 12 to 18 in. depending on how large the plants are and how rapidly you want coverage. Keep well watered until established. Mulch plants for best results.

ADVICE FOR CARE

In sun, dwarf astilbe will need watering during dry spells. With sun and dry soil, the foliage cups, indicating water stress, or it may scorch. In soils of low fertility, fertilize plants in the spring with a light application of balanced fertilizer such as 10-10-10. You can remove the flowering spikes if you don't like their appearance as they turn brown. If left on the plant, however, they will persist into winter, providing attractive contrast against snow. To increase your planting, divide plants in the spring when the foliage is emerging. Dig sections to be divided, and separate into pieces with a knife or sharp spade. Replant at the same level, and keep well watered until new roots form. You can also use a spade to make divisions without lifting the entire planting.

ADDITIONAL INFORMATION

The flowering spike opens slowly from the bottom up. This lengthens the blooming period but also leads to a stage where some flowers are pink and others are brown. For an interesting tapestry of ground-covering plants, use dwarf Chinese astilbe with the shiny leaves of European ginger, bigroot geranium, and hosta in partial shade.

ADDITIONAL SPECIES, CULTIVARS, OR VARIETIES

Plants sold as *Astilbe chinensis* var. *pumila* may vary somewhat in height and color. Plants may also be given the cultivar name 'Pumila'. 'Finale' (15 to 18 in.) is larger, and the flowers are a soft mauve-pink. A few other cultivars exist. They are not as spreading as those above. 'Serenade' (14 in.) has more feathery rose-red flowers. The clump-forming hybrid astilbe, *Astilbe × arendsii*, makes a suitable groundcover in partial shade and cool, moist soil and is particularly attractive when combined with hosta. It will not spread to cover the ground, however.

Lily-of-the-Valley

Convallaria majalis

Height: 6 to 8 in.
Flowers: White or pale pink
Bloom Period: Late spring
Zones: 3, 4, 5, 6
Light Requirement:

About the same time that daffodils are blooming, the sturdy green shoots of lily-of-the-valley are pushing up from the soil. By mid-May, dainty stalks arch over the leaves and bear the white ball-like buds. As they open, lily-of-the-valley releases its sweet fragrance, which for many gardeners is the essence of spring. Lily-of-the-valley is easy to grow in well-drained soil and partial shade. It spreads by rhizomes, or underground stems, and will quickly carpet an area with part sun, part shade, or even full shade. In fact, lily-of-the-valley is such a strong grower that it can be invasive. Keep it within bounds with barriers, or place it where the plant's spreading nature is a plus, such as a groundcover under shrubs. Do not plant lily-of-the-valley in perennial borders. Each plant has 2 pointed leaves 6 to 8 in. long and 3 in. wide with a stiff, somewhat coarse effect. Its value as a groundcover is in late spring and summer. By August, the leaves begin to look ratty, especially if the plants are grown in sun and there has been little rain. Still, lily-of-the-valley has its strengths, including the ability to grow under shade trees where few other plants will survive. The fragrant white bell-like flowers of May and early June are more than enough reason to grow this perpetual favorite.

When to Plant

Container-grown plants may be planted from April through September. Sections of lily-of-the-valley rhizome or underground stem with 2 to 3 pips, which are shoots or "eyes," should be planted in spring.

Where to Plant

Place in part to full shade. Lilies-of-the-valley prefer moisture-retentive soil but will grow nearly anywhere that isn't under water. If the plants are grown in full sun and it is hot and dry, the leaves will become yellow and beat-up looking as the summer progresses. The best use is as a groundcover in a defined shady area that will not receive foot traffic. Lily-of-the-valley is valuable for covering slopes to prevent erosion. Combine it with ferns, hostas, and astilbes.

HOW TO PLANT

Pot-grown plants should be spaced 8 to 12 in. apart. Sections of rhizome can be set 6 in. apart and 1 to 2 in. deep.

ADVICE FOR CARE

Once established, lilies-of-the-valley need little care. Water during hot dry periods to extend the life of the foliage. After leaves die in the fall, rake out the foliage. Some gardeners topdress the plants with well-rotted compost or aged manure in late fall. Plants grown beneath trees will require additional water and fertilizer. Plants that are producing fewer flowers than in previous seasons may be dug and divided in spring or fall.

ADDITIONAL INFORMATION

Cut stems to place in small vases for a closer view of this unique flower. Note, though, that lily-of-the-valley is toxic, including the red-orange fruits it sometimes bears in fall.

ADDITIONAL SPECIES, CULTIVARS, OR VARIETIES

'Fortin's Giant' (12 to 15 in.) has large leaves and flowers and is a vigorous grower. 'Flore Pleno' has double flowers. 'Rosea' has flowers in pale pink and is not as invasive as the other two.

GROUNDCOVERS

Mother-of-Thyme

Thymus praecox var. arcticus

Other Name: Creeping Thyme
Height: 1 to 6 in.
Flowers: Rose-lavender
Bloom Period: Late spring to early summer
Zones: 4, 5, 6
Light Requirement:

The fine-textured mats of mother-of-thyme blanket the ground. When the plant is crushed or trod upon, a fragrance both savory and invigorating fills the air. It's not surprising that thyme has been used for centuries as a healthful tonic. Mother-of-thyme, sometimes called creeping thyme, forms carpets of small glossy leaves topped in late spring and early summer with round clusters of tiny rose-lavender flowers. Full sun and sandy, light soil are the only requirements for healthy growth. The height of plants offered as creeping thymes varies from 1 to about 6 in., and cultivars offer reliable size and a range of flower colors. This creeping groundcover is perfect for planting by sunny patios, on rock walls, and in perennial beds and as a complement for sun-loving perennials such as lavender, lamb's ears, and stonecrop. Although widely used as a groundcover and in perennial gardens, thyme is still considered first and foremost an herb. So when shopping for mother-of-thyme, look in the herb section of nursery catalogs and garden centers or you may miss out. Plants are available with purple, red-purple, pink, and white flowers. The flowers are very attractive to bees, and a mass in full flower will be abuzz. Use thyme to advantage by letting it spill over onto pathways or walks or over the top of rock walls. Mother-of-thyme is useful for filling in between pavers or the risers of sunny steps, but it can't withstand the pressures of heavy traffic. The fine texture and low form of this aromatic herb make it useful for weaving together a range of perennials. For a sunny patio, combine a variety of thymes with lavender, cheddar pinks, stonecrops, and bloody cranesbill, and accent with the ornamental onion called star-of-Persia. In places where thyme is growing well—full sun and well-drained soil—underplant with botanical tulips or dwarf bulbous iris for a spring treat.

WHEN TO PLANT

Plant thyme in the spring to early summer.

WHERE TO PLANT

Thyme prefers full sun and dry, free-draining soil of moderate to low fertility. It will grow in heavier soils and a bit of shade, but growth will be leggy in partial shade. It won't tolerate poor drainage. Use in any full sun situation. Thyme is wonderful bordering walks and patios and on top and in the crevices of rock walls where it will spill downward.

HOW TO PLANT

Space plants of creeping thyme about 12 in. apart. Smaller selections should be spaced closer together. Dig holes and position the plant so that the soil level is the same as it was in the pot. Don't plant too deep or plants may rot. Firm the soil and water well. Keep moist until established.

ADVICE FOR CARE

If located in sun and dry soil, thyme will have few pest and disease problems. It shouldn't need to be watered. Rot can be a problem in wet sites. Thyme doesn't like to be heavily mulched. Some thymes develop a semi-woody habit. In the spring your plants may have a lot of dieback. Cut back hard to live wood to promote compact growth. Thyme is easily divided in spring. Dig clumps and pull apart into sections for replanting.

ADDITIONAL INFORMATION

Keep in mind its bee appeal before planting if you are allergic to bee stings or have small children.

ADDITIONAL SPECIES, CULTIVARS, OR VARIETIES

Mother-of-thyme suffers from a confusing array of botanical names and is offered for sale by several. *Thymus praecox* var. *arcticus* is the current accepted name, but plants are often offered for sale as *Thymus serpyllum*. The cultivar 'Coccineus' has deep reddish-purple flowers on dark stems and small dark green leaves. It turns bronzy in the winter. 'Album' (3 in.) has white flowers and is very prostrate. Woolly thyme, *Thymus pseudolanuginosa* (2 in.), has sporadic pink flowers. It is grown for its small fuzzy silver-gray leaves, which form attractive gray mats. Try it combined on a stone wall with lamb's ears and hens-and-chicks. Plant botanical tulips and pasque-flower for spring interest. *Thymus vulgaris* (8 to 15 in.), the culinary thyme, is hardy to Zone 5.

Pachysandra

Pachysandra terminalis

Other Name: Japanese Spurge
Height: 6 to 10 in.
Flowers: White
Bloom Period: Late winter to early spring (pachysandra is really grown for its foliage)
Zones: 4, 5, 6
Light Requirement:

Among the Big Three evergreen groundcovers, pachysandra is the most popular. Unlike ivy and vinca, however, pachysandra does not have the potential to be invasive, so it is a fine choice for gardeners throughout much of Michigan. Its glossy green, notched leaves—each about 2 in. long—are pachysandra's trademark. Although the leaves dull and droop a bit during extremely cold weather, they remain a welcome sight all year. The white flowers usually appear in late winter to early spring. Easy to grow, pachysandra is at home in the casual woodland garden as well as at a formal estate. It is often planted as an elegant groundcover to sweep around the bases of trees and shrubs, forming a carpet about 6 to 10 in. tall. Even heavy shade, such as the kind found under maples, will not deter pachysandra from creating a lush swath of green.

WHEN TO PLANT

Container-grown pachysandra may be set out in spring or summer. The plants may be divided in spring to early summer.

WHERE TO PLANT

Pachysandra is a gorgeous evergreen groundcover for full to partial shade. Send it spreading under deciduous trees and shrubs or tall evergreens such as hemlocks. Plant bulbs such as daffodils within beds of pachysandra to add seasonal interest. Although it will not be as vigorous where exposed to full afternoon sun, pachysandra will survive if it receives adequate moisture. Plants in sun may develop leaf scorch, however. It is better to plant pachysandra in part to full shade to ensure healthy, attractive growth. As pretty as pachysandra is when well grown, it loses its appeal and becomes disease-prone when stressed.

HOW TO PLANT

Set 6 in. apart for good cover. Pachysandra is a slower grower than some other groundcovers. If spaced farther apart, it will take several years to fill in, increasing the need for weeding. Mulch new plants to conserve moisture and discourage weeds.

ADVICE FOR CARE

Soaker hoses are useful to water large plantings. Pinch off any browned leaves in late winter to improve the plant's appearance. At that point, the pachysandra may be fertilized with 10-10-10 or a fertilizer for acid-loving plants and watered well.

ADDITIONAL INFORMATION

Once pachysandra is established and covering the soil surface, it is so dense that weeds are usually not a problem. Leaf blight can infect stressed pachysandra plantings and ruin them. Outbreaks are most frequent in warm, humid weather in late spring and summer and on plants that were previously injured from winter damage, recent transplanting, or shearing, or stressed from placement in full sun. Healthy, vigorous plants resist leaf blight.

ADDITIONAL SPECIES, CULTIVARS, OR VARIETIES

Pachysandra terminalis 'Green Carpet' (6 to 8 in.) is a favorite. *Pachysandra terminalis* 'Variegata' has green-and-white variegated leaves that shine in deep shade, although it is less vigorous. *Pachysandra terminalis* 'Green Sheen' has remarkable leaves that are so glossy, they look as though they had been dipped in varnish. *Pachysandra procumbens* is the Alleghany spurge, native to woodlands of the southeastern U.S. It is somewhat taller than *P. terminalis* and grows in slowly spreading, broad clumps. It is attractive with spring wildflowers and hardy to Zone 5.

'Palace Purple' Alumroot

Heuchera micrantha 'Palace Purple'

Height: 12 to 24 in.
Flowers: White
Bloom Period: Summer
Zones: 3, 4, 5, 6
Light Requirement:

Purple in spring, the leaves of 'Palace Purple' fade to bronze-green while the leaf underside remains deep wine red. The richness of the foliage color nearly glows in a perennial border or landscape planting. The scalloped and veined basal leaves, similar in shape to geranium or maple leaves, grow near the base in a cluster and stay attractive into late fall and early winter. The leaf underside is slightly fuzzy. While groundcovers such as bugleweed spread quickly, heuchera is slower growing and remains in clumps. Plant it to bring attention to a smaller, defined area that you want noticed, or use it in drifts to add interest to a planting of groundcovers such as hostas, astilbe, foamflower, and hardy geraniums in a woodland garden. The bronze-purple color of 'Palace Purple' is a subtle foil for blues and purple and turns exotic when played against reds and oranges. Try it with *Allium aflatunense* for a stunning contrast of dark maroon with the ornamental onion's tall lilac-colored sphere. 'Palace Purple' is increasingly propagated by seed, which has created a range of color variation. Many are not as purple as the original selection. Some vegetatively propagated forms are being sold, including 'Molly Bush' and 'Bressingham Bronze'.

WHEN TO PLANT

Add container-grown plants to the garden from late April through September. Keep watered as they get established, especially if planting in summer.

WHERE TO PLANT

The foliage will scorch in hot sun if the site is dry. The best soil is well drained and high in organic material. Amend if needed before planting. Clumps of *Heuchera* make an interesting groundcover for a small area, lining a walk or massed in a border. Although the leaves stay about 12 in. high, the flower stalks reach 24 in. Some gardeners remove the flower stalks so that they do not distract from the effect of the foliage. The plant's spread is about 12 in. Do not plant alumroot where it will be walked on.

How to Plant
Plant about 12 in. apart. Established plants may be divided in spring.

Advice for Care
Water after planting. Remove flowering stalks when they begin to fade. 'Palace Purple' alumroot does better with adequate moisture. Mulch with shredded bark to conserve moisture, keep the soil cool, and lessen competition from weeds. Keep a mulch-free zone about 2 to 3 in. around the base of the plant. If the soil where they are planted is infertile, these perennials may be fed with 10-10-10 in early spring as they emerge from the ground. They do not require fertilizer every year. Alumroot is usually free from serious pests and diseases in well-drained soils. Divide the plants when they become overgrown and bare in the center.

Additional Information
Don't cut back the foliage in fall. It is semievergreen. In protected locations, the foliage will remain attractive for much of the winter. Remove old foliage in early spring.

Additional Species, Cultivars, or Varieties
Heuchera micrantha 'Ruffles' has lobed leaves and white flowers. *Heuchera micrantha* 'Bressingham Bronze' (12 to 24 in.) has a fade-resistant purple-bronze color. *Heuchera americana* 'Pewter Veil' has an unusual metallic-pewter finish with prominent green-purple veins. It does best in partial shade.

Spotted Dead Nettle

Lamium maculatum

Height: 8 to 12 in.
Flowers: Rose-pink, pink, white
Bloom Period: Late spring
Zones: 3, 4, 5, 6
Light Requirement:

Spotted dead nettle brings a touch of silver-white to the shade. Each green leaf is marked with a stroke, splash, or almost complete coat of silver, adding light to dim parts of the garden. In part shade and moist, well-drained soil, spotted dead nettle grows quickly, rooting at the leaf joints to form an appealing ground-cover. The short spikes of hooded flowers, although not the main attraction, create quite a show. They are produced in late May to early June and are typically deep rose-pink, but cultivars exist with pale pink and white flowers. Use spotted dead nettle as a groundcover under trees and shrubs, on a shaded slope, in shade gardens, and as a cover for bulbs. The prettiest and most useful types are those with a broad stripe of silver down the middle of the leaf. The variegation creates movement, mimicking the appearance of dappled light. It looks attractive in mass and combines well with shade-loving perennials. Cultivars such as 'Beacon Silver' are so heavily frosted that only a trace of green remains around the margin. The silver variegation sets off the color of blue-foliaged hostas. Try the vase-shaped hosta 'Krossa Regal' underplanted with *Lamium maculatum* 'White Nancy' for an elegant mix of silver, white, and green.

WHEN TO PLANT

Plant container-grown spotted dead nettle in the spring and late September. With adequate watering, they may also be planted in summer.

WHERE TO PLANT

Lamium prefers moist, well-drained soil in partial shade. It tolerates most soils. The silver-touched foliage adds life to shade but can become straggly in dry shade where there is too much competition from tree roots. Plant in light shade as a groundcover or edging plant, or combine it with perennials and bulbs.

How to Plant

Plant spotted dead nettle 12 to 18 in apart. Dig holes and position the plant so that the soil level is the same as it was in the pot. In partial shade, plants will fill in quickly. Water well after planting.

Advice for Care

Water spotted dead nettle during dry spells, especially where there is competition from tree roots. In the average shady garden, *Lamium* won't need extra fertilizer. Shear back after flowering to keep plants compact and create denser cover. Dead nettle is easy to divide. In spring or early summer, dig sections and pull apart. Replant and keep new divisions moist until established in their new location. Mulch to conserve moisture.

Additional Information

Spotted dead nettle can get leggy and sparse if planted where there is too much root competition, such as under a maple. Shear it back to keep it compact and force fresh new foliage. Use *Lamium* in drifts with other shade lovers for an attractive mix. Try spotted dead nettle with the coarse heart-shaped foliage of Siberian bugloss, 'Palace Purple' alumroot, and tall pink 'Ostrich Plume' astilbe to complete a shade garden combination. The silver-streaked foliage of dead nettle is attractive with bulbs, particularly those with white flowers such as summer snowflake and *Narcissus* 'Thalia'. In the fall, use white autumn crocus (*Colchicum* sp.) for extra interest.

Additional Species, Cultivars, or Varieties

Cultivated selections of dead nettle have various amounts of variegation, different flower color, and more compact, spreading growth. They are preferred to the species. 'Chequers' has rose-purple flowers and a center stripe of silver. 'Beacon Silver' has rose-purple flowers and silver leaves with narrow green borders. These silver-leaved forms should be used in smaller drifts because a large silver mass is too assertive in the shade. 'White Nancy' is very attractive and has slightly wider green margins than 'Beacon Silver'. 'Shell Pink' and 'Pink Pewter' have pale pink flowers. 'Aureum' has the novel combination of yellowish-green leaves with a creamy stripe. Don't get *Lamium maculatum* confused with *Lamiastrum galeobdolon* 'Variegatum'(12 in.), the variegated yellow archangel, a somewhat similar plant with a rampant nature. Use it only in restricted areas. 'Herman's Pride' has attractive silver stippling and is much more restrained.

GROUNDCOVERS

CHAPTER THREE

Hardy Bulbs

*H*ARDY BULBS ARE BURIED IN THE GARDEN AS COLDER WEATHER HINTS AT THE APPROACH OF WINTER, leaves fall from the trees, and garden flowers are turning brown and dying. Yet even surrounded by unmistakable cues that one season is ending, the gardener who plants hardy bulbs celebrates the certain renewal of life come spring.

In winter's final and spring's earliest days, nothing is more welcome than buttercup yellow winter aconites or a crisp white snowdrop nodding from a bright green stem. Later in the growing season, when showier plants are in flower, these tiny blossoms might go unnoticed. But at the end of a grueling winter, they are a harbinger of spring and a cause for joy.

Spring bulbs add bloom to a season of little color. They create dramatic displays, offer surprises around the base of a tree, and make elegant combinations with shrubs and perennials.

Many hardy bulbs excel in woodland gardens, where their natural beauty is perfect under trees. The bulbs will get enough sun to bloom before the trees finish leafing out in the spring and shade the area. Plant hardy spring-blooming bulbs in perennial beds and where annuals will be planted in late May or early June. Naturalize bulbs in turf and lower-maintenance areas as well as under roses, in groundcovers, and under shrubs.

PLANTING AND CARING FOR YOUR HARDY BULBS

Hardy bulbs, which also include certain corms, tubers, and rhizomes, are planted in the fall, spend the winter in the frozen ground, and bloom the following season. Among the most popular are the ones that bloom in the spring such as daffodils, crocuses, tulips, grape hyacinths, snowdrops, and squills.

Chapter Three

Tender bulbs such as cannas and dahlias will not survive a Michigan winter outdoors. They must be dug up in the fall and stored inside or treated as annuals and replanted every year.

Hardy bulbs are planted in September and October and generally flower from March to late May. Lilies, which bloom in summer, are planted in fall or spring.

Many bulbs are available locally or through specialty mail-order firms. When buying bulbs, select the largest ones and avoid any that are shriveled, soft, or moldy.

As with all garden plants, it is important to prepare the bed before planting bulbs. They will rot if they stand in water in the winter, so good drainage is necessary.

Improve the likelihood of success in sandy or heavy soil by digging in organic material such as well-rotted compost or leaf mold. Loosen the soil to about 12 to 14 in. deep and remove weeds and debris.

There are several ways to add a fertilizer specifically made for bulbs or a general-purpose fertilizer. If putting fertilizer in individual holes, dig the holes deeper and mix fertilizer well with the soil to avoid burning the bulbs. With a larger bed, incorporate the fertilizer into the entire area before planting, or scratch it into the surface afterward.

Your arrangement of the bulbs depends on the effect you're seeking. Many bulbs are best planted in drifts; others, such as tulips, are appropriate for more formal designs. Check each entry in this section for suggestions. Avoid planting bulbs in single file.

Planting depth depends on the bulb size. The general rule is to plant so the base of the bulb is three times as deep as the bulb is wide, although tulips may be planted deeper to extend their life. Check individual plant entries for more specific planting information. Although it can be tempting to cheat on this step if you're planting dozens of bulbs, best results will be achieved when the bulbs are planted at the proper depth. Make sure no air pockets remain under the bulb. Once the bulbs are planted, replace the soil, firm it, and water the area well.

Until the ground freezes, continue watering the bulbs when the soil is dry. When the ground freezes, newly planted bulbs may be mulched with shredded bark, evergreen boughs, or shredded leaves.

When the bulb's first shoots appear in spring, gradually remove the mulch and expose the emerging bulbs. Hardy spring bulbs will not be harmed by a sudden dip in temperatures. During the first year, the bulbs won't need extra fertilizer. In subsequent years, an early spring fertilizer may be beneficial, especially in soils with poor fertility. Bulbs planted in beds with other flowering plants that are fertilized generally don't need extra feedings.

After the bulbs bloom, leave the foliage on the plants until it turns papery and yellow or brown. While it is still green, the leaves are producing nutrients that aid the bulb in its production of next spring's flowers.

The hardy bulbs' yellowing or ripening foliage, left intact to nourish the bulbs for next year's show, can be hidden by growing perennials and annuals. Hostas are often used for this purpose. Their leaves emerge at just the right time to cloak the declining leaves of daffodils and tulips.

Most bulbs will continue flowering for years. Certain tulips, however, may bloom well for only one or two years, then show only leaves thereafter. When flower production declines, these bulbs should be dug and discarded.

Many bulbs are suited to forcing indoors in the winter. Pot them in October or November, placing the bulbs close enough together in potting soil or soilless mix to nearly touch. Place the containers in a cool area such as an unheated garage or basement, or in the refrigerator. In about 8 to 14 weeks, depending on type, the bulbs should be ready to bring back into room temperatures, where they will quickly begin to grow. After the bulbs flower, let the foliage ripen on the plant. Daffodils and crocuses may then be planted outdoors, where they usually rebloom in subsequent years.

Chapter Three

Hardy bulbs generally have few pest or disease problems. The biggest threat at planting time is from squirrels, which enjoy digging up and eating certain bulbs. Put an old window screen or wire mesh over the newly planted bed for a few weeks. It also helps to clean all bulb debris, such as the papery outer skins, from the ground around the planting site. Commercial repellents may be applied. Dutch gardeners plant crown fritillarias (*Fritillaria imperialis*) around bulb beds in the belief that rodents are put off by the skunky scent.

In spring, deer and rabbits may nibble bulb foliage and flowers; fencing is about the only permanent solution. Daffodils are usually unappealing to deer.

Daffodils and other hardy bulbs are a smart investment. They are relatively inexpensive to plant by the dozens or even hundreds. In the right location, many hardy bulbs will multiply and bloom for years. Many are also lovely as cut flowers. Like annuals, bulbs are an excellent choice for a splash of color in a beginner's garden, and they are equally capable of sophisticated effects.

Autumn Crocus

Colchicum species and hybrids

Other Name: Meadow Saffron
Height: 6 to 12 in.
Flowers: Pink, lavender, mauve, white
Bloom Period: Late summer and fall
Zones: 5, 6
Light Requirement:

The wispy, goblet-shaped flowers of autumn crocus emerge on bare stems in late summer and fall. This oddity of timing and form explains one of this curious plant's nicknames—the wonder bulb. Colchicum grows from a corm, a compressed underground stem that resembles a bulb without scales. It produces flowers at the approach of autumn, during the plant's dormant stage. The following spring, colchicum launches into its vegetative cycle, growing dark green leaves in mounds 10 to 15 in. high and wide. The leaves present a challenge to gardeners. Although initially attractive, the foliage turns yellow by late spring or early summer but must remain in place until the leaves die back naturally. Removing them too early robs the plant of the opportunity to make and store nutrients for flowers later in the season. The best place for colchicum is where the ripening foliage won't be an eyesore. That may be among perennials that will grow and obscure the yellowing leaves in early summer. Colchicum also makes an effective display in groundcover at the edge of a woodland planting or an area of mixed shrubs and trees. These areas are not usually scrutinized as closely as a flower garden, so the yellow leaves are not as noticeable. Like Japanese anemones, another fall-bloomer, the flower shape and pastel shades of colchicum are reminiscent of spring even though it blooms as the season is winding down.

When to Plant

Autumn crocus corms are sold June to early September. Plant them immediately. Colchicum is on a schedule all its own, and it will flower on time, whether the corm is stashed on a windowsill or a store shelf or planted in the ground.

Where to Plant

Plant autumn crocus in well-drained, moisture-retentive soil in sun to part sun. In a woodland setting, place autumn crocus near the front edge where there is more sunlight. Colchicum is also an excellent bulb for rock gardens, under perennials, and among ground-covers. Try pink colchicum with *Ajuga* 'Burgundy Glow' or a white colchicum with *Lamium* 'White Nancy'. The groundcover backdrop makes the colchicum flowers show up.

How to Plant

Place the corm so the base is 3 to 4 in. deep and 6 to 9 in. apart. Plant in clusters so the flowers are easier to see. Water after planting. Colchicum tolerates heat and dry periods but needs moisture when the foliage is growing. The flowers are thin and may be beaten down by rain. To combat this, plant colchicum so that it is surrounded by grass or low-growing groundcovers to support the fragile flowers.

Advice for Care

Once planted, colchicum sends up its flowers within weeks. The plants will slowly form colonies if left undisturbed or may be lifted, divided, and replanted, if desired, after 3 years. Autumn crocus needs no additional care.

Additional Information

If colchicum is planted in a lawn, do not cut the grass in that area until the colchicum foliage dies down. Note that this plant is considered toxic. Use gloves when digging corms to divide if they become crowded. The time to do this is after the foliage matures. Even though colchicum's common name is autumn crocuses, it is not really a crocus. There are, however, fall-blooming types of true crocus. *Crocus speciosus* has small violet-blue flowers.

Additional Species, Cultivars, or Varieties

Colchicum autumnale is a rosy lilac and 8 in. tall. The cultivar 'Alba' (4 in.) has small white flowers. *C. autumnale* var. 'Alboplenum' is white and double. *Colchicum speciosum* has larger flowers of rose-pink. Many showy colchicums, including 'Waterlily', 'Lilac Wonder', and 'The Giant', are hybrids. They are available in singles and doubles in shades of pink, lavender, and white. 'Autumn Queen' (6 in.) is dark pink and flowers earlier than other varieties. 'Lilac Wonder' has large pink-purple blossoms. The flowers of 'The Giant' (8 to 12 in.) are mauve with white centers. 'Waterlily' (6 in.) is a favorite hybrid with double flowers and many petals. It really does resemble a waterlily.

Botanical Tulip

Tulipa tarda

Height: 3 to 4 in.
Flowers: Yellow with white point
Bloom Period: Spring
Zones: 4, 5, 6
Light Requirement:

Tulipa tarda, a sunny little tulip with yellow petals tipped in white, is only one example of the numerous botanical or species tulips available. These aren't the grand hybrids, massed by the truckload and underplanted with pansies. These are small and unpretentious but with the underlying appeal that sparked the hysteria of tulipomania and resulted in the hundreds of showy Darwin, cottage, and triumph tulips now commonplace. Dozens of species tulips are offered in the trade and not all are easy to grow. Some, native to high rocky hillsides in central Asia, require specialized treatment, but others are an easy addition to the garden. With sun and good drainage, these tiny charmers will perennialize and return to your garden year after year, long after the fancy hybrids have disappeared. A good example is *Tulipa tarda*. Blooming in late April and early May, this botanical tulip flowers in bunches displayed low to the ground against the strap-like foliage. Each flower opens from the bud to create a flat yellow-and-white star. Clumps multiply rapidly to form a spring groundcover of bloom. Combine it with grape hyacinth or Siberian squill in bulb plantings. Or use this little tulip in perennial beds coming up through thyme or carpeting sedums. Try woolly thyme, *Tulipa tarda*, and the downy nodding purple flowers of *Anemone pulsatilla*, the pasqueflower, for an early spring association. A selection of other recommended species tulips is listed below.

WHEN TO PLANT

Plant the bulbs of botanical tulips in October through November. Leave species tulip bulbs for last when planting bulbs in fall. These don't mind late planting.

WHERE TO PLANT

Plant the bulbs in well-drained, fertile soil and full sun. Good drainage is important for success with most botanical tulips. *Tulipa tarda* will tolerate partial shade, but some botanical tulips won't. For the most part, the bulbs like to be warm and dry in the summer, so plant them where you won't be watering. Use them in the front of perennial beds, by sunny patios, along front walks, or combined with sun-loving—but not too aggressive—groundcovers. Ideal locations are rock gardens or the top of stone retaining walls.

HOW TO PLANT

Dig holes and plant the bulbs so that the base is 4 to 5 in. below the soil surface. Don't leave any air pockets under the bulb. Space 2 to 3 in. apart in natural-looking groups. A strong, narrow bulb-planting trowel marked with the proper depth is ideal for this job. A bulb booster-type fertilizer (9-9-6) could be incorporated into the soil at this time. Water the bulbs after planting.

ADVICE FOR CARE

Tulipa tarda will self-sow and spread in ideal locations. Provided with good drainage, it should not have pest or disease problems. Don't skimp on the planting holes. As with all tulips, the best result occur when bulbs are planted at the full depth recommended.

ADDITIONAL INFORMATION

Plant these small tulips in groups of at least a dozen for the best effect. Many botanical or species tulips are now available. Be sure the bulbs are commercially propagated and not collected from the wild. Shop with reputable merchants. *Tulipa tarda* is sometimes offered as *T. daystemon*.

ADDITIONAL SPECIES, CULTIVARS, OR VARIETIES

T. kaufmanniana, the waterlily tulip, is creamy yellow brushed with red on the exterior of the petals. It is one of the earliest flowering tulips, usually blooming in April. Many selections and hybrids exist, but the species is still worth consideration. Plant a full 8 in. deep. These grow 8 in. tall. *T. batalinii*, which is 5 to 6 in. tall, has fragrant, creamy yellow to bronze-yellow fully shaped flowers. Try the selections 'Bronze Charm' or 'Apricot Jewel'. *T. clusiana* (12 to 14 in.), sometimes called the lady tulip, has white flowers with a crimson stripe on the outside petals. 'Cynthia' is gold and rose. *T. sylvestris* (6 to 8 in.) is unusual in that it prefers partial shade. Beautiful in a partial shade location with Chinese forget-me-not, this small yellow tulip with a tendency to spread is also fragrant. It is not as hardy as *Tulipa tarda*.

Camas

Camassia cusickii, Camassia leichtlinii

Other Name: Wild Hyacinth
Height: 3 to 4 ft.
Flowers: Blue, white
Bloom Period: Late spring to early summer
Zones: 4, 5, 6
Light Requirement:

If you have experience with the familiar hardy spring bulbs such as daffodils and tulips and are looking for something different, try camas. Your reward will be spikes of starry blooms that look a little like Siberian squills on steroids. Camassia leaves are narrow, deep green, somewhat leathery in appearance, and long— up to 24 in., almost like long blades of grass in a clump around the plant's base. The dozens of flowers appear on a tall spike or raceme. They have 6 slender petals about 1 in. long and open wide, creating a feathery effect of pale blue or white stars. This is a hardy bulb for creating a grand sweep of form and color, and camassia flowers remain attractive for 2 to 3 weeks. It may be naturalized, mixed into a bed of groundcovers or added to a perennial border, where it will bloom in May and early June. *Camassia cusickii* (3 to 3½ ft.), native to Oregon, has icy blue flowers. *Camassia leichtlinii* is slightly taller (3½ to 4 ft.) and has blue blooms; the cultivar 'Alba' has white flowers. It is native to the western U.S. and British Columbia. Camas makes an unusual and attractive cut flower.

When to Plant

Plant the bulbs in September. If squirrels are a problem in your area, cover the new planting with screen or wire, or soak the bulbs in a repellent before planting.

Where to Plant

Plant camassia in full sun and rich, moist soil, such as along the margins of water gardens, ponds, and streams. Camas will also grow in lightly shaded areas and tolerates heavy soils. It will not thrive in locations that stay hot and dry in summer. Camassia is magnificent planted in mass. Try it in a woodland garden, near a pond where the flowering spikes will reflect in the water, or under tall trees. Pair it with daylilies, which will hide the declining camassia foliage as the daylilies begin to fill the area with new growth in late spring.

How to Plant
Plant so the base of the bulb is 4 to 6 in. deep. Space 6 to 8 in. apart.

Advice for Care
After several years, camassia bulbs may be dug up and divided to increase your supply or to share with friends. Division is rarely necessary for rejuvenation, however. Ripe seeds may be sown in sandy soil, left undisturbed for 2 to 3 years, and then moved to a permanent spot in the garden. It will take 3 to 4 years for the bulbs to reach flowering size. Camassia has no serious pest or disease problems.

Additional Information
Native Americans and early explorers sometimes cooked and ate camassia bulbs.

Additional Species, Cultivars, or Varieties
Camassia leichtlinii 'Alba' has white flowers with bright yellow anthers, while 'Blue Danube' is a dark blue cultivar that has done well in mid-Michigan. A creamy white double form, 'Semiplena', is also available. *Camassia quamash* is sometimes available from bulb suppliers. It is a favorite and often invites comment in the garden compared to the more familiar hardy bulbs. *C. quamash* grows to 1 to 2 ft. Some forms have deep blue flowers.

Crocosmia

Crocosmia × crocosmiiflora 'Lucifer'

Other Name: Montbretia
Height: 3 to 4 ft.
Flowers: Scarlet-red
Bloom Period: Mid- to late summer
Zones: 5, 6
Light Requirement:

The fiery red tubular flowers of *Crocosmia* 'Lucifer' steal the show from mid-July through August. Equally important but in a supporting role, the broad swordlike, pleated foliage provides a bold accent from June until fall. *Crocosmia* 'Lucifer' quickly grows from a bulb-like structure called a corm to a bold, season-long presence in the garden. Montbretia appears tropical and difficult, and, in fact, many books and catalogs will tell you it isn't hardy in Michigan. It's true that most montbretia can't handle our cold winters, but 'Lucifer', although you wouldn't suspect it from the name, is reliably cold tolerant and easy to grow in Zones 5 and 6. Gardeners in colder areas can lift the corms and store them for the winter if they want to grow these plants. 'Lucifer' *Crocosimia* prefers full sun and well-drained soil and prospers with little care. The flowers provide a jolt of red in the late summer while its bold foliage, unusual in the sunny garden, draws the eye, combining effectively with almost everything. The flowers, however, are this plant's most spectacular asset. Arranged in zigzags high on upward arching stems, the bright tubular trumpets attract hummingbirds. Plant 'Lucifer' near windows and outdoor living areas to enjoy this feature. Combine 'Lucifer' with the hot colors of summer—sneezeweed, coreopsis, sunflower heliopsis—or temper the red with a backdrop of bronze fennel or ornamental grasses. Although montbretia mingles successfully with other tall plants, it shines on its own where its architectural presence can be appreciated. Try it in a prominent location rising up from a frothy mass of lavender-blue 'Six Hills Giant' catmint.

WHEN TO PLANT

Plant container-grown plants in the spring to early summer. Corms can be planted in the spring around the frost-free date.

Where to Plant

Plant 'Lucifer' crocosmia in full sun and fertile, well-drained soil. Plants will tolerate some shade but not soggy conditions. Use in sunny perennial beds or mixed plantings in a mass or as an accent plant. Use this plant's dramatic form and flowers as a focal point. Take advantage of its hummingbird appeal, and place near a sunny patio, porch, or deck.

How to Plant

For corms, dig holes and plant 5 in. deep to the base of the corm, then water in. Bulb booster-type fertilizer (9-9-6) or a low formulation general fertilizer (10-10-10) could be incorporated into the holes. Plant groups of 5 to 7 corms, spaced 2 in. apart, for attractive results. Typically, 'Lucifer' is sold in garden centers and from mail-order nurseries as a potted perennial. The unplanted corms are more difficult to find. Container-grown crocosmia should be planted in the garden at the same level it was growing in the container.

Advice for Care

No special fertilization beyond what is provided for other perennials is needed. Although somewhat drought-tolerant, crocosmia will be healthier with adequate moisture. Don't be too quick to remove the spent flowers; the seedpods remain attractive until the stalks begin to yellow. Cut back the foliage in the fall or spring.

Additional Information

Divide in early spring if needed. Mulch to keep the roots cool and to protect for winter. In Zones 3 and 4, corms should be lifted in the fall and overwintered indoors. Pack the corms in peat or vermiculite, and store them for the winter in a dark and cool location (about 50 degrees Fahrenheit).

Additional Species, Cultivars, or Varieties

Many other montbretias are available, but most are not hardy this far north. *Crocosmia* 'Lucifer' is actually a hybrid between *Crocosmia masonorum* and *Crocosmia paniculata*. Other selections from these crosses may prove useful in Michigan.

Crocus Hybrids

Crocus vernus hybrids

Height: 5 to 6 in.
Flowers: Yellow, white, purple, lavender, blue, stripes
Bloom Period: Early spring
Zones: 3, 4, 5, 6
Light Requirement:

The large flowers of Dutch crocus are the most familiar and most loved of the early spring bulbs. Their appearance confirms the arrival of spring even if the temperature outdoors still feels like winter. With the right selection, the crocus season can span several weeks in March and April. The smaller snow crocus (*Crocus chrysanthus*) blooms about 2 weeks earlier than the large-flowered Dutch crocus hybrids and is increasingly popular. It has smaller flowers, but its earlier appearance is a most welcome feature. Plant crocuses where you will pass them often, such as along the driveway, near the doorway, and in beds and rock gardens close to the house. They are charming nestled next to tree trunks. Crocuses may also be planted and naturalized in lawns if you're willing to wait to mow until the narrow, threadlike leaves die back on their own. In pale or vivid shades of yellows, purples, and whites, crocuses symbolize the beginning of springtime. Plant generously. Five dozen crocuses with flowers the color of melted butter wrapping around the base of a tree will soon grow into a swath of yellow bright enough to boost the spirits of an entire spring-starved neighborhood. Select both Dutch and snow crocuses to extend the season of bloom. Make crocuses part of a succession of spring bulbs, including snowdrops, squills, daffodils, tulips, and hyacinths. Crocuses and daffodils are especially good performers, increasing in number and strength every year.

WHEN TO PLANT
Plant the corms in September.

WHERE TO PLANT
Crocuses do well where they receive sun in spring. They may be naturalized or planted randomly under shade trees because the crocuses will finish flowering and their leaves ripen before the tree leaves appear. Bulbs planted against a south-facing wall will warm and flower earlier than others, as will those in full sun. Crocuses

prefer well-drained soil. Amend heavy clay before planting. Use crocuses for early spring flowers in borders, rock gardens, and spots you walk or drive by every day, such as near doorways and drives. They look best in clusters of at least 7 corms; more is better, and sometimes crocuses are available by 50s or 100s at substantial discounts. Their foliage must ripen in place, but this is a much faster process, and the thin crocus leaves are less noticeable, than with larger bulbs. In beds and borders, crocuses will be finished and the foliage brown before most perennials begin to grow, so interplant them at will.

How to Plant

Plant the large-flowered Dutch crocuses about 4 in. deep and 4 in. apart. Follow the general rule by planting them 3 times as deep as the bulbs measure in diameter.

Advice for Care

Mix bulb fertilizer with the soil before planting, and water the area afterward. Crocuses require no additional care. They may be fed again in the fall and divided after several years if performance has dwindled. They are usually disease-free. Squirrels and mice find them irresistible, however. Cover the newly planted area with mesh screening or chicken wire, apply a commercial repellent, or enlist the patrol assistance of a cooperative cat or dog.

Additional Information

Many crocus hybrids are excellent for forcing indoors in winter.

Additional Species, Cultivars, or Varieties

Dutch crocus selections include the white 'Jeanne d'Arc', 'Yellow Mammoth', 'Pickwick', which has lavender stripes on blue-white flowers, and the blue-violet 'Remembrance'.

Snow crocus, or *Crocus chrysanthus*, blooms about 10 to 14 days earlier than the Dutch crocus and has smaller flowers. Plant snow crocus 4 in. deep and 3 to 4 in. apart. Many hybrids are available, such as 'Blue Bird' and the cheery 'Snowbunting', which is white with purple veins and a yellow throat. Saffron, which is added to food for flavor and its yellow-orange color, is made from the dried stigmas of another crocus, *Crocus sativus*, which blooms in the fall. It is too tender to survive reliably in Michigan.

Daffodil

Narcissus species and hybrids

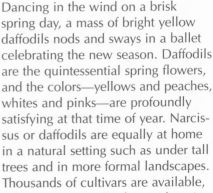

Other Names: Narcissus,
   Jonquil
Height: 6 to 18 in.
Flowers: Yellow, pink, peach,
   white, green
Bloom Period: Spring
Zones: 3, 4, 5, 6
Light Requirement:

Dancing in the wind on a brisk spring day, a mass of bright yellow daffodils nods and sways in a ballet celebrating the new season. Daffodils are the quintessential spring flowers, and the colors—yellows and peaches, whites and pinks—are profoundly satisfying at that time of year. Narcissus or daffodils are equally at home in a natural setting such as under tall trees and in more formal landscapes. Thousands of cultivars are available, and most will not only return but also increase in number each spring for many years. Daffodils are easy bulbs to grow where the soil is well drained and they receive full to part sun. Interplant daffodils with perennials such as daylilies or hostas. These begin to grow in late spring as the daffodils decline, hiding the yellowing leaves. These bulbs are all classified as narcissus. There are distinctions between daffodils and jonquils. People who move here from the South may use all 3 names for different classes of daffodils. When they say "narcissus," they're usually referring to the white or white-and-yellow varieties with flowers in clusters. Whatever you call them and however you use them, plant these hardy bulbs. No yard can have too many daffodils.

WHEN TO PLANT

Plant daffodil bulbs in September or early October at the latest. They need about a month to establish roots before the weather turns cold and the ground freezes.

WHERE TO PLANT

The ideal site is in full sun in early spring but shady by summer when deciduous trees leaf out. Daffodils want plenty of moisture in spring. They tolerate somewhat drier conditions in summer. Plant some bulbs along a south-facing wall for an early display. The soil should be well drained and average to rich in organic matter. Improve the soil with well-rotted compost or leaf mold if necessary before planting. Daffodils may be arranged formally, but they have a more natural appeal planted in quantity as sweeping drifts in beds or at the edge of a wooded area. Select cultivars recommended for naturalizing because those bulbs will be hardy and long-lived. Daffodils also work well in beds and groundcover, near doors, and as an understory for hedges. When selecting a spot for daffodils, remember that the foliage must stay in place as it turns yellow.

HOW TO PLANT

Plant large trumpets 6 to 8 in. deep and 4 to 6 in. apart. Smaller varieties should be 4 to 6 in. deep and 4 in. apart. Many kinds of daffodils are available as larger bulbs, which produce larger flowers the first year, or as smaller or landscape bulbs, which are more economical for naturalizing. The bulb merchant should have specific instructions on how deep to plant the type purchased. If you are using a bulb-booster fertilizer, incorporate it well in the soil before planting to lessen the chance of burning the bulbs.

ADVICE FOR CARE

In the spring after flowering, snap off the flower head, but leave the foliage intact while it ripens. With daffodils, this can be a commitment of 6 weeks or even longer. Some people braid or tie the fading leaves to make them less noticeable, but this is not recommended. It impairs the plants' ability to make and store food, which nourishes the bulb and ensures plentiful blooms for next year. In fall, apply a fertilizer for bulbs if desired. Every 5 to 10 years, the bulbs may be dug and divided to increase stock or reduce crowding.

ADDITIONAL INFORMATION

Daffodils usually withstand diseases and pests, including hungry deer or rabbits. The bulbs and possibly other parts of daffodils are toxic. Daffodils are excellent cut flowers.

ADDITIONAL SPECIES, CULTIVARS, OR VARIETIES

Trumpet daffodils, the traditional favorite, bloom in early to mid-spring and have center trumpets at least as long as their petals, such as the yellow 'Dutch Master' and 'Golden Harvest'. Large-cup daffodils are similar in shape but the trumpets are slightly shorter. Among them are 'Salome' and 'Ice Follies'. These flower in early to mid-spring. The pheasant's eye or *Narcissus poeticus* is among the latest of daffodils. Others of special appeal are the early-season cyclamineus hybrids, with their long, tube-like centers and turned-back form, such as 'Jack Snipe'. They are typically less hardy than the trumpet types. Species daffodils are small and early- to mid-season bloomers. If you garden in Zone 3 or 4, check local sources and catalogs for daffodils that will be hardy in your area.

Dwarf Bulbous Iris

Iris reticulata

Height: 5 in.
Flowers: Blue, purple, violet
Bloom Period: Spring
Zones: 4, 5, 6
Light Requirement:

The miniature blooms of *Iris reticulata* invite close examination. Coming as they do in early spring, this can lead to wet knees—but that small price is worth it to discover the sweet fragrance and to admire these exquisite flowers. The flowers are similar in form to the Dutch iris often seen in florists' bouquets only much more diminutive, just 5 in. high. Among the earliest plants to flower, dwarf iris competes with snowdrops and crocus for first place. Dwarf bulbous iris isn't as dependable as crocus or glory-of-the-snow—it needs sharper drainage and sun. But where it finds a suitable home, it will persist and increase. The distinctive iris flowers, with upright standards and downward falls in shades of deep purple and blue, are nestled among the linear, four-angled foliage. The falls are often marked with a white blotch and a stripe of yellow-orange. These bloom early and are most attractive at close range, so place dwarf iris where it will be easily noticed in March and not in an out-of-the-way location. Plant groupings of a dozen or so dwarf iris for best effect, but note that this bulb is not one to mass in carpets in the fashion of scilla or windflower. Plant dwarf iris in the front of a sunny border, on top of a rock wall, near a front walk, or wherever good drainage can be provided. A gravelly free-draining spot or a rock garden is ideal. Combine it with other early-blooming bulbs, or use it to add spring interest to a planting of low-growing sedums and thymes. The original species is deep purple. Cultivars are available with sky blue, indigo blue, and a range of color variations.

WHEN TO PLANT
Plant the beige teardrop-shaped bulbs of dwarf iris in September through mid-October.

WHERE TO PLANT
Iris reticulata prefers well-drained soil in full sun. It will bloom in partial shade, but it won't thrive. Its miniature size and preference for sharp drainage make it a perfect choice for planting in rock gar-

dens and on the top of stone retaining walls. It's also adaptable to garden conditions if you can provide some sun and good drainage.

HOW TO PLANT

Dig holes and plant the bulbs 4 to 5 in. deep, measured from the base of the bulb to the soil surface. Don't leave any air pockets under the bulb. Space bulbs 1 to 2 in. apart in natural-looking groups. Water the bulbs after planting to settle and moisten the soil. For an attractive group, plant 12 or more bulbs.

ADVICE FOR CARE

Iris reticulata is not always as dependable as other early performers such as glory-of-the-snow and scilla. Poor drainage will doom these bulbs. They have no significant pest or disease problems.

ADDITIONAL INFORMATION

Dwarf bulbous iris will perennialize and increase in ideal conditions. The dark purple selections don't stand out well against dark soil and mulch. Use them to better effect in areas with a gravel mulch. As the foliage matures, it grows to almost 12 in. tall. It's narrow and presentable in appearance and then disappears quickly.

ADDITIONAL SPECIES, CULTIVARS, OR VARIETIES

Several cultivars and some hybrids of *Iris reticulata* are available, differing in color and markings. 'Cantab' is pale sky blue with a yellow blotch. 'Purple Gem' is dark purple with a white blotch. *Iris histrioides* (3 in. tall) has larger blue flowers, which appear slightly earlier than *I. reticulata*. Hybrids exist between the two, such as 'Harmony', a two-tone sky blue and royal blue with a yellow blotch. Fragrant *Iris danfordiae* (4 in. tall), a dear little yellow iris with brown spots, is less likely to perennialize. Deep planting a full 4 to 5 in. is recommended. It is suitable for forcing in pots.

Glory-of-the-Snow

Chionodoxa luciliae

Height: 4 to 5 in.
Flowers: Blue
Bloom Period: Early spring
Zones: 4, 5, 6
Light Requirement:

As befits their name, the cheery flowers of glory-of-the-snow often get caught by an early spring snow, a fairly common occurrence in Michigan. Glory-of-the-snow comes on the heels of snowdrops and winter aconites, and all three are a delight to the winter weary. Glory-of-the-snow has lilac-blue to sky blue star-shaped flowers about 1 in. wide, with 8 to 10 per spray or stem. The arching stem's relaxed habit causes the flowers to face skyward, revealing the distinctive white eye that distinguishes *Chionodoxa* from *Scilla*, the Siberian squill, with which it is sometimes confused. Well adapted to garden culture, glory-of-the-snow is perfectly hardy and easy to grow in full sun or light shade. It naturalizes both by seed and offsets to form a memorable blue carpet. Plant glory-of-the snow where its spring bloom will be noticed—for example, along walkways, by front entrances, or in view from windows. It combines well with early tulips and daffodils but is perhaps best used on its own in a group of at least 100, naturalized in grass or in the front of perennial and shrub beds. Although this may seem extravagant, large quantities of bulbs can be obtained at a substantial price break. In late March and April, *Chionodoxa* provides an extra layer of interest under small trees and shrubs. Plant naturalistic groupings—not perfect circles—under small trees such as star magnolia and serviceberry or shrubs such as Korean rhododendron. Combine glory-of-the-snow with the earliest blooming perennials such as the Lenten rose, *Helleborus orientalis*, and underplant an 'Arnold Promise' witchhazel to create a special place in the spring garden. Glory-of-the-snow and other small bulbs are perfect for providing interest in areas that won't have flowers for months. For an early spring lift, try a few dozen in your rose beds or in a perennial herb garden. Most places would benefit from the starry blue appeal of glory-of-the-snow.

WHEN TO PLANT

Plant the small, teardrop-shaped bulbs of glory-of-the-snow in September through early October.

WHERE TO PLANT

Glory-of-the-snow grows well in all but poorly drained soils. It prefers full sun but tolerates light shade with ease. It will grow through groundcovers and turfgrass and under trees. Use sweeps of its blue flowers to add interest to perennial and shrub beds.

HOW TO PLANT

Dig holes and plant the bulbs so that they are 3 to 4 in. deep, from the base of the bulb to the soil surface. Space bulbs 1 to 3 in. apart in natural-looking groups. A strong, narrow bulb-planting trowel marked with the proper depth is ideal for this job. Don't leave any air pockets under the bulb. These small, relatively inexpensive bulbs can be planted rapidly and with less care than a tulip or large daffodil bulb. Use large quantities, at least 50 to 100 bulbs, for the best effect and economy.

ADVICE FOR CARE

Chionodoxa needs no special care. Bulb booster-type fertilizer (9-9-6) could be used at planting, but this is an extra and can be difficult when digging many small planting holes. When using glory-of-the-snow in a prepared bed with other bulbs, it is easy to incorporate fertilizer at planting. If naturalizing *Chionodoxa* in lawns, let the foliage mature before mowing.

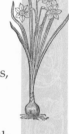

ADDITIONAL INFORMATION

Glory-of the-snow, while superb on its own, also combines well with other early-spring bulbs. Try it as a complement for waterlily tulips, *Tulipa kaufmanniana*, or small early daffodils such as 'Tete a Tete'.

ADDITIONAL SPECIES, CULTIVARS, OR VARIETIES

A few cultivars of *Chionodoxa luciliae* are available, offering larger flowers and different colors, but it's hard to beat the delicate form and white-eyed lavender-blue flowers of the species. 'Alba' is a white-flowered form. 'Blue Giant', a taller (6 to 8 in.) and more upright form, has a consistent deep blue color. 'Pink Giant' (6 to 8 in.) is its pink counterpart. *Chionodoxa gigantea* has 1- to 2-in., upward-facing flowers. 'Alba' is its white counterpart. *Chionodoxa sardensis* (4 to 6 in. tall) has 3/4-in. flowers in a beautiful shade of clear bright blue with a tiny white eye. It naturalizes freely; a large mass can stop you in your tracks.

Grape Hyacinth

Muscari armeniacum, Muscari botryoides

Height: 6 to 8 in.
Flowers: Purple-blue, white, yellow
Bloom Period: Mid-spring
Zones: 3, 4, 5, 6
Light Requirement:

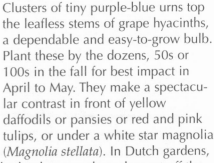

Clusters of tiny purple-blue urns top the leafless stems of grape hyacinths, a dependable and easy-to-grow bulb. Plant these by the dozens, 50s or 100s in the fall for best impact in April to May. They make a spectacular contrast in front of yellow daffodils or pansies or red and pink tulips, or under a white star magnolia (*Magnolia stellata*). In Dutch gardens, "rivers" of muscari run through the landscape, where they set off the flaming hues of tulips. Although they are native to the Mediterranean region, grape hyacinths are hardy enough for most Michigan gardens. Each tapered cluster of flowers, called a raceme, resembles a cluster of grapes. In a favorable location with plenty of sun and fertile soil, grape hyacinths multiply readily. The plants die back after flowering and disappear. In early fall, the narrow, grass-like leaves sprout again and remain evergreen, although somewhat disheveled, for much of the winter. Some gardeners put this characteristic to work for them and plant grape hyacinths around the fringes of bulb beds to mark the boundaries. Then in the fall, when it's time to plant more bulbs or to fertilize ones already in the ground, the grape hyacinth leaves will indicate the location of existing beds and lessen the chance of a tulip or daffodil bulb being dug up by mistake. Grape hyacinths are excellent bulbs for naturalizing in landscapes. They will multiply to form large colonies in groundcovers. Use them generously along with other spring bulbs for naturalizing, including squills and daffodils.

WHEN TO PLANT

Grape hyacinths are planted in September along with other small bulbs, including crocus, winter aconite, snowdrops, and squills. They should be planted immediately because the foliage will begin to grow in the fall.

WHERE TO PLANT

Use generous quantities of these small bulbs to ensure they are visible and appreciated in mid-spring. Plant them in curving sweeps or drifts under trees and shrubs where they can spread and remain undisturbed. They are useful in rock gardens and along a path. Combine them with yellow daffodils and red tulips for spectacular contrast. Although typically used in drifts and masses, in smaller gardens grape hyacinths can be used in small-scale combinations with early perennials and bulbs, taking advantage of grape hyacinths' long-lasting blue color. Try muscari coming up through the sprawling stems of myrtle euphorbia (*Euphorbia myrsinites*), the grape hyacinth's blue flowers setting off the euphorbia's yellow-green.

How to Plant
Plant the bulbs 3 in. deep and 3 in. apart in sun and well-drained, fertile soil. Amend the area as necessary with compost, shredded leaves, or other organic material. Mix in a bulb fertilizer before planting, or top dress with fertilizer afterward. If squirrels are a persistent problem in your garden, protect newly planted bulbs by covering the area with screening or chicken wire or using a commercial repellent.

Advice for Care
Water after planting and during dry periods until the ground freezes. Grape hyacinths need little additional care and are easy to grow. Deadhead if you wish to prevent them from self-sowing, although self-sowing is the best way to establish large drifts.

Additional Information
Although small, grape hyacinths make nice cut flowers, especially in old-fashioned May baskets or bouquets. *Muscari* species are native to southern Europe and Asia Minor.

Additional Species, Cultivars, or Varieties
Of this genus, *Muscari armeniacum* is the most widely planted. Cultivars are available in several shades of blue to bluish-purple. Each raceme consists of roughly 20 to 30 flowers on a straight stalk. 'Early Giant' has deep blue flowers rimmed in white. 'Blue Spike' is almost fluffy looking with double flowers of clear blue. This one is sterile but increases through bulb division. *Muscari botryoides* is smaller but hardy to Zone 3. It has sky blue flowers, does not spread as quickly and blooms a little earlier than *Muscari armeniacum*. Cultivated since 1576 in Europe, it is considered the original grape hyacinth. *Muscari armeniacum* was introduced in the 1870s. A white-flowered version is *Muscari botryoides* 'Album'. Several other species may be of interest, although they are not as widely available as *Muscari armeniacum*. *Muscari latifolium* (10 in.) has dark blue lower flowers and lighter ones higher up the raceme.

Lily

Lilium hybrids

Height: 18 in. to 6 ft.
Flowers: White, yellow, gold, orange, pink, red
Bloom Period: Summer
Zones: 3, 4, 5, 6, depending on selection
Light Requirement:

This is the real lily—not an impersonator like the daylily, waterlily, and others that attempt to raise their stature by association with this most exotic and beautiful of garden flowers. Lilies suffer from a reputation of being difficult, tracing back to when bulbs arrived in Europe, dry and desiccated, from the far reaches of Asia. This is no longer the case. Now lilies are available fresh and ready to plant from growers in the United States. It's true that some species can be tricky, but after years of breeding, easy-to-grow hybrid lilies are well adapted to garden culture. Pendant trumpets, upward-facing stars, ruffled, spotted, fragrant—lily flowers are dazzling. Their exotic yet graceful flowers are produced in almost every color but blue. In perennial beds or mixed plantings, a group of lilies raises the ordinary to the extraordinary. Good drainage is essential for lily growth. This is not a suggestion but a caveat; lilies will not grow in poorly drained gardens. The selection can be staggering, and some are more difficult to grow than others. The Asiatic hybrids—easy, long-lived, and less fussy about drainage—are the best place to start.

WHEN TO PLANT

Plant the bulbs in late October or as soon as they are received from the grower. Lilies are shipped later in the season than daffodils. Spring planting is a second choice. Either way, have the ground ready, and plant the bulbs immediately. Lily bulbs don't have a protective covering and can dry out quickly.

WHERE TO PLANT

Drainage is of critical importance for lilies. Most prefer moist but well-drained, humus-rich garden soil and full sun. Many will tolerate partial shade. Lilies don't compete well with aggressive spreading groundcovers or perennials; plant them in the gaps between clumping perennials, or cover with low-growing annuals. You can also plant lilies in shrub beds or naturalize them in low-maintenance areas. Raised beds improve drainage.

How to Plant

Plant bulbs 5 to 8 in. deep, depending on the size of the bulb, following specific instructions that arrive with it. Incorporate bulb-booster-type fertilizer into the hole. For attractive groupings, plant bulbs of the same variety in triangular groups of 3, spaced from 12 to 18 in. apart. Mark or label your bulbs; in the spring, lily shoots can be crushed by a misplaced foot.

Advice for Care

Lilies should be fertilized for the best results. Apply a well-balanced granular fertilizer such as 10-10-10 in the spring as the shoots emerge. Or use a dilute liquid feed or a generous application of well-rotted manure. For the most sumptuous growth, fertilize once a month with a liquid feed until the foliage begins to yellow. Water during dry spells. Deadhead hybrid lilies before seeds form, but leave as much foliage as possible. The foliage feeds the bulb for next year's blooms. Divide clumps as they start to lose vigor, usually every 5 to 6 years. Do this in the fall after the foliage has died back. Lift bulbs, separate, and replant. There will be lots of extras to share.

Additional Information

Some tall lilies with large flowers may need to be staked, especially if grown in partial shade. For blossom-heavy sorts, stake just as the buds begin to open, and take care to avoid piercing the bulb with the stake. Lilies are generally pest- and disease-free if you provide good drainage and some sun. Purchase only healthy bulbs. If bulbs look moldy or dried out and have no roots, don't buy them. Healthy bulbs are readily available from specialty mail-order nurseries.

Additional Species, Cultivars, or Varieties

For the gardener mainly interested in lilies and lots of them, the widely available naturalizing mixtures are a great value. Other lilies good for beginners are the Asiatic hybrids 'Enchantment' (2 to 3 ft.), 'Connecticut King' (3 to 4 ft.), and 'Connecticut Yankee' (4 to 5 ft.); and the Aurelian hybrid (trumpet-type) 'Moon Temple' (4 to 5 ft.). The later-blooming Oriental hybrids are more difficult to cultivate. A good one to start with is the pure white 'Casa Blanca' (4 ft.). The royal lily, *Lilium regale* (4 to 6 ft.), is another easy choice.

Ornamental Onion

Allium aflatunense

Height: 20 to 30 in. **Flowers:** Lilac-purple **Bloom Period:** Late spring **Zones:** 4, 5, 6 **Light Requirement:**

Everyone knows that onions, garlic, shallots, and chives are indispensable in the kitchen. But many people don't realize that scores of onions (*Allium* sp.) are grown in the garden for their ornamental value alone. *Allium aflatunense*, one such ornamental onion, shows off dense, spherical flower heads held high on strong, straight stems. Flowering in late May and into June, its lilac-purple to rose-purple flowers in 4-in.-wide balls are a superb accent to a range of other perennials. Each flower bursts from the bud to form a perfect globe, lasting in flower for close to 3 weeks. After bloom, the spent flower heads continue to be attractive for months until they finally begin to deteriorate. No trouble to grow in sun and average garden soil, this ornamental onion provides an interesting complement to May- and June-flowering perennials and then disappears, as bulbs do, only to return the following spring for a repeat performance. The globular heads of flowers are best used in groups of at least 5 but a dozen is even better. Groups of *Allium aflatunense* placed at regular intervals provide an interesting accent and a unifying rhythm to a perennial border. Combine ornamental onion with perennial salvia, catmint, blue false indigo, peonies, and other late spring flowers. Grow it up through 'Valerie Finnis' artemisia. Combine with hardy geraniums and the yellow-green flowers of lady's mantle. This ornamental onion is also highly prized for cut flowers and can be included in vegetable or cut flower gardens for this use. Only a few cultivars exist. The selection 'Purple Sensation' (3 ft.) offers a deeper, rose-purple hue.

WHEN TO PLANT

Plant the plump, rounded, white-skinned bulbs in late September to early October.

WHERE TO PLANT

Plant alliums in full sun. A bit of shade may be tolerated. They prosper in average to rich, well-drained soil. Use them in perennial beds, cottage gardens, and mixed plantings.

How to Plant

Dig holes and plant the bulbs, placing them so the base of the bulb is 5 in. below the soil surface. Don't leave any air pockets under the bulb. Plant at least 3 in each group, spaced 3 to 5 in. apart. Water the newly planted bulbs. Bulb-booster-type fertilizer (9-9-6) could be added to the planting hole to improve performance.

Advice for Care

In well-drained soil, ornamental onion should not have pest and disease problems. The leaves are attractive as they appear but begin to look ratty as the flower matures. This is easily remedied by growing the flower up through other perennials, creating a double tier effect and masking the browning foliage.

Additional Information

Ornamental onion will self-sow modestly. This can be prevented by removing the heads before they scatter their seed. Ornamental onion works well in mixed plantings. A memorable planting from Cranbrook House in Bloomfield Hills featured the spherical flowers of ornamental onions as an accent among purple perennial salvias, pink petunias, grey artemisia, and ornamental kale. The characteristic oniony odor of *Allium* is noticeable only when the foliage is crushed.

Additional Species, Cultivars, or Varieties

Allium giganteum, the 3- to 4-ft. giant onion, is the large purple globular flower often seen towering over an admiring child in bulb catalogs. Sometimes confused with the onion discussed above, the giant onion is impressive. It's more difficult to use in the garden, more expensive, and not as easy to grow, however. Plant bulbs 8 in. deep and 8 to 10 in. apart. Use in groups as an accent plant. The seed heads are attractive long after the flowers fade. *Allium sphaerocephalum*, the drumstick allium, has a lithe habit in comparison. Tall (15 to 30 in.) with elliptical, dark rose-purple flowers, this onion needs to be grown through another perennial to obscure its unattractive, spindly foliage. At the Michigan State University DeLapa Perennial Garden, drumstick allium grows through Sedum 'Autumn Joy' and in front of Russian sage to great effect. Plant 5 in. deep and 2 to 3 in. apart in full sun.

Siberian Squill

Scilla siberica

Height: 4 to 6 in.
Flowers: Blue
Bloom Period: Early spring
Zones: 3, 4, 5, 6
Light Requirement:

The electric blue of Siberian squills is almost bold enough to send out shock waves. This early bloomer won't be ignored. Planted thickly along walkways or scattered in lawns, these small hardy bulbs grow into a mat of rich color so intense that it nearly sparkles, accounting for their long popularity with gardeners. Some squill plantings have remained viable for a half century or longer. Their pendant star-shaped flowers are among the earliest to open, following snowdrops. Whether they are found at the edge of a woodland or in a rock garden or lawn, squills are favorites for mass plantings over large areas where they will multiply to form huge colonies. Play up their diminutive size to edge a path or patio, to encircle a star magnolia or redbud, or to use at the front of a planting of bulbs or perennials. Their deep green leaves and bright color, sometimes called Prussian blue, are bold contrasts for yellow or white daffodils. Squills planted in lawns will complete their flowering stage and the foliage will usually ripen and die before the grass gets shaggy and needs mowing. For a relatively low-cost spring splash, buy squills by the hundreds.

WHEN TO PLANT

Plant squills, like the other small or minor bulbs, in September.

WHERE TO PLANT

Use squills generously at the edge of trees, in lawns, in rock gardens, and along paths. Although squills need sun in spring, they tolerate shade in summer; it is fine to plant them beneath deciduous trees because the squills will be finished with their show by the time the trees leaf out. Plant squills in large numbers because the flowers are quite small and plenty of company will make them easier to see. Eventually, they will multiply by bulblets and seed into colonies in a suitable location. The grasslike seedlings will reach blooming size after 4 to 5 years.

How to Plant

These bulbs prefer areas with sun to part sun and well-drained soil. Plant them 3 in. deep, and space them 3 in. apart. A bulb fertilizer may be mixed into the area before the bulbs are planted. After planting, firm the soil around the bulbs, and water the area well.

Advice for Care

Let the squill foliage ripen and turn brown before removing or cutting it. If squills are planted in the lawn, do not mow the grass until the squill leaves turn brown. Until that time, the plant is making food inside the leaves that will fuel the bulb and next year's flowers. The area where squills are planted may be fertilized in the fall or dressed with a top layer of compost in the fall every few years. They can be left undisturbed indefinitely. If you want to share bulbs with friends or move them to a new location, squills may be divided and replanted after 3 to 5 years. Squills make few demands. They are generally disease- and pest-free.

Additional Information

Squills, which are members of the lily family, are wonderful to brighten the early spring landscape before daffodils and most other bulbs or flowers begin to open. Their intense blue flowers and green leaves draw the eye while the landscape is just beginning to come to life.

Additional Species, Cultivars, or Varieties

'Spring Beauty' has blue flowers. It is large and vigorous with more flowers per stem than others. The blooms tend to last well, but this squill does not self-sow as quickly as others. 'Alba' is white. Twin-leaf squill, or *Scilla bifolia*, is an excellent choice for naturalizing and very graceful. Its starlike blue flowers are arranged loosely on 6-in. stems. The selection 'Praecox' has larger blooms, 'Rosea' is a faint pink, and 'Alba' is white. *Scilla tubergeniana*, sometimes called *S. mischtschenkoana*, has 1/2-in. pale-blue flowers in very early spring on 4-in. stems. Spanish bluebells have sometimes been called *Scilla*, but now botanists classify them as *Hyacinthoides hispanica*.

Snowdrop

Galanthus nivalis

Height: 6 in.
Flowers: White
Bloom Period: Early spring
Zones: 3, 4, 5, 6
Light Requirement:

Few sights any time of the year bring more joy to gardeners than the first snowdrop. These petite beauties pop up as early as February and March, often while there is still snow on the ground. Their white nodding flowers are small but distinctive, with 3 flaring petals and a central notched tube marked with green. The green leaves are smooth and about 6 in. long. Snowdrops can be planted in part to full shade, such as under evergreens or trees or in a shady border. They thrive in well-drained, moisture-retentive soil where they will eventually multiply. Like squills, snowdrops bloom and the leaves ripen so early that they are finished well before they might be an eyesore. The area where snowdrops are planted can then be turned over to annuals. Or plant snowdrops in a low-growing groundcover. Along with squills and grape hyacinths, snowdrops often appear in broad swaths and clumps in old gardens. Snowdrops are enjoying great popularity in the United Kingdom, with gardeners eager to buy and grow named varieties that show even the slightest variation, according to bulb historian Scott Kunst of Ann Arbor. Whatever kinds you grow, you'll be rewarded with tiny but exquisite flowers during the final days of winter. A miniature arrangement of cut snowdrops on a windowsill is a real heart-warmer.

WHEN TO PLANT

Plant snowdrops with other minor bulbs in September. They may take a year or two to get established. For faster results, plant snowdrops "in the green." After they flower in the spring, snowdrops may be dug and shared with friends or spread around your own garden.

WHERE TO PLANT

Snowdrops prefer light to partial shade and moist but well-drained soil that is high in organic material. Sandy soils should be amended. Don't plant in hot, dry areas. Use snowdrops planted randomly under trees, between shrubs, in a woodland setting, or at the front of a shady border. Put some near your front door where they will be easy to spot.

HOW TO PLANT
The bulbs should be 3 to 4 in. deep and spaced 4 in. apart.

ADVICE FOR CARE
Select firm bulbs, not ones that are dry and desiccated. Snowdrops appreciate the qualities of a wooded, natural setting—moist, fertile soil, shade, and nutrients found in organic materials. They may be dug and divided when they form large, vigorous clumps as the bulbs finish flowering. Snowdrops are not troubled by pests and diseases.

ADDITIONAL INFORMATION
As with many other spring bulbs, the snowdrop season can be pushed up if you plant them close to the foundation along the south side of the house. Snowdrops with a protected exposure will bloom several weeks ahead of those in a more exposed location. The flowers are quite small, so plant in quantities. Snowdrops are particularly lovely with the yellow flowers of winter aconite.

ADDITIONAL SPECIES, CULTIVARS, OR VARIETIES
Galanthus nivalis (4 to 5 in.) is the common or garden snowdrop. It generally opens late February to March and is not damaged by snow or freezing temperatures. The cultivar 'Flore-Pleno' has double flowers. Another cultivar, *G. nivalis* 'Viridiapicis' (8 to 10 in.), has more prominent green markings. *Galanthus elwesii*, at 8 to 10 in., is the giant snowdrop.

Star-of-Persia

Allium christophii

> **Height:** 10 to 20 in.
> **Flowers:** Silvery lilac
> **Bloom Period:** Late spring to early summer
> **Zones:** 4, 5, 6
> **Light Requirement:**
>
>

Star-of-Persia opens like a starburst—first a few star-shaped flowers, then finally the whole thing explodes to a tremendous sphere of celestial lavender flowers. These perfect, starry globes, each close to 10 in. wide, are a novelty in perennial beds, cottage gardens, and rose gardens. Each flower head holds close to 100 6-pointed flowers. The color is a lilac-purple with a silvery luster, and each has a small green center. The loose flower heads on stout stems provide interest at ground level, combining well with lavender, pearly everlasting, woolly thyme, and other perennials with silvery foliage. Plant star-of-Persia in groups of at least 3. A dozen or more will create a spectacular display. The flowers of *Allium christophii* bloom for 2 to 3 weeks, but the large spheres remain attractive in the garden for months. Leave them until they begin to deteriorate, or harvest them early to use as an everlasting. The gray-green foliage of star-of-Persia is fairly narrow and somewhat hairy. Although they begin to brown as the flowers come into bloom, the leaves are not a significant detraction. Take advantage of the flowers' metallic purple cast by planting them in well-drained locations with blue oat grass and low-growing sedums. The dusky plum foliage of *Sedum* 'Vera Jameson' provides an attractive contrast. Or grow star-of-Persia at the base of shrub roses with catmint and the pastel cheddar pink, 'Bath's Pink'. Sun and adequate drainage are all this wonderful ornamental onion needs to persist and bloom year after year.

WHEN TO PLANT

Plant the white-skinned bulbs of star-of-Persia in late September to mid-October.

WHERE TO PLANT

Star-of-Persia and other alliums should be planted in full sun (a bit of shade may be tolerated) in average to rich, well-drained soil. Use them in perennial beds, cottage gardens, and mixed plantings. Star-of-Persia makes a great accent when planted to come up through sun-loving groundcovers such as thyme, lamb's ears, and sedum.

How to Plant

Dig holes and plant the bulbs, setting them so the bottom of the bulb is 5 in. below the soil surface. Don't leave any air pockets under the bulb. Plant at least 3 in each group, spaced 8 to 12 in. apart. Water the newly planted bulbs. Bulb-booster-type fertilizer (9-9-6) could be added to the planting hole to improve performance.

Advice for Care

In well-drained soil, star-of-Persia should not be troubled by pest or disease problems. It is drought tolerant later in the summer, but while the plant is in bloom, give it adequate moisture. In soils of average fertility, this ornamental onion will not require extra fertilization.

Additional Information

The seed heads of star-of-Persia, if cut before they begin to deteriorate, can be used as an everlasting. Just 3 or 5 will fill a medium-sized vase. You can also use them as a fresh-cut flower but only if you plant many extras. They are almost too beautiful to take from the garden. *Allium christophii*, when ideally situated, will self-sow. The seedlings will take 2 to 3 years to reach flowering size. Star-of-Persia is also offered for sale as *A. albopilosum*.

Additional Species, Cultivars, or Varieties

Allium karataviense, 8 in. tall and flowering in late May to June, also has large, globular flowers that are 6 in. wide. They aren't nearly as appealing as star-of-Persia. The broad, flat leaves, however, are gray-green edged with purple, pleated, and very attractive. The ribbed foliage sets off the white-to-pink flower heads and doesn't begin to decline until the flowers are on the wane. It, too, prefers sun and good drainage.

Summer Snowflake

Leucojum aestivum

Height: 14 to 24 in.
Flowers: White
Bloom Period: Late spring
Zones: 5, 6
Light Requirement:

Summer snowflake dangles white bell-shaped flowers, each petal marked with green, from upright stems and glossy straplike leaves. Despite its common name, this snowflake actually blooms in late spring, flowering for 2 to 3 weeks in May. Summer snowflake is graceful, not flashy. Its dainty, nodding flowers, produced among robust foliage, add subtle beauty to the garden. The overall effect is one of green foliage decorated with small white bells. Summer snowflake, native to wet fields, woods, and swamps of Europe and western Asia, tolerates and perhaps prefers moist soils. It will grow in all but the wettest sites. The fresh white bells are particularly attractive reflecting in the water of a pond or gracing the bank of a stream. *Leucojum aestivum* thrives in moist soil and full sun but will also tolerate partial shade. Use summer snowflake in perennial beds and cottage gardens, as an accent for groundcover plantings, and naturalized in a sunny, moist location. It's a great choice for adding interest to a moist, partly shaded location at the edge of a shrub bed or a damp location near the foundation of a house. Try summer snowflake with the spotted foliage of Bethlehem sage, flowers of blue woodland phlox, and ferns in a corner of the garden with filtered shade. Or grow it with globeflower, *Trollius*, and cushion spurge in a moisture-retentive, sunny location. The selection 'Gravetye Giant', the best choice for garden use, is taller and more floriferous.

WHEN TO PLANT
Plant the daffodil-like bulbs of summer snowflake in late September through early October.

WHERE TO PLANT
Summer snowflake flourishes in rich, well-drained soil, but—unusual among bulbs—it also grows well in moist and less than perfectly drained sites. Moist soil, not sodden, and full sun to light shade are ideal. Sandy spots that become hot and dry in the summer

will not be acceptable. The graceful white bells are spectacular waterside. Plant summer snowflake beside ponds and streams.

How to Plant

Dig holes and plant the bulbs so that the base of the bulb is 4 to 5 in. below the soil surface. Don't leave any air pockets under the bulb. Space bulbs 3 to 5 in. apart in natural-looking groups. A bulb planter or a large trowel is suitable for digging the holes. When using a bulb planter, you don't need to extract the soil to finish the job. As you dig the next hole, the soil will pop out the top. A bulb-booster-type fertilizer (9-9-6) could be incorporated into the soil at planting. Water the bulbs after planting.

Advice for Care

Summer snowflake is pest- and disease-free and needs no special care. You can carefully move it while it is in leaf, and this is a useful way to establish the plant elsewhere or to share with other gardeners. If plants become congested and blooming decreases, dig and separate them into single bulbs. Let the foliage mature fully before removing.

Additional Information

Bulbs will take several years to form mature-sized clumps. *Leucojum* will naturalize and spread, particularly in a moist, sunny location. The graceful nodding flowers are a nice addition to flower arrangements.

Additional Species, Cultivars, or Varieties

'Gravetye Giant', which grows 20 to 24 in. tall and is a superior selection, was named for Gravetye Manor, home of William Robinson, the 19th-Century English gardener and garden writer who was one of the first to promote the naturalizing of bulbs. It is widely available. *Leucojum vernum*, the spring snowflake, is often confused with the snowdrop; they are a similar size and prefer similar growing conditions. Snowflakes have bell-shaped flowers touched with green, not the distinctive central tube of the snowdrop. Each stem of the spring snowflake carries 1 or 2 pendant bells, which open as the snowdrops go over. Spring snowflake prefers moist soil as well.

Tulip

Tulipa hybrids

Height: 6 to 30 in.
Flowers: Red, white, peach, pink, salmon, yellow, purple, maroon-black, lavender, solid or combinations
Bloom Period: Spring
Zones: 3, 4, 5, 6
Light Requirement:

Stately and formal in a geometric massed planting or casual and cheery in a clump near the front door, tulips are a colorful staple unparalleled in the spring garden. Even a modest grouping of 2 dozen bulbs can jazz up the view from a window or walkway. Tulips start coming into bloom at the end of April, and the bulk opens in May after the minor bulbs finish flowering and toward the end of the daffodils' show. As with daffodils, tulips display an immense range of colors, shapes, bloom periods, and heights. Some tulip flowers are the familiar chalice shape, but there are many others to consider. Double late tulips such as 'Angelique' resemble peonies. The parrot tulips have distinctive frilled edges. A lily-flowering tulip called 'White Triumphator' is elegant and graceful, perfect to use in a perennial bed. Although they will live for more than one season, many tulips decline in flowering stamina after one to several seasons. Some gardeners treat them as annuals, discarding them after they finish blooming and then planting new tulips in the fall. If you want tulips with more staying power, choose carefully. Some will perform for several seasons, such as the single early and single late tulips. Bulbs sold as "perennial tulips" usually bloom well for 3 to 5 years. Tulips have a long history of cultivation. They were so popular in Holland during the 1600s that a craze known as tulipomania swept the country and single bulbs sold for the equivalent of thousands of dollars. These hardy bulbs have been grown in the United States since the earliest European settlers arrived and continue to be among the most widely planted today, especially in mass displays that herald spring.

WHEN TO PLANT

Tulips may be planted in October to November or as long as the soil can be worked. Tulips do better planted later than other bulbs.

WHERE TO PLANT

Tulip displays are most dramatic when the bulbs are planted in quantity or clumps. Use groups of one color for a sophisticated effect or mixed colors for an informal party of color. Tulips need sun and a well-drained soil. Before planting, dig the soil to a depth of 12 in. Unlike daffodils, large hybrid tulips are not suited to naturalizing since the bulb display cannot be counted on for more than a year. Regular fertilization will increase bulb longevity.

HOW TO PLANT

Plant larger bulbs 6 to 8 in. deep. Space 4 to 6 in. apart. Smaller tulip bulbs are planted 4 to 5 in. deep and apart. It is important to plant tulips to the full recommended depth. A deep planting will be longer lived and less likely to be invaded by rodents.

ADVICE FOR CARE

After tulips finish blooming, allow the foliage to stay intact until it turns yellow. Leave the bulbs in place, or dig them up, divide, and store in mesh bags in a cool, dry place to replant in fall. Or treat tulips as annuals and discard. Fertilize tulips at planting by working bulb food into the soil. Feed lightly as the first leaves emerge in spring. Fertilize again in fall with bulb food, or top dress with compost.

ADDITIONAL INFORMATION

Plant bulbs only in well-drained locations to avoid potential problems. In heavy clay soils or locations where they stay wet in summer, tulips will perform poorly, will be prone to winter injury, and eventually will rot.

ADDITIONAL SPECIES, CULTIVARS, OR VARIETIES

With so many tulips to choose from, the best way to select is to spend time with a bulb catalog and then experiment. Single and double early tulips usually start blooming in mid-April. Peony flowering tulips are also called double late tulips. 'Angelique' is pale pink and blooms in early May, an inviting combination with deep-blue pansies. Triumph tulips such as 'Apricot Beauty' are crosses between Darwins and early tulips with large flowers, and they bloom in late April. Green or viridiflora tulips, which have flowers with a green band or vein on the petal, bring unusual color combinations to the garden. They bloom in May. There are also multi-flowering and lily-flowering tulips, single and double lates, and Rembrandt or striped tulips. See the separate entry on botanical tulips.

Windflower

Anemone blanda

Height: 4 in.
Flowers: Blue, white, pink
Bloom Period: Early spring
Zones: 5, 6
Light Requirement:

The blue daisylike flowers of windflower, *Anemone blanda*, are uniquely appealing in early spring. Perhaps the yellow-centered blue daisies, resembling asters, suggest the lush growing season to come. Or maybe it's just that daisy flowers, so common in high summer, are uncommon in early spring. Whatever the reason, a carpet of windflowers is a delight on a sunny Michigan spring day. Windflowers are among the earliest bulbs—combining with snowdrops, winter aconite, and squill—but hang on for weeks, remaining in bloom for the daffodils and early tulips. The flowers, more closely related to buttercups than daisies, are set off by ground-hugging, deep green, dissected leaves. Like winter aconites and snowdrops, windflowers prefer filtered sun and moist, well-drained, rich soil. Use them beneath deciduous trees and shrubs, which provide sun in the early spring and dappled shade later. Plant them in drifts under river birch, crabapple, or corneliancherry trees. Add daffodils to enliven the show. Many beautiful combinations can be devised; try white emperor tulips underplanted with pink windflowers or red tulips with mixed blue shades. Windflower is impressive planted in mass; it's not enough to plant just a few. Windflower can often be purchased in lots of 50 or 100 for a substantial price break. The tubers can be planted with ease. Come spring, you won't regret the effort.

WHEN TO PLANT

Plant the brown bumpy tubers from late September until mid-October. Windflowers can also be split and moved after flowering—or, for that matter, while in flower—in the same way as winter aconite. Dig them up, disturbing the roots as little as possible, and replant in the desired location. This is a good way to spread windflowers to other parts of the garden.

WHERE TO PLANT

Anemone blanda prefers moist, well-drained soil that is high in organic matter. The ideal location is sunny in early spring and partially shady later, such as a woodland garden, borders under high trees, and the edges of shrub beds. Windflowers will also grow in full sun with adequate moisture and combine well with daffodils and early tulips. They can be naturalized in woodland gardens and low-maintenance grassy areas under trees. Hardiness may be variable; before investing in large quantities, grow a few to be sure they will be hardy in your garden.

How to Plant

Soak purchased tubers in water overnight. Dig holes and plant the tubers so that the base is 2 to 3 in. below the soil surface. Look carefully for eyes or buds, and plant them facing up. If you can't determine which end is up, plant the tubers on their sides. Space bulbs 2 to 3 in. apart in natural-looking groups. Don't lose them! The tubers resemble a piece of mulch and can be overlooked. A strong, narrow bulb-planting trowel marked with the proper depth is ideal for this job. These small, relatively inexpensive bulbs can be planted more quickly and with less care than a tulip or large daffodil bulb. Use large quantities (50 to 100 bulbs) for the best effect and economy.

Advice for Care

Windflowers need no special care and are virtually trouble-free. They can be difficult to establish if the tubers are desiccated. Watering may be necessary in an extended dry period. Apply a mulch to overwinter *Anemone blanda* in the colder parts of Zone 5.

Additional Information

In ideal conditions, windflower spreads and seeds to form beautiful flower carpets. Seedlings will bloom the second or third year from seed.

Additional Species, Cultivars, or Varieties

Purchase only nursery-propagated windflowers. Choosing cultivated selections ensures this. 'Blue Shades' is a mix of blue hues. 'White Splendor', with its beautiful flowers against dark foliage, lights up woodland gardens. Several pink selections are available including 'Rosea', which is soft pink, and 'Charmer', which is a brighter shade. 'Radar' is almost gaudy with magenta flowers and a white bull's-eye. Mixes of white, blue, and pink are also commonly sold.

Winter Aconite

Eranthis hyemalis

Height: 3 to 5 in.
Flowers: Buttercup yellow
Bloom Period: Early spring
Zones: 4, 5, 6
Light Requirement:

Once you know where winter aconites grow, watching for them becomes a favorite early spring ritual while the tall trees are still bare and the ground is covered with leaves or even patches of snow. Impatiently, you look and look again and finally, one day, spot these golden yellow flowers poking up toward the sun, blooming proof that winter is almost over. Winter aconites are cohorts of squills, crocuses, and snowdrops in that they fall into the category of the so-called minor bulbs. That label is misleading, though. Winter aconites and their fellows are small in size, but they have a major impact on gardeners because they come so early in the season and are inexpensive to plant in quantity. These yellow flowers are about 1 in. wide and appear surrounded by a rufflike collar of green. Naturalize winter aconites, which grow from tubers, and they'll continue to bloom and multiply under trees and shrubs for years. The bright yellow makes a colorful contrast with white snowdrops and creates spring's earliest floral display. Winter aconites are also excellent for rock gardens and borders.

When to Plant

Plant winter aconites along with the other small bulbs in September or as soon as they are available. They profit from as much time to get established as possible before the ground freezes. A more reliable way to plant them is to dig and divide established plantings in spring, while the plants are still green. Dig carefully, disturbing the roots as little as possible, and replant.

Where to Plant

Locate these plants by the dozens or hundreds under deciduous trees and in borders, rock gardens, and beds. They need sun in early spring but will be finished blooming and maturing by the time the trees and shrubs leaf out. The bulbs require well-drained, moisture-retentive soil that does not dry out completely in summer, particularly if they are planted in full sun. A better choice is an area that remains cool and moist in summer with high or dappled shade. Combine with snowdrops for a white-and-yellow display in earliest spring. Use under trees and shrubs, in borders and beds. Winter aconite makes a splash on a slope where the flowers will make a carpet of buttercup yellow.

How to Plant
Soak the dried tubers in water overnight before planting. Space the tubers 3 in. apart and plant 3 in. deep. Or plant from divisions. Use winter aconites in drifts rather than straight lines.

Advice for Care
Winter aconite is carefree after planting and will spread rapidly in ideal conditions. Mix fertilizer with the soil before setting the bulbs in the ground. If rodents regularly ravage bulbs in your yard, cover a new planting with wire screening or chicken wire, or apply a commercial repellent, which is available at garden centers. The bulbs will gradually multiply if left undisturbed in subsequent years. They have no serious diseases.

Additional Information
Winter aconite blooms from new tuberous roots produced each year, which send up a flower in the spring. The plant's botanical name, *Eranthis*, means "flower of spring."

Winter aconite is not a good choice for naturalizing in a lawn. It is short and does not compete well with grass. These plants have a reputation for being difficult to establish in fall planting. Seed from the ripening seed heads can be scattered in areas of a woodland garden where you want winter aconites to spread. These will take 3 to 4 years to reach blooming size.

Additional Species, Cultivars, or Varieties
Eranthis hyemalis is the most widely available winter aconite. It is similar to *Eranthis cilicica*, which has slightly deeper yellow flowers.

Lawns

$\mathscr{P}$EOPLE WHO LIVE IN MICHIGAN LOVE THEIR LAWNS.
An expanse of healthy green turf is attractive and functional,
and grass is soft and inviting. It's a tempting place to spread a blanket and read a book, enjoy a picnic, or savor a comforting moment
of solitude.

A lawn's textured, horizontal surface sets off the rest of the
landscape—flowers, trees, and shrubs. It is relatively easy and inexpensive to install and maintain. A neat, well-tended lawn can even
boost property values.

Keys to maintaining a robust lawn are selecting the right type of
grass, mowing high, and watering and fertilizing properly. A
healthy lawn is best able to resist diseases and insects.

Most people want some grass in their yards. The question is,
how much grass should be grown—and how much work should a
lawn be? There are many possible answers, and it comes down to
a personal choice. Make a realistic assessment of what you want
from a lawn and how much work you're willing to exert to achieve
your goal.

Your ideal lawn may be quite different from the one you grew up
with. People have long associated an intensely manicured, weed-
free lawn with prosperity and responsibility, and some home
owners cheerfully classify themselves as lawn obsessed. Their
favorite weekend activity is tending the turf.

Others, however, are looking for ways to keep some grass while
decreasing the overall amount of mowing, watering, and fertilizing
required. They may decide to develop a low-care utility lawn in
which nongrass but green plants are perfectly welcome. They may
incorporate groundcovers and paving materials into grassy areas.

Chapter Four

To figure out what kind of lawn you want and need, consider how the lawn will be used. Will it get lots of traffic? Will children play on it? Will its main function be as a visual link to the flower borders or the vegetable garden?

Then assess how much sun the area receives. If it's in sun all or most of the day, you have a good shot at maintaining turf successfully. Check the sunlight and soil requirements for the four turfgrasses in this chapter. An area that gets just an hour of light a day is better suited for perennial groundcovers or even a hardscape such as brick or pea-sized pebbles than for turfgrass.

The drainage of the soil and its fertility are also considerations. Nearly all plants require soils that hold some moisture but also drain well. Drainage and fertility will be improved with the addition of organic materials such as well-rotted compost.

Soil preparation is especially crucial for lawns around brand-new houses, where subsoil from the basement excavation may have been spread about and traffic from heavy equipment has compacted the soil.

Take a soil test to see what nutrients are needed before beginning a new lawn. Your county's office of the MSU Extension can tell you how to take the samples and submit them for analysis. When installing a brand-new lawn, you may also want to consider hiring a professional landscaper to assess the situation.

Whether you maintain your lawn or hire someone else to do it, understanding a few principles of grass care can help achieve the type of lawn you want.

PLANTING AND CARING FOR YOUR LAWN

The best time to establish a lawn from seed or to renovate bare patches is mid-August to mid-September, or August 10 to September 1 in northern Michigan. By then, the nighttime temperatures are beginning to cool, the days are still warm, and rainfall is increasing. Weeds are not growing as actively as they were earlier in the year. All these conditions are good for grass seed germination. If you can't do the work at that time, the next best period to sow grass seed is mid-April to mid-May.

Besides simply sowing seed, another way to begin is by hydroseeding. In this process grass seed is mixed with mulch and fertilizer and then sprayed on the soil. Hydroseeding is best done in spring or fall.

Sod may be laid from April through late fall as long as the soil temperature is above 40 degrees Fahrenheit. Before installing sod, moisten the soil to a depth of 6 inches, and keep the area watered afterward until roots are established.

Starting a lawn from seed is the least expensive way to begin a new lawn. It also requires more work and takes longer to achieve good results. Sod, while more costly, provides an "instant lawn."

When you undertake a new lawn or want to seed bare patches, evaluate the existing conditions. If the soil and grade are acceptable, the only preparation required is to scratch or roughen up the surface to a depth of at least 2 inches.

Heavy clay or infertile or sandy soil may be improved by adding well-rotted compost, aged manure, and other organic materials. These will improve the soil's ability to drain as well as its capacity to retain moisture.

Dig up any weeds or kill them with a herbicide. In a new lawn, this is the time to install an in-ground irrigation system if desired.

Some seed packages contain more filler than others, so check the label of the seed mixtures or blends to see what percentage is selected seed. When buying grass seed, it's a better bargain to pay more initially for higher quality.

Although it is sometimes advertised for sale, zoysia grass is not a good choice for Michigan lawns. It is a warm-season grass that thrives in hot weather but turns brown when temperatures fall, both in spring and in fall. Bentgrass is another type to avoid for residential lawns. It is beautiful on golf course greens but requires a higher level of maintenance than most home owners can provide.

Chapter Four

After planting, lightly roll or firm the area to make sure the seed gets in contact with the soil. Water and then cover the surface with a mulch such as clean straw or a paper-based mulch such as the kind in hydroseed. A new paper mulch available in pellets contains a substance that absorbs and then gradually releases water. When the pellet gets wet, the mulch absorbs water and expands to cover the newly seeded area. A light application of fertilizer (half the normal recommended rate) may be done at seeding.

The main reason grass seed fails to grow is that it dries out. If the weather is warm and windy, it may be necessary to water the newly seeded area several times a day. After about 3 weeks, the straw mulch may be removed. Mow when the new grass is 3 inches tall.

Ideas about mowing have changed in the last decade or so. Lawn experts now recommend mowing high—2$^{1}/_{2}$, 3, or even 3$^{1}/_{2}$ inches. With more surface area, the grass can manufacture more nutrients to nourish its roots and stems. Longer blades also shade the soil surface, making it harder for crabgrass seeds to germinate.

Mow often enough so that no more than the top $^{1}/_{3}$ of the grass blade is removed at one time. Mowing is easier if beds are defined with edging and there is a circle left free of grass around the base of trees. This also protects the tree trunks from close encounters with a lawn mower.

Besides mowing high, turf experts advise leaving the grass clippings to disintegrate where they fall on the lawn. The cut pieces are mostly water. As they break down, they return nutrients to the soil and the grass roots.

For information about when and how much to fertilize, see the individual entries. Turf experts at Michigan State University recommend that high-care lawns of blended Kentucky bluegrass need 3 to 5 pounds of nitrogen per 1,000 square feet a year. Low-care or utility lawns with a mixture of grasses will perform well with 1 to 2 pounds nitrogen per 1,000 square feet

The question of how often to fertilize gets back to what kind of lawn you want. A low-care or utility lawn won't look as uniform or deeply green as a high-care lawn—but it won't need as much fertilizer, mowing, or watering, either. Nitrogen is the most important nutrient in a fertilizer for lawns.

Organic fertilizers, which are made from natural products such as animal manures, are not as concentrated, so more fertilizer will be needed to apply the recommended rate of nitrogen. This can make organic fertilizers more expensive to use. Their lower concentration, however, means there is less danger of runoff, and they rarely burn the grass.

Nonorganic fertilizers are mixtures of chemical salts and inert substances that break down quickly when they are watered into the soil. They are concentrated, so less of the product is needed, but they must be used at the proper rate to avoid burning, and they should not be used around rivers or lakes.

Slow-release fertilizers, which release the nutrients gradually over several months, are a better choice for waterside locations because there is less chance of pollution from runoff. As a precaution, leave at least a 10- to 20-foot strip that is not fertilized next to the water.

Crabgrass control is a traditional concern for those who maintain lawns. In the past, the forsythia in full bloom has been a signal for many people to apply a preemergent chemical to stop crabgrass and other weed seeds from germinating. Before spreading a preemergent over the whole lawn, however, analyze the extent of the problem. It may be possible to deal with crabgrass on a spot basis rather than to treat the entire lawn, which may not need it. If perennial weeds such as dandelions are a concern, dig them with a long fork, pull by hand, or, if desired, spot treat them with a herbicide.

The best way to prevent the appearance of crabgrass and other weeds is to keep the lawn healthy through proper mowing, watering, and fertilizing. These steps keep the grass dense and tall, shading the soil so crabgrass won't germinate. Tests at Michigan State University showed that simply using the right amount of fertilizer cut the number of weeds in lawns significantly.

Cool-season grasses, the kind recommended for Michigan lawns, grow most vigorously when the temperature is 60 to 85 degrees

Chapter Four

Fahrenheit. They go dormant in hotter weather. This is a natural process and does not harm the grass, which will green up again when the weather turns cooler.

If you choose to keep the grass from going brown and dormant, you will have to water often in hot, dry weather. Turfgrasses require about 1 inch of water a week during the growing season, from rain, a sprinkler, or an irrigation system. The current recommendation is to water frequently—even every day—for short periods rather than to wait several days and then apply a longer soaking. Watch the lawn for signs of drought stress such as wilting or a blue-gray cast to the leaves.

Aerating a lawn is another tactic to keep the grass vigorous, especially in heavy clay or compacted soils. Core aerators are heavy large drums covered with spikes. As they pass over the turf, they cut out round sections several inches deep and throw them on the surface. This process creates thousands of small holes in the lawn, exposing the root area to additional air, water, and nutrients. It also helps reduce thatch or accumulated debris around the base of the grass plants. If the aeration is done in spring, the grass will recover fairly quickly. Aeration does not have to be done each year.

In fall, keep tree leaves from forming a thick mat on the grass. The usual way to remove leaves is with a rake or blower. Another approach is to mow the leaves and let them stay on the lawn. If they are cut finely with a mulching mower or two passes of a regular lawn mower, the leaves will decompose and will not contribute to thatch. In a study at Michigan State University, a 6-inch layer of leaves was mowed and left on a lawn without harmful effect. As a result, many Michigan golf courses are now mowing the leaves and letting them stay on the grass each fall.

Keeping the grass healthy by selecting the proper seed, watering, mowing, and fertilizing is the best way to achieve a handsome, resilient lawn.

Fineleaf Fescues

Festuca species

Zones: 3, 4, 5, 6
Light Requirement:

The fine fescues perform better in shady areas than other turfgrasses recommended for Michigan lawns. They may be mixed with Kentucky bluegrass to increase shade tolerance or to use for a low-care utility lawn that tends to stay dry and includes some shade. Fine fescues require a well-drained soil and should not be watered excessively. In fact, fescues that stay wet during warm summer weather are more susceptible to fungal diseases such as leaf spot. Fine fescues that are sometimes mixed with Kentucky bluegrass include creeping red fescue (*Festuca rubra* var. *rubra*), chewings fescue (*Festuca rubra* var. *commutata*), and hard fescue (*Festuca longifolia*). A few fine fescue cultivars are available with moderate disease resistance from endophytes, a fungus that helps repel chinch bugs, billbugs, sod webworms, and aphids. The fungus is concentrated on the part of the turf above ground level. Fescues require less fertilizer per growing season than Kentucky bluegrass or perennial ryegrass. The fine fescues need 1 to 2 lb. actual nitrogen per 1,000 sq. ft. of lawn per year. In open sun, fine fescues will usually perform better with some irrigation.

WHEN TO PLANT

Sow seed from mid-August to mid-September when night temperatures are cool and rain is usually plentiful. In northern Michigan, sow from August 10 to September 1. In late summer and early fall, there is less competition from weeds than at other times of the growing season. The second choice for sowing grass seed is mid-April to mid-May.

WHERE TO PLANT

Use fineleaf fescues on partially shaded lawns that remain on the dry side. The soil must be well drained.

How to Plant

Sow fine fescue seed at the rate of 3 to 5 lb. per 1,000 sq. ft. of turf. Be patient because fineleaf fescues take a while to fill in. See the instructions on site preparation in the introduction to this chapter. After sowing seed, mulch with clean straw or paper-based product. Mulch helps keep in moisture and protects the seed from washing away. Water often enough to keep the soil moistened while the seed germinates and gets established. It is normal to have weeds come up in a new lawn. Many weeds will be controlled by subsequent mowing. The remainder may be pulled or killed with a spot treatment of herbicide. If using a herbicide, however, wait 6 weeks after seeding. Fine fescues are more susceptible to injury if treated too soon.

Advice for Care

Michigan State University turf experts suggest fertilizing a fine fescue lawn at Memorial Day and Labor Day. The total actual nitrogen applied per season should be 1 to 2 lb. per 1,000 sq. ft. of lawn, with no more than 1 lb. applied at one time. Mow as high as possible, especially in hot weather. Set the mower blade at 2½ to 3 in. Mow often enough to remove no more than ⅓ of the blade height at any one time.

Additional Information

Fineleaf fescues are prone to develop leaf spot diseases during humid, wet summers. A fine fescue lawn that is thinning may be fertilized at half the usual rate to encourage dense growth and recovery.

Additional Species, Cultivars, or Varieties

Researchers are testing new cultivars every year. Buy the best quality seed you can find.

Kentucky Bluegrass

Poa pratensis

Zones: 3, 4, 5, 6
Light Requirement:

Kentucky bluegrass is the most widely planted lawn grass in Michigan. People admire its rich appearance, deep green color, and texture. Kentucky bluegrass forms a dense, carpet-like turf. This grass is best suited to areas with full or nearly full sunlight and requires more upkeep—both watering and fertilizing—than most other grasses. If that doesn't bother you and your goal is a near perfect lawn, a blend of Kentucky bluegrasses is the right choice. Like the other grasses profiled in this chapter that are recommended for Michigan lawns, Kentucky bluegrass is a cool-season grass, showing most vigorous growth when the temperatures are between 60 and 85 degrees Fahrenheit. When the weather is hot and dry, Kentucky bluegrass will go dormant. Dormancy is a natural process of self-preservation, and a dormant lawn will green up again when cooler, wetter weather returns. To keep a Kentucky bluegrass lawn looking its best, however, supplemental irrigation is a necessity. An in-ground system is easiest to use. Most lawns planted in Kentucky bluegrass use several cultivars in a blend—or combine improved types of Kentucky bluegrass with other recommended turfgrasses, such as perennial ryegrass or fine fescues. The best choices for full-sun, high-quality lawns are the improved cultivars of Kentucky bluegrass. You can tell them by their specific cultivar names, such as 'Baron' or 'Touchdown'. For Michigan lawns, turf experts at Michigan State University recommend a mixture of different grasses based on the site conditions and the care the lawn will receive. A mixture has advantages over a monoculture, or planting of all one type, because it is better able to resist diseases and performs well despite variations in soil, environment, and maintenance.

WHEN TO PLANT

Sow seed from mid-August to mid-September when night temperatures are cool and rain is usually plentiful. In northern Michigan, sow seed from August 10 to September 1. In late summer to early fall, there is less competition from weeds than at other times of the growing season. The second choice for sowing grass seed is mid-April to mid-May. Lay sod any time that grass roots are growing, from April to late November, when the soil temperature is 40 degrees Fahrenheit or higher.

WHERE TO PLANT

Select Kentucky bluegrass for a high-quality lawn in a location that receives at least 6 hours of full sun a day. Some cultivars are moderately shade tolerant. It performs best in rich, well-drained soils; amend the soil if needed before planting.

HOW TO PLANT

See instructions on site preparation in the introduction to this chapter. Sow at the rate of 1 to 2 lb. of seed per 1,000 sq. ft. of lawn. Make a light application of fertilizer, using 1/2 lb. nitrogen per 1,000 sq. ft., or half the usual rate. Mulch with clean straw or paper-based product. Mulch helps keep in moisture and protects the seed from washing away. Water and keep the soil moistened several times a day as needed for about 3 weeks while the seed germinates and gets established. Don't worry if it takes a while. Kentucky bluegrass is slow to begin growing. It is normal to have weeds come up in a new lawn. Many will be controlled by subsequent mowing. The remainder may be pulled or killed with a spot treatment of herbicide. If using a herbicide, however, wait until after the grass has been mowed 3 or 4 times.

ADVICE FOR CARE

Kentucky bluegrass requires multiple feedings a season, usually at Memorial Day, the Fourth of July, Labor Day, and Halloween. During the growing season, improved cultivars of Kentucky bluegrass require a total of 3 to 5 lb. of nitrogen per 1,000 sq. ft. of lawn, according to turf experts at Michigan State University. Do not apply more than 1 lb. of actual nitrogen per 1,000 sq. ft. in any one application. Lawns with in-ground irrigation systems normally will need the higher amount of nitrogen. If you allow the lawn to go dormant during the hottest part of the summer, do not apply nitrogen during that time. Mowing the lawn high, with the mower blade set between 2¹/₂ and 3¹/₂ in., improves overall quality. Mow often enough to remove no more than 1/3 of the blade height at any one time.

ADDITIONAL INFORMATION

Kentucky bluegrass has excellent cold hardiness.

ADDITIONAL SPECIES, CULTIVARS, OR VARIETIES

Researchers are testing new cultivars every year. Buy the best quality seed you can find.

Perennial Ryegrass

Lolium perenne

Zones: 3, 4, 5, 6
Light Requirement:

Perennial ryegrass—another deep green, cool-season grass—germinates and grows quickly. Mixed together, Kentucky bluegrass and perennial ryegrass form the basis of a tough, attractive lawn for high-traffic areas. Perennial ryegrass needs frequent moisture and goes dormant in extreme heat and drought. Its watering and fertilization needs are similar to those of Kentucky bluegrass. Annual or Italian ryegrass, *Lolium multiflorum*, is not recommended for lawns in Michigan. A small amount may be useful in a seed mixture that contains mainly other turfgrasses because annual rye germinates quickly. But it is coarse, may outcompete other grasses, and usually does not live more than a year. Perennial ryegrass cultivars are reasonably cold hardy. Use improved types of perennial ryegrass, which are better able to withstand low temperatures and have a finer texture than common ryegrass. A fungus called an endophyte occurs on some cultivars of perennial ryegrass. Turf experts have found a way to concentrate the endophyte on the grass above the soil level, where it helps repel aphids, chinch bugs, sod webworms, and other pests.

WHEN TO PLANT

Sow seed from mid-August to mid-September, when night temperatures are cool and rain is usually plentiful. In northern Michigan, sow seed from August 10 to September 1. In late summer and early fall, there is less competition from weeds than at other times during the growing season. The second choice for sowing grass seed is mid-April to mid-May.

WHERE TO PLANT

Perennial ryegrass performs best in well-drained soils of average fertility and in sun or part shade. Combine it with Kentucky bluegrass for a lawn that can withstand wear. This is also a good combination for an embankment.

How to Plant

See instructions on site preparation in the introduction to this chapter. Make a light application of fertilizer—1/2 lb. nitrogen per 1,000 sq. ft., or half the normal recommended rate—at planting. Apply 4 to 5 lb. of seed per 1,000 sq. ft. of lawn. Mulch with clean straw or paper-based product. Mulch helps keep in moisture and protects the seed from washing away. Water and keep the soil moistened several times a day as needed for about 3 weeks while the seed germinates and gets established. It is normal to have weeds come up in a new lawn. Many will be controlled by subsequent mowing. The remainder may be pulled or killed with a spot treatment of herbicide. If using a herbicide, however, wait until after the grass has been mowed 3 or 4 times.

Advice for Care

Perennial ryegrass has about the same water and feeding needs as Kentucky bluegrass. According to turf experts at Michigan State University, a nonirrigated lawn would need 2 to 3 lb. of nitrogen per year per 1,000 sq. ft., using 1 lb. nitrogen per 1,000 sq. ft. per application. Twice-yearly applications can be made at Memorial Day and Labor Day. A third application can be timed around the Fourth of July. An irrigated lawn may require 3 to 5 lb. nitrogen per 1,000 sq. ft. of lawn per year. Mow at 2 1/2 to 3 1/2 in. and often enough so that no more than 1/3 of the blade's height is cut off at any one time.

Additional Species, Cultivars, or Varieties

Researchers are testing new cultivars every year. Buy the best quality seed you can find.

Turf-type Tall Fescues

Festuca arundinacea

Zones: 5, 6
Light Requirement:

Turf-type tall fescues are coarse-textured grasses that grow in bunches or clumps. When planted alone or as the main grass in a mix, the tall fescues can form a good uniform sod. They have wide leaf blades and prominent veins. Tall fescues may be mixed with a smaller percentage of Kentucky bluegrass or perennial ryegrass seed. Older tall fescues were considered inappropriate for lawns because of their coarseness. Newer cultivars have a narrower leaf texture and are less inclined to form bunches. They can withstand dry periods, heat, and traffic, including the rough-and-tumble demands of a playing field. They also tolerate some shade and resist pests and diseases to some degree. Tall fescues have been used successfully where a tough, resilient lawn is required, such as on the strip of lawn between a curb and sidewalk. Tall fescues resist stress from either temperature or use. They have proven to be hardy in southeastern Michigan. Some turf-type tall fescues grass seed is enhanced with endophytes, a fungus that improves the grass's ability to resist aphids, sod webworms, chinch bugs, and billbugs.

WHEN TO PLANT

Sow seed from mid-August to mid-September when night temperatures are cool and rain is usually plentiful. In northern Michigan, sow grass seed from August 10 to September 1. In late summer and early fall, there is less competition from weeds than at other times of the growing season. The second choice for sowing grass seed is mid-April to mid-May.

WHERE TO PLANT

Use tall fescues on banks that are subject to erosion, on playing fields, or in other utility applications for a tough, low-care lawn. They may be planted in sun or shade and in a wide variety of soil types, including sand. Michigan State University research indicates they are hardy in southeastern parts of the state and possibly elsewhere.

How to Plant

See instructions on site preparation in the introduction to this chapter. At planting, make a light application of fertilizer—$1/2$ lb. nitrogen per 1,000 sq. ft., or half the usual recommended rate. Sow seed for tall fescues at the rate of 4 to 8 lb. per 1,000 sq. ft. of lawn. Mulch with clean straw or a paper-based product. Mulch helps keep in moisture and protects the seed from washing away. Water and keep the soil moistened several times a day or as needed for about 3 weeks while the seed germinates and gets established. It is normal to have weeds come up in a new lawn. Many will be controlled by subsequent mowing. The remainder may be pulled or killed with a spot treatment of herbicide. If using a herbicide, however, wait until after the grass has been mowed 3 or 4 times.

Advice for Care

Tall fescues can withstand drought. This type of grass does best with infrequent but deep watering. Mow at 3 to 4 in. or at the highest mower blade setting, and let the clippings remain on the lawn where they will quickly decompose and return nutrients to the soil. Mowing the lawn high improves overall quality. Mow often enough to remove no more than $1/3$ of the blade height at any one time. Tall fescues should receive about 3 lb. nitrogen per season per 1,000 sq. ft. of lawn, applied about the end of May, early July, and early September, according to Michigan State University turf experts. Apply 1 lb. nitrogen per 1,000 sq. ft. per application.

Additional Information

Avoid the older types of tall fescues. They are coarse and may not be reliably winter hardy.

Additional Species, Cultivars, or Varieties

Researchers are testing new cultivars every year. Buy the best quality seed you can find.

CHAPTER FIVE

Ornamental Grasses

*O*RNAMENTAL GRASSES, WHICH ARE AMONG THE
EASIEST PERENNIALS TO GROW, ARE UNBEATABLE FOR
MULTISEASON IMPACT. Their beauty is natural, never contrived,
and their appearance is reminiscent of prairies and meadows.

Then why don't more gardeners grow ornamental grasses?
Perhaps some people overlook them because their flowers aren't
bright and showy. Others may be leery of grasses in general, fearing
they will become weedy, like crabgrass.

In fact, ornamental grasses that are selected and sited correctly
add elegance, a rustling sound, and graceful movement to the garden in a way few other plants can. Plant ornamental grasses in drifts
or swathes or as accents in the shrub or perennial border, where
their fine texture makes for dramatic contrast.

Grasses and spring bulbs make a happy pairing. The bulbs bloom
while the grasses are still dormant. By the time the bulb foliage
starts to yellow, the grasses start to grow. Cut back the grasses in
late winter, and the bulbs are ready to start the cycle again.

Ornamental grasses play an important role in the New American
garden, a style of landscaping that uses grasses massed with other
perennials. The Frederik Meijer Gardens in Grand Rapids features a
New American garden designed by James van Sweden, a Washington, D.C., landscape architect and a native of Grand Rapids. Another
place where you can see how ornamental grasses can be combined
with other perennials is the Horticultural Demonstration Gardens at
Michigan State University.

HOW ORNAMENTAL GRASSES GROW
Most ornamental grasses are perennials. They grow in two different
ways. Running grasses spread quickly by vigorous rhizomes.

Chapter Five

Clump-forming grasses increase in size slowly. Clump-formers are the best choice for home gardeners.

Grasses are categorized according to the temperatures in which they grow best. Cool-season grasses prefer temperatures of 60 to 75 degrees Fahrenheit. They produce foliage in spring or early summer. Some go dormant in hot weather, then resume growth in the fall.

The warm-season grasses, which thrive when it is 75 degrees Fahrenheit or warmer, stay dormant until late spring and then grow rapidly, flowering in late summer. They often turn color in the fall and add interest to the winter garden.

Most grasses do best in full sun, although some will tolerate part shade. Grasses are adaptable to different soil types. Many prefer rich, loamy soil, but some perform well even on poorly drained sites. Once established, most ornamental grasses will withstand drought. They rarely require fertilizer.

GROWING ORNAMENTAL GRASSES IN MICHIGAN

The ideal time to observe ornamental grasses is late summer and fall, when they are at their peak. Plant in the spring so grasses have time to get established before the heat of summer. They often take two years to achieve their mature effect.

Space the grasses as far apart as their height at maturity. Moving them closer together in a mass planting creates the effect of an ocean of grass. Spacing them farther apart emphasizes each plant's form.

Cutting back the foliage of ornamental grasses is the most important maintenance activity. Most grasses are cut back in late winter to early spring, before new growth begins.

We selected these grasses because they are reliable performers for Michigan gardens and none has fast-running roots. All are hardy to Zone 5. This attractive and diverse group can open new design possibilities for the garden.

Blue Oat Grass

Helictotrichon sempervirens

Height: 3 ft.
Flowers: Blue-gray changing to beige
Bloom Period: Late spring to early summer
Zones: 4, 5, 6
Light Requirement:

The metallic foliage of blue oat grass shimmers in the garden. A cool-season grass, *Helictotrichon sempervirens* gets a jump on the season, producing foliage in the early months of spring. Spiky tufts of blue leaf blades augment the pink, purple, and magenta flowers of the late spring and early summer garden. While most ornamental grasses save their flowers for late summer, those of blue oat grass dance in the spring breeze. Although blue oat grass is grown for its foliage, the delicate flowers waving high above it are lovely. In warmer climates, the flowering is sporadic, but in Michigan gardens blue oat grass will put on quite a display. Blue oat grass forms distinct clumps or tussocks of spiky foliage about 18 to 24 in. high. The flowers on silvery gray arching stems rise above the foliage by 1 to 2 ft. Planted in the foreground of a garden bed, the tall flowering stems add unexpected height, but their delicacy allows a see-through effect. The blue-gray tussocks of blue oat grass are persistent in the winter garden. Choose a full sun location with well-drained soil for blue oat grass. It can be massed but is at its best alone or in groups of 3 as an accent plant among perennials or shrubs. Enjoy the steely blue foliage of blue oat grass with the flowers of June. Use it as an anchor with a profusion of bloom—lavender-blue catmint, deep purple 'May Night' salvia, magenta cheddar pinks, and 'White Swirl' Siberian iris. Or plan for a late summer combination with blue spirea (*Caryopteris* × *clandonensis*) and 'Autumn Joy' showy stonecrop.

When to Plant
Plant blue oat grass in spring or September.

Where to Plant
Blue oat grass prefers full sun and well-drained, fertile soil. It tolerates a range of soils but not heavy, wet conditions. Plants will tolerate light shade for part of the day.

How to Plant

Plant blue oat grass in the landscape 2$^1/_2$ to 3 ft. apart. Plants that are too close together can't show off their dramatic form. Dig a hole and position the plant so that the soil level is the same as it was in the pot. Water thoroughly, and keep moist until established.

Advice for Care

Blue oat grass needs some grooming but not the severe haircut given to many grasses. Don't cut back blue oat grass to the ground; cut only to the top of the clump or tussock. For the best spring show, cut back the plants in the fall or early winter; otherwise, you risk an ugly haircut right before the main event. An alternative is to groom the plants in spring when clumps have a mixture of blue and beige leaf blades. Gently tug and remove the old foliage. This is effective if you have a few plants, but would soon get tedious for a mass planting. Remove the flowering stems (culms) when they are no longer appealing, usually by midsummer. Blue oat grass doesn't need any special fertilization. Plants appreciate water during drought.

Additional Information

Plants occasionally need division, which is best done in the spring. Dig plants and divide them into sections with a sharp spade or knife. Divisions often take 1 to 2 years to develop their characteristic tufted form. In hot, humid summers, foliar rust may occur. Avoid this with wide spacing and good air circulation. Blue oat grass can be planted with shrubs or even shrub roses. Try blue oat grass with purple smokebush and Russian sage. Add white tulips and the purple globes of ornamental onion, *Allium aflatunense*, or star-of-Persia, *Allium christophii*, for extra interest.

Additional Species, Cultivars, or Varieties

A smaller grass with a similar blue landscape effect is *Festuca ovina* 'Elijah Blue' (10 in.), a selection of blue fescue. Many blue fescues need division every 2 years and suffer from summer brownout. 'Elijah Blue', the best of the lot, has neither of these characteristics.

ORNAMENTAL GRASSES

Feather Reed Grass

Calamagrostis × acutiflora

Height: 5 to 6 ft.
Flowers: Purplish-green changing to gold
Bloom Period: Early summer
Zones: 5, 6
Light Requirement:

Few herbaceous plants offer the ever-changing interest of feather reed grass. As the year unfolds, it transforms itself for almost 10 months in the garden. If you're unsure about adding ornamental grasses to your yard, start with this natural beauty. If you grow ornamental grasses and haven't tried feather reed grass, add it to your shopping list right away! A cool-season grass, feather reed grass quickly forms fresh green clumps, maturing at about 3 ft. By late spring and early summer, when many grasses are just starting, feather reed grass sends forth tall (5 or 6 ft.), loose plumes of bronzy purple-tinged flowers. Next the flowers turn a golden wheat color and stiffen into an architectural vertical form. Moving with the slightest breeze, the upright flowers literally form amber waves. As late fall arrives, the plant becomes a light tan and remains an upright but swaying presence until February. Feather reed grass is well behaved in every way. A naturally occurring hybrid, it is sterile and never self-sows. In full sun, the tall, upright stalks never need staking. Summer rain and winter snow may weigh them down, but they always resume their vertical posture. Although tall, feather reed grass is not a giant. Its lithe nature and vertical habit make it appropriate for even small gardens. Use it with perennials of all types. It's attractive as a backdrop for blue false indigo in June and daylilies in July. A horizontal golden swath of feather reed grass sets off all the flowers of fall. The cultivar 'Karl Foerster' is the best.

WHEN TO PLANT

Plant feather reed grass in the spring to establish roots before the heat of summer.

WHERE TO PLANT

Feather reed grass prefers full sun but will tolerate some shade. Too much shade will decrease flowering, and clumps may flop. Feather reed grass is very adaptable, tolerating drier and heavier soils but preferring moist, well-drained conditions. Use the vertical form of feather reed grass as an accent or drift in perennial beds, with shrubs, as a screen, or in meadowlike mass plantings with other grasses and perennials.

How to Plant
Plant feather reed grass in the garden 2 to 2¹/₂ ft. apart. Dig holes and position the plant so that the soil level is the same as it was in the pot. If plants are potbound, loosen the root ball. Water thoroughly, and keep moist until established. Mulch will help to conserve moisture.

Advice for Care
Feather reed grass is easy to grow and requires little care. Cut back clumps to 6 in. from the ground in midwinter, a month or so earlier than warm-season grasses. Feather reed grass starts growing early, and an inopportune buzz cut will remove the tips of new foliage. Feather reed grass doesn't need frequent division, but clumps can be split for propagation or when they start to die in the center. Dividing clumps of feather reed grass will take some exertion. Lift clumps out of the ground, and split apart. A sharp shade and good gardening boots should do the trick. Discard the woody unproductive center, and replant healthy sections from the outside of the clump. Replant sections at the same level at which they were growing, and keep moist until established. This step is critical because feather reed grass produces foliage early and is more prone to desiccation. Make divisions in the spring.

Additional Information
Rust will occasionally appear on the foliage, particularly in moist areas with poor air circulation. It isn't a significant problem. Use the flowers and foliage for indoor arrangements.

Additional Species, Cultivars, or Varieties
'Stricta' is very similar to 'Karl Foerster'. For small gardens, we recommend *Calamagrostis × acutiflora* 'Overdam'. It possesses all the attributes of feather reed grass and also has attractive, cream-striped foliage. It reaches 3 to 4 ft. when in bloom, but the foliage forms an 18-in. clump. In late spring, the fresh clumps of variegated foliage combine attractively with pink coral bells and the hardy geranium 'Johnson's Blue'.

The Korean feather reed grass, *Calamagrostis arundinacea* var. *brachytricha* (3 to 4 ft.), is an attractive addition to the garden but isn't a superstar like *Calamagrostis* 'Karl Foerster'. It tolerates more shade, blooms in September, and has self-sowing tendencies.

Fountain Grass

Pennisetum alopecuroides

<table>
<tr><td>

Height: 3 to 4 ft.
Flowers: Pinkish-green or
  whitish-tan
Bloom Period: Midsummer
Zones: 5, 6
Light Requirement:

</td></tr>
</table>

Fountain grass attracts attention with elegance, not flamboyance. Truly resplendent, the glossy narrow foliage and pinkish foxtail flowers cascade loosely, catching the summer light to mimic a sparkling fountain. A warm-season grass, fountain grass is not much to look at in spring, but by early summer, the graceful bright-green foliage clumps are an attractive addition to the garden. By midsummer, the pinkish-purple bottlebrush flowers appear on the stems. The flowers begin to shatter by October. The foliage bleaches to an almond tan by December, catching snow and adding volume to the winter garden. Use fountain grass to provide contrast with coarser textured plants such as showy stonecrop and 'Goldsturm' black-eyed Susan. This combination has been used extensively in the Washington, D.C., area as a component of the New American landscape style and is also seen in public plantings in Michigan. Try fountain grass as a refined companion to annuals. Plant daffodils to add spring interest around the late-developing foliage.

WHEN TO PLANT

Plant fountain grass in the spring so that the roots have a chance to develop before the heat of summer.

WHERE TO PLANT

Fountain grass appreciates full sun and moisture-retentive, well-drained soil. It is adaptable to a wide range of soil conditions. Use it as a specimen plant to show off its full, cascading habit. One mature clump in a perennial bed or by a patio fills a corner or softens edges in summer and early fall. Or use several plants as permanent anchors for a bed of summer annuals. For massing or use as a groundcover, we suggest the dwarf cultivar 'Hameln'.

HOW TO PLANT

Space fountain grass at least 3 to 3½ ft. apart. Closer spacing, unless you want a meadowlike effect, will crowd the plants and obscure their splendid form. Dwarf selections such as 'Hameln' can be spaced closer. Dig a hole and position the plant so that the soil level is the same as it was in the pot. If plants are potbound, loosen the root ball. Water thoroughly, and keep moist until established. Mulch will help to conserve moisture.

ADVICE FOR CARE

In full sun, fountain grass is very adaptable and easy to grow. Cut it back anytime from late fall to early spring to several inches from the ground. For large clumps and/or mass plantings, this is easily accomplished with a hedge trimmer. Mature clumps will eventually start to die in the middle and split open. Plants may need rejuvenation every 3 to 5 years. Divide clumps in the spring when the foliage is just emerging and you can determine which parts of the plant are alive. This is not a quick, easy job. Lifting the entire clump takes a lot of muscle; recruit an assistant. Divide the clump with an ax and maul. Don't swing the ax, but position the ax head and pound with the maul to split the clump apart. Remove and discard the woody center portion; divide the remaining healthy sections into pieces. Small divisions will take longer to reach mature size, but they won't need division as soon. Keep new divisions well watered. Desiccation is the leading cause of death for new grass divisions.

ADDITIONAL INFORMATION

Fountain grass is not completely hardy in Zone 5. In unusually cold winters and exposed locations, portions of the clump or rarely the entire plant may winter kill. Also, fountain grass will self-sow to some extent, perhaps a dozen or so seedlings. If unwanted, seedlings should be pulled before their root systems develop. A specimen plant can be deadheaded or cut to the ground in early fall to prevent self-sowing. In warmer areas of the country, self-sowing is a nuisance. Because of this characteristic, we don't recommend planting fountain grass in natural areas.

ADDITIONAL SPECIES, CULTIVARS, OR VARIETIES

A dwarf cultivar of fountain grass called 'Hameln' (2^1/$_2$ to 3 ft.) is an excellent choice. It is not as dramatic as the species but is hardier and easier to site. It has fine-textured foliage and smaller, white flowers appearing about 2 weeks earlier. 'Hameln' hasn't self-sown for us. We don't recommend the black-seeded cultivars like 'Moudry'. They are less hardy and prolific self-sowers. Purple fountain grass, *Pennisetum setaceum* 'Rubrum' (3 ft.), is a tender grass with burgundy foliage and purplish plumes. It makes a spectacular centerpiece for a large container and backdrop for annuals or perennials. It is not hardy and will winter kill in Michigan. It produces no viable seed.

Japanese Silver Grass

Miscanthus sinensis

Other Name: Eulalia
Height: 6 to 8 ft.
Flowers: Purplish bronze, changing to silver white
Bloom Period: Late summer to early fall
Zones: 5, 6, depending on cultivar
Light Requirement:

Tall and poised, Japanese silver grass has the noble bearing of a garden aristocrat. Cultivated in Japan for centuries and fairly common in American gardens at the turn of the century, Japanese silver grass is back in vogue. Its attractive shape, adaptability, fall color, gleaming plumes, and winter presence are just a few of the reasons. Dozens of cultivars are now available; however, it can be difficult to determine the best selections for a Michigan garden. Of primary importance is hardiness. Many selections of Japanese silver grass thrive in Zone 5, but some won't survive the cold winters. Another important factor is flowering time. Silver grass refers to the silvery plumes, breathtaking against a blue autumn sky. If the flowering stalks are frosted before they emerge, you've lost the *raison d'être*. Early flowering types are better for Michigan gardens. The cultivar 'Purpurascens', sometimes called flame grass, is a good first choice. It is more compact (to 5 ft.), flowers in August, and has striking orange- to deep red fall color beginning as early as September. Its small size makes it easier to use. It lacks, however, the elegant vase shape of some of its clan. Plant with 'Snowbank' boltonia or calico aster (*Aster lateriflorus*) for an attractive fall combination. Cultivars are available with variegated, banded, fine-textured, and coarse-textured foliage. All provide unfailing winter interest. The fluffy plumes catch the snow, and the plants remain attractive until spring.

WHEN TO PLANT
Plant Japanese silver grass in the spring.

WHERE TO PLANT
Moist rich soil is ideal, but this adaptable grass tolerates a wide range of conditions, from wet to somewhat dry. Japanese silver grass prefers full sun but will take some shade. In too much shade, clumps will sprawl open and need to be staked. It is superb as a specimen and an excellent choice for planting by a pond or water feature.

How to Plant

Space fountain grass at least 3 to 6 ft. apart depending on the cultivar. Don't crowd this grass; let it have room to display its elegant form. Dig a hole and position the plant so that the soil level is the same as it was in the pot. Water thoroughly, and keep moist until established. Mulch will help to conserve moisture.

Advice for Care

Water clumps during drought. The leaf blades will roll, indicating stress, when they need moisture. In late winter or early spring, cut clumps to several inches from the ground. For large clumps or mass plantings, this is easily accomplished with a hedge trimmer. For just a few plants, pruner or loppers will do the trick. Wear long sleeves and gloves because miscanthus leaves are sharp and can scratch and irritate your skin. Plants may need rejuvenation every 5 to 7 years. Divide clumps in the spring when the emerging foliage allows you to determine which parts of the plant are alive. This is not a quick, easy job. Divide the clump with an ax or saw. Remove and discard the woody center portion; divide the remaining healthy sections into pieces. Keep new divisions well watered. Desiccation is the leading cause of death for new grass divisions.

Additional Information

Clumps planted in partial shade or those in need of rejuvenation may split open and require staking.

Additional Species, Cultivars, or Varieties

Flame grass, *Miscanthus sinensis* 'Purpurascens' (5 ft.), is described above. It also makes a great backdrop or screen. We highly recommend 'Graziella' (5 to 6 ft.) for its early flowers held high above the foliage and orange fall color. 'Gracillimus' (5 to 8 ft.), or maiden grass, has been widely grown for its elegant fine-textured foliage. Grow it for its foliage effect, but don't count on the flowers, which are often lost to frost. 'Morning Light' (5 to 6 ft.) is grown for its finely variegated foliage, which appears silvery. 'Variegatus' (5 to 7 ft.) has wide variegated foliage and an almost white effect in the garden. The tropical-looking porcupine grass 'Strictus' (5 to 7 ft.) has leaves horizontally striped with creamy yellow. It is widely confused with zebra grass 'Zebrinus', which is similar but somewhat less hardy. Some other species of *Miscanthus* are available with spreading roots. They can colonize large areas and should be avoided.

Switch Grass

Panicum virgatum

Height: 4 to 7 ft.
Flowers: Pinkish-green
Bloom Period: Midsummer
Zones: 4, 5, 6
Light Requirement:

Switch grass, an American native, is highly adaptable. It grows in almost every state, occurring in tall-grass prairies, dunes, and open, moist woodlands. Switch grass creates a diaphanous pinkish cloud when in bloom. In the autumn, its early fall color—often yellow, orange, and purplish-red—adds an incendiary glow to the garden. By winter the leaves bleach to straw, and its sturdy silhouette contributes to the garden until early spring. Full sun is all you need to grow switch grass. It is not particular about soil type or drainage. A warm-season grass, switch grass gets a slow start in spring and eventually forms clumps of foliage about 3 to 4 ft. high. By August, the hazy cloud of flowers rises another foot or two over the foliage. The overall effect is subtle, but when the foliage begins to color, the plants have an arresting fiery beauty, especially when backlit by the sun. The species varies in height, habit, and fall color, and it is best used in meadows, in prairie-style gardens, or for wildlife cover. Gardeners should look for the cultivated selections (cultivars), which offer compact uniform size, upright habit, and attractive autumn colors. Almost any combination of fall-blooming perennials will benefit from the addition of switch grass. In a moist, sunny bed, the burgundy-leaved selection, 'Rotstralbusch', dramatically sets off the simple white flowers of *Anemone* × *hybrida* 'Honorine Jobert' with a haze of deep color. If you have the space, add the deep purple-red Joe-pye weed 'Gateway' for added drama. Combine switch grass with pearly everlasting, Russian sage, pink turtlehead, or 'Snowbank' boltonia.

WHEN TO PLANT
Plant switch grass in the spring so that the roots will have time to grow before the heat of summer.

WHERE TO PLANT
Switch grass is very adaptable and will grow in a wide range of soil types and conditions. It prefers full sun and moist, fertile soil but accepts dry and moist situations. In very dry sites, plants are

stunted. Use it in perennial beds as a specimen, in small groups or large sweeps. Switch grass makes an excellent backdrop for perennials. It is well suited to massing in natural meadow-style gardens with prairie plants.

HOW TO PLANT

Plant switch grass in the garden 3 ft. apart. Dig a hole and position the plant so that the soil level is the same as it was in the pot. Remove any excess soilless mix, and incorporate it into the planting hole. Water thoroughly, and keep moist until established. Mulch will help to conserve moisture.

ADVICE FOR CARE

Cut back switch grass in late winter or early spring to 4 or 5 in. If plants begin to split open in late summer, the clump should be divided. Divide clumps in spring as the foliage is emerging. Lift clumps out of the ground, and split apart with a sharp shade. Discard the unproductive center, and replant healthy sections from the outside of the clump. Replant at the same level at which they were growing, and keep moist until established.

ADDITIONAL INFORMATION

The delicate flowers and colorful foliage are wonderful as cut flowers. Cut long stems for large arrangements. You can create a meadow or prairie-style planting by combining switch grass with native prairie plants such as purple coneflower, yellow coneflower (*Ratibida pinnata*), blazing star, and Culver's root.

ADDITIONAL SPECIES, CULTIVARS, OR VARIETIES

Many cultivars are available. A favorite is red switch grass or 'Rotstralbusch' (4 ft.). Its burgundy color develops by September or earlier. 'Strictum' (4 to 5 ft.) is upright and has orange to purplish-red fall color. 'Haense Herms' (4 to 4½ ft.) has fiery fall color and a more compact habit. 'Heavy Metal' (4 to 5 ft.) is upright with steely blue foliage. It complements a pastel autumn scene with 'Clara Curtis' chrysanthemum, the dwarf lavender-blue aster 'Professor Kippenburg', and pale pink anemones. 'Cloud Nine' at 6 to 8 ft. makes a fine specimen plant.

Tufted Hair Grass

Deschampsia caespitosa

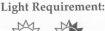

Height: 2 to 3½ ft.
Flowers: Pale green changing to golden yellow
Bloom Period: Late spring to early summer
Zones: 3, 4, 5, 6
Light Requirement:

From a modest clump of arching dark green foliage just 1 ft. tall, tufted hair grass generates a tremendous cloud of loose delicate flowers almost 3 ft. high. The flowers emerge in late spring a soft silky bronze-green, but, as they mature, they stiffen to form a billowing mass of yellow or gold. Flowering begins as early as late spring, but tufted hair grass is in its glory in midsummer when its bright airy flowers create an remarkable backdrop for broad-leaved perennials. Tufted hair grass is a cool-season grass, well suited to Michigan's chilly spring and sometimes cool summer. The dense clumps of slender arching foliage are a presence in the early spring garden, when many ornamental grasses still appear lifeless. In addition, unlike most grasses, tufted hair grass will grow in partial shade. The evergreen grassy clumps add a new dimension to the shade garden, providing effective contrast for bold hostas and lacy ferns. In full sun, tufted hair grass is the most floriferous, but the soil must be rich and moist for good results. Tufted hair grass can be used under shrubs or on the edges of a woodland garden or massed on a bank. A large drift creates a cloud of color when in bloom. Superb in moist soil, it may be planted pond-side with the dramatic foliage of big-leaf ligularia, *Ligularia dentata* 'Desdemona', and the yellow flag iris. In a sunny but moisture-retentive garden, take advantage of its colorful fine-textured flowers as a contrast to other perennials. The golden haze of *Deschampsia* 'Goldstaub' and the lavender mist of Russian sage make an unforgettable backdrop for the red-violet daisies and the coarse foliage of purple coneflower.

WHEN TO PLANT
Plant tufted hair grass in early spring or in September.

WHERE TO PLANT
Tufted hair grass prefers light shade but will thrive in full sun with adequate moisture. It is one of the few grasses that will grow in

shade. Too much shade will decrease flowering. It prefers moist, rich soil and tolerates fairly wet, heavy soils. It will not survive in a hot, dry location. Use it in perennial beds, by ponds, in groundcover plantings, and under shrubs.

How to Plant

Plant tufted hair grass in the landscape 2 to 3 ft. apart. Dig a hole and position the plant so that the soil level is the same as it was in the pot. Water thoroughly, and keep moist until established. Mulch will help to conserve moisture.

Advice for Care

In full sun, tufted hair grass will need watering during dry spells. Remove the flowering stems in late summer or early fall when the inflorescences begin to break up and look disheveled. In fact, shearing the whole clump back in late summer is probably the best option. New foliage will appear to form a fresh green clump by mid-fall and will remain evergreen through the winter. After 3 or 4 years, clumps of hair grass may need rejuvenation. Divide plants in early spring when new growth is emerging. Dig the clumps and split into pieces with a sharp spade or knife. Remove the inner dead sections, and replant healthy, vigorous pieces. Water new divisions frequently until established. A layer of mulch will help to conserve moisture.

Additional Information

Unlike many grasses, hair grass is not at its peak in late summer and early fall. At that point, the flowers are beginning to deteriorate. Keep this in mind when planning mass plantings in high-use areas. The flowers are wonderful in fresh or dried arrangements. The silky flowering stems are an intriguing complement to a bouquet of lily-flowered tulips or iris.

Additional Species, Cultivars, or Varieties

There are many good cultivars, but the names don't trip off your tongue. 'Bronzeschleier' (Bronze Veil) grows to 3 ft. The flower effect is bronze-green changing to bronze-yellow. 'Goldschleier' (Gold Veil) has brighter golden yellow flowers. 'Goldstaub' (Gold Dust) forms 1 ft. foliage clumps and later a 3-ft. golden cloud.

Wild Oats

Chasmanthium latifolium

Height: 2 to 3 ft.
Flowers: Green changing to coppery brown
Bloom Period: Midsummer
Zones: 5, 6
Light Requirement:

Few perennials have the winter appeal of wild oats. Their copper-tan dangling spikelets, when backlit by the low winter sun, create a garden picture as memorable as peonies in June. Cut wild oats down only when the first crocus assures you that spring really is on the way. Wild oats excels in 3 seasons—with fresh foliage and flowers in summer, with rich bronze color in autumn, and with its vase-like form and persistent spikelets in winter. Wild oats offers natural beauty, graceful movement, and a soft rustle to the garden. It is native to rich woodlands and river-banks of the eastern United States. Its natural range just reaches into the southwest corner of Lower Michigan. Due to its native woodland home, it is one of the few grasses that prefers partial shade. A warm-season grass, it begins to grow as warm temperatures return. The wide green leaf blades held roughly perpendicular to the stems have a bamboo-like, almost tropical appearance in late spring. By early summer, the flowers arise, and, when mature, the thread-like stems barely support the 1-in. flattened spikelets, creating a nodding habit. Spangle grass, another common name, alludes to the dangling spikelets as they sway in the slightest breeze, reflecting light. The flowers start out green and gradually change to a copper brown. Take advantage of wild oats' shade tolerance, and add its attractive foliage and flowers to shade gardens. Contrast its wide flat leaf blades with the airy flowers of Bowman's root and the coarse heart-shaped foliage of Siberian bugloss. Or punctuate a mass of bigroot geranium with the upright form and nodding flowers of wild oats. In a moisture-retentive sunny bed, back dwarf fountain grass and 'Goldsturm' black-eyed Susan with wild oats. Add extra interest by interplanting the tall red-purple flowers of Brazilian verbena. And don't forget winter. Plant wild oats where its free spirit will uplift you in the doldrums of February.

WHEN TO PLANT
Plant wild oats in the spring to allow time for its roots to grow before summer's heat.

Where to Plant

Wild oats prefers moist, well-drained, humus-rich soil and partial shade. With adequate moisture, plants will thrive in full sun; the foliage will be lighter green. It prefers moist, rich soil and tolerates fairly heavy soils. It is somewhat drought-tolerant but will not thrive in a hot, dry location. Use it in moisture-retentive or shady perennial beds, by streams and ponds, as an accent in a ground-cover planting, and in naturalized areas.

How to Plant

Plant wild oats in the landscape 1¹/₂ to 2 ft. apart. Dig a hole and position the plant so that the soil level is the same as it was in the pot. Remove any excess soilless mix, and incorporate into the planting hole. Water thoroughly, and keep moist until established. Mulch will help to conserve moisture.

Advice for Care

Plants located in full sun will need water during dry spells. Cut back wild oats to the ground in early spring. Clumps can be divided in the spring as the foliage is just emerging. Dig clumps and split apart with a sharp spade or large knife. Remove any old woody sections, and replant healthy, vigorous pieces in the garden at the same level. Water frequently until new roots are formed.

Additional Information

Wild oats self-sows. This can be welcome, and the extra plants can be moved to enlarge your planting or shared with friends. In some situations, however, it can be a nuisance. A thick layer of mulch will discourage self-sown seedlings. Wild oats makes a wonderful cut flower and everlasting. The drooping stems and flattened spikelets create an elegant outline in a large vase. Stems can be harvested at any stage. If cut while young, they will maintain a greenish cast; later, the stalks will be coppery brown.

Additional Species, Cultivars, or Varieties

There aren't any cultivars. Occasionally, wild oats is referred to as "sea oats." This is another plant, *Uniola paniculata*, that grows in sandy coastal areas of the eastern United States.

CHAPTER SIX

Perennials

ITH CAREFUL PLANNING, A PERENNIAL GARDEN
CAN GLOW WITH COLOR and beauty from early spring to
late fall. Unlike annual flowers, which look the same all season,
perennials are constantly changing as new plants come into their
prime. Week to week, the focus moves with a seasonal rhythm,
beckoning the gardener to explore and observe the unique aspects
of each plant.

Part of the gardener's pleasure comes from orchestrating a whole
year of interest and planning seasonal combinations of flowers as
well as foliage, the backbone of the perennial garden. Attractive
leaves add a charm and texture all their own and form a unifying
ribbon that ties the garden together.

Perennials grow in diverse conditions. Some prefer sun, some
shade; some tolerate wet spots, and others prefer to be on the dry
side. Perennials range in size from just one inch tall to as large as
seven feet, and their range of possible effects is endless. They are
important in the garden's design, along with woody plants and
annuals, bulbs, and groundcovers.

The plants chosen for this chapter have proved to be good plants
in Michigan gardens. They are generally long-lived and adaptable,
and they resist pests and diseases if planted in the right site and
properly maintained. Bed preparation is especially important since
perennials often remain in place for many years. Before planting,
test the soil and amend it as required.

SELECTING PERENNIALS

With new and beautiful perennials coming on the market all the
time, it's tempting to want one of each. Certain qualities can help
you identify which ones will be hardy and high achievers in
your garden.

Chapter Six

The easiest ones will be those that seldom need staking or special treatment for diseases or pests. Ones that spread moderately or stay in clumps will blend well with the rest of the garden without trying to take over. Seek out perennials with attractive foliage. Many bloom for just a week or two, but their leaves can be an important element in the garden all season long.

Perhaps rather than low-care perennials, you're looking for plants that will offer a wider range of diversity and be more challenging to grow. Many gardeners find that caring for perennials is relaxing and a good way to tap into their creative and artistic talents.

Either way, maintaining your garden should be a pleasure and an expression of your personality. Grow what you like, experiment, and learn.

PLANTING YOUR PERENNIALS

Many perennials require periodic division for rejuvenation. Take your cue from the plants. Those that die in the middle, are producing fewer flowers than they used to, or are splitting open are ready to be divided.

In most cases, the plants are dug out of the garden and cut apart. Don't be afraid to work with your perennials. Most are tough and forgiving. Specific guidelines on division are included with each plant entry in this chapter. When you divide perennials, take the opportunity to dig in compost, then replant the healthy portions. Caring for newly divided plants is critical while they get established.

In the fall, while your memory of the season is still fresh, make notes about your garden to review during the winter and spring. Jot down what plants are splitting open or spreading out of bounds, and put them on the list for division. Also note which plants to move to improve seasonal combinations or to fine-tune design.

Perennials bring variety, color, and romance to the garden. They entice the gardener to try new tactics, to move and experiment, to extend the season of bloom. For these reasons, as well as for sheer beauty, growing perennials is satisfying and rewarding—as more and more gardeners are discovering every year.

Artemisia

Artemisia ludoviciana

Other Names: White Sage, Western Mugwort
Height: 2 to 3 ft.
Flowers: Whitish, insignificant; artemisia is grown for its silver foliage
Zones: 4, 5, 6
Light Requirement:

In the garden realm, the royal pair 'Silver King' and 'Silver Queen' are not the best behaved of monarchs. Though they are not exactly tyrants, their spreading ways strike some gardeners as overbearing. Still, they're worth planting. These artemisias offer silvery foliage that calms nearby bright colors. They provide textural interest and they shine in their own right. Use artemisia to create a backdrop for other plants or to fashion a ribbon of silver that ties together a summer planting. 'Silver King' grows to about 3 ft. tall and has slender stems and fine-textured narrow silvery leaves. It creates a noticeable billow of silver gray in the garden. The flowers add extra delicacy. 'Silver Queen' is more variable. It is generally shorter, about 2 ft., and has wider leaves with jagged edges and more tenacious roots. A new choice of hybrid origin is 'Valerie Finnis', with wide silver foliage and a spreading but not aggressive habit. (If all this talk of invading roots is frightening, skip to the bottom and read about *Artemisia* 'Lambrook Silver' and 'Silver Mound', which are better-behaved silver plants.) Artemisias such as 'Silver King' will tolerate drought and sandy, light soils. These are the conditions in which their spread is most rampant, however. In heavier soil, it is easy to keep them in check by removing unwanted portions in the spring. Perhaps these plants shouldn't be used in small or formal gardens, but they come into their own when planted in drifts as part of a large, sweeping display. 'Silver Queen' sparks the already vibrant combination of yellow yarrow and violet-blue salvia. 'Silver King' can set off orange daylilies, 'Lucifer' crocosmia, and yellow coreopsis. Where there is room, add the steely blue spheres and silvery foliage of globe thistle (*Echinops*).

WHEN TO PLANT
Container-grown artemisia can be planted from spring into summer.

WHERE TO PLANT

Plant artemisia in full sun and any soil. Though tolerant of heavy soil, plants will sprawl if the site is too moist. Plant it in informal areas where its spread will be welcome.

HOW TO PLANT

Plant white sage 2 to 3 ft. apart. Dig a hole twice as wide as the pot, and position the plant so that the soil level is the same as it was in the pot. Fill in with soil around the roots about halfway up, firm gently, and water well. Add more soil to completely fill the hole. Water regularly until plants are established.

ADVICE FOR CARE

Artemisia does not need extra watering or fertilization. Too much fertility will lead to soft sprawling growth. Every spring, evaluate your planting and remove unwanted sections. Underground runners may have spread several feet from the main clump. Take a sharp spade and cut down to sever all roots. Pull up and remove. When the clump starts to die in the middle, dig it up and replant vigorous pieces from the outside edges. These plants can be grown like mint, in a bottomless bucket, to prevent spreading. Artemisia may be pruned back at any time during the growing season to shape its growth, tame floppy stems, or eliminate flowers. Remove flowers on 'Valerie Finnis' as they appear; they detract from the foliage effect.

ADDITIONAL INFORMATION

All these plants are wonderful for cutting and drying. The fine texture of 'Silver King' makes a wonderful filler for arrangements and base for herbal wreaths.

ADDITIONAL SPECIES, CULTIVARS, OR VARIETIES

Wormwood, *Artemisia absinthium*, is a semi-evergreen shrub-like artemisia with silvery gray, finely divided foliage. 'Lambrook Silver' (2¹/₂ ft.) is probably the best ferny silver plant for Michigan gardens. Plant it in average or sandy, well-drained soil, and cut it back in the spring. A related plant is *Artemisia* 'Powis Castle'; it has not proven to be hardy in Zone 5. *Artemisia schmidtiana* 'Silver Mound' (6 to 8 in.) forms perfect little buns of filigreed silver foliage. If grown in rich soil, 'Silver Mound' splits open. Cut it back hard to force new foliage.

Astilbe Hybrids

Astilbe × arendsii

Height: 1¹/₂ to 3¹/₂ ft.
Flowers: White, red, pink, peach
Bloom Period: Late spring and summer
Zones: 5, 6
Light Requirement:

The "right plant, right place" message can be clearly demonstrated with astilbe. In partial shade and humus-rich, moist soil, astilbe is beyond compare. Clouds of feathery plumes float above glossy divided foliage. In sun and dry soil, though, astilbe bakes. The foliage sears and the flowers stunt. Grow astilbe in the sun if you must, but be prepared to make frequent runs for the hose. Hybrid garden astilbes are esteemed plants for light shade and moist soil. They adorn the shady garden with color and long-lasting handsome foliage. The flowers appear above the foliage in open feathery sprays or slender upright plumes. They can be subtle, in shades of cream, pale pink, or peach, or obvious with deep reds, intense whites, or bright pinks. Flowers are in peak color for about one month. With different cultivars, astilbe can be in bloom in the garden from late spring and through much of the summer. Astilbe's shiny, lush foliage persists throughout the growing season—an attractive feature in the woodland garden where many plants go dormant—and is often tinged with bronze or crimson in spring. The feathery plumes may be left for winter interest if desired. In the right location, astilbe is easy to grow and carefree. Clumps will require rejuvenation about every 3 to 5 years. Plant ribbons of astilbe with hostas, 'Palace Purple' alumroot, and Solomon's seal. A mass display of assorted astilbe cultivars provides more bright color in the shade than any other perennial.

When to Plant
Plant container-grown astilbe in the spring so the roots become established before summer's heat.

Where to Plant
Choose moist, humus-rich soil in partial shade. Plentiful moisture but not standing water is essential for healthy plants. Astilbe will tolerate sun but only if it has almost constant moisture. Instead, plant astilbe in shady, moist beds, in borders and woodland gardens, and by ponds and water features.

How to Plant

Plant astilbes 1¹/₂ to 2 ft. apart. Dig a hole twice as wide as the pot, and position the plant so that the soil level is the same as it was in the pot. Fill in with soil around the roots about halfway up, firm gently, and water well. Add more soil to fill the hole. Water regularly until plants are established. A layer of mulch will conserve moisture.

Advice for Care

Keep plants moist. In extended dry periods the leaves will brown and die. Feed plants in the spring by topdressing with well-rotted compost or an application of general fertilizer such as 10-10-10. After about 3 to 5 years, clumps will start to lose vigor. For rejuvenation or propagation, divide plants in the spring as the foliage is emerging. The roots are tough. Dig up the clumps, and split apart the woody fibrous-rooted crowns with a sharp spade or large knife. Before replanting, enrich the soil with organic matter to hold moisture and increase fertility. Work in well-rotted compost or other organic amendments. Split the astilbe clumps into pieces and replant. Keep new divisions well watered and mulch to keep them moist.

Additional Information

Astilbe makes an attractive cut flower. Harvest stems when the flowers are only half open. Deadheading astilbe (removing the spent flowers) is a judgment call. Tidy gardeners often find the browning flowers unappealing and remove them from the plant. Flowering stems left in place will provide an effective contrast with the snow. Remove them in early spring.

Additional Species, Cultivars, or Varieties

There are many cultivars. A favorite is 'Ostrich Plume' (3 ft.) for its tall pink arching flowers. 'Fanal' (2 ft.) is renowned for its deep red flowers and bronzy leaves. *Astilbe simplicifolia* 'Sprite' (12 in.) with shell-pink flowers and bronzy foliage creates a delicate effect. For a bolder statement, plant *Astilbe taquetii* 'Superba' (4 ft.). It blooms in mid- to late summer with tall upright spires of rose-purple.

Bethlehem Sage

Pulmonaria saccharata

Other Name: Lungwort
Height: 9 to 12 in.
Flowers: Pink, blue, white
Bloom Period: Early to late spring
Zones: 3, 4, 5, 6
Light Requirement:

In the shade garden, foliage plants with unusual variegation or leaf colors stand out and draw the attentive eye of the gardener. The Bethlehem sage or lungwort is a spectacular foliage plant offering tremendous variation in foliage markings and highlights that can brighten dark corners in the shade and make spectacular contrasts in a mixed planting. The lungworts form mounding, low-growing (9 to 12 in.) clumps of foliage with a diversity of silvery patterns on dark green leaves. In some cultivars, the leaves are almost completely silver-white with only a green edge remaining. Others have varying degrees of silver, from spots to splatters to completely drenched. The foliage certainly carries this plant through the seasons, but the early spring flowers are beautiful in a range of colors from pure white to pink to the deepest azure. Typically, the flowers are bright pink in bud and open to blue, giving the appearance of different-colored flowers on the same plant. Planted as a low-growing edging plant or as a groundcover in mass, few shade plants can compare in foliage and flower. Plant Bethlehem sage with spring bulbs, woodland wildflowers, and other shade lovers such as Siberian bugloss and barrenwort. The silvery-spotted foliage adds interest to plantings of astilbes, hostas, and ferns.

WHEN TO PLANT
Plant container-grown Bethlehem sage in the spring or fall.

WHERE TO PLANT
The lungworts prefer moist, humus-rich soil and partial to full shade. In full sun, plants experience leaf burning, and the attractive foliage turns crispy brown. Plant lungworts in woodland gardens and shady beds and under shrubs. Use them to edge a wooded path or to soften a shady patio.

How to Plant

Plant pulmonarias 12 to 18 in. apart. Dig a hole twice as wide as the pot, and position the plant so that the soil level is the same as it was in the pot. Fill in with soil around the roots about halfway up, firm gently, and water well. Add more soil to completely fill the hole. Water regularly until plants are established. Mulch plants to conserve moisture.

Advice for Care

Water in times of prolonged drought to avoid foliar scorch. Plants will need some grooming throughout the season in highly maintained areas. The flowering stalks can be removed when the display is over. In midsummer, the older foliage begins to look worn. Remove it to make way for new, fresh foliage. Clumps rarely need division but may be split easily for propagation. Divide after flowering in the spring. Dig clumps and separate into pieces with a sharp spade or knife. Replant vigorous pieces at the same level at which they were growing. Keep well watered until established.

Additional Information

In dry conditions, plants are susceptible to powdery mildew. Water plants in the morning. The common name "lungwort" comes from the spotted foliage's resemblance to a diseased lung.

Additional Species, Cultivars, or Varieties

'Sissinghurst White' has silvery-spotted foliage and large white flowers. 'Mrs. Moon' has silvery-spotted foliage and flowers that open pink, then fade to blue. 'Argentea' has almost completely silver foliage and blue flowers. For the best effect, use these silver-foliage pulmonarias as accents and small drifts. Many other cultivars are available. The long-leaf lungwort, *Pulmonaria longifolia*, is another exceptional plant for shady sites. It has pink buds that open to deep blue flowers. The foliage is narrower than the Bethlehem sage and has a white spotting. It make a nice groundcover, growing 9 to 12 in. in height and combining well under shrubs such as 'Cornell Pink' Korean rhododendron. 'Roy Davidson' grows 12 to 15 in. in height and has dark green leaves spotted with silver and flowers that are sky blue. The blue lungwort, *Pulmonaria angustifolia*, has very early spring flowers that are cobalt blue and quite noticeable from a distance. The foliage is a rather plain green. The plant grows to a height of 8 to 12 in.

Black Snakeroot

Cimicifuga racemosa

Other Names: Bugbane,
    Black Cohosh
Height: 5 to 6 ft.
Flowers: White
Bloom Period: Midsummer
Zones: 3, 4, 5, 6
Light Requirement:

So many woodland plants hug the ground, soaking in sunlight as it hits the forest floor. Tall and bold plants add much-needed contrast that brings the shade garden to life. For noticeable coarse-texture foliage and lofty flowers, black snakeroot, *Cimicifuga racemosa*, is a dramatic choice. A woodland native at home in rich soil and open shade, black snakeroot is at the northern edge of its range in Michigan. At maturity, it forms large, beautiful 3-ft. clumps of dark green dissected foliage. In summer, slender stems topped with white bottlebrush-shaped flowers rise above the foliage, reaching more than 6 ft. Before opening, the buds resemble tiny pearls, and after flowering, the pale green seedpods remain attractive. Snakeroot needs deep, rich soil and ample moisture to be at it best. Where these condition exist, snakeroot is easy and trouble-free. The wandlike stems of black snakeroot are not stiffly upright unless staked. They bend and lean with grace. It's a shame to stake them so they are ramrod straight. Use snakeroot as an accent plant in the woodland garden or as an elegant addition to the moist, lightly shaded perennial border. Its dark divided foliage makes for interesting contrast with hostas, ferns, and woodland wildflowers. In light shade and moist soil, the flowers stand out against the purple-tinged green flowers of feather reed grass. On a shady slope, black snakeroot can form a memorable groundcover planting all on its own.

WHEN TO PLANT
Plant container-grown snakeroot in the spring.

WHERE TO PLANT
Choose a location with moist, humus-rich soil in partial shade. Add organic matter to sandy or clay soils. Snakeroot will grow in full sun with ample moisture but is at its best in light shade. Like astilbe, its

leaves will scorch when the soil dries out. Use snakeroot as an accent in shade gardens and woodland edges. It makes an interesting tall groundcover.

How to Plant

Plant snakeroot 3 ft. apart. Dig a hole twice as wide as the pot, and position the plant so that the soil level is the same as it was in the pot. Fill in with soil around the roots about halfway up, firm gently, and water well. Add more soil to completely fill the hole. Water regularly until plants are established. Mulch to conserve moisture.

Advice for Care

In partial shade and rich, well-drained soil, snakeroot should be trouble-free. The tall flower stalks have a tendency to lean. This has a lovely informal appearance, but tidy gardeners often secure each stalk with a slender green stake. Don't hurry to remove the flowers. The seedheads are ornamental for quite a while. Snakeroot's clumps increase slowly, and division is rarely necessary. For propagation, the large fibrous-rooted crowns can be divided in the spring. Plants of snakeroot take several years to reach their full potential.

Additional Information

Gardening books sometimes show pictures of black snakeroot blooming merrily in full sun with garden phlox and daylilies. Black snakeroot will survive nicely in sunny borders with rich soil and ample moisture. Lacking these, the foliage will scorch. It is more at ease in a shady, woodland home.

Additional Species, Cultivars, or Varieties

The American bugbane, *Cimicifuga americana*, is a similar plant. Native to Siberia, the Kamchatka bugbane, *Cimicifuga simplex* (3 to 4 ft.), is the last of snakeroots—or, for that matter, the last of the perennials—to flower. 'White Pearl' is the cultivar usually offered. Often the white airy wands catch brightly colored foliage as it drops from the trees in October. This garden vision is fraught with risk, though; flowers can get nipped by the first frost. *C. ramosa* 'Brunette', once rare, has now become available in the United States. This cultivar of a Japanese bugbane has very dark purple foliage.

Black-eyed Susan

Rudbeckia fulgida ssp. *sullivantii*

Other Names: 'Goldsturm'
Daisy, Orange Coneflower
Height: 2 to 3 ft.
Flowers: Orange-yellow
Bloom Period: Mid- to late
summer
Zones: 3, 4, 5, 6
Light Requirement:

Everything about the brilliant yellow-orange daisies and chocolate-brown centers of *Rudbeckia* 'Goldsturm' screams black-eyed Susan. Actually just a cousin to the real black-eyed Susan, this plant is a good one to illustrate the confusing nature of common names. The true black-eyed Susan, *Rudbeckia hirta*, transformed by hybridizers into the gloriosa daisy (see the chapter on annuals), is an annual or a short-lived perennial. In horticultural books and botanical field guides, *Rudbeckia fulgida* is called orange coneflower, but anyone who sees it in the garden can't help letting "black-eyed Susan" slip from his or her lips. All this aside, this perennial, which for here and now we will call *Rudbeckia* 'Goldsturm', is among the very best for Michigan gardens. It produces masses of 3-in. yellow-orange flowers with dark centers over coarse, deep green foliage from midsummer until frost. In full bloom, it lends a sunny meadow feeling to any garden. The center cones continue to be appealing through the winter. The species, a Michigan native occurring in the Lower Peninsula's meadows, wet ground, swamps, and prairie fens, is a worthy garden plant in its own right. 'Goldsturm', a German selection that flowers for 2 or even 3 months, is more compact and has dark green, boldly textured foliage and a greater number of larger flowers. Plant 'Goldsturm' in moist soil and full sun for the best results. A standard component of the New American garden style of landscaping, it is often seen in combination with 'Autumn Joy' stonecrop and ornamental grasses—so often, in fact, that it is becoming a cliché. If you want to try a different combination, use the bright yellow-orange daisies set off by blue asters and softened by the subtle haze of switch grass.

WHEN TO PLANT

Plant container-grown rudbeckia in the spring and early summer. Provide plenty of water if planted later in the season.

WHERE TO PLANT

Choose a location with full sun and average soil for rudbeckia 'Goldsturm'. Plants prefer moist, well-drained soil and are tolerant of heat but not extended drought. Rudbeckia responds dramatically to moisture. Clumps in moist areas will be taller and outperform those in dry areas. Some light shade is tolerated, but plants will flower less profusely, which can subdue the brilliant color a bit.

HOW TO PLANT

Plant rudbeckia 2 to 2½ ft. apart. Dig a hole twice as wide as the pot, and position the plant so that the soil level is the same as it was in the pot. Fill in with soil around the roots about halfway up, firm gently, and water well. Add more soil to completely fill the hole. Water regularly until plants are established.

ADVICE FOR CARE

Water plants during dry periods. Fertilization is usually not needed. Rudbeckia is a vigorous grower, and clumps will need to be divided about every 3 to 4 years as the centers die out. This chore isn't difficult. Lift the clumps and amend the soil in which the plants were growing with well-rotted compost. Separate them into pieces, and discard the worn-out middle sections. Replant at the same level at which they were growing, and water well. Keep new divisions watered. Divisions usually bloom the first year.

ADDITIONAL INFORMATION

The raised brown cones in the middle of the flowers can provide winter interest.

ADDITIONAL SPECIES, CULTIVARS, OR VARIETIES

The cultivar 'Goldsturm' should be vegetatively propagated to maintain its special qualities; however, seed-grown strains are also sold. These will be attractive, just more variable. Many other garden-worthy rudbeckia are available. To provoke comment, try *Rudbeckia maxima*. Its large glaucous gray leaves—often more than 1 ft. long—have an appearance almost like cabbage. In late summer and early fall, 5- to 6-ft. stems rise above, bearing flowers with drooping petals and a large 3-in. central cone. This species may not be hardy in Zone 4. Where there is room, the tall (6 ft.) *Rudbeckia nitida* 'Herbstonne' (Autumn Sun) is spectacular. It has drooping petals and a greenish central disk. If you enjoy self-sowing plants, try the short-lived perennial *Rudbeckia triloba*. A Michigan native of wet prairies and marshy ground, it forms plump yellow-orange daisies. Let it self-sow and it will come back each year.

Blazing Star

Liatris spicata

Other Names: Spiked Blazing Star, Gayfeather
Height: 2 to 3 ft.
Flowers: Rosy purple
Bloom Period: Early to late summer
Zones: 4, 5, 6
Light Requirement:

Blazing star is a spectacular perennial with long, fat spikes of rose-purple flowers and narrow foliage. Often seen in florists' bouquets, this native wildflower is more at home on the prairie. Several species are cultivated. The spiked blazing star, *Liatris spicata*, is the easiest to grow and the best for gardens. Spiked blazing star grows in the southern third of Michigan's Lower Peninsula in meadows, marshes, wet prairies, and other moist, open places, although its natural habitat is decreasing. A label on a herbarium specimen collected in 1896 states "thousands of acres covered with it about Lake St. Clair." That image alone is enough reason to try this plant in your garden. Blazing star's thick spires are made up of clustered, wispy rose-purple flowers held on stems clothed with narrow grasslike foliage. The leaves increase in size as they descend the stem. The vertical effect is sculptural—feathery and at the same time dramatic. The flowers open from the top down and are a favorite of butterflies. Blazing star is at its best in prairie and meadow plantings where the lanky (close to 3 ft.) stems are held up by grasses and other meadow flowers such as Culver's root, sunflower heliopsis, black-eyed Susan, and others. In the garden, the tall spires may need to be staked. The cultivar 'Kobold' (15 to 18 in.), also called 'Gnome', is a good choice. It has bright red-violet flower spikes and a more compact habit, eliminating the need for staking. In all but the largest perennial borders, blazing star is best used in groups of three or as a single specimen. The bold form stands out and would be too extreme in larger groups. Blazing star contrasts effectively with fine-textured plants such as tufted hair grass or Russian sage. Blazing star and purple coneflower are a natural combination.

WHEN TO PLANT
Plant blazing star in the spring to early summer. Keep new plantings moist during hot weather.

WHERE TO PLANT

Plant blazing star in average to rich, moist soil in full sun. Plants like moisture but not poor drainage. *Liatris spicata* tolerates moisture better than other blazing stars, and its upright form is attractive in perennial borders or island beds.

HOW TO PLANT

Plant blazing star 2 ft. apart. Dig a hole twice as wide as the pot, and position the plant so that the soil level is the same as it was in the pot. Fill in with soil around the roots about halfway up, firm gently, and water well. Add more soil to completely fill the hole. Water regularly until plants are established. Blazing star corms are sometimes sold in the spring unpotted like summer-flowering bulbs. These should be planted so that the pinkish buds are 2 in. below the soil surface. Firm the soil lightly, and water.

ADVICE FOR CARE

Blazing star is easy to grow and pest- and disease-free. Water during extended dry spells; although drought-resistant, blazing star grows best in moist soils. Voles and mice will eat the fleshy corms. Division is seldom needed. Corms can be lifted and separated or cut apart in the spring to increase stock. In formal plantings, deadhead the spikes as they fade. In more natural areas, leave the seedheads for the birds.

ADDITIONAL INFORMATION

The spiky blooms make splendid cut flowers. Tall plants may flop and need to be staked. Plant shorter cultivars such as 'Kobold' to avoid this inconvenience.

ADDITIONAL SPECIES, CULTIVARS, OR VARIETIES

'Floristan White' (2$\frac{1}{2}$ to 3 ft.) is an excellent white-flowered cultivar. Its partner 'Floristan Violet' (3 ft.) is a taller rose-purple selection. These were bred for cut flower production. Many other blazing stars are suitable for cultivation particularly in informal meadow-style gardens. All attract butterflies in bloom and goldfinches when in seed. A Michigan native, the rough blazing star, *Liatris aspera* (4 to 5 ft.), grows in dry, sandy fields and dry prairies as well as jack pine woodlands and blooms in late summer. *L. scariosa* (3 ft.) has button-like flower clusters and also prefers dry, sandy soil. There is a showy cultivar called 'September Glory'. Both prefer drier conditions in the garden and need good drainage.

Bleeding Heart

Dicentra spectabilis

Height: 2 to 3 ft.
Flowers: Deep pink and white, white
Bloom Period: Mid-spring
Zones: 3, 4, 5, 6
Light Requirement:

Common names are often descriptive and "bleeding heart" depicts the distinctive pink heart-shaped flowers of *Dicentra spectabilis* with inner petals resembling a drop of liquid. Turn them upside down to see the "lady in the bathtub," a lighthearted common name that is a favorite of preschoolers for this old-fashioned beauty. In mid-spring, bleeding heart gladdens viewers with its beauty as well as the memory it often evokes of a parent's or grandparent's garden. A full-grown clump of bleeding heart, 1 yd. high and equally wide, creates a magnificent display. The arching stems dangle pink-and-white flowers like heart-shaped lockets. The divided blue-gray foliage is also attractive. Quite easy to grow, bleeding heart needs only the right location—rich, moist soil and partial shade—to flourish. It has one significant flaw, the tendency for the foliage to yellow and die by late summer. That is easily accommodated, however. Plant it with ferns, large-leaved hosta, or bluestar to fill in the gap. Bleeding heart is a traditional part of the spring perennial border. Combine it with the green-yellow of cushion spurge, blue woodland phlox, and white tulips. Fill a lightly shaded corner near the house with a bleeding heart, and underplant it with white-flowered bigroot geranium. The elegant white bleeding heart glows among the dark green foliage and blue forget-me-not blooms of Siberian bugloss. Bleeding heart can also be tucked in with spring-flowering shrubs and groundcovers.

WHEN TO PLANT
Plant container-grown bleeding heart in the spring.

WHERE TO PLANT
Choose a location with moist, well-drained, humus-rich soil in partial shade. Bleeding heart tolerates sun with adequate moisture, but the foliage will go dormant prematurely. Add organic matter to light soils. Don't choose hot, dry, or windy locations.

How to Plant

Plant bleeding heart 18 to 24 in. apart. Dig a hole twice as wide as the pot, and position the plant so that the soil level is the same as it was in the pot. Fill in with soil around the roots about halfway up, firm gently, and water well. Add more soil to completely fill the hole. Water regularly until plants are established. Use mulch to conserve moisture.

Advice for Care

Water plants during dry spells. Adequate moisture prevents the foliage from declining. Bleeding heart shouldn't need dividing but can be divided to yield more plants in early spring. Dig it and divide before the stems elongate because they're brittle and apt to break.

Additional Information

When the foliage starts to deteriorate, cut it down to the ground. If you can spare them from the garden, the arching sprays of bleeding heart are a superb cut flower.

Additional Species, Cultivars, or Varieties

The white-flowered types of bleeding heart are 'Alba' or 'Pantaloons'. A related plant of high merit is *Dicentra eximia*, the fringed bleeding heart. Growing to a height of 9 to 18 in., this forest native of the eastern United States forms carpets of lovely blue-gray dissected foliage. The flowers in pink or white have an elongated heart shape and are not as showy or as tall as the common bleeding heart. They bloom for an extended period, however, often flowering heavily in spring and continuing sporadically through October, and the foliage does not go dormant. Fringed bleeding heart is an excellent choice for woodland gardens and shady beds, associating well with spring wildflowers, groundcovers, ferns, and hostas. Moist, humus-rich soil and partial shade are ideal. Several cultivars and hybrids exist. 'Snowdrift' (12 in.) has white flowers. 'Bountiful' (12 to 15 in.) and 'Luxuriant' (15 in.) are both hybrids with the Pacific bleeding heart, *Dicentra formosa*. They are larger and have showier floral displays.

Bloody Cranesbill

Geranium sanguineum

Height: 8 to 12 in.
Flowers: Magenta, red-purple, white
Bloom Period: Late spring through early summer and on
Zones: 4, 5, 6
Light Requirement:

Though the flower structure and finely cut foliage of bloody cranesbill are delicate, the blossoms pack a punch, opening to a bright magenta that smolders like an ember in the garden. This cranesbill spreads out eagerly, forming low, mounded clumps that turn dark red in the fall. Use it as a filler plant with other perennials such as the yellow-green flowers of lady's mantle, the cheery pastel flowers of hybrid columbine, and the clear blues of Siberian iris. Hardy geranium's weaving habit makes it an effective groundcover and accent around taller perennials. Bloody cranesbill, as well as other hardy geraniums, are easy-care, hardworking additions to the garden.

WHEN TO PLANT

Plant in the spring. Bloody cranesbill can be planted later with adequate moisture during hot weather.

WHERE TO PLANT

Choose locations with moist, well-drained, average to humus-rich soil for bloody cranesbill. Full sun with adequate moisture is ideal, but partial shade is readily tolerated. Its form will be looser in shade. Bloody cranesbill is fairly drought-tolerant due to its fleshy roots. This plant is very versatile. It's wonderful in perennial gardens, cottage gardens, and rock gardens and in other parts of the landscape as groundcover or edging.

HOW TO PLANT

Plant bloody cranesbill 1¹/₂ to 2 ft. apart. Dig a hole twice as wide as the pot, and position the plant so that the soil level is the same as it was in the pot. Fill in with soil around the roots about halfway up, firm gently, and water well. Add more soil to completely fill the hole. Water regularly until plants are established.

ADVICE FOR CARE

Bloody cranesbill is very easy to grow. Provide water during drought. This hardy geranium rarely needs division, but, in tight situations, division may be needed to keep its spreading growth in check. This is easily accomplished in the spring. Dig clumps, and pull them apart into sections. Replant, and water well until established. Add some organic matter to replenish the soil before replanting. A layer of mulch will conserve moisture. To increase your supply of plants, you don't even have to dig up the whole clump of bloody cranesbill. Just use a sharp spade to cut off pieces from around the edge. Then replant following the directions above.

ADDITIONAL INFORMATION

After the first flush of bloom, plants may be sheared back to remove the seedpods and to promote rebloom. Some hardy geraniums such as 'Johnson's Blue' begin to deteriorate in midsummer and should be sheared to the ground to promote fresh foliage. Bloody cranesbill looks good all season.

ADDITIONAL SPECIES, CULTIVARS, OR VARIETIES

Geranium sanguineum var. *striatum* or *lancastriense* is a very low grower with ferny foliage. Its light pink flowers are etched with rose. *Striatum* makes an excellent groundcover or edging plant for shrub roses, and this is a first-rate perennial for use in either sun or partial shade. 'Album' (10 to 18 in.) has white flowers, is taller, and has a looser habit. Other cultivars exist and are not dramatically different from the species. A few are lower and make a prostrate groundcover. Hardy geraniums are lovely and easy garden plants. Among those to choose from are the following: *Geranium cinereum* 'Ballerina', the grayleaf cranesbill, grows into small clumps only 4 to 6 in. tall. Its exquisitely veined flowers contrast with the gray-green foliage. It needs good drainage. *Geranium psilostemon* (4 ft.), the Armenian geranium, has tall, brilliant magenta flowers that can be staked or allowed to "weave" in and out of neighboring plants. It self-sows. *Geranium wallichianum* 'Buxton's Blue' (12 in.), with China blue flowers with a white center, is another excellent groundcover with an abundance of bloom. For more on geraniums, see the groundcover chapter entry on bigroot geranium, and, in the woodland wildflowers and ferns chapter, see the profile of wild geranium.

Blue False Indigo

Baptisia australis

Height: 3 to 4 ft.
Flowers: Blue-violet
Bloom Period: Late spring
Zones: 3, 4, 5, 6
Light Requirement:

Blue false indigo combines strength and beauty. The tall spires of blue-violet flowers add grace to the late spring garden, and the mounds of soft gray-green foliage create an elegant backdrop right into autumn. Once established, the clumps will last a lifetime with no special care.

Blue false indigo is a native wildflower growing in woodland edges and prairies south and east of Michigan. Its common name refers to its use as a blue dye. It forms thick, deep roots and, when mature, large clumps that are often more than 3 ft. high and just as wide. In the garden, it couldn't be easier. Plant it once, give it a few years to grow, and enjoy. This plant requires sun and plenty of room. In partial shade, plants often split open. Full-grown clumps are large and difficult to move, so select a permanent location. The stems of blue false indigo push up quickly in the spring garden. It has its big moment in June, when the intense blue pea-like flowers open on tall stalks that are a handsome complement to peonies. Later, the three-lobed cloverlike foliage adds soft gray-green color, textural form, and structure to the garden. Try blue false indigo as part of a late spring combination. Add the vertical form and lovely flowers of Siberian iris, blue or magenta hardy geraniums, blue star, and coral bells. Add drifts of hybrid anemones and red switch grass for late season interest. In a cottage-style garden, use blue false indigo as a complement to peach-leaf bellflower, peonies, and shrub roses.

When to Plant

Plant blue false indigo in the spring.

Where to Plant

Choose locations in full sun with moist, well-drained, average to fertile soil. Clumps will tolerate light shade but will flop in too much. Plants are drought-tolerant once established. Give each plant ample room. Blue false indigo is versatile and may be planted in formal borders, informal cottage gardens, island beds, or meadow-like gardens or even massed as a shrub for hedges or foundation plantings.

How to Plant

Plant blue false indigo 3 to 4 ft. apart. Dig a hole twice as wide as the pot, and position the plant so that the soil level is the same as it was in the pot. Fill in with soil around the roots about halfway up, firm gently, and water well. Add more soil to completely fill the hole. Water regularly until plants are established.

Advice for Care

Blue false indigo needs little care. Plants are slow to establish and best left alone. Division is not recommended. If you must divide them, however, dig clumps in the spring as early as possible. A large clump can be quite a job to get out of the ground. In adequate sun, plants will not need staking. In too much shade, clumps may split open and flop. It's almost impossible to stake them unobtrusively and retain their natural character. Better to plan a spring move to a sunnier part of the garden or try lightly pruning back the foliage after flowering to keep plants compact.

Additional Information

Blue false indigo takes 3 to 4 years to reach maturity, but it's worth the wait. Full-grown plants are very long-lived and require little care. The seedpods of blue false indigo are puffy and fat. Remove them as they form so the pods don't weigh down the stems, or leave the pods and stems for winter interest and cut back in spring.

Additional Species, Cultivars, or Varieties

White false indigo, *Baptisia alba* (2¹/₂ to 3 ft.), hardy to Zone 5, is a choice plant with creamy white pealike flowers on dark stems and blue-gray foliage. *Baptisia leucantha*, also called white or prairie false indigo, also has beautiful gray-green foliage and a tall, shrub-like habit. It grows on prairies and dry open roadsides in southern Michigan. Look for *Baptisia* 'Purple Smoke' (4¹/₂ ft.), a new hybrid between *B. alba* and *B. australis*. It has an abundant stalk of purple flowers, dark stems, and attractive bluish-green leaves.

Blue Star

Amsonia tabernaemontana

Other Name: Amsonia
Height: 2 to 3 ft.
Flowers: Pale blue
Bloom Period: Late spring
Zones: 4, 5, 6
Light Requirement:

Blue star has a shrubby form and small celestial flowers. A plant of considerable, yet subtle, beauty, it is underappreciated or even unknown by many gardeners. Not every plant can be a celebrity, and some plants play supporting roles that are just as important as the lead. Blue star makes other plants look good. When in bloom, the icy blue flowers of blue star or amsonia are attractive and refreshing but not scene stealers. The starry domed clusters push up quickly on stems with slender leaves. They make excellent companions for peonies, blue false indigo, Oriental poppies, and other late spring flowers. As the flowers pass, the willowy foliage grows to form a 2- to 3-ft. shrub-like mass that contributes structure to the perennial border. This shiny green foliage effect, which lasts all season, provides a pleasant backdrop for annuals and perennials. In the fall, the foliage changes color, enhancing the garden with a rich yellow. Few perennials offer reliable fall color, and amsonia is one of the best. Amsonia is easy to grow. It is long-lived, rarely needs division, and is pest- and disease-resistant. Full sun leads to increased flowering and superior fall color, but partial shade is suitable as well. Try blue star with all shades of Siberian iris, a drift of gray 'Valerie Finnis' artemisia, or a grouping of peonies. Use blue star as a shrub, and mass it for a low-maintenance but tall groundcover or foundation plant. Capitalize on blue star's fall color by planting clumps with ornamental grasses, asters, and Japanese hybrid anemones.

WHEN TO PLANT
Plant container-grown blue star in the spring.

WHERE TO PLANT
Plant blue star in moist, well-drained soil of average to rich fertility and in full sun or partial shade. Deep, moist soils and sun are ideal. Avoid hot, dry sites. Use blue star in perennial beds or borders, in mixed plantings, with shrubs, or in natural areas.

How to Plant

Plant blue star 2¹/₂ to 3 ft. apart. Dig a hole twice as wide as the pot, and position the plant so that the soil level is the same as it was in the pot. Fill in with soil around the roots about halfway up, firm gently, and water well. Add more soil to completely fill the hole. Water regularly until plants are established. A layer of mulch is beneficial.

Advice for Care

Blue star needs little care. It is drought-tolerant once established, although some water during dry spells is beneficial. We have never experienced a pest or disease problem with blue star. Long-lived with a woody, fibrous-rooted crown, this plant usually will not require division, but, if it is desired, division to increase stock may be done in spring.

Additional Information

Plants can be pruned to create dense, compact growth. Try this with plants in partial shade that may have more of a tendency to sprawl. Use pruners (don't shear) to cut back by about half after flowering. Plants will produce new shoots. The foliage and pods of blue star are attractive in arrangements.

Additional Species, Cultivars, or Varieties

There are few, if any, cultivars of this native of the southern United States, but several other species and forms are available. The var. *montana* is lower growing, reaching only 2 to 2¹/₂ ft. It has a more lax habit. The Arkansas amsonia, *Amsonia hubrectii*, is worth seeking out. It has fine-textured, almost feathery foliage, reaching a height of 3 ft., and beautiful orange-yellow fall color. The foliage stands on its own the whole season as a billowing mass. It has survived in Michigan's Zone 5 but may not be hardy in Zone 4.

Boltonia

Boltonia asteroides

Height: 3 to 6 ft.
Flowers: White
Bloom Period: Late summer into fall
Zones: 4, 5, 6
Light Requirement:

The white 1-in. daisies of boltonia engulf its foliage with flowers from late summer into fall. This aster-like plant is called false aster in some field guides, and the two are quite similar. Boltonia's flowers are more delicate, however, and the foliage—gray-green and willow-like—doesn't succumb to the diseases that attack some asters. Like many asters, boltonia is a North American native. It is usually found growing in moist soils and gravelly shores. It occurs south of Michigan, although it has been found in a few of our southernmost counties. With adequate moisture and full sun, plants can reach close to 6 ft. Given its tremendous height, the species isn't suitable for most gardens. A cultivar called 'Snowbank' is a better choice. 'Snowbank' grows to 3 or 4 ft. and is smothered with shaggy yellow-centered daisies when in bloom. This easy-to-grow perennial is an excellent addition to formal and informal perennial gardens, to meadows, or to a rustic fence. Boltonia produces blue-green, willow-like leaves on straight pencil-thin stems. The foliage is handsome, but the stiff upright habit is best softened by lower-growing plants. Its clouds of white flowers with a delicate texture are reminiscent of baby's breath. The flowers contribute to the garden from late August into fall. A striking late-season combination is blue spirea (*Caryopteris*) and boltonia in front of the silvery plumes of flame grass (*Miscanthus sinensis* 'Purpurascens'). By early fall, the white daisies glow in front of the rich red-and-orange foliage of the grass. Boltonia's gray-green foliage and airy blooms provide satisfying contrast with coarser plants such as 'Gateway' Joe-pye weed or purple coneflower. Add New England asters and switch grass for a late-season meadow garden.

WHEN TO PLANT
Plant container-grown boltonia in the spring.

WHERE TO PLANT

Choose a location with moist, average to fertile, well-drained soil in full sun. Boltonia tolerates some light shade, but plants won't be as upright. Plants grow tallest in moist soil. Use in natural meadow-type gardens. The cultivar 'Snowbank' is suitable for the back of perennial borders, for the center of island beds, and for mixed plantings. The bottoms of the straight tall stems are too upright and bare for the garden's foreground.

HOW TO PLANT

Plant boltonia 'Snowbank' 2 ft. apart. The species should be spaced at 3 ft. Dig a hole twice as wide as the pot, and position the plant so that the soil level is the same as it was in the pot. Fill in with soil around the roots about halfway up, firm gently, and water well. Add more soil to completely fill the hole. Water regularly until plants are established.

ADVICE FOR CARE

Boltonia is resistant to pests and disease. Somewhat drought-tolerant, clumps will be shorter in dry soils. Water during drought for more lush growth. Divide clumps every 3 to 4 years to restore vigor and control spread. This is easily accomplished in the spring. Dig clumps, split into sections, and pull apart the pieces. Replant vigorous divisions. Water well until established.

ADDITIONAL INFORMATION

The cultivar 'Snowbank' is usually self-supporting. The species may grow too tall and require staking, particularly in rich soil or light shade. To avoid staking, cut back the plants by about half in late spring or early summer. The flowers of boltonia are a delicate filler for arrangements.

ADDITIONAL SPECIES, CULTIVARS, OR VARIETIES

'Snowbank' (3 to 4 ft.) is a superior compact, although still tall, selection. 'Pink Beauty' (4 ft.) has tousled pale pink daisies and blue-gray foliage. It has a sprawling habit even in full sun. Cut it back in early summer to promote compact growth, or plant it tightly with more upright plants such as feather reed grass. The soft pink and wispy nature of the plants is more delicate than a pink aster.

Bowman's Root

Gillenia trifoliata

Height: 2 to 4 ft.
Flowers: White
Bloom Period: Summer
Zones: 4, 5, 6
Light Requirement:

Bowman's root, an overlooked North American native, is an immensely satisfying plant to grow. It offers ever-changing beauty throughout the growing season. Never flashy, although it has its brilliant moment in the fall, bowman's root is always noteworthy for it refined presence.

Once you have added bowman's root to your garden, you may never want to be without it. The season begins with the patterned texture created by the repeating shapes of the thrice-divided leaves. In summer a lacy display of delicate white flowers veils the foliage. The five-petaled star-shaped blooms are held loosely in open clusters on wiry pink stems. The flowers seem to hover over the foliage, creating an effect of ethereal beauty. An astilbe looks brazen in comparison. After the flowers drop, the wine-colored sepals, a leafy floral part under the petals, persist, giving the plant a subtle pinkish cast, and the foliage remains attractive. In fall, an extra surprise is the wonderful color, a warm combination of yellow, orange, and red all on the same plant. Later, the stems have a chestnut color in the winter garden. Bowman's root has a shrubby habit and grows from 2½ to 4 ft. tall. A native of rich woods slightly south and east of Michigan, it grows with little trouble in partial shade and moist, humus-rich soil but also thrives in sun with ample moisture. Plants will be shorter in full sun and attain their full stature in partial shade. The airy flowers add light to the shady garden. In a moist, sunny perennial bed, try bowman's root with peonies and blue star for dramatic foliage effect right into fall. Cottage gardeners combine it with shrub roses and hardy geraniums. Drifts of bowman's root can be used to tie together other plantings. Try a ribbon of bowman's root among ferns, bigroot geranium, and spotted dead nettle. Bowman's root may be a bit hard to find, but it is worth seeking out. Try it first in a lightly shaded garden or woodland edge. Once it wins you over, you'll be adding this plant to other parts of your garden.

WHEN TO PLANT

Plant bowman's root in the spring.

WHERE TO PLANT

Plant bowman's root in moist, fertile soil and partial shade to full sun. Plants need moisture-retentive soil in full sun. Add organic matter to light soils. Use the plant in a lightly shaded woodland garden, a sunny, moist perennial bed, or a cottage garden. It also softens walks and patios. Its airy texture is accentuated by massing, but a single clump creates a lovely detail among lower, ground-covering perennials.

HOW TO PLANT

Plant bowman's root 2 ft. apart. Dig a hole twice as wide as the pot, and position the plant so that the soil level is the same as it was in the pot. Fill in with soil around the roots about halfway up, firm gently, and water well. Add more soil to completely fill the hole. Water regularly until plants are established. Mulch to conserve moisture.

ADVICE FOR CARE

Bowman's root needs little care if sited correctly. Water plants, especially those in full sun locations, during drought. Division of the deep, thick roots is rarely needed but can be attempted in the spring. The shiny brown stems remain upright and provide moderate winter interest.

ADDITIONAL INFORMATION

Plants take a few years to develop into mature clumps and are best left undisturbed. Bowman's root is sometimes listed as *Porteranthus trifoliatus*. A refined combination for partial shade pairs an elegant specimen or drift of bowman's root with blue-leaved hostas, 'Palace Purple' alumroot, and the drooping spikelets of wild oats. Add Siberian bugloss and Bethlehem sage for spring flowers.

ADDITIONAL SPECIES, CULTIVARS, OR VARIETIES

Gillenia stipulata, a similar plant but not as showy, is sometimes available.

Butterflyweed

Asclepias tuberosa

Other Name: Butterflyflower
Height: 18 to 24 in.
Flowers: Orange
Bloom Period: Early to
  midsummer
Zones: 4, 5, 6
Light Requirement:

Bright orange grabs your attention. That's why butterflyweed, the flamboyant star of the milkweed family, is one of the most recognizable summer-blooming wildflowers. Native to a vast area of the United States, butterflyweed grows in most of Michigan's Lower Peninsula in woodland openings, sandy roadsides, old fields, and grassy meadows. It gets noticed even at 65 miles per hour. Butterflies also take note; this plant is a magnet for monarchs. A more complimentary common name is butterflyflower; another common name, pleurisy root, describes its use as a remedy for respiratory illness. Butterflyflower has unusual flowers shaped like a crown above flaring reflexed petals. When mature, dozens of stems grow up to about 2 ft. from a large taproot. The orange flowers are produced in clusters on upright stems with linear leaves. Although a milkweed, it doesn't have milky sap. Its long (4 to 6 in.), tapered seedpods are ornamental and open to release the standard milkweed seeds, each with a fluffy parachute. Butterflyflower is easy to grow in full sun and average to sandy soil where drainage is good. Plants can be massed for brilliant effect; however, they are more effective used as an accent. One clump creates a remarkable focal point. Orange flowers are sometimes criticized for being difficult to use, but often orange adds a spark to a garden. Try butterflyflower interplanted with shrubby lavenders and the tall rose-purple spires of Brazilian verbena. Or front ornamental grasses, blue false indigo, and the yellow-orange sunflowers of heliopsis with butterflyweed, yellow coreopsis, the deep blue-violet of mealy-cup sage, and pale blue 'Butterfly Blue' pincushion flower. Watch out for the butterflies!

WHEN TO PLANT
Plant container-grown butterflyweed in the spring.

WHERE TO PLANT

Plant butterflyweed in full sun and in poor to average, well-drained soil. Sandy loam is ideal; good drainage is paramount. Plants are tolerant of dry soils and drought. Avoid poorly drained or heavy clay sites. Use in meadow gardens or the front to middle of sunny perennial beds.

HOW TO PLANT

Space clumps of butterflyweed 1 1/2 to 2 ft. apart. Dig a hole at least as wide as the pot, and position the plant so that the soil level is the same as it was in the pot. Be gentle with the brittle tuberous root. Fill in with soil around the roots about halfway up, firm gently, and water well. Add more soil to completely fill the hole. Water regularly until plants are established.

ADVICE FOR CARE

Butterflyweed needs little special care. The deep, fleshy taproots resent disturbance; young plants should be left alone to develop into mature clumps, which will take at least 2 to 3 years. Plants often self-sow if seed is allowed to disperse. Division is usually unnecessary. If you must move plants or are just adventurous, try division in early spring when the plant is still dormant. Cautiously dig the whole root, being careful not to slice through the root with the spade. Split it with a sharp knife into sections, each containing at least one bud. Plant with buds 1 in. below the soil surface. Keep new divisions moist but not sodden. New divisions, like young plants, will take several years to reach their full potential.

ADDITIONAL INFORMATION

Butterflyweed is one of the last perennials to appear, and it's easy to damage its roots while planting annuals or weeding in the spring garden. Mark butterflyweed's place with a label, or, when cutting back plants, leave 6 in. of stem to remind you of its location.

ADDITIONAL SPECIES, CULTIVARS, OR VARIETIES

'Gay Butterflies Mix' (24 to 30 in.) is a seed-grown strain with showy flowers in shades of deep red, orange, and yellow. The swamp milkweed, *A. incarnata*, grows throughout Michigan. Typically, the flowers are a deep rose. It prefers heavy, wet soils and grows to 4 ft. A beautiful white-flowered selection, 'Ice Ballet' (4 to 5 ft.), makes an unusual addition to a perennial garden. Try it with turtlehead in a moist, sunny spot. Swamp milkweed is very attractive to butterflies.

Catmint

Nepeta × *faassenii*

Other Names: Hybrid
  Catmint, Faassen's
  Nepeta
Height: 2 to 3 ft.
Flowers: Lavender-blue
Bloom Period: Late spring
  through midsummer
Zones: 4, 5, 6
Light Requirement:

Long-flowering perennials are favorites of garden designers. Their steady presence bridges the gap between seasons, allowing the creation of many garden "pictures." Hybrid catmint, *Nepeta* × *faassenii*, is such a perennial. This easy plant for sun and well-drained soil has grayish-green foliage and clouds of blue-purple flowers creating a soft, misty appearance. It opens its first flowers in late spring, but its lavender haze continues through midsummer or even beyond. At first, catmint is upright, growing to 2 to 3 ft. Then stems begin to flop as the season progresses. The polite way to describe this tendency is to identify the plant as a weaver. Catmint is a weaver; its natural habit is to sprawl. Locate plants where this relaxed habit will be welcome. Let it intermingle with other perennials such as iris, daylilies, or 'Lucifer' crocosmia. Catmint is often seen bordering herb, vegetable, and rose beds in British gardens. Its romantic, billowing form can be a nuisance next to lawns, however. Place it farther back in the bed, or plant it where it will border brick or stone. Catmint's subdued coloring harmonizes with pastels and flatters vibrant jewel tones. Try catmint with Siberian iris and purple perennial sage for a late spring combination. In early summer, combine catmint with the yellow 'Coronation Gold' yarrow and paler yellow 'Moonbeam' coreopsis. Even later, catmint softens the impact of summer-flowering daylilies. The cultivar 'Six Hills Giant' is worth seeking out. Bloom continues for months. Plant a grouping as a misty lavender-blue complement to a clump of yellow hybrid lilies. Or try this catmint with hardy geraniums, lamb's ears, and bright pink shrub roses.

WHEN TO PLANT
Plant container-grown catmint in the spring.

WHERE TO PLANT

Choose locations with well-drained to sandy soil of average fertility in full sun. In heavier or richer soils or partial shade, plants will split open and sprawl. Wet sites will lead to rot.

HOW TO PLANT

Plant catmint 2 ft. apart. The selection 'Six Hills Giant' should be spaced at 2½ to 3 ft. Dig a hole twice as wide as the pot, and position the plant so that the soil level is the same as it was in the pot. Fill in with soil around the roots about halfway up, firm gently, and water well. Add more soil to completely fill the hole. Water regularly until plants are established.

ADVICE FOR CARE

Catmint is carefree and needs only a little pruning. After the first flush of bloom, cut back the stems to tidy the plants and to encourage rebloom. Clumps that split open in the middle are a signal that the catmint needs dividing or a sunnier exposure. Do this in early spring as the fuzzy foliage is just emerging. Dig clumps, and split into sections with a sharp spade. Replant, and keep watered until established.

ADDITIONAL INFORMATION

The true *N. × faassenii* won't self-sow. If your plants are *Nepeta mussinii*, self-sown seedlings will appear and may be weeded out where unwanted. Catnip, *Nepeta cataria*, is the plant that cats go crazy for, although some gardeners report feline interest in catmint.

ADDITIONAL SPECIES, CULTIVARS, OR VARIETIES

'Six Hills Giant', a fine garden plant, is bigger than other cultivars and creates a cloud of lavender-blue. It grows to a height and spread of 3 ft. 'Dropmore' (18 to 24 in.) is shorter. *Nepeta sibirica* (3 to 3½ ft.) is a superb garden plant with upright tiered flowers of blue-violet. It's very hardy, long-flowering, and beautiful. Ann Hancock at the Michigan State University Horticultural Demonstration Gardens reports that the seeds attract flocks of goldfinches. It prefers well-drained soil of average fertility. A cultivar called 'Souvenir d'Andre Chaudron', or more simply 'Blue Beauty', is 1½ to 2 ft. Calamint, *Calamintha nepetoides* (12 in.), is another useful perennial in the mint family. It has performed well in Zone 5 in Michigan. This compact aromatic plant produces a haze of tiny pale bluish-white flowers from summer until fall. The flowers turn pale lavender when cool temperatures set in. It's a delicate addition to the garden.

Cheddar Pinks

Dianthus gratianopolitanus

Height: 9 to 12 in.
Flowers: Pink
Bloom Period: Late spring to midsummer
Zones: 4, 5, 6
Light Requirement:

Cheerful and fragrant, the cheddar pinks begin blooming in late spring with 1-in. wide flowers in various shades of pink and rose. These are easy-to-grow perennials with abundant, fragrant flowers over an evergreen mat of narrow, grass-like blue-gray foliage. A particularly nice cultivar is 'Bath's Pink', which has pale pink fringed flowers and a scent of clove. Combine the cheddar pinks with other gray-foliaged plants, such as salvias, lamb's ears, lavender, blue oat grass, and catmint. They are also effective with creeping thyme, blue flax, and hardy geraniums. The cheddar pinks called 'Tiny Rubies' has 1/2-in. double flowers in a deep shade of rose. This is an apt cultivar name because the flowers sparkle like jewels over the clumps of blue-gray foliage. Cheddar pinks are cold hardy and perform well in a sunny spot as long as the soil is well drained. In heavy clay or moist sites, however, they may rot. Deadheading, or removing the faded flowers, will prolong their floral display. Combine cheddar pinks with other perennials, and place them in the front of borders and beds. Lining a walkway, cheddar pinks form a low-growing mat that invites visitors into your garden.

WHEN TO PLANT
Plant container-grown cheddar pink in the spring.

WHERE TO PLANT
Choose locations with average to sandy, well-drained soil in full sun. Pinks dislike acid soils. Avoid poorly drained sites, which will lead to rot. Use in perennial beds and borders, in rock gardens, and along edges of brick or stone patios.

HOW TO PLANT
Plant cheddar pinks 2 ft. apart. Dig a hole twice as wide as the pot, and position the plant so that the soil level is the same as it was in the pot. Fill in with soil around the roots about halfway up, firm

gently, and water well. Add more soil to completely fill the hole. Water regularly until plants are established.

ADVICE FOR CARE

Properly sited in areas of the garden with good drainage, cheddar pinks will not need any special care. Plants shouldn't need watering or fertilization. Avoid piling mulch around the mats of foliage because this can lead to rot. After they finish flowering, deadhead the flowering stalks, removing them back to the basal foliage, to promote rebloom. Be careful not to cut foliage; remove only the flowering stalks. Divide clumps when they begin to die out in the middle. Lift mats, and divide with a sharp knife into healthy, vigorous pieces. Replant, taking care not to set the plants too deep. Keep watered until established. Allow space between plants to promote good air circulation, which promotes health.

ADDITIONAL INFORMATION

The mats of foliage are evergreen. Do not attempt to cut off the plants at ground level during fall cleanup. Cut some of the delicate spicy flowers for small windowsill arrangements.

ADDITIONAL SPECIES, CULTIVARS, OR VARIETIES

The maiden pinks, *Dianthus deltoides* (6 to 18 in.), form very low, spreading clumps and are suitable for the front of a perennial garden or a rock garden. The small bright flowers create mats of color. 'Brilliant' has deep rose-pink flowers while 'Flashing Light' has deep ruby-red flowers. The bright flowers of sweet William, *Dianthus barbatus*, are an old-fashioned favorite. Although described as a biennial, sweet William often behaves as a short-lived perennial. It prefers moist, rich soil and in these conditions self-sows to perpetuate itself in the garden. The China pinks or annual pinks, *Dianthus chinensis*, sold with the bedding plants, also behave as short-lived perennials in Michigan. These plants have been covered with flowers in annual trials at Michigan State University.

Coral Bells

Heuchera × brizoides

Height: 1 to 2 ft.
Flowers: Red, pink, magenta, white
Bloom Period: Late spring to early summer
Zones: 4, 5, 6
Light Requirement:

If there are "fairies at the bottom of our garden," as the old poem goes, they may be lurking among the coral bells. These sprightly flowers on thin stems seem to float magically over the foliage with elfin charm. Coral bells are sentimental favorites, plants that many of us recall from our grandparents' gardens. The airy clusters of tiny bell-shaped flowers are held high over the clump of evergreen foliage—green or mottled with a deep green-gray color—with their scalloped, lobed, or wavy edges. The flowers, which continue to be attractive for 4 to 8 weeks, attract hummingbirds. Plant drifts of coral bells with white or pastel bearded irises, columbine, and hardy geraniums. Even though the stems are tall, they are so delicate that they may be placed near the front of the border.

WHEN TO PLANT

Plant coral bells in the spring. They are subject to winter heaving and need time to develop roots.

WHERE TO PLANT

Choose locations with moist, well-drained, humus-rich soil in full sun or light shade. Coral bells flower more abundantly in the sun but need adequate moisture. Avoid hot, dry, and poorly drained sites. Plant in perennial beds, cottage gardens, or drifts in the lightly shaded garden; use for edging walks and beds.

HOW TO PLANT

Plant coral bells 1 ft. apart. Dig a hole twice as wide as the pot, and position the plant so that the soil level is the same as it was in the pot. Fill in with soil around the roots about halfway up, firm gently, and water well. Add more soil to completely fill the hole. If the plants have begun to develop a woody base, they may be set slightly deeper. Water regularly until plants are established. Mulch to conserve moisture.

ADVICE FOR CARE

Water coral bells during dry spells. Deadhead (remove the finished flowering stalks) to promote rebloom. Let the foliage remain in place in the fall; it stays evergreen all winter. After 3 to 5 years, flowering will decrease, and plants will become bare and woody at the base. This is the signal to divide. Dig up the clumps, and gently pull them apart. Discard old, woody sections, and plant young, vigorous pieces each with a rosette of foliage, woody root, and some attached fibrous roots. Bury the piece to the level of the foliage; coral bells are an exception to standard advice of replanting at the same level. Be sure to augment the soil with additional organic material before replanting. Coral bells are susceptible to the strawberry root weevil. Infested plants may appear stunted or die. Look for the white C-shaped grubs on the roots. The safest control is to remove and discard infected plants. Call your county's office of the MSU Extension for current recommendations. Replant healthy coral bells in another section of the garden.

ADDITIONAL INFORMATION

Plants are shallow-rooted and subject to heaving, the alternate freezing and thawing that can force plants out of the ground during winter. A nonmatting material such as evergreen boughs used as a winter mulch can prevent this. Apply the mulch after the ground freezes, and remove before growth begins in spring. New plantings and new divisions are more prone to heaving; a winter mulch is strongly recommended. A reliably thick cover of snow provides superior insulation.

ADDITIONAL SPECIES, CULTIVARS, OR VARIETIES

There are several to choose from with different colored flowers. 'Chatterbox' (20 in.) has blooms that are a blend of pink and rosy coral. 'Pluie de Feu' ('Rain of Fire') is brilliant red and grows to 18 in. The 'Bressingham Hybrids' (22 in.) are mixed colors in pink, red, coral, and white. See the groundcover chapter entry for *Heuchera micrantha* 'Palace Purple' for information on alumroot, another member of the coral bell clan.

Culver's Root

Veronicastrum virginicum

Height: 4 to 6 ft.
Flowers: White, pale pink
Bloom Period: Mid- to late summer
Zones: 3, 4, 5, 6
Light Requirement:

With its sheer vertical form and elegant, airy effect, Culver's root is a native plant that successfully makes the transition to the garden. It can be found in southern Michigan's prairies, fens, and meadows, along rivers, and in deciduous woodlots. The roots were formerly used for medicines. When it comes to garden use, Culver's root is a frequent accent plant in European perennial borders, where its distinctive form contrasts with sneezeweed, asters, and purple coneflower for a striking architectural effect. The stems of Culver's roots are encircled by clusters of five narrow, toothed leaves. Growing to 6 in. long, these horizontal leaves create an interesting texture below the elegant branched spires. The tapered spikes, appearing in mid- to late summer, are most often white but occasionally pale lavender. Play up the tall, vertical habit of Culver's root by combining it with the mounded form and chubby bright gold-orange daisies of *Helenium*. Culver's root has a tall, lofty presence, making it a strong character in the perennial border, useful as a specimen plant or in a shrub border. Culver's root is easy to grow in sun, where it will achieve the best form. It is not particular about soil, thriving in sites with average fertility, but it does require a well-drained site.

WHEN TO PLANT

Plant container-grown Culver's root in the spring.

WHERE TO PLANT

Choose locations with full sun to partial shade and moist but well-drained, average to fertile soil. Avoid deep shade; clumps grown there may lose their vertical habit and need staking. Use Culver's root in back of a perennial border or at the center of an island bed. It is also suited for sunny, moist meadows, for woodland edges, by ponds, and in natural areas. Avoid windy or shady spots, which may cause the plant to flop.

How to Plant

Plant Culver's root 2 to 3 ft. apart. Dig a hole twice as wide as the pot, and position the plant so that the soil level is the same as it was in the pot. Fill in with soil around the roots about halfway up, firm gently, and water well. Add more soil to completely fill the hole. Water regularly until plants are established. Mulch clumps to conserve moisture.

Advice for Care

Culver's root needs no special care, although it should be watered during times of drought. The clumps rarely need division but may be divided in the spring. Dig up the clumps, and split them apart with a knife. Replant them at the same level, and keep the plants moist until they are established.

Additional Information

The elegant spires of Culver's root are wonderful in large arrangements. Sometimes this plant will be listed as *Veronica virginica*.

Additional Species, Cultivars, or Varieties

A pale pink form, 'Rosea', is very attractive and makes an excellent show with 'Prairie Blue Eyes' daylily, rose-pink obedient plant (*Physostegia virginiana*), and the paler pink 'Brilliant' showy stonecrop. Another tall native plant for moist soil is Joe-pye weed. Similar to Culver's root, Joe-pye weed (*Eupatorium fistulosum*) is a tall, back-of-the-border plant that has been used for years to anchor British perennial gardens. Joe-pye weed has dusky rose flowers in domed clusters and large, deep green foliage, and it grows to 5 or 6 ft. The best form of it for the garden is 'Gateway', which is somewhat shorter (4¹/₂ ft.) and has attractive, deep maroon stems and wine-red flowers. Culver's root and Joe-pye weed softened by an airy cloud of switch grass make a pleasant combination for large natural areas.

Cushion Spurge

Euphorbia polychroma

Height: 18 to 24 in.
Flowers: Chartreuse-yellow
Bloom Period: Mid-spring
Zones: 4, 5, 6
Light Requirement:

Cushion spurge's neatly mounded foliage is brightened in spring with early green-to-yellow, almost fluorescent flowers that add zest and fresh color to the garden. The eye-catching bloom is actually a bract, or modified leaf, similar to the red bracts of the cushion spurge's relative, the poinsettia. This group of plants has no petals or sepals. After the flowering period, the foliage remains attractive all season and turns a warm orange-red in the fall. Put this accommodating perennial to good use by placing cushion spurge in perennial beds and borders with tulips and moss phlox. It may also be planted so that ornamental onions such as *Allium aflatuenese* grow up through it. Try it with blue dwarf bearded iris and lamb's ears in a well-drained, sunny area. Or in light shade, plant cushion spurge with bleeding heart. Cushion spurge thrives in areas that enjoy full sun and well-drained to even dry soils. It may be used as a specimen or planted among other perennials. The high-quality foliage makes it invaluable in the garden. It is also useful for growing with flowering shrubs or in partial and somewhat dry shade, where it may be used with Solomon's seal and epimediums. Cushion spurge, like many of its relatives, has milky sap that can cause skin irritation.

WHEN TO PLANT
Plant container-grown cushion spurge in the spring.

WHERE TO PLANT
Choose locations with average well-drained soil in full sun or partial shade. Cushion spurge tolerates poor sandy soils and dislikes wet sites. In rich soil and partial shade, the mounded foliage may sprawl. Use in perennial beds and borders, in cottage gardens, with tulips, and in mass plantings.

How to Plant

Plant cushion spurge 12 to 18 in. apart. Dig a hole twice as wide as the pot, and position the plant so that the soil level is the same as it was in the pot. Fill in with soil around the roots about halfway up, firm gently, and water well. Add more soil to completely fill the hole. Water regularly until plants are established.

Advice for Care

Cushion spurge, when sited correctly, is long-lived and needs no special care. Clumps do not require division. In moist soil and partial shade, plants may become overgrown and split open to reveal the middle. With most perennials, this is the signal to divide, and although this can be attempted in spring with cushion spurge, the large rootstock resents disturbance. A more dependable way to replace overgrown plants is to purchase new container-grown cushion spurge; this time, plant it in a sunnier location.

Additional Information

All spurges produce a milky sap that can be irritating to the skin. Wear gloves when handling plants. Self-sown seedlings may appear in some locations and are easily pulled. Cushion spurge is generally trouble-free.

Additional Species, Cultivars, or Varieties

An unusual low-growing (6 to 9 in.) evergreen spurge is *Euphorbia myrsinites*, sometimes called the myrtle euphorbia or donkey-tail spurge. This plant has prostrate snake-like stems clothed in waxy blue-green leaves. It flowers early, at the same time as grape hyacinths and daffodils, with brilliant yellow-green flowers (bracts) at the ends of the stems. It needs well-drained soil and is excellent planted at the top of a rock wall. This spurge is hardy in Michigan's Zone 5. It self-sows, and the little seedlings with their succulent gray-green leaves are distinctive.

Daylily

Hemerocallis hybrids

Height: 12 to 48 in.
Flowers: Yellow, orange, red, pink, lavender
Bloom Period: Early to late summer
Zones: 3, 4, 5, 6
Light Requirement:

Daylilies are among the easiest and most attractive of all perennials to grow. They form dense clumps that are covered with tall stalks bearing multiple flowers. Although each blooms for just one day, the plant continues to produce flowers for several weeks. By choosing early, mid-season, and late daylily cultivars, it is possible to extend the season of bloom for much of the summer. Thousands of hybrid cultivars exist, and hundreds more are being introduced each year. The trend among hybridizers is to search out cultivars that are longer flowering. Perhaps the most well-known of these is 'Stella d'Oro', with flowers the somewhat gaudy yellow of egg yolks and sporadic rebloom all season. 'Happy Returns' is another rebloomer with a softer yellow color. As with hostas, it is possible to spend a considerable amount of money on a rare daylily cultivar, and collectors with thousands of plants are always looking for the new and unusual. Other daylilies are available for more modest prices, however, allowing them to be used in quantity in the landscape. Daylilies are spectacular and long-lived on their own or planted in a bed with daffodils, which die back as the daylilies start to grow rapidly in late spring. They are also attractive teamed with the finely textured plants such as purple fennel, Russian sage, and 'Moonbeam' coreopsis.

WHEN TO PLANT

Container-grown daylily plants can be planted anytime from spring through early fall. If planting in hot weather, provide ample water, and shade the clumps with cardboard boxes or bushel baskets. Daylilies' bareroot divisions are usually shipped in spring or early fall.

WHERE TO PLANT

Daylilies tolerate a wide range of soils and full sun to light shade. For the best results, choose moist, well-drained, average to fertile soil in full sun. Plant in perennial beds in drifts or groups of three.

Daylilies can also be used to mass with shrubs, to cover banks, to edge driveways, and to deal with problem areas where a tough plant is needed.

How to Plant

Plant daylilies 2 to 3 ft. apart, depending on the ultimate size of the selection. Dig a hole twice as wide as the pot, and position the plant so that the soil level is the same as it was in the pot. Fill in with soil around the roots about halfway up, firm gently, and water well. Add more soil to completely fill the hole. Water regularly until plants are established. Mulch to conserve moisture.

Advice for Care

Daylilies are long-lived, easy to grow, and generally problem-free. Although they are drought-tolerant once established, they prefer moist soil. Water during dry periods. Daylilies rarely need division but are so durable that they may be divided at almost any time during the growing season. The best time is in spring, when the foliage is just emerging. Dig them up, and pull or slice them apart. One way to do this is with two spading forks held back to back. Insert them in the clump and then pry them and the clump apart. Add organic material to enrich the soil, then replant divisions and keep them well watered. Remove faded flowers daily to keep the plants well groomed. The larger the flower, the more unappealing the faded flowers become. This is a good first gardening job for a preschooler, although you may lose a few buds in the process.

Additional Information

Daylily foliage can start to look tired later in the season. Pull and remove browning foliage, or shear brown tips if desired. Remove flower stalks after the flowers have finished.

Additional Species, Cultivars, or Varieties

Consider color, size of flower, stem height, time of bloom, and the amount you want to spend when selecting daylilies. As with hostas and peonies, it's hard to make specific cultivar recommendations because there are so many to choose from. 'Bitsy' is a small-flowered trumpet that begins blooming in early summer. The blooms of 'Prairie Blue Eyes' (28 in.) are large and purple-pink. The old favorite daylily 'Hyperion', with large yellow flowers, blooms in mid- to late summer on 40-in. stems. Or, for a change of pace, try one of the species daylilies. *Hemerocallis dumortieri* has funnel-shaped fragrant flowers that are a light orange-yellow, and its overall height is 18 to 24 in.

Garden Phlox

Phlox paniculata

Height: 3 to 3¹/₂ ft.
Flowers: Pink, white, lavender, red
Bloom Period: Early to late summer
Zones: 3, 4, 5, 6
Light Requirement:

Garden phlox is the flamboyant prima donna of the summer garden. With its bright colors and large, pyramidal heads, phlox is often considered the backbone of the summer border. It does require some tending, however. Phlox is often hit hard by powdery mildew, which turns its leaves grey and dusty-looking and can make it a garden liability rather than an asset. Spraying is an option but is probably not worth the effort for most gardeners. Use thinning, proper spacing, frequent division, watering at ground level, and the selection of resistant cultivars. If these measures don't solve the mildew problem, try another perennial in that location. Meadow phlox, *Phlox maculata*, is more resistant, though still not immune, to mildew. Its flowering panicle is more cone-shaped, and the foliage is narrow, leathery, and a rich, dark glossy green. The cultivar 'Miss Lingard' has earlier beautiful white flowers and has been in cultivation for more than 80 years. 'Omega' has white flowers with a pink eye, and 'Alpha' is lavender-pink. If phlox grows well for you, take advantage of its colorful July and August blossoms by combining garden phlox with the cool airy spires of Russian sage and balloonflower. It is also excellent in combination with shasta daisies, daylilies, coreopsis, boltonia, heliopsis, globe thistle, and purple coneflowers.

WHEN TO PLANT
Plant container-grown phlox in the spring.

WHERE TO PLANT
Choose locations with moist, well-drained, fertile soil in full sun. Plants must have moisture and good air circulation to avoid powdery mildew. Use in perennial beds, borders and cottage gardens.

HOW TO PLANT
Plant garden phlox 2 to 3 ft. apart. Plant taller selections farther apart. Don't crowd plants. Dig a hole twice as wide as the pot, and

position the plant so that the soil level is the same as it was in the pot. Fill in with soil around the roots about halfway up, firm gently, and water well. Add more soil to completely fill the hole. Water regularly until plants are established. Mulch to conserve moisture.

ADVICE FOR CARE

Phlox needs special attention to be an asset in the garden. Provide ample moisture, and water deeply during dry spells but avoid wetting the foliage, which encourages powdery mildew. Fertilize clumps in early spring with an application of general fertilizer (10-10-10) or a layer of compost. Additional side-dressing with fertilizer later in the season will promote strong growth and flowering. Deadhead to avoid self-sown seedlings, which won't resemble the parent plant. Regular deadheading may encourage a second flush of flowers. Phlox clumps should be divided every 2 to 4 years. Dig clumps, and divide the fibrous-rooted crowns into sections with a sharp spade. Take only vigorous divisions from the outside of the clump, and discard the weak and unproductive center. Augment the soil with plenty of well-rotted compost or other organic soil amendments. Replant at the same level at which they were growing, and keep well watered.

ADDITIONAL INFORMATION

Clumps of phlox should be thinned early in the season to improve air circulation and to direct the plant's energy into a few impressive and strong stems. When foliage is about 6 to 8 in. tall, remove all the small and weak stems, and thin the remainder to about 5 to 6 stems.

ADDITIONAL SPECIES, CULTIVARS, OR VARIETIES

If you wish to grow garden phlox, experiment with the cultivars that will perform the best in your garden. The spectacular cultivar 'Mt. Fujiyama', with its trusses of white flowers, may be mildew-free in some gardens or even in some years. Other years it is unsightly in the Lansing area. A gardener with a view of Lake Superior reports no problems there with mildew on phlox, however. In other words, it's impossible to make blanket recommendations. Seek out resistant cultivars. 'David', a tall (to 4 ft.) phlox with enormous heads of fragrant white flowers and thick dark green leaves, appears to be mildew-resistant. Try the cultivars of meadow phlox, *Phlox maculata*, mentioned above. 'Miss Lingard' is especially nice. A completely different phlox is the well-loved moss phlox or moss pink, *Phlox subulata*. It forms semi-evergreen mats of prickly foliage and creates brilliant splashes of color in early spring. These need full sun and well-drained soil.

Goat's Beard

Aruncus dioicus

Height: 4 to 7 ft.
Flowers: White
Bloom Period: Early to midsummer
Zones: 3, 4, 5, 6
Light Requirement:

A fine North American native, goat's beard has splendid foliage; its sheer size makes it an impressive addition to any shady garden. Goat's beard offers a combination of outstanding features that make it valuable in a mixed perennial planting. When the blooms of spring have passed and summer is approaching, goat's beard produces an impressive display of creamy white flowers on tall branches, a graceful addition to a distinctly shrubby plant. Goat's beard thrives in moist areas and is perfect for a pond planting or near the water's edge where its roots can draw upon a plentiful water supply. The ultimate size of goat's beard (4 to 7 ft.) makes it ideal for a grand accent or the back of the border. A mass planting spills forth a frothy bloom that brightens the dimmer areas of a woodland garden. The attractive dark green compound foliage adds mass and structural interest. Combined with hosta, Solomon's seal, and other perennials, goat's beard creates a dynamic textural contrast. Male and female flowers appear on separate plants and have different bloom characteristics. The male flowers are more showy with the upright plumes that make a grand display. The female blooms are pretty but bend with the weight of newly developing seeds. When you purchase a goat's beard, you take your chances. There is no way to identify the sex from a clump of foliage! If given enough moisture, goat's beard will grow well in a full sun perennial border. Nothing can compare to its best use as a tall highlight for the woodland border. Few plants have such a refined architectural stature, and habit.

WHEN TO PLANT

Plant container-grown goat's beard in the spring or fall.

WHERE TO PLANT

Choose a location with partial shade and a moist, well-drained, humus-rich soil. While goat's beard tolerates sun, it will languish in a hot, dry site and require frequent irrigation. Put it to its best use in a lightly shaded garden or a rich, moist location that receives morning sun and afternoon shade. Use it as an accent plant in a woodland garden, a tall specimen for the shady border, or a foundation plant near the house, or mass it with shrubs.

How to Plant

For a mass planting, space goat's beard 4 to 5 ft. apart. Dig a hole twice as wide as the pot, and position the plant so that the soil level is the same as it was in the pot. Fill in with soil around the roots about halfway up, firm gently, and water well. Add more soil to completely fill the hole. Water regularly until plants are established. Add mulch to conserve moisture.

Advice for Care

Sited correctly, goat's beard is trouble-free. Water during dry spells. Goat's beard forms a tough, woody crown and generally does not need division. Mature clumps can be divided with significant effort, but this is generally not needed to maintain the plant's vigor. Female plants produce numerous seedlings that can be transplanted to other areas of the garden if desired. Female flowers can be cut and dried for flower arrangements.

Additional Information

With its love of moist soils, consider planting goat's beard with Siberian iris, *Iris sibirica*. The sword-like foliage of the iris combines wonderfully with the divided compound foliage of the goat's beard. The dark foliage also contrasts well with the bold blue-scalloped leaves of *Hosta* 'Halcyon' and the vase-shaped hosta called 'Krossa Regal'. The hosta's pale lavender-blue flowers are enhanced by the handsome foliage of the *Aruncus*.

Additional Species, Cultivars, or Varieties

'Kneiffii' is an exceptional cultivar with finely divided foliage and a smaller stature, reaching only 2^1/$_2$ to 3 ft. It has creamy white plumes in early summer. Grow it in light shade with the peach-leaf bellflower and pale pink hardy geraniums (*Geranium sanguineum* var. *striatum*). *Aruncus aethusifolius*, a diminutive Korean goat's beard reaching only 1 ft. in height, has finely dissected foliage and creamy white flowers. Place it in partial shade in the front of the border or with other woodland plants. This dwarf goat's beard develops brilliant fall color where it receives some sun.

Goldenrod

Solidago species and hybrids

Height: 2 to 5 ft.
Flowers: Yellow
Bloom Period: Late summer to fall
Zones: 3, 4, 5, 6
Light Requirement:

More than 35 species of goldenrod grow in Michigan, creating a golden glow over meadows and hillsides late in the season. With all the beauty goldenrod brings to our natural landscape, this showy native is often maligned in the garden as an undesirable weed that causes hay fever. It doesn't. Reconsider this natural beauty, and welcome goldenrod into your garden. Grow it as the Europeans do in formal perennial beds, or use it in natural areas with asters and grasses. Many hybrid cultivars, most developed in Europe, are excellent garden plants. They offer compact habits and showy plumed clusters of golden yellow from later summer into fall. They combine naturally with aster, boltonia, and ornamental grasses and are the best choice for the formal perennial border or bed. Species of goldenrod are well suited for planting in meadows, large "wild" borders, and naturalized areas. Be careful when choosing a species goldenrod. Find out first if it has a clumping or running habit. Some goldenrods are well behaved, but others can be assertive spreaders. Nonetheless, many of our native goldenrod species are fit for garden use. The prairie or stiff goldenrod, *Solidago rigida*, growing from 3 to 5 ft., is one of the best species of goldenrod to grow in the garden. It has large flat-topped clusters of golden yellow flowers and reddish fall color. This golden native grows in the southern half of the Lower Peninsula in prairies, dry fields, and roadsides. The rough-leaved goldenrod, *Solidago rugosa*, is another good clump-forming species for the garden. The yellow flowers appear on arching sprays on 2¹/₂- to 3-ft. plants. A new cultivar called 'Fireworks' has a striking horizontal blooming habit. The rough-leaved goldenrod is more tolerant of moist soils and appreciates water during dry periods.

WHEN TO PLANT

Plant container-grown goldenrod in the spring.

WHERE TO PLANT

Plant in average, well-drained soil in full sun. Sandy or loamy soil is preferred; rich soil may lead to floppy growth. Most species and hybrids of goldenrod are drought-tolerant. Use in perennial beds, meadow or prairie gardens, and natural areas or along rustic fences or with ornamental grasses.

How to Plant

Plant goldenrod 18 to 36 in. apart, depending on the species or cultivar. Dig a hole twice as wide as the pot, and position the plant so that the soil level is the same as it was in the pot. Fill in with soil around the roots about halfway up, firm gently, and water well. Add more soil to completely fill the hole. Water regularly until plants are established.

Advice for Care

Goldenrod properly sited will need no special care. Watering and fertilization can lead to soft, weak growth, and plants will need staking to stay upright. A few goldenrods, native to moister areas, appreciate water during drought. Many goldenrods produce self-sown seedlings. Weed them out in spring. Goldenrod may need division to rejuvenate the plant or control its spread. Most of the garden selections are not rapid spreaders. Do this in the spring. Dig clumps, and split them into pieces with a sharp spade or old kitchen knife. Replant vigorous pieces from the outside of the clumps, and discard the unproductive middle. Keep new divisions well watered until established.

Additional Information

Although it is widely believed to cause hay fever and allergies, goldenrod has heavy pollen that is transported by bees, not the wind. Ragweed, a more inconspicuous plant that blooms at the same time as goldenrod, is the real culprit.

Additional Species, Cultivars, or Varieties

Showy goldenrod, *Solidago speciosa*, has long wands of golden yellow. Many hybrid goldenrods are suitable for Michigan gardens. They have compact habits, showy flowers, and less tendency to self-sow. A few good ones are 'Goldenmosa' (2 to 3 ft.), which blooms in late summer; 'Peter Pan' (2 to 3 ft.), with showy yellow flowers in early fall; 'Cloth of Gold' (18 to 24 in.), a dwarf selection with deep yellow flowers; and 'Golden Thumb' (12 to 14 in.), a very short, front-of-the-border goldenrod. × *Solidaster luteus* is a cross between aster and goldenrod with tiny soft yellow daisies. It is widely grown as a florist's cut flower.

Heliopsis

Heliopsis helianthoides ssp. *scabra*

Other Names: Ox-eye Sunflower, Sunflower Heliopsis
Height: 3 to 4 ft.
Flowers: Bright yellow, orange-yellow
Bloom Period: Early to late summer
Zones: 3, 4, 5, 6
Light Requirement:

For a blast of eye-popping yellow-orange, plant heliopsis in a sunny border or island garden. This plant—native to Michigan prairies, meadows, and roadsides—has sunflower-like flowers and a long season of bloom, from July to September. Heliopsis has gold-orange daisy flowers with raised centers. Like the bold and brassy shades of *Rudbeckia* 'Goldsturm' and the other bright daisies of summer, it can be tricky to combine with the garden's more subdued colors without blasting them out of the water. Still, it is useful to provide long-lasting and bright color to the summer garden. Add heliopsis to parts of the garden that peaked in June. The vibrant flowers add late color to plantings of blue false indigo and blue star. Or to mimic the yellow-orange and purple combination found in prairies, use it with blazing star and purple coneflowers. Tempering these combos liberally with ornamental grasses will make the colors less jarring. Specific cultivars of heliopsis are preferable for garden use because they are more compact and upright and less coarse in appearance. 'Summer Sun' (2 to 3 ft.) is easy to grow. More possible combinations with heliopsis in a hot-colored summer garden are sneezeweed, butterflyweed, threadleaf coreopsis, daylilies, and 'Lucifer' crocosmia, as well as the ornamental grasses such as feather reed grass and switch grass.

WHEN TO PLANT
Plant container-grown heliopsis in the spring.

WHERE TO PLANT
Choose locations with full sun and well-drained, average soil. Heliopsis is adaptable to a wide range of soils including clay, sand, and poor soils, and it is also drought-tolerant. Clumps may sprawl

in moist, rich soil. Plant for intense color in perennial border and island beds, meadow plantings, and cutflower gardens and with ornamental grasses.

How to Plant

Plant heliopsis 2¹/2 to 3 ft. apart. Dig a hole twice as wide as the pot, and position the plant so that the soil level is the same as it was in the pot. Fill in with soil around the roots about halfway up, firm gently, and water well. Add more soil to completely fill the hole. Water regularly until plants are established.

Advice for Care

Sunflower heliopsis is trouble-free but will need division for rejuvenation when stems become crowded and flower production decreases. This could happen in 3 to 4 years. In the spring when the foliage is just emerging, dig up the clumps, and split them into pieces with a sharp spade. Lifting large clumps out of the ground can be moderately difficult. Replant vigorous pieces at the same level at which they were growing. Water well until established. Deadheading (removing the old flowers) is necessary to improve heliopsis's appearance and to increase the flowering period. Taller forms may profit from staking.

Additional Information

The gold-orange flowers on tall stems make excellent cut flowers. Plants often self-sow, although not to excess.

Additional Species, Cultivars, or Varieties

These cultivars are superior for the garden: 'Summer Sun' (3 to 4 ft.) has a long blooming period and comes true from seed. 'Karat' (3 to 4 ft.) is a single-flowered selection. A new German cultivar called 'Ballerina' (3 to 4 ft.) has semi-double flowers and a blooming period that approaches 3 months. 'Incomparabilis' (2 to 3 ft.) is shorter and has orange-yellow semi-double flowers. 'Golden Plume' (3 to 3¹/2 ft.) has full double flowers.

Hosta

Hosta species and hybrids

Other Name: Plantain Lily
Height: 6 to 48 in.
Flowers: White, lavender
Bloom Period: Midsummer
  to late summer
Zones: 3, 4, 5, 6
Light Requirement:

Along with daylilies, hostas are getting plenty of attention these days as easy-to-grow, dependable perennials for Michigan gardens. Although they have attractive, sometimes fragrant flowers on tall stems, hostas are usually more prized for their foliage and the ability to bring color and interest to shady corners of the garden. With leaves in greens, blues, chartreuse, and variegated colors as well as various textures, hostas form clumps ranging from just a few inches to several feet wide. They make a bold statement in a perennial bed, under trees, along a shaded walkway, or around a brick patio. Some leaves are puckered or veined so much they look as if they had been quilted. Edges may be smooth or wavy. From the array of plants suitable for shade, hostas emerge as among the best. They are long-lived and rarely require division. They are hardy and attractive from late spring through fall, often turning an attractive gold in autumn. Their clumps enlarge, but they are never invasive. The variegated forms, especially, bring light into the garden. Although attractive on their own, their chief use is as a contrast to fine-textured denizens of the shade such as ferns, astilbe, fringed bleeding heart, and wild blue phlox. Hostas make a valuable cover for early spring bulbs and spring woodland plants, which often disappear after they flower. Hostas are also useful as a groundcover under a specimen tree or shrub.

WHEN TO PLANT
Plant bareroot plants in the spring. Plant container-grown hosta at anytime during the growing season. Provide plenty of moisture to plants in the heat of summer.

WHERE TO PLANT
Choose locations with moist, well-drained, humus-rich soil in partial to full shade. Add well-rotted compost or other organic amendments to light or infertile soil. Some hostas will tolerate more sun, but most do best in partial shade. Hostas are bold additions to woodland gardens, shady perennial beds, foundation beds, and

edges of ponds and pools. They may also be used as edging plants and groundcovers. Large specimens create a dramatic accent.

How to Plant

Space small hostas 1¹/₂ to 2 ft. apart and large ones 2, 3, or even 4 ft. apart, depending on the cultivar. Avoid planting too close. Dig a hole twice as wide as the pot, and position the plant so that the soil level is the same as it was in the pot. Fill in with soil around the roots about halfway up, firm gently, and water well. Add more soil to completely fill the hole. Water regularly until plants are established. Use mulch to conserve moisture.

Advice for Care

Hostas planted in the appropriate location will need little care. Water during hot, dry weather. Although hostas rarely need it, division is an inexpensive way to increase your supply of plants. Divide in spring as the hostas' fat shoots emerge. Dig up the clumps, and cut them into pieces with a large sharp knife. Replant at the same level as which they were growing. Water new divisions frequently. Slugs can be a problem in moist, shaded areas. Set out traps such as moist newspaper, an old board, or cabbage leaves. Check the undersides daily, and destroy the prisoners to get populations under control. Another method is to set out shallow pans of beer at night to attract and drown the slugs.

Additional Information

Flower stalks should be removed after bloom in highly visible areas if desired.

Additional Species, Cultivars, or Varieties

'Sum and Substance' (30 in.) is a wide-spreading plant with chartreuse-gold leaves. It tolerates more sun than many other hostas. 'Krossa Regal' (36 in.) is an impressive, vase-shaped mound with bluish-gray-green foliage that is best in the shade. It is named for the late Gus Krossa of Saginaw. 'Gold Standard' (18 to 22 in.) has gold leaves with green edges. It is good in part sun as well as shade. 'Gold Standard' was introduced by the late Pauline Banyai of Madison Heights. The fragrant white flowers of 'Royal Standard' (24 to 36 in.) are noteworthy, along with its rich green foliage. *Hosta sieboldiana* 'Elegans' is a classic shade plant with large gray-green leaves. It forms clumps about 4 ft. wide. *Hosta plantaginea* is the old-fashioned, fragrant plantain lily with shiny green leaves and large, waxy, fragrant white flowers in mid- to late summer.

PERENNIALS

Japanese Anemone

Anemone × hybrida

Other Name: Hybrid
Anemones
Height: 3 to 4 ft.
Flowers: White, pink
Bloom Period: Late summer
to early fall
Zones: 5, 6
Light Requirement:

Japanese hybrid anemones add an element of surprise to the garden. For most of the year, they remain a low clump of attractive but unremarkable foliage. But just when the garden is gearing down, hybrid anemones burst on the scene with hundreds of startlingly spring-like flowers in shades of pink, rose, and white. Hybrid anemones never fail to get noticed. The most useful perennials display attractive foliage, even when flowers are nowhere to be seen, and hybrid anemones are a model example. The divided leaves are handsome, bold, and textured, and they reach a height of 1 to 1½ ft. The foliage is late to start growing in spring but stays attractive all season. In late summer, Japanese anemone's 3- to 4 ft.-tall branching stems push up, topped with round silvery-furred buds. These open to reveal the elegant, yet simple, flowers, single or double, with pink or white petals surrounding a green button and yellow stamens. The flowers sway in the breeze from late summer until the first frost. Of course, no plant is perfect. Hybrid anemones have a spreading habit, but most cultivars are more friendly than bothersome. There are always extras to share, and many a gardening friendship has been strengthened with the gift of a clump or two lifted during spring cleanup. Grow anemones in moist and fertile, well-drained soil in sun or a bit of shade. Combine the late flowers with ornamental grasses and other fall bloomers. Try the elegant white 'Honorine Jobert' in front of the rich fall color of switch grass. Or create a spring-like color scheme with the pink 'Queen Charlotte', blue 'Professor Kippenburg' asters, and the abundant pink daisies of 'Clara Curtis' chrysanthemum. Hybrid anemones are superior for providing a late accent to a garden that peaked in the spring.

WHEN TO PLANT

Plant anemones in the spring. Container-grown plants can be planted later if given adequate moisture.

Where to Plant

Choose a location with rich, moist soil in sun or light shade. Hybrid anemones don't like a hot, dry site and will tolerate heavier soils. Too much shade will cause the flowering stalks to sprawl. Take advantage of this plant's spreading nature by planting it as ground-cover with other spreading perennials.

How to Plant

Plant hybrid anemones 2 ft. apart. Dig a hole twice as wide as the pot, and position the plant so that the soil level is the same as it was in the pot. Fill in with soil around the roots about halfway up, firm gently, and water well. Add more soil to completely fill the hole. Water regularly until plants are established. Add an organic mulch to conserve moisture.

Advice for Care

Water anemones during dry spells. In humus-rich soils, fertilization may not be necessary. A light application of fertilizer in poorer soil is beneficial. The rhizomes are attractive to rodents such as voles. In the spring, control any plants that have spread into undesirable areas by digging. Clumps can also be divided at this time. Often the soil falls away from the roots, and you are left with smallish pieces. These will take a few years to develop into mature clumps.

Additional Information

In Michigan's Zone 5 areas, hybrid anemones will occasionally get nipped by an early frost. A winter mulch may allow some Zone 4 gardeners to overwinter hybrid anemones. Nevertheless, early frost can be a problem in Zones 4 and 5.

Additional Species, Cultivars, or Varieties

These cultivars have performed well in Michigan: 'Honorine Jobert' (3 to 4 ft.) is a single white heirloom cultivar that has been unsurpassed for more than 100 years. 'Whirlwind' (3 ft.) has many semi-double white flowers. 'Queen Charlotte' (3 ft.), another favorite, has 4-in. silvery pink semi-double flowers, while the blooms of 'Prince Henry' (2 ft.) are deep rose-pink and semi-double. *Anemone tomentosa* 'Robustissima' (4 ft.) has pale pink flowers that appear earlier than the hybrid anemones. An aggressive spreader, it's best used where it can run—for example, as a groundcover in front of a rustic fence.

Lady's Mantle

Alchemilla mollis

Height: 12 to 18 in.
Flowers: Chartreuse
Bloom Period: Late spring to early summer
Zones: 3, 4, 5, 6
Light Requirement:

Lady's mantle is a gracious garden companion. Its attractive mounds of scalloped foliage and airy chartreuse flowers are rarely out of place. The frothy flowers of lady's mantle extend spring right into summer. The color, a fresh yellow-green reminiscent of the early flowers of some trees, complements any nearby plant. The foliage of lady's mantle is just as appealing as the flowers. Rounded light-green leaves emerge pleated and enlarge to form lobed fans with wavy edges. The surface is softly hairy. Raindrops bead up on the fuzzy foliage and shine like jewels. Their overlapping shapes and lax habit create an intriguing patterned carpet that sets off other perennials. Adaptable and easy to grow, lady's mantle will thrive just about anywhere except hot, dry sites. In fact, in moist soil and partial shade, it can self-sow with abandon, a trait either admired or disliked depending on your esteem for the plant. In a casual garden, lady's mantle adds serendipity, coming up between flagstones and under shrubs to great advantage. The flowers billow onto stone and brick walks. Lady's mantle intensifies any color scheme. It sets off deep tones, brights, pastels, and white with equal aplomb. Used in drifts and sweeps, lady's mantle is a mixer, unifying diverse plantings and pulling the design together. In a sunny, moist location, try lady's mantle in swaths with hardy geraniums and clustered bellflower as a groundcover. Plant pink tulips among the soft green foliage to highlight the display. A cloud of lady's mantle is a fine underplanting for Siberian iris. Or edge a stone path with lady's mantle, purple-foliaged coral bells, and astilbe in partial shade. A natural in a cottage garden, the frothy flowers complement shrub roses, spiked speedwell, peach-leaf bellflower, violet-blue hybrid salvia, cottage pinks, and ornamental onions.

WHEN TO PLANT

Plant container-grown lady's mantle in the spring.

WHERE TO PLANT

Choose locations with moist, well-drained, average to fertile soil in partial shade or sun. Add organic matter to sandy soils. Avoid hot, dry, sunny sites; the foliage will scorch. Lady's mantle is an attractive addition to perennial beds and borders, herb gardens, lightly shaded woodland gardens, and cottage gardens. Mass it as a groundcover with other perennials, or use it as an informal edging for brick or stone paths. It will sprawl, so in a bed bordering the lawn, plant lady's mantle some distance from the edge.

HOW TO PLANT

Plant lady's mantle 2 ft. apart. Dig a hole twice as wide as the pot, and position the plant so that the soil level is the same as it was in the pot. Fill in with soil around the roots about halfway up, firm gently, and water well. Add more soil to completely fill the hole. Water regularly until plants are established. Mulch to conserve moisture.

ADVICE FOR CARE

Lady's mantle needs little special care. Water plants in full sun during dry spells. Clumps rarely need division, but division is easily accomplished in early spring. Dig clumps, split into pieces with a sharp spade, and replant. Keep new divisions moist. A layer of mulch will assist with this. In sunny locations, clumps may begin to look unkempt. Plants can be prettied up by the removal of old foliage; in several weeks, new foliage will grow.

ADDITIONAL INFORMATION

Lady's mantle self-sows abundantly in moist, partly shaded locations. Young plants are easy to move, or remove the flowering stems before they set seed to prevent self-sowing. The flowers of lady's mantle are excellent for cutting and for drying. The chartreuse flowers complement any color scheme, and the airy sprays can be used like baby's breath to fill in an arrangement. When dried, the flowers retain a pale green color. Pick stems before the flowers begin to brown, and hang upside down in a well-ventilated location until dry.

ADDITIONAL SPECIES, CULTIVARS, OR VARIETIES

Two small lady's mantles are interesting additions to the garden. *A. erythropoda* (6 in.) has sprays of tiny little chartreuse flowers and gray-green scalloped leaves. *A. conjuncta* is just 8 in.

Lamb's Ears

Stachys byzantina

Other Name: Lamb's Tongue
Height: 12 to 15 in.
Flowers: Red-purple
Bloom Period: Late spring
  to early summer
Zones: 4, 5, 6
Light Requirement:

Who can resist petting the fuzzy silver leaves of lamb's ears? They form dense, woolly velvet mats that almost glow in some lights, beckoning both youngsters and grown-ups to touch. Their alternate common name—lamb's tongue—perhaps more aptly describes the shape of the leaves, which remain attractive all season, although the foliage is at its best in spring. As spring turns to early summer, the square flowering stalks bear small rosy purple flowers in furry, chunky clusters. The stems may turn floppy and need to be removed. If you find the flower stalks unattractive, look for lamb's ears cultivars that are free, or nearly free, of flowers. Use lamb's ears, which spread by creeping fibrous-rooted rhizomes, with other plants that have silvery or bluish foliage, such as lavender, creeping thyme, and the prickly texture and steely blue-gray color of sea hollies. It is also attractive with purple fennel and the pale shades of the Galaxy hybrid yarrows. Russian sage, catmint, pearly everlasting, salvia, blue oat grass, and star-of-Persia are other good companions. Try lamb's ears growing beneath shrub roses with hardy geraniums.

When to Plant

Plant container-grown lamb's ears in the spring.

Where to Plant

Choose locations with light, sandy soil and full sun for the healthiest growth. Lamb's ears will also grow well in average to rich loamy soil but will be prone to rot in heavy, poorly drained sites. Plants are drought-tolerant. Use lamb's ears in perennial gardens, dry gardens, and cottage gardens, under shrub roses, and as edging for a brick or stone path.

How to Plant

Plant lamb's ears 1 to 2 ft. apart. Dig a hole twice as wide as the pot, and position the plant so that the soil level is the same as it was in

the pot. Fill in with soil around the roots about halfway up, firm
gently, and water well. Add more soil to completely fill the hole.
Water regularly until plants are established.

ADVICE FOR CARE

Deadhead the flower stalks as they begin to look unappealing. Some
gardeners who feel that the flowers detract from the silvery leaves
remove them immediately. The cultivar 'Silver Carpet' eliminates
this chore because it doesn't produce flowers. Lamb's ears are
drought-tolerant and rarely require irrigation. When watering, avoid
getting the foliage wet, which can promote foliar disease. Divide
clumps when they become woody and unproductive in the center or
are spreading into areas where they are not wanted. This is easy to
accomplish. In spring, dig up the clumps, and split them into pieces.
Use vigorous divisions from the edge of the clumps, and discard the
woody center. Replant at the same level at which they were growing, and water well. There will be lots of extra pieces to share or to
use in other areas of the garden. Division is usually needed every 3
to 4 years. Plants will need more frequent division in rich soil. Pieces
of lamb's ears can be separated easily from the mother plant without
lifting the entire clump. Just use a sharp spade to sever a piece, and
fill in the hole with soil.

ADDITIONAL INFORMATION

In the spring, plants will need a little grooming to look their best.
Gently pull out any brown and unattractive foliage. In hot and
humid summers, lamb's ears can deteriorate, although the plant
performs well most years in Michigan.

ADDITIONAL SPECIES, CULTIVARS, OR VARIETIES

'Silver Carpet' (4 to 6 in.) is a non-flowering selection that forms a
dense, felt-like silver mass. Another beautiful lamb's ears is 'Helene
von Stein', also called 'Big Ears' in the trade. It forms 12-in. clumps
of broad foliage that is not as silver-white as typical lamb's ears but
a very soft silvery gray-green. It produces an occasional flower stalk
and is more adaptable to hot, humid weather. Try it with the pale
pink variety of bloody cranesbill, regal lilies, and deep pink shrub
roses. A lesser-known *Stachys* is the big betony, *Stachys macrantha*
(1 to 2 ft.). In contrast to lamb's ears, it has green crinkly foliage and
very attractive flowers. The pinkish-purple flowers are held in tiered
whorls, or groups that circle the stem.

Lavender

Lavendula angustifolia

Other Name: English Lavender
Height: 18 to 30 in.
Flowers: Lavender, purple
Bloom Period: Early summer to midsummer
Zones: 5, 6
Light Requirement:

Lavender has been cultivated for thousands of years for its fresh, clean, and singular fragrance. All parts of the plant are fragrant. What gardener can pass a lavender plant without reaching down to crush a leaf, releasing the refreshing scent? Lavender doesn't always make it into the perennial books. Often, it is included with the herbs or even with the shrubs. Whatever its classification, English lavender, *Lavendula angustifolia*, is an indispensable addition to the sunny garden. Lavender forms rounded, shrubby mounds of needle-like gray-green foliage. In early summer, hundreds of purple spikes on square stems transform the plants into a fragrant swell of purple. Lavender likes it hot and dry; in fact, the sunnier and the hotter the location, the more fragrant its flowers will be. To grow lavender well in Michigan, the soil must be light and well drained. Plants will not prosper in heavy, wet soil. Where the soil is less than well drained, raised beds are a good option. The billowing nature of lavender spills over, softening the edges. On its edge of hardiness in the colder parts of Zone 5, lavender offers northern Michigan gardeners more of a challenge. Good drainage seems to be the key for winter hardiness. Where the right conditions can be found, lavender needs no water or other tending beyond a yearly shearing or two. It can be planted as an edging for a rose garden or stone path, combined with other perennials, or massed as a groundcover. Anywhere silver-foliaged plants thrive, lavender is a willing companion. Combine it with cheddar pinks, lamb's ears, sea holly, and thyme to envelop a sunny patio. A gardener with a home near one of Michigan's many lakes planted a sandy hillside with lavender and butterflyweed. In midsummer, the planting is a breathtaking sea of deep purple-blue punctuated by brilliant orange flowers.

WHEN TO PLANT
Plant container-grown lavender in spring.

WHERE TO PLANT

Choose locations with sandy, well-drained soil and full sun for the best performance. Lavender will also grow in average, loamy, well-drained soil. Neutral or slightly alkaline soils are preferred. Good drainage is critical; avoid wet areas. Lavender grows very well in raised beds. Use it in perennial beds and borders, cottage gardens, herb gardens, and dry gardens, or use it for massing and edging.

HOW TO PLANT

Plant lavender 2 to 3 ft. apart. Dig a hole twice as wide as the pot, and position the plant so that the soil level is the same as it was in the pot. Fill in with soil around the roots about halfway up, firm gently, and water well. Add more soil to completely fill the hole. Water regularly until plants are established.

ADVICE FOR CARE

Lavenders grown in well-drained soil and sun are very long-lived and trouble-free. They don't require watering or fertilization. Division is inadvisable due to their woody shrub habit. In mid-spring when new growth is breaking, clip the shrubs back to live wood. Look for the green center portion of the stem. In harsh winters, this could mean cutting the clumps back to 1 or 2 in. above the ground. In mild winters, you still may wish to trim the plants way back to promote stocky, compact growth, particularly for a formal edging. Shear flowering stalks when the flowers are no longer attractive. Lavender will often have some repeat bloom later in the season. Plants are more susceptible to winter kill in heavy, wet soils. Plants have survived in Zone 4 of the Upper Peninsula where there is sandy soil and deep snow cover.

ADDITIONAL INFORMATION

To use lavender for sachets, scented pillows, or other uses, the stems must be harvested just as the whole spike shows color. This is a dubious job, removing the flowers just before their best show! Hang them upside down in small bunches in a well-ventilated location.

ADDITIONAL SPECIES, CULTIVARS, OR VARIETIES

The plain unselected English lavender, *Lavendula angustifolia*, is the best choice for massing, herbal harvests, and dry gardens. The differences among the plants add interest. The cultivars are especially useful when you need uniformity as for an edging, low hedge, or grouping in a perennial border. 'Hidcote' is a famous deep purple selection, growing from 18 to 22 in. 'Munstead Dwarf' is slightly lower, growing from 12 to 15 in. with lavender flowers. 'Jean Davis' is a pale whitish pink.

Lenten Rose

Helleborus orientalis

Other Name: Hellebore
Height: 15 to 18 in.
Flowers: White to deep
  purple and shades in
  between
Bloom Period: Very early to
  mid-spring
Zones: 4, 5, 6
Light Requirement:

Each year, gardeners watch and wait for signs of spring, and one of the plants greeting us early is the Lenten rose. In late February and early March, you can push the snow off the evergreen leaves of hellebore to discover the thick, tight flower buds patiently waiting for warmer temperatures. In due time, the flowers appear as nodding waxy blooms emerging directly from the crown. The flowers are made of petal-like sepals. The colors vary from soft white to rose to deep purple and often are stippled with crimson and maroon. The bloom period of the Lenten rose can extend beyond 8 weeks. The cool spring air preserves the flowers. Hellebores may be planted in clumps or grown as a single accent plant. The attractive evergreen foliage of Lenten rose is thick and leathery, and, when planted in mass, Lenten roses make an attractive groundcover. Plants are slow to develop, but, once they are established, they are tough customers, withstanding drought for short periods of time. They prefer moist shade. Lenten roses make fine companion plants with other herbaceous and woody plants, not only for the exquisite early flowers but especially for the dark evergreen leaves. Plant Lenten roses alongside the variegated dead nettle *Lamium maculatum* 'White Nancy' for a nice foliage combination. Or use the hellebore as an underplanting for the Koreanspice viburnum or other spring-blooming shrubs. Interesting foliage collages are created when combining the Lenten rose with the fine-textured foliage of the fringed bleeding heart, *Dicentra eximia*, or the silvery ferny foliage of the Japanese painted fern.

WHEN TO PLANT
Plant container-grown Lenten rose in the spring.

WHERE TO PLANT
Plant in a moist, humus-rich soil in shade to partial sun. Hellebores in general will not tolerate hot, dry conditions, and the foliage will

brown out and lose its luster in sunny exposed conditions. Add
Lenten roses to shady borders and woodland gardens, and tuck
them under shrubs and small flowering trees. Be sure to plant them
where they'll be noticed in early spring.

HOW TO PLANT

Space plants of Lenten rose $1^1/_2$ to 2 ft. apart. Dig a hole twice as
wide as the pot, and position the plant so that the soil level is the
same as it was in the pot. Fill in with soil around the roots about
halfway up, firm gently, and water well. Add more soil to completely fill the hole. Water regularly until plants are established.
Mulch to conserve moisture.

ADVICE FOR CARE

Water plants during extended dry periods. Remove any brown
foliage in early spring to allow for the development of new leaves.
Be careful; avoid clipping or damaging the flower buds that rest
close to the ground. Lenten rose expands slowly over time and takes
a few years to develop an impressive clump of evergreen foliage.
Division is possible but not recommended. Hellebore black spot can
be an occasional problem with hellebores. Dark spots appear on the
leaves, stems, and flowers, causing leaf yellowing, foliage loss, and
wilted flowers. Chemical controls are not recommended. Instead,
remove and discard infected leaves and flowers to control the
spread of the disease.

ADDITIONAL INFORMATION

In moist situations with a generous organic mulch, new seedlings
will appear at the base of clumps. These may be transplanted to
other areas in the garden or passed along to a gardening friend.

ADDITIONAL SPECIES, CULTIVARS, OR VARIETIES

New hybrids of Lenten rose offering a range of flower colors are
arriving from European breeders in unprecedented numbers. While
it is easy to become enamored with their resplendent beauty, time
will tell which selections are ultimately adaptable to our northern
climate. Many of them are listed under the name *Helleborus* ×
hybridus. The Christmas rose, *Helleborus niger*, can also be grown
in Michigan.

New England Aster

Aster novae-angliae

Height: 18 in. to 5 ft.
Flowers: Lavender-blue, pink, white
Bloom Period: Late summer to fall
Zones: 3, 4, 5, 6
Light Requirement:

In late summer, asters are a familiar sight along Michigan's roadsides. Perhaps because they are so common, Americans have overlooked their merit as garden plants. In Europe, though, this wild American has been long popular among gardeners, and it's beginning to increase in status in the United States as well. More than 25 different asters are native to Michigan. The New England aster, the well-known purple daisy, grows native in moist ground, in meadows and fields, as well as our wet prairies and fens. In nature, New England asters can be gangly, growing to 5 ft., but capable of generating a profusion of bloom. In the garden, New England asters are not carefree. They need fairly frequent division. Some are susceptible to mildew, and taller types may flop without pinching or staking. Early in the season, their appearance is green, leafy, and sometimes coarse. Still, their performance in the late summer and fall eclipses these shortcomings. Asters need sun and moist but well-drained soil. The taller types are suitable for natural gardens and the back of the border; shorter types can be used in the front. Cultivars and hybrids of New England aster are available that overcome some flaws. Combine asters with the similar hues of Japanese hybrid anemones, white boltonia, turtlehead, and showy stonecrop. Or bring the Michigan meadow to your garden—plant goldenrod and asters together.

WHEN TO PLANT
Plant container-grown asters in the spring or early summer.

WHERE TO PLANT
Choose locations with moist, normal to fertile soil in full sun. Asters like moist soil and tolerate heavier clay soils. Plant asters in borders, mixed plantings, and meadow or prairie-style gardens.

HOW TO PLANT
Plant New England asters 3 to 4 ft. apart. Smaller cultivars can be spaced closer. Don't crowd them; asters need good air circulation.

Dig a hole twice as wide as the pot, and position the plant so that the soil level is the same as it was in the pot. Fill in with soil around the roots about halfway up, firm gently, and water well. Add more soil to fill the hole. Water regularly until plants are established.

ADVICE FOR CARE
Water asters during drought and dry spells. Always water at the base of the plant; wet foliage creates a favorable environment for foliar disease. Division is necessary every 2 to 4 years to keep the plants vigorous. When the center of the clump starts to die, it's time to divide. Do this in the spring when the foliage is just beginning to grow. Dig up the clump, and divide with a spade or knife into healthy sections. Discard the unproductive middle. Replant divisions at recommended spacing, and water well until established. New divisions grow quickly and bloom the first year.

ADDITIONAL INFORMATION
Pinching keeps asters short, compact, and freely flowering. It is only necessary with the tall types. Pinch out the growing tip of each stem when it reaches 6 in. high. In formal gardens, tall asters may need to be staked, but this is usually not necessary with full sun and the right plant choice. Try New England aster in a prairie-style garden with black-eyed Susan, yellow coneflower, and native grasses.

ADDITIONAL SPECIES, CULTIVARS, OR VARIETIES
'Purple Dome' is a mass of purple on compact plants. 'Purple Pixie' is another compact form. 'Alma Potschke' (3 to 3^1/2 ft.) has brilliant magenta flowers and a full rounded form. Try it with Russian sage, feather reed grass, and blue spirea. 'Honeysong Pink' (3 to 3^1/2 ft.) has clear rich pink flowers, and 'Hella Lacy' is a tall (3^1/2 ft.) royal purple selection. *Aster novi-belgii*, the New York aster, is native to the East Coast. Scads of cultivars originating in Europe exist. Some are more susceptible to mildew and other foliar diseases. A dwarf cultivar is the lavender-blue 'Professor Kippenburg' (12 in.). Its compact form and rich color make it ideal for the front of a perennial garden. Several other native Michigan asters are appealing garden residents. The flowers of the calico aster, *Aster lateriflorus* (4 ft.), have small white petals and rose-purple centers. The foliage darkens to plum color in September. Heath or white prairie aster, *Aster ericoides*, grows in prairies, marshy shores, meadows, and roadsides. Like the calico aster, it has a delicate effect from multitudes of tiny starry white flowers and small leaves on wiry stems. Heath aster tolerates dry soils. Cultivars are available in pink and blue.

Peach-leaf Bellflower

Campanula persicifolia

Height: 2 to 3 ft.
Flowers: Blue, white
Bloom Period: Early to
midsummer
Zones: 3, 4, 5, 6
Light Requirement:

Peach-leaf bellflower is full of old-fashioned charm. Its profuse and large, cup-shaped bells in blue or white rise above neat mats of bright-green leathery leaves. The flowering stems grow from 1 to 3 ft., each carrying a mass of delightful bells that are usually lavender-blue, China blue, or pure white. Neat folded buds open to reveal the idyllic flowers. After they bloom, the flowering stems may be cut back to promote later reblooming. Easy to grow in moist, well-drained, and somewhat fertile soil, peach-leaf bellflower is a welcome addition to a mixed planting of shrub roses, annuals, and perennials. Try blue- and white-flowered bellflowers with the hazy purple-blue of catmint and a pink rose such as 'Betty Prior' or 'Carefree Wonder'. Let the tall stems and pendant trumpets of regal lily rise above. Add small-flowered petunias and flowering tobacco or purple heliotrope for a nostalgic cottage garden mix. Peach-leaf bellflower makes beautiful drifts of color in sunny perennial borders with phlox and Russian sage, or in light shade with hardy geranium, hosta, and astilbe. Add it to areas where peonies and iris bloomed in June.

When to Plant

Plant container-grown peach-leaf bellflower in the spring. This is an easy plant to grow from the smaller cell-packs that may be available.

Where to Plant

Choose locations in moist, well-drained soil in full sun or light shade. Hot, dry sites will not do; evenly moist soil with a bit of shade is best. Plant in perennial beds, cutflower gardens, and cottage gardens and with shrub roses. The foliage, although somewhat attractive, is not a point of interest; narrow drifts and small groups achieve the best effect.

How to Plant

Plant peach-leaf bellflower 1½ to 2 ft. apart. Dig a hole twice as wide as the pot, and position the plant so that the soil level is the same as it was in the pot. Fill in with soil around the roots about halfway up, firm gently, and water well. Add more soil to completely fill the hole. Water regularly until plants are established.

Advice for Care

Water plants during drought. Deadhead (remove spent flowers as they fade), cutting back the whole stem to encourage rebloom on new stems. Plants may become crowded and lose vigor over the years and can be divided or replaced. The slowly spreading clumps can be divided every 3 to 4 years. Add organic material to the soil when dividing or replacing clumps.

Additional Information

Tall stems of bellflower, particularly in light shade, may be pounded in a heavy rainstorm. Salvage what you can by cutting the stems and bringing the beaten-down stems inside for an arrangement. Peach-leaf bellflower can self-sow, although this is not likely if you diligently deadhead. Flowers may or may not come true from seed. During fall cleanup, don't remove the basal foliage. It is evergreen.

Additional Species, Cultivars, or Varieties

'Telham Beauty' (3 to 4 ft.) is a tall, vigorous cultivar with large China blue flowers. The white forms are very attractive with blue- and purple-flowered perennials. 'Alba' is 2½ ft. tall with delicate white bells. Double forms are sold. These sacrifice simple charm for blowsy flowers. Many other bellflowers are easy garden plants. The Carpathian bellflower, *Campanula carpatica* (6 to 9 in.), is a low, mat-forming plant perfect for edging, rock gardens, and the front of perennial beds. Many types are available; all form charming bells on low tussocks of foliage. Popular seed-grown choices are 'Blue Clips' and 'White Clips' (6 to 8 in.). The clustered bellflower, *Campanula glomerata* (1 to 3 ft.), has clusters of purple starry bells on stiff stalks and a spreading nature. It offers early summer color and easy culture but not the charm of the plants mentioned above. Use it where its spread will be an advantage. Try drifts of clustered bellflower with lady's mantle and bloody cranesbill on a moist slope.

Peony

Paeonia lactiflora and hybrids

Height: 20 to 36 in.
Flowers: White, pink, red, single or double
Bloom Period: Late spring to early summer
Zones: 3, 4, 5, 6
Light Requirement:

Peonies are fragrant old-fashioned perennials that celebrate the arrival of early summer. The flowers are 3 to 6 in. wide and may be single, semi-double, or double—and full as fluffy petticoats. Japanese peonies have a single row of large petals. All these are the herbaceous peonies, which die back to the ground each winter. In contrast, tree peonies are woody plants that can reach 6 ft. tall. Even after the herbaceous peonies finish flowering, their glossy deep green foliage remains attractive into fall. The plants form mounds that are 20 to 36 in. tall and wide. Peonies may be used as specimens or as an herbaceous hedge or integrated into perennial borders. Newer cultivars as well as single peonies tend to bloom earlier and stand up better to wind and rain than older and double types of the common peony, *Paeonia lactiflora*. One of Michigan's most extensive plantings of old peonies, established in 1922, is at Nichols Arboretum in Ann Arbor. The beds are now renovated and filled with bloom in June. But for some years during the 1960s and 1970s, the peonies were ignored and actually mowed. Nevertheless, many original plants survived and recovered, a testament to this sturdy perennial's tenacity.

WHEN TO PLANT
Plant peonies in September.

WHERE TO PLANT
Peonies prefer full sun and deeply cultivated, well-drained soil that is moisture retentive and rich in organic material. Without adequate sun, peonies produce lush foliage but few flowers. They should not be planted where they will have to compete with tree roots. Peonies are long-lived, so good site preparation will pay off for decades.

HOW TO PLANT
Dig a hole at least three times the size of the roots, or about as big as a bushel basket. With the soil removed to form the planting hole,

work in a handful of fertilizer that is high in phosphorus and low in nitrogen. Replace and firm some of this soil in the hole so the peony won't settle when planted. Place the crown so the buds or "eyes" are facing upward. The depth is especially important when planting peonies. The buds should be 1 to 1$^{1}/_{2}$ in. below the soil surface. Peonies planted too deeply will not flower, and those planted too near the surface are prone to winter damage. Continue filling the planting hole, and water. Space peonies at least 3 ft. apart.

ADVICE FOR CARE

Deadhead or remove faded flowers. For the first winter after planting, mulch the peony after the ground freezes. Remove the mulch in early spring, taking care not to damage the new red growth. Water regularly. The roots need water as the buds develop. Peonies may be fertilized in early spring with a general food such as 10-10-10. Avoid high-nitrogen fertilizers, which stimulate foliage growth but not flowers. Peony cages or supports should be placed around the plants in spring as the peonies begin to grow. Remove peony foliage in the fall. Do not compost the leaves, which may contain botrytis blight. This causes streaked or discolored foliage. Remove any leaves that show these symptoms. A fungicide may be needed in severe cases. Move or divide peonies in September. Each division should have 3 to 5 eyes. Peonies resent being disturbed and may take 3 years to reach peak flower production.

ADDITIONAL INFORMATION

There are several reasons why peony buds may fail to open. These include inadequate moisture, unusually cool spring weather, too much shade, and too few nutrients. Peonies make beautiful cut flowers. They are also favorites of ants, which visit the buds seeking sugar.

ADDITIONAL SPECIES, CULTIVARS, OR VARIETIES

With the proper plant selection, it is possible to stretch the season of peony bloom to as long as 6 weeks. Fernleaf peony, *Paeonia tenuifolia* (20 in.), which has finely dissected foliage and bright red flowers, is among the earliest to bloom. A late peony is 'Elsa Sass' (30 in.), a fragrant white double. Tree peonies (*Paeonia suffruticosa*) are the epitome of elegance, reaching 4 to 6 ft. tall and displaying dozens of large flowers that tend to open just before old-fashioned double peonies.

Purple Coneflower

Echinacea purpurea

Height: 2 to 4 ft.
Flowers: Rose-pink, white
Bloom Period: Early to late
  summer
Zones: 3, 4, 5, 6
Light Requirement:

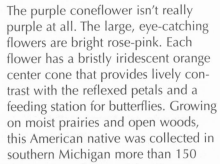

The purple coneflower isn't really purple at all. The large, eye-catching flowers are bright rose-pink. Each flower has a bristly iridescent orange center cone that provides lively contrast with the reflexed petals and a feeding station for butterflies. Growing on moist prairies and open woods, this American native was collected in southern Michigan more than 150 years ago but typically occurs to the south and west of the Great Lakes state. Native Americans have long used purple coneflower and its relatives for medicine, and today echinacea is enjoying a renewed popularity in health food stores as a treatment for the common cold. Plants form basal clumps of lance-shaped toothed foliage. The large daisy-style flowers are usually deep rose-pink, paler pink, or white. They appear in large quantities from early to late summer, growing to 3 or 4 ft. tall. The prominent prickly center cone glows orange. Outer petals are typically reflexed, but many cultivars have spreading petals, which gives the flower more of a flat daisy look. Purple coneflower isn't a graceful plant. The flowers are big and bold, the form stiffly upright, and the foliage coarse. It may not be tame, but it's wildly bright, easy to grow, and dependable. A favorite combination is purple coneflower with a lavender-blue cloud of Russian sage. Add the narrow gray-green foliage and airy white flowers of boltonia for even greater contrast. Team it with ornamental grasses, such as the flaxen mist of 'Golden Veil' tufted hair grass or switch grass. The orange center cone allows purple coneflower to both clash and blend with hot-colored flowers. In a meadow-style garden, the pink blooms add zip to the multitudes of yellow-orange daisies such as sunflower heliopsis, sneezeweed, and black-eyed Susan.

WHEN TO PLANT
Plant purple coneflower in the spring.

WHERE TO PLANT

Purple coneflower tolerates a wide range of soil types, including both dry and heavy soils. Moist, well-drained, average to rich soil is ideal. Full sun is best, although it will tolerate light shade for part of the day. Use purple coneflower in perennial beds, mixed plantings, cutting gardens, meadow-style gardens, and natural areas.

HOW TO PLANT

Plant purple coneflower 2 ft. apart. Dig a hole twice as wide as the pot, and position the plant so that the soil level is the same as it was in the pot. Fill in with soil around the roots about halfway up, firm gently, and water well. Add more soil to completely fill the hole. Water regularly until plants are established.

ADVICE FOR CARE

Purple coneflower is an undemanding garden resident. Plants are heat- and drought-tolerant and seldom need water. Fertilization is usually not necessary. The slowly increasing clumps rarely need division. Deadheading (removing the faded flowers) will prolong bloom. Later in the season, leave the flowers to develop into seed-heads, which provide fall and winter food for birds.

ADDITIONAL INFORMATION

Plants can self-sow, although this isn't a significant problem. These seedlings will bloom by the second or third year and will not be identical to the parent plant. For natural areas and meadows, this should not be a concern. In more formal gardens, weed out the seedlings.

ADDITIONAL SPECIES, CULTIVARS, OR VARIETIES

Many cultivars are available, and some are seed propagated. All are more ornamental or at least less variable than the species. Seed-propagated types include 'Bright Star' (30 in.), which has rose-red flowers with more horizontal petals; 'Bravado', with 4-in. flat daisies; and 'White Swan' (24 to 30 in.), a compact white form with copper-orange cones. These are propagated vegetatively: 'Magnus' (36 in.) has flat pink petals, and 'White Lustre' (30 in.) has white drooping petals and gold-orange cones. *Echinacea angustifolia* (2 ft.) and *Echinacea pallida* (3 to 4 ft.) have long, drooping pale pink petals. These species are the ones used most for medicinal purposes. The native yellow coneflower, *Ratibida pinnata* (4 to 5 ft.), has shuttlecock-like flowers with yellow petals drooping from a prominent central cone. This prairie plant has a natural if somewhat lanky grace.

Russian Sage

Perovskia atriplicifolia

Height: 3 to 4½ ft.
Flowers: Lavender-blue
Bloom Period: Early summer
  to fall
Zones: 5, 6
Light Requirement:

The delicate flowers of Russian sage, *Perovskia atriplicifolia*, create a lavender-blue haze above gray-green foliage in the garden. The flowering effect lasts for months, combining with purple coneflower in July and later with ornamental grasses in September. Russian sage's graceful 3- to 4-ft. stems hold thousands of small flowers, but its delicate appearance belies its ease of culture. At its best in groupings of three or more, Russian sage provides a light and airy backdrop for perennials such as daylily and 'Autumn Joy' sedum, mixes beautifully with pink shrub roses, and also works well in the foreground of a landscape bed. Russian sage needs full sun and good drainage for optimum growth; it is adaptable to a wide range of soil types. The dissected foliage has a noticeable odor when crushed, similar to but not as appetizing as culinary sage. It isn't used in the kitchen unless it appears in a floral arrangement—the delicate flowers on tall stems are perfect for cutting. Russian sage is a subshrub. It doesn't die back completely like most herbaceous perennials. It grows each year from woody branches near the base of the plant. The silvery white stems provide winter interest in the garden until spring.

WHEN TO PLANT
Container-grown Russian sage can be planted in spring or summer. Don't wait until fall. The roots need time to establish before winter. Bareroot plants should be planted in the spring.

WHERE TO PLANT
Russian sage thrives in full sun. Some shade is tolerable, but plants will lean toward the light and may sprawl. Plant drifts of Russian sage in perennial borders or in mixed plantings of annuals, perennials, and shrubs. Try them by a sunny patio or behind a bench with a full sun exposure.

How to Plant

Plant Russian sage 2 to 2¹/₂ ft. apart. Dig a hole twice as wide as the pot, and position the plant so that the soil level is the same as it was in the pot. Fill in with soil around the roots about halfway up, firm gently, and water well. Add more soil to completely fill the hole. Water regularly until plants are established. After that, plants are quite drought-tolerant.

Advice for Care

Don't cut down plants in the fall; leave the silvery stems for winter interest. Wait to cut back Russian sage until signs of new growth appear in the spring. At this time, remove with pruners any dead or weak branches, and cut remaining branches back, leaving 4 to 6 healthy buds. In an unusually cold winter, plants may die back to the ground and resprout from below soil level. Due to its shrub-like habit, division of Russian sage is unnecessary and inadvisable. Plants prefer soil on the lean side, so extra fertilization isn't necessary. There are no serious pest and disease problems. Good drainage and full sun will lead to healthy plants.

Additional Information

The extended blooming period of Russian sage, among the longest of any perennial, allows for a wide range of successful plant combinations. In July, combine the delicate texture of Russian sage with the larger flowers of purple coneflower, daylilies, and phlox. In August, the orange-yellow daisies of sunflower heliopsis and black-eyed Susan offer vivid contrast. Finally, in September, the hazy blue flowers and silvery stems of Russian sage glow in front of the burgundy foliage of red switch grass. Add 'Autumn Joy' sedum and white boltonia or pink New England asters for a memorable fall combination. Russian sage may also be grown in Zone 4 with the protection of a winter mulch. It will die back to the ground.

Additional Species, Cultivars, or Varieties

Several cultivars are available, offering uniformity and improved characteristics. 'Blue Spire' grows to 3 ft.; it has bluer flowers, deeply cut foliage, and a more erect habit. 'Filigran' (to 2¹/₂ ft.) has finely dissected leaves. 'Longin', a very upright selection, has silvery leaves that are not as divided. It's more formal but not as graceful in the garden. Russian sage may also be sold by nurseries under the name *Perovskia × suberba*. Most plants in cultivation are believed to be a hybrid of *P. atriplicifolia* and *P. abrotanoides*.

Salvia

Salvia × *superba*

Other Names: Hybrid Sage, Perennial Salvia
Height: 18 to 24 in.
Flowers: Violet, blue
Bloom Period: Late spring to midsummer
Zones: 4, 5, 6
Light Requirement:

Red, orange, and yellow flowers vie for attention in the garden. Hybrid perennial salvia doesn't use a hot-tempered display to get noticed; it coolly attracts admiring glances with its deep violet-blue pools of color. Perennial hybrid salvia or violet sage provides months of saturated purple-blue color on upright spikes. In late spring, its flowers are early enough to complement peonies or Siberian iris. But a few weeks later the purple flowers are at their peak, providing dramatic contrast for the yellow daisies of threadleaf coreopsis or the flat-topped clusters and ferny gray foliage of 'Coronation Gold' yarrow. Like these two, violet sage needs full sun to perform at its best. The dense spikes arise by the score from mounds of gray-green foliage. The flowers are effective for several months, and the spikes retain an attractive red-violet cast even after the flowers drop. The deep violet-blue of perennial salvia makes for electric contrast with bright yellow flowers. Add silver-foliaged plants such as 'Silver King' artemisia for a calming influence. Salvia's rich purple-blue is stunning with magenta, pink, and lavender, and it makes silver foliage shine. Try salvia 'May Night' with the intense pink flowers of bloody cranesbill, 'Bath's Pink' cheddar pinks, catmint, lamb's ears, and 'Valerie Finnis' artemisia.

When to Plant

Plant perennial salvia in the spring so the roots can become well established before winter.

Where to Plant

Choose locations with average to fertile, well-drained garden soil. Full sun is preferred, but light shade is tolerated. Hybrid salvia is tolerant of drought but performs best with adequate moisture. Plants in heavy soil and partial shade will not achieve their full potential and will sprawl. Avoid poorly drained sites. Use in formal and informal perennial borders and cottage gardens.

How to Plant

Plant perennial salvia 1¹/₂ to 2 ft. apart. Dig a hole twice as wide as the pot, and position the plant so that the soil level is the same as it was in the pot. Fill in with soil around the roots about halfway up, firm gently, and water well. Add more soil to completely fill the hole. Water regularly until plants are established. Young plants establish quickly and usually bloom well the first year.

Advice for Care

Correctly sited, hybrid perennial salvia will need little care other than removing the spent flower stalks. This deadheading will encourage a second flush of bloom. Cut back hard to the basal foliage. Salvia is drought-tolerant and will survive without supplemental irrigation, but water during drought may improve performance. Clumps seldom need division but may be divided in the spring. Carefully split clumps apart with a sharp spade or knife. New divisions take a few years to settle in and return to full performance.

Additional Information

These salvia are hybrids, and plants are sometimes sold as *Salvia nemerosa* or *Salvia sylvestris*. Deep snow cover—or, where it can't be relied upon, a winter mulch of evergreen boughs applied after the ground freezes—will help to overwinter plants in Zone 4.

Additional Species, Cultivars, or Varieties

'May Night' (18 to 24 in.) is a wonderful garden plant with deep violet-blue flowers on long spikes for an extended period. 'East Friesland' (20 to 24 in.) and 'Lubeca' (15 to 18 in.) are lower growing with purple flowers. 'Blue Hill' (20 in.) has flowers that are more blue than purple. Pink- and white-flowered forms are also offered. *Salvia verticillata* 'Purple Rain' (18 to 20 in.) has smoky purple flowers in whorls over wavy, heart-shaped gray-green foliage. Although not as showy as hybrid salvia, it flowers over a long period (July into early September) and has a spreading habit. The culinary sage, *Salvia officinalis,* has several selections that add wonderful foliage interest to sunny perennial beds, herb gardens, and containers. Look for them in the herb section of nurseries and catalogs. 'Icterina' has a lovely fresh combination of green and yellow-green. 'Tricolor' has sage-green foliage variegated with cream and pink-purple, and 'Purpurea' has green and purple foliage. They are evergreen and form a shrub-like mound. In spring, cut back to live wood to shape the plants. These colorful foliage plants have been hardy in Michigan's Zone 5.

Sedum 'Autumn Joy'

Sedum 'Autumn Joy'

Other Name: Showy
  Stonecrop
Height: 1 to 2 ft.
Flowers: Pink maturing to
  red-pink
Bloom Period: Midsummer
  through fall
Zones: 3, 4, 5, 6
Light Requirement:

Sedum 'Autumn Joy' is the kind of perennial that can earn a new gardener's confidence. It is undemanding and easy to grow, with attractive light green, fleshy foliage all summer. When it is in bud, the chunky heads resemble broccoli. This sedum's flowers attract bees and butterflies. By mid- to late summer, the flat heads of tiny pink flowers change to deep rose, open, and gradually mature to a rich mahogany color, remaining upright all winter, even when dusted with snow. In fact, this sedum is so trouble-free, it is becoming common in both home gardens and municipal plantings. It is often seen with black-eyed Susans, purple coneflower, and ornamental grasses, sometimes in beds adorned by spring bulbs for early-season color. Although these pairings are becoming almost routine, it's hard to hold overuse against a plant with as many positive attributes as sedum 'Autumn Joy'.

WHEN TO PLANT

Plant sedum 'Autumn Joy' from spring through early fall. Keep new plants well watered, particularly in hot weather, until established. Cut back tall plants for late-season planting.

WHERE TO PLANT

Choose locations with full sun and average soil. Plants will grow in fertile soil but will be taller and more prone to split open. Avoid poorly drained sites; good drainage is the key to success. Stonecrop is heat- and drought-tolerant. Use in the perennial border, mixed plantings, massing as in the New American garden style of landscaping, and dry gardens.

HOW TO PLANT

Plant 'Autumn Joy' 2 ft. apart. Dig a hole twice as wide as the pot, and position the plant so that the soil level is the same as it was in the pot. Fill in with soil around the roots about halfway up, firm gently, and water well. Add more soil to completely fill the hole. Water regularly until plants are established.

ADVICE FOR CARE

'Autumn Joy' stonecrop needs almost no input from the gardener. Clumps may get overcrowded and split open in the center, occurring more quickly in rich, moist soils. This is the sign to divide the clumps. Stonecrops are a cinch to divide. Lift the clumps in spring. They split apart easily with a sharp spade. Remove the unproductive center, and replant healthy, vigorous pieces from the outside of the clump. Replant, and keep well watered. Even small pieces with a bit of root will establish with little care.

ADDITIONAL INFORMATION

Plants in rich soil are inclined to get too tall. Pinch them back when shoots are 6 to 8 in. high to promote more compact growth. Aphids are attracted to the succulent stems but don't seem to bother the plants. Keep populations in check by washing them off with a direct stream of water. Cut back the dried seedheads in early spring to make way for new growth.

ADDITIONAL SPECIES, CULTIVARS, OR VARIETIES

Stonecrops offer the gardener a wide range of useful and easy-to-grow plants. Some are wonderful border plants, and others are suitable for groundcovers and rock walls. Experiment with several if you have full sun and good drainage. 'Brilliant', a selection of showy stonecrop *Sedum spectabile*, has dense, soft pink heads from late summer to early fall. *Sedum maximum* 'Atropurpureum' has very deep purple foliage. Several hybrids are excellent border subjects, offering attractive foliage coloring. *Sedum* 'Vera Jameson' (9 to 12 in.) has purplish gray-green leaves and dusky pink flowers. It is very nice with blue oat grass. *Sedum* 'Rosy Glow', also called 'Ruby Glow' (12 in.), has gray-green foliage tinged maroon and ruby-red flowers. *Sedum kamtschaticum* 'Weihenstephaner's Gold' flowers in late spring to midsummer with golden yellow clusters over dark green toothed leaves. It is an excellent plant for a groundcover in a sunny site and grows to about 8 in. Another great groundcovering stonecrop is the two-row sedum, *Sedum spurium*. The flowers are a deep rose-pink. Older foliage often takes on a burgundy-maroon color contrasting with the green rosettes of new foliage. 'Dragon's Blood' is a familiar purple-bronze form. Variegated types are available.

Siberian Bugloss

Brunnera macrophylla

Height: 12 to 18 in.
Flowers: Blue
Bloom Period: Mid- to late
   spring
Zones: 3, 4, 5, 6
Light Requirement:

Opening with the daffodils, the tiny sky blue starry flowers of Siberian bugloss deserve to be a standard feature in every spring garden. They resemble forget-me-nots held aloft on thin stalks, and the flowers continue to be attractive for 3 to 4 weeks. Unlike some other spring charmers, Siberian bugloss continues to play a role in the summer garden, even after its flowers are gone. The plants grow as clumps in partial shade, and their showy, coarse dark green leaves gradually enlarge, reaching up to 8 in. across by summer's end. The leaves are shaped like hearts. Easy to grow in partial shade, Siberian bugloss requires little care other than the occasional division. It excels in a wooded setting, as a groundcover under shrubs, and in any place where it can naturalize. The coarse and textured foliage functions as does that of hosta in shade, providing contrast with the more common finely textured foliage of other shade-loving plants such as ferns, astilbes, and fringed bleeding hearts. Siberian bugloss may also be used with daffodils, hostas, pulmonaria, variegated Solomon's seal, and epimediums for a gorgeous display.

WHEN TO PLANT
Plant container-grown Siberian bugloss in the spring.

WHERE TO PLANT
Choose locations with moist, well-drained, humus-rich soil in partial shade. Siberian bugloss will tolerate some sun but may need more frequent watering in sunny locations. Use it in woodland gardens, shady borders, and foundation beds and as a groundcover under trees.

HOW TO PLANT
Plant Siberian bugloss 1^1/$_2$ to 2 ft. apart. Dig a hole twice as wide as the pot, and position the plant so that the soil level is the same as it was in the pot. Fill in with soil around the roots about halfway up,

firm gently, and water well. Add more soil to completely fill the hole. Water regularly until plants are established. Mulch to conserve moisture.

ADVICE FOR CARE
Properly sited, Siberian bugloss needs no special care. Water during drought. Foliage will brown if the conditions are too dry. Eventually, clumps may split open in the center and need dividing. This is easily accomplished in the spring. Dig up the clumps, and split them apart with a sharp spade or large knife. Discard the unproductive center, and replant the healthy pieces. Water frequently until established. Mulch new divisions to conserve moisture.

ADDITIONAL INFORMATION
Siberian bugloss self-sows in moist, shady gardens. Seedlings may be moved to other locations, weeded out, or allowed to grow. Where self-sowing is prevalent, brunnera will spread to form large masses. The dark green, heart-shaped leaves of Siberian bugloss make a striking contrast with hardy spring bulbs. The clear blue flowers are especially lovely interplanted with bright yellow daffodils.

ADDITIONAL SPECIES, CULTIVARS, OR VARIETIES
Some interesting cultivars exist, but they may be difficult to find. 'Variegata' has large leaves that are mostly to partly white. It requires a shady, moist location. The leaves of 'Hadspen Cream' are light green with off-white margins. 'Alba' has green foliage and white flowers.

PERENNIALS

Siberian Iris

Iris sibirica

Height: 2 to 4 ft.
Flowers: Blue, purple, red-violet, white
Bloom Period: Late spring to early summer
Zones: 3, 4, 5, 6
Light Requirement:

The exquisite flowers of Siberian iris add grace to the garden. With their upright standards and downward falls, the blooms have classic, clean lines that are both beautiful and elegant. The falls, often with intricate veining and a marking called a blaze, are smooth, unlike their more flouncy and demanding relative, the tall bearded iris. When in bloom, the blue, purple, or white flowers of Siberian iris dance aloft, looking almost as if they could take flight against the blue sky. After their blooming period, the iris's arching foliage adds vertical structure to the garden all summer long. Siberian iris are easy to grow. Moist, well-drained soil and sun ensure success, but these long-lived, disease-resistant plants also tolerate wet sites and partial shade. The clumps need infrequent division. Use Siberian iris as an accent plant among peonies, blue false indigo, lady's mantle, hardy geraniums, and tufted hair grass. The blue or purple flowers shine above a pool of white-and-yellow 'May Queen' daisies or pale yellow-golden marguerites (*Anthemis* 'Moonlight'). Many cultivars of Siberian iris are available, and some of the older selections that have stood the test of time are still worth considering. 'Caesar's Brother' (2½ ft.) is a deep dark purple with graceful flowers. 'Ego' (2 ft.) is a medium blue, and 'Super Ego' (2 to 2½ ft.) is a delicate pale blue beauty with falls veined deep blue-violet. 'Ruffled Velvet' (2 ft.) is a deep velvety reddish-purple. 'White Swirl' (3 ft.) is an attractive white selection. Many beautiful Siberian iris are being developed in Michigan. Look for the award-winning 'Jewelled Crown' (24 in.), a stunning wine-red iris with ruffled falls with a light gold blaze and a vigorous habit.

WHEN TO PLANT
Plant container-grown Siberian iris from spring into early fall.

Where to Plant

Choose locations with moist, humus-rich soil in full sun to partial shade. Siberian iris are very tolerant of moisture. Plant clumps along streams or ponds but not where the roots will be submerged. In sandy, poor soils, add organic material to increase the water-holding capacity of the soil. Plant these iris in perennial beds, mixed plantings, and cottage gardens and in drifts by water features.

How to Plant

Plant Siberian iris 1^1/$_2$ to 2 ft. apart. Dig a hole twice as wide as the pot, and position the plant so that the soil level is the same as it was in the pot. Fill in with soil around the roots about halfway up, firm gently, and water well. Add more soil to completely fill the hole. Water regularly until plants are established. Mulch to conserve moisture.

Advice for Care

Siberian iris are easy to grow and much more resistant to the problems that affect bearded iris. Water them during dry spells if they are planted in sandy soil. Clumps may be fed lightly with a low-nitrogen fertilizer in the spring. Remove the flowering stalks when the display is finished. Eventually, the clumps of Siberian iris will produce fewer flowers and become dead in the center. Divide them in spring when the foliage is 4 to 6 in. high. Large clumps can be difficult to lift out of the ground. Split the clump into pieces with a sharp spade, a large knife, or even a saw. Discard the woody center, and replant vigorous pieces from the outside of the clump. Add additional organic material to the soil. Keep new divisions well watered until established. Mulch to conserve moisture. New divisions will take a few years to reach their full potential.

Additional Information

Plants shouldn't require staking. If clumps are splitting open or flopping, divide them or move them to a sunnier location. Cut back the foliage of Siberian iris in the fall. Foliage left standing for the winter will flop providing the perfect hiding place for rodents, which love to eat the roots.

Additional Species, Cultivars, or Varieties

Bearded iris are a familiar garden favorite. They require well-drained, average to fertile soil in full sun and profit from division every 3 or 4 years after flowering. They can be prone to problems such as iris borer.

Sneezeweed

Helenium autumnale

Height: 3 to 5 ft.
Flowers: Yellow, orange-red, rust
Bloom Period: Early summer to late summer
Zones: 3, 4, 5, 6
Light Requirement:

Sneezeweed produces mobs of bright chubby daisies lighting up the summer border. Each flower has a knobby center and flaring wedge-shaped notched petals. But with a name like sneezeweed, it's hard to achieve popularity. Some perennial catalogs have taken to calling it Helen's flower in a marketing attempt to upgrade sneezeweed's image. The common name "sneezeweed" describes not an allergic reaction but the use of the dried flowerheads to produce a sort of snuff. In field guides, *Helenium autumnale* is sometimes called the swamp sunflower, and a swamp is where you might find it growing in the Great Lakes state. Sneezeweed can be found in both the Upper and the Lower Peninsula in swamps and wet meadows and along the banks of rivers and streams. This lanky native, often growing to 5 ft., has been civilized and hybridized by European growers into a range of beautiful, floriferous, and more compact garden plants. The height is lower, the stems are stronger, and the flower colors range from bright yellow to warm copper-orange and mahogany-red. It retains its penchant for moisture; moist soil is the secret to growing it well. Sneezeweed adds life to the summer garden. The colors are bright and rich and can be combined with 'Coronation Gold' yarrow, threadleaf coreopsis, and 'Lucifer' crocosmia for a splendid effect. Or tone down the flowers, and plant with butterfly-bush (*Buddleia*), violet-blue perennial sage, an airy mass of purple fennel, and the tall stems and rose-purple flowers of Brazilian verbena. Add a few clumps of yellow coreopsis or a hot-colored daylily to balance the color scheme.

WHEN TO PLANT
Plant container-grown sneezeweed in the spring.

WHERE TO PLANT
Choose locations with moist, average to fertile soil in full sun. Plants are tolerant of wet soils, and adequate moisture promotes healthy

growth. Avoid dry sites. Use sneezeweed in moist, sunny perennial beds and borders, wet areas, cottage gardens, and natural meadow-type plantings.

HOW TO PLANT

Plant sneezeweed 2 to 3 ft. apart. Dig a hole twice as wide as the pot, and position the plant so that the soil level is the same as it was in the pot. Fill in with soil around the roots about halfway up, firm gently, and water well. Add more soil to completely fill the hole. Water regularly until plants are established. Mulch to conserve moisture.

ADVICE FOR CARE

In moist soils, sneezeweed is usually pest- and disease-free. Water plants during dry spells if they are not planted in a moisture-retentive site. Deadhead flowering stems after the first flush of flowers to encourage more bloom, or take the shears to clumps and cut back plants by half. Rebloom isn't as showy. Although often relegated to the list of plants needing frequent division, sneezeweed clumps can often go for 4 to 6 years without it. Always take your cue from the plants and not from a chart in a book. If flowering diminishes and clumps begin to die out in the center, divide plants the following spring. To divide, dig clumps, and split the fibrous-rooted crown into pieces. Replant vigorous sections from the outside of the clump.

ADDITIONAL INFORMATION

If plants start flopping, try pinching out the growing tips when the shoots are about 6 in. high. This will delay flowering and promote stockier growth. Some cultivars may be more self-supporting than others. Staking is also an option. Sneezeweed makes an excellent cut flower and is lovely in large bunches. It is often seen in large British perennial borders with other North American natives such as Culver's root, Joe-pye weed, asters, and goldenrod.

ADDITIONAL SPECIES, CULTIVARS, OR VARIETIES

The cultivars are preferred over the species for garden use. Choose the shorter selection to avoid the need for staking or pinching. 'Butterpat' (3^1/$_2$ to 4 ft.) is a gorgeous sunny yellow selection. Another favorite is 'Moerheim's Beauty' (3 ft.), which has rich copper-red flowers with dark centers. 'The Bishop' (2 to 2^1/$_2$ ft.) with yellow flowers and 'Wyndley' (2 to 2^1/$_2$ ft.) with copper-orange flowers are compact selections.

Spiked Speedwell

Veronica spicata

Height: 1 to 2 ft.
Flowers: Blue, pink, white
Bloom Period: Early to
  midsummer
Zones: 4, 5, 6
Light Requirement:

Yellow flowers abound in the summer garden, but blue flowers are all too rare. Spiked speedwell, often just called veronica, sends forth tapering spikes of deep or light blue, adding vertical lift to the mounds and mats of the garden's foreground. The long, graceful spikes bloom for almost 6 weeks, appearing in profusion atop neat clumps of green foliage. Some, such as 'Blue Peter', are fairly tall—almost 2 ft.—and are suitable for the middle of a perennial bed or border. The upward spires provide visual relief from the chunky trusses of phlox or the flat-topped clusters of yarrow. Other are more diminutive. 'Red Fox'—they aren't *all* blue—throws 9- to 12-in. red-violet spikes from a low clump of small foliage. The woolly speedwell, *Veronica spicata* subsp. *incana*, is grown not only for its 10-in. blue-violet spikes but also for its prostrate mats of silvery foliage. A cultivar of woolly speedwell called 'Silver Slippers' doesn't flower at all! New hybrid veronicas offer a range of desirable characteristics. *Veronica* 'Goodness Grows' is a low-growing (to 12 in.) perennial for edging or for the front of the border. It has narrow spires of dark indigo-blue over mounds of green foliage. We highly recommend this free-flowering speedwell. It has bloomed in mid-Michigan (with deadheading) from June through October. The vertical spires of spiked speedwell are a natural complement to the rounded form of many perennials. The soft yellow and mounded form of 'Moonbeam' coreopsis makes an attractive pairing with the dark blue 'Goodness Grows' or the lighter 'Blue Peter'. Spiked speedwell is welcome in mixed plantings and cottage gardens. Try it under shrub roses, with hardy geraniums, lady's mantle, and cheddar pinks.

WHEN TO PLANT
Plant container-grown spiked speedwell in the spring.

WHERE TO PLANT
Choose a location with average, well-drained soil in full sun. Good drainage is important for success. Plant spiked speedwell in peren-

nial beds and borders, cottage gardens, and rock gardens, and use for edging.

How to Plant

Plant spiked speedwell 18 to 24 in. apart. Dig a hole twice as wide as the pot, and position the plant so that the soil level is the same as it was in the pot. Fill in with soil around the roots about halfway up, firm gently, and water well. Add more soil to completely fill the hole. Water regularly until plants are established. Mulch to conserve moisture.

Advice for Care

In full sun and well-drained soil, speedwell is pest- and disease-resistant. Water plants during dry spells. Remove the flowering spikes to promote rebloom. Don't overfertilize. Too much fertilizer will lead to flopping. When flowering decreases, about every 4 to 5 years, divide clumps for rejuvenation. This is easily accomplished in the spring. Dig clumps, and split apart with a knife or sharp spade. Replant vigorous pieces from the outside of the clumps. Keep new divisions watered until established.

Additional Information

The silvery foliage of the woolly speedwell is an attractive ground-cover when not in bloom. Combine it with other silver-foliaged plants in a well-drained location. Add lamb's ears, 'Tricolor' sage, 'Rosy Glow' sedum, woolly thyme, 'Moonshine' yarrow, and hens-and-chicks (*Sempervivum* sp.) for a silvery mosaic.

Additional Species, Cultivars, or Varieties

A nice selection is 'Blue Peter' (2 ft.) with branched stems of dark blue flowers. 'Blue Spires' (18 in.) is another spiky blue veronica. 'Icicle' (18 to 20 in.) is a fine white cultivar with deep green foliage and spires of white flowers over a long period. 'Red Fox' is a shorter (12 to 15 in.) spiked speedwell with red-violet flowers. For true azure blue, grow the Hungarian speedwell, *Veronica teucrium*. The cultivar 'Crater Lake Blue' produces thousands of brilliant blue flowers in loose spikes from late spring to early summer. This plant is prone to splitting open and needs staking with shrubby twigs to maintain its form. Cut it back after flowering. The stiffly upright, award-winning *Veronica* 'Sunny Border Blue' (18 to 24 in.) has per-formed poorly in mid-Michigan, developing foliar disease that causes the leaves to drop. Even when healthy, this long-bloomer has clubby spikes and little of the elegant grace characteristic of many speedwells.

Threadleaf Coreopsis

Coreopsis verticillata

Height: 18 in. to 3 ft.
Flowers: Yellow
Bloom Period: Early summer to fall
Zones: 3, 4, 5, 6
Light Requirement:

Many perennials are transitory in the garden, blooming only a few weeks at most. The threadleaf coreopsis 'Moonbeam', though, blooms on and off from early summer into fall, peaking at midsummer. Besides its long season of bloom, 'Moonbeam' is unusual for its pale, almost icy yellow color that blends harmoniously with blues, purples, and whites without being intense. Other types of threadleaf coreopsis are a brighter golden yellow. The finely textured foliage is airy and attractive before and during flowering. Threadleaf coreopsis, a native to the southeastern United States, needs little care such as staking, pinching, or watering. In light soils and full sun, threadleaf coreopsis spreads quickly. Leave it uncut in late fall, and the small dark brown buttonlike seedheads will remain attractive all winter over the tangle of stems. It makes a fine groundcover combined with other spreading perennials such as common yarrow, 'Silver King' artemisia, and hardy ageratum (*Eupatorium coelestinum*). For a long blooming combination, pair 'Moonbeam' with salvia 'May Night', 'Butterfly Blue' pincushion flower, and 'Six Hills Giant' catmint.

WHEN TO PLANT
Plant threadleaf coreopsis in spring or early summer.

WHERE TO PLANT
Choose locations with full sun and moist but well-drained, average soil. Clumps tolerate light shade. Threadleaf coreopsis is drought-tolerant once established. Its fine-textured foliage and starry flowers are a welcome addition to perennial borders and island beds. Also use it for massing as edging, as a groundcover, or with grasses in a landscape design.

HOW TO PLANT
Plant coreopsis 2$\frac{1}{2}$ to 3 ft. apart. 'Moonbeam' should be spaced at about 2 ft. Dig a hole twice as wide as the pot, and position the

plant so that the soil level is the same as it was in the pot. Fill in with soil around the roots about halfway up, firm gently, and water well. Add more soil to completely fill the hole. Water regularly until plants are established.

ADVICE FOR CARE

Threadleaf coreopsis needs little care. The clumps are pest- and disease-resistant. Watering is rarely needed. After about 4 years, plants will begin to die in the middle, flower less profusely, or spread into areas where they are unwelcome. This is the time to divide. In the spring, lift the mats of spreading rhizomes and fibrous roots, and cut into sections. Replant healthy, vigorous pieces. Water well until established. 'Moonbeam' forms clumps more slowly and is less likely to need division. Still, division is simple; the clumps split apart easily. This is a great way to obtain more plants. 'Moonbeam' was a frequent pass-along plant before it became widely available at nurseries. Even small divisions the diameter of a quarter will bloom for months.

ADDITIONAL INFORMATION

After the first flush of flowers, some gardeners deadhead threadleaf coreopsis by shearing back the plants to promote rebloom. But even without shearing, plants—especially 'Moonbeam'—produce lots of bloom, and those that were not sheared may have better form going into winter. Try both shearing and not shearing to see what works best in your garden. Cut back the brown stems to the ground in the spring. The dark brown seedheads, particularly of 'Moonbeam', can be very ornamental in the winter.

ADDITIONAL SPECIES, CULTIVARS, OR VARIETIES

'Moonbeam' (12 to 18 in.), which has become increasingly popular over the last decade, forms a mound of dark green foliage and pastel yellow flowers. It is especially effective with blues, purples, and whites. 'Golden Showers' (2 to 3 ft.) is larger and more vigorous. It may need more frequent division than other types of threadleaf coreopsis. 'Zagreb' (12 to18 in) is a dwarf form useful for edging. *Coreopsis grandiflora* (1 to 2 ft.), grown as an annual or short-lived perennial, has yellow-orange flowers and simple leaves rather than the fern-like foliage of threadleaf coreopsis. 'Early Sunrise' is a compact plant with double yellow-orange flowers. Pink coreopsis, *C. rosea*, sometimes described as the pink 'Moonbeam', doesn't live up to this comparison. It is not tolerant of dry soil and not as useful, attractive or adaptable as 'Moonbeam'.

Turtlehead

Chelone obliqua

Height: 2 to 3 ft.
Flowers: Rose-pink
Bloom Period: Midsummer to early fall
Zones: 3, 4, 5, 6
Light Requirement:

Rose turtlehead, *Chelone obliqua*, has a fascinating appearance due to the unusual structure of its flowers. Each deep rose tubular bloom resembles a turtle's head with lower lip protruding and mouth agape. It's a strange image, but the satiny pink flowers arranged in spikes like snapdragons are gorgeous. The lush dark green leaves provides the perfect complement. Native to but rare in southeastern Michigan, rose turtlehead can occasionally be found along rivers and in wet places blooming at the end of summer. In locations where moist soil can be found—a condition not uncommon in Michigan gardens—turtlehead is an easy, long-lived, and engaging garden plant. Where content, turtlehead forms large clumps of attractive foliage. The stiffly upright stems, reaching 2 to 3 ft., are clothed in handsome, deep green glossy leaves. The spikes of satiny pink flowers add something different to the garden. Healthy plants will produce a large number of stems blooming over an extended period from late summer into fall. Turtlehead is well adapted to a place by a stream or a pond, but it also adapts well to garden conditions as long it is not dry. If the plant is to succeed in the perennial border, the soil must be moisture-retentive and humus-rich. Use mulch to retain moisture. In a moist, sunny perennial bed, contrast rose turtlehead's dark foliage and rose flowers with the gray foliage and milky white flowers of the three-veined pearly everlasting. Lavender-blue asters and burgundy-tinted switch grass would be an attractive addition. In a naturalized damp garden, plant rose turtlehead with the tall smoky purple clusters of Joe-pye weed and the white flowers of 'Ice Ballet' swamp milkweed. Or in a lightly shaded, moist area, try it with the bottle gentian, *Gentiana andrewsii* (another Michigan native of swampy ground), with its clusters of dark blue flowers for a stunning combination.

WHEN TO PLANT
Plant container-grown turtlehead in the spring.

WHERE TO PLANT

Choose locations with moist, humus-rich soil in full sun or light shade. Plants are taller in partial shade. Turtlehead is not tolerant of dry soils; moisture is the key to success. Use turtlehead in moist perennial borders, along ponds and streams, and in wet spots and natural areas.

HOW TO PLANT

Plant turtlehead 2 ft. apart. Dig a hole twice as wide as the pot, and position the plant so that the soil level is the same as it was in the pot. Fill in with soil around the roots about halfway up, firm gently, and water well. Add more soil to completely fill the hole. Water regularly until plants are established. Mulch to conserve moisture.

ADVICE FOR CARE

If sited in moist soil, turtlehead will need no special care. In well-drained areas, water during dry spells. If plants stretch and flop, relocate to a sunny position. Division is rarely needed, but the fleshy rooted crowns of turtlehead can be divided in the spring.

ADDITIONAL INFORMATION

Some gardeners pinch the shoot tips when the stems are about 6 in. tall to promote branching. In full sun, this shouldn't be necessary.

ADDITIONAL SPECIES, CULTIVARS, OR VARIETIES

The pink turtlehead, *C. lyonii*, has pale pink flowers and has narrower foliage. It is also suitable for garden culture in moist sites. The white turtlehead, *C. glabra*, grows throughout Michigan in low ground along streams and rivers, blooming in midsummer. It has dark green narrow foliage and the same snapdragon-like arrangement of flowers. Plant in rich, moist soil in the garden. The rose turtlehead is better adapted to growing in typical garden conditions than the pink and white turtlehead. But with rich soil and consistent moisture, all will thrive.

Yarrow

Achillea 'Coronation Gold'

Other Name: Hybrid Yarrow
Height: 2¹/₂ to 3 ft.
Flowers: Golden yellow
Bloom Period: Early summer
   to late summer
Zones: 3, 4, 5, 6
Light Requirement:

Radiating the warm glow of summer, the mustard-yellow, flat-topped floral clusters of *Achillea* 'Coronation Gold' catch the sun's rays and reflect them. This striking hybrid yarrow is one of the very best for the garden. The 3- to 4-in. upward-facing flowerheads are produced on strong 3-ft. stems over aromatic feathery gray-green foliage. The color glows against the soft muted leaves. Lasting for almost 2 months, the flattened clusters offer pleasing contrast to the sunflowers and daisies of the summer garden. The foliage, attractive all season, is particularly appealing in spring, forming ferny silver-green mounds. As the flowers develop, the woolly buds are silvery white, opening to the radiant golden yellow for which this cultivar is named. For cutting and drying these bright flat-topped flowerheads are beyond compare. Some yarrows sprawl and require staking, some have flowers that fade in the sun, and others spread aggressively, requiring yearly division. With sun and average soil, the clump-forming 'Coronation Gold' stands tall and bright in the summer garden. Combine this gold yarrow with the purple spires of perennial salvia for an eye-catching contrast of form and hue. Or use it as a complement to orange daylilies set among soft lavender-blue catmint. Another beautiful hybrid yarrow to grow is *Achillea* 'Moonshine'. It has softer yellow flowers, ferny silver-green foliage, and a more compact size, growing to 2 ft. Flowering starts earlier, usually in late spring or early summer. It tends to need more frequent division to look its best, often every 2 to 3 years. Cut it back hard after flowering to stimulate rebloom.

WHEN TO PLANT
Plant 'Coronation Gold' yarrow in the spring.

WHERE TO PLANT
Choose locations with well-drained, average soil in full sun. Yarrow is tolerant of sandy soils and drought. Avoid shade and locations with moist, rich soil. Use hybrid yarrow in perennial beds and

borders, cottage gardens, dry gardens, cutflower gardens, and mixed plantings.

How to Plant

Plant hybrid yarrow 2 to 2^1/$_2$ ft. apart. Dig a hole twice as wide as the pot, and position the plant so that the soil level is the same as it was in the pot. Fill in with soil around the roots about halfway up, firm gently, and water well. Add more soil to completely fill the hole. Water regularly until plants are established.

Advice for Care

In well-drained soil, yarrow needs little special care. Plants in rich soil may be tall and weak and require staking. Avoid heavy layers of mulch. Deadhead the long-lasting flower heads when they become brown. After a few years, usually 3 to 4, clumps will need division for rejuvenation. This is easily accomplished in the spring. Dig the clumps, and split with 2 spading forks or a sharp spade. Take vigorous pieces from the outside of the clumps. Replant at the same level at which they were growing, and keep watered until established.

Additional Information

Yarrow makes a colorful cut flower and everlasting. For drying, cut the stems when the flowers are just beginning to open and before the pollen develops. This will preserve the bright yellow color.

Additional Species, Cultivars, or Varieties

The common yarrow *Achillea millefolium* (1 to 2 ft.), blooming in early to midsummer with magenta-red flowers and green ferny foliage, is a fast spreader and needs division almost every year to control its growth. 'Rosea' has a long period of bloom and magenta-red flowers. *Achillea* 'Summer Pastels' (2 ft.), an All-America Selection winner, blooms the first year from seed and then behaves as a perennial. This mix comes in a range of colors and sizes for a hodgepodge effect. The Galaxy hybrids are a group of cultivars developed in Germany with various colors. Most open one color in early summer and fade to a softer tint, giving the plant a two-tone appearance. Many are quite beautiful but not as dramatic or sturdy as 'Coronation Gold'. 'Weser River Sandstone' (30 in.) has brick-red flowers aging to a dusty rose. 'Citronella' (30 in.) has butter-cream flowers fading to buff. These yarrows are attractive with the dark foliage of purple fennel, shrubs of lavender, and lamb's ears.

Why Garden in Michigan?

Because it's a pleasure.
The landscape stages its own
theater, a natural drama in four
acts. The plot unfolds with new
life in spring that turns lush
and green in summer, transforms
to brilliant golds and reds in
autumn and lies serenely
dormant in winter.

The

Gardener

who plans

reaps

the

Greatest

Reward

COOL
SPRINGS
PRESS

The Michigan Gardener's Guide

Photographic gallery of featured plants

Brazilian Verbena
Verbena bonariensis

Cleome
Cleome hasslerana

Coleus
Coleus × hybridus

Cosmos
Cosmos bipinnatus

Dusty Miller
Senecio cineraria

Flowering Tobacco
Nicotiana alata

Geranium
Pelargonium × hortorum

Globe Amaranth
Gomphrena globosa

Gloriosa Daisy
Rudbeckia hirta

Heliotrope
Heliotropium arborescens

Hyacinth Bean
Lablab purpureus

Impatiens
Impatiens wallerana

Love-in-a-Mist
Nigella damascena

Marigold
Tagetes species

Mealy-cup Sage
Salvia farinacea

Melampodium
Melampodium paludosum

Moss Rose
Portulaca grandiflora

Pansy
Viola × wittrockiana

Petunia
Petunia × hybrida

Pot Marigold
Calendula officinalis

Purple Fennel
Foeniculum vulgare var. *purpureum*

Snapdragon
Antirrhinum majus

Sunflower
Helianthus annuus

Wax Begonia
Begonia "Semperflorens hybrids"

GROUNDCOVERS

Zinnia
Zinnia angustifolia

Barrenwort
Epimedium × versicolor 'Sulphureum'

Bigroot Geranium
Geranium macrorrhizum

Bugleweed
Ajuga reptans

Creeping Juniper
Juniperus horizontalis

Dwarf Chinese Astilbe
Astilbe chinensis var. *pumila*

Lily-of-the-Valley
Convallaria majalis

Mother-of-Thyme
Thymus praecox var. *arcticus*

Pachysandra
Pachysandra terminalis

HARDY BULBS

'Palace Purple' Alumroot
Heuchera micrantha
'Palace Purple'

Spotted Dead Nettle
Lamium maculatum

Autumn Crocus
Colchicum species
and hybrids

Botanical Tulip
Tulipa tarda

Camas
Camassia leichtlinii

Common Tulip
Tulipa hybrids

Crocosmia
Crocosmia × crocosmiiflora 'Lucifer'

Crocus Hybrids
Crocus vernus hybrids

Daffodil
Narcissus species and hybrids

Dwarf Bulbous Iris
Iris reticulata

Glory-of-the-Snow
Chionodoxa luciliae

Grape Hyacinth
Muscari armeniacum

Lily Hybrids
Lilium 'Enchantment'

Ornamental Onion
Allium aflatunense

Siberian Squill
Scilla siberica

Snowdrop
Galanthus nivalis

Star-of-Persia
Allium christophii

Star-of-Persia
Allium christophii

Summer Snowflake
Leucojum aestivum

Summer Snowflake
Leucojum aestivum

Windflower
Anemone bland

Windflower
Anemone bland

Winter Aconite
Eranthis hyemalis

Winter Aconite
Eranthis hyemalis

Blue Oat Grass
Helictotrichon sempervirens

Feather Reed Grass
Calamagrostis × acutiflora

Fountain Grass
Pennisetum alopecuroides

Japanese Silver Grass
Miscanthus sinensis

Switch Grass
Panicum virgatum

Tufted Hair Grass
Deschampsia caespitosa

Wild Oats
Chasmanthium latifolium

Artemisia
Artemisia ludoviciana

Astilbe Hybrids
Astilbe × arendsii

Bethlehem Sage
Pulmonaria saccharata

Black Snakeroot
Cimicifuga racemosa

Black-eyed Susan
Rudbeckia fulgida ssp. *sullivantii*

Blazing Star
Liatris spicata

Bleeding Heart
Dicentra spectabilis

Bloody Cranesbill
Geranium sanguineum

Blue False Indigo
Baptisia australis

Blue Star
Amsonia tabernaemontana

Boltonia
Boltonia asteroides

Bowman's Root
Gillenia trifoliata

Butterflyweed
Asclepias tuberosa

Catmint
Nepeta × faassenii

Cheddar Pinks
Dianthus gratianopolitanus

Coral Bells
Heuchera × brizoides

Culver's Root
Veronicastrum virginicum

Cushion Spurge
Euphorbia polychroma

Daylily
Hemerocallis hybrids

Garden Phlox
Phlox paniculata

Goat's Beard
Aruncus dioicus

Goldenrod
Solidago species and hybrids

Heliopsis
Heliopsis helianthoides ssp. *scabra*

Hosta
Hosta species and hybrids

Japanese Anemone
Anemone × *hybrida*

Lady's Mantle
Alchemilla mollis

Lamb's Ears
Stachys byzantina

Lavender
Lavendula angustifolia

Lenten Rose
Helleborus orientalis

New England Aster
Aster novae-angliae

Peach-leaf Bellflower
Campanula persicifolia

Peony
Paeonia lactiflora and hybrids

Purple Coneflower
Echinacea purpurea

Russian Sage
Perovskia atriplicifolia

Salvia
Salvia × superba

Sedum 'Autumn Joy'
Sedum 'Autumn Joy'

Siberian Bugloss
Brunnera macrophylla

Siberian Iris
Iris sibirica

Sneezeweed
Helenium autumnale

Spiked Speedwell
Veronica spicata

Threadleaf Coreopsis
Coreopsis verticillata

Turtlehead
Chelone obliqua

Yarrow
Achillea 'Coronation Gold'

'Bonica' Shrub Rose
Rosa 'Bonica'

'Frau Dagmar Hastrup' Rugosa Rose
Rosa rugosa 'Frau Dagmar Hastrup'

'Peace' Hybrid Tea Rose
Rosa 'Peace'

'Sunsprite' Floribunda Rose
Rosa 'Sunsprite'

'William Baffin' Climbing Rose
Rosa 'William Baffin'

Anglojap Yew
Taxus × media

Arborvitae
Thuja occidentalis

'Arnold Promise' Witchhazel
Hamamelis × intermedia 'Arnold Promise'

Arrowwood Viburnum
Viburnum dentatum

Bayberry
Myrica pensylvanica

Bluebeard
Caryopteris × clandonensis

Bottlebrush Buckeye
Aesculus parviflora

Carolina Allspice
Calycanthus floridus

'Carol Mackie' Daphne
Daphne × burkwoodii

Chinese Juniper
Juniperus chinensis

Climbing Hydrangea
Hydrangea petiolaris

'Cornell Pink' Korean Rhododendron
Rhododendron mucronulatum

Dwarf Fothergilla
Fothergilla gardenii

Forsythia
Forsythia × intermedia

Fragrant Winter Hazel
Corylopsis glabrescens

Gray Dogwood
Cornus racemosa

'Green Velvet' Boxwood
Buxus 'Green Velvet'

Koreanspice Viburnum
Viburnum carlesii

Leatherleaf Viburnum
Viburnum rhytidophyllum

Lilac
Syringa vulgaris

Michigan Holly
Ilex verticillata

'Miss Kim' Korean Lilac
Syringa patula 'Miss Kim'

Panicle Hydrangea
Hydrangea paniculata

Redtwig Dogwood
Cornus stolonifera

Staghorn Sumac
Rhus typhina

Russian Arborvitae
Microbiota decussata

Star Magnolia
Magnolia stellata

Summersweet
Clethra alnifolia

Weigela
Weigela florida

American Smoketree
Cotinus obovatus

Amur Chokecherry
Prunus maackii

Baldcypress
Taxodium distichum

Black Gum
Nyssa sylvatica

Corneliancherry
Cornus mas

Dawn Redwood
Metasequoia glyptostroboides

Flowering Crabapples
Malus

Ginkgo
Ginkgo biloba

Hop-Hornbeam
Ostrya virginiana

Katsuratree
Cercidiphyllum japonicum

Kentucky Coffeetree
Gymnocladus dioicus

Littleleaf Linden
Tilia cordata

Norway Spruce
Picea abies

Pagoda Dogwood
Cornus alternifolia

Paperbark Maple
Acer griseum

Pawpaw
Asimina triloba

Red Oak
Quercus rubra

Redbud
Cercis canadensis

River Birch
Betula nigra

Saucer Magnolia
Magnolia × soulangiana

Shadblow
Amelanchier canadensis

Sweetgum
Liquidambar styraciflua

Tuliptree
Liriodendron tulipifera

White Ash
Fraxinus americana

White Fir
Abies concolor

White Pine
Pinus strobus

Yellowwood
Cladrastis kentukea
synonymous with
Cladrastis lutea

WOODLAND WILDFLOWERS & FERNS

Bloodroot
Sanguinaria canadensis

Christmas Fern
Polystichum acrostichoides

Foamflower
Tiarella cordifolia

Large-Flowered White Trillium
Trillium grandiflorum

Maidenhair Fern
Adiantum pedatum

Marginal Shield Fern
Dryopteris marginalis

Solomon's Seal
Polygonatum biflorum

Virginia Bluebell
Mertensia virginica

Virginia Bluebell
Mertensia virginica

Wild Blue Phlox
Phlox divaricata

Wild Columbine
Aquilegia canadensis

Michigan's motto—
"If you seek a pleasant
peninsula, look about
you"—is as true of
its gardens as of its
sandy lakeshores,
fields, and woods. The
state's unique climate,
geography, and
natural features make
it a special place to
tend a plot of land.

Roses

𝒲HILE UNDENIABLY LOVELY AND ROMANTIC, ROSES HAVE A REPUTATION FOR BEING NEEDY PLANTS. Hybrid teas especially have detailed regimes for pruning, spraying, and preparing for the winter.

True rose enthusiasts dismiss these tasks as a small price to pay for a long season of exquisite bloom. But other gardeners, even though they admire roses in flower, are reluctant to take on the extra work, especially the disease-prevention treatments that some roses require.

Fortunately, many roses are rugged and dependable landscape plants that can grow in the right place with modest amounts of care. That's good because roses have much to offer in the garden. Their flowers are lush and often fragrant. Roses may be used singly as specimen plants, integrated into a bed with annuals and perennials, planted to form hedges, or positioned to climb a trellis or an arbor. Roses are also wonderful cut flowers.

Rosarians have divided roses into many classes. Here are a few of special interest:

- The classic and long-stemmed hybrid teas are the most popular rose. Hybrid teas bloom from June to fall and come in a rainbow of colors, from pale and polite to neon bright. They are 2 to 6 feet tall and require winter protection in Michigan.

- Old garden roses and antique roses are a diverse group of refined beauty, many with exquisite fragrance. Most bloom just once in early summer. Modern hybridizers are creating new repeat-blooming roses that have the old-fashioned appeal of the antiques as well as increased disease resistance. The full-flowered David Austin or English roses fall in this category, although they also may be considered shrub roses.

Chapter Seven

- The tough rugosa rose and its hybrids are often separated into a group called the hybrid rugosas or lumped with the modern shrub roses.

- Shrub roses grow vigorously and usually survive the winter without extra protection. Hybridizers in Canada have developed a truly rugged group of shrub and climbing roses that are hardy to Zone 3 without protection, including the Canadian Explorer series and others. Shrub roses offer advantages in hardiness and lower care requirements that make them suited for use as hedges and screens in many gardens. Many have ornamental hips.

- Climbing roses include ramblers, everbloomers, large-flowered climbers, and climbing hybrid teas, among others. Some are hardier, but all require winter protection in Michigan, although some Canadian selections are hardy to Zone 3.

If you're thinking about planting roses, spend some time with a good reference book or several mail-order catalogs to learn more about the different types. You have thousands of roses to choose from. You may also want to contact your local chapter of a rose society for recommendations about specific roses.

Rose hardiness, particularly that of hybrid teas and floribundas, can be tricky. Snow cover, exposure, and cultural practices such as watering and fertilizing all play a role in the hardiness of these plants.

PLANTING YOUR ROSES

Sun and soil are the most important factors in success with roses. The site should get full sun or at least 6 to 8 hours a day; morning sun is best. Place roses where they won't have to compete with roots of shrubs or trees.

The soil should be well drained and of at least average fertility. Most roses prefer neutral to slightly acidic soil. Contact your county's MSU Extension office for information on soil tests. Avoid future problems by analyzing your soil and making any necessary adjustments.

Chapter Seven

Bareroot roses are planted in April to early May. Container-grown roses may be planted in spring or early summer, but it will be easier on them if you avoid planting in hot summer weather.

Soak the roots of bareroot roses in water for 12 to 24 hours before planting. Meanwhile, dig a hole larger than the roots, at least 18 inches deep and wide. With the soil removed from the hole, mix one tablespoon superphosphate and well-rotted compost. Use this mixture to make a mound of soil in the bottom of the planting hole.

Prune off any broken or dead canes and any damaged roots. Cut back long canes to 12 inches. Make any cuts on a 45-degree angle and slightly above an outward-facing bud. Use scissor or bypass pruners to avoid crushing the stems.

Position the bareroot rose on the mound, gently spreading out the roots. Fill in with the soil mixture, firm it so there are no air pockets, and water well. If the rose is grafted, it should be growing so the bud union (the knobby spot where the top and bottom were grafted together) is level with the surrounding soil or, in northern parts of the state, slightly below the soil. In colder regions, hybrid roses grown on their own roots (not grafted) are preferred for increased hardiness.

Water and check the rose's position again. Then mound soil around the newly planted bareroot rose about 10 to 12 inches deep to prevent desiccation while the rose gets established. After several weeks, when the rose is showing signs of growth, the mounded soil may be hosed away.

Container-grown roses should not be soaked first and do not have to be planted on a mound. When removing the rose from the container, leave the root ball as undisturbed as possible. Container-grown roses do not have to be protected with the soil mound after planting.

After planting, apply a 3-inch layer of mulch such as shredded bark or cocoa shells around the rose, leaving a 6-inch mulch-free circle around the base of the plant. The mulch will conserve mois-

Chapter Seven

ture around the roots, keep the temperature around the roots moderate, and discourage weeds.

Roses need at least 1 inch of water a week. It's best to soak deeply and avoid wetting the foliage because moist leaves are more prone to develop disease. In subsequent years, most roses are pruned in spring, and hybrid teas in particular may suffer extensive winter dieback.

Roses can be a smorgasbord for diseases such as black spot and powdery mildew and insects such as aphids, Japanese beetles, rose chafers, and midges. Buy healthy plants and space them properly. If you don't want to buy into a routine of spraying or dousing to prevent these attacks, choose a resilient type of rose such as rugosas and modern shrub roses.

Roses differ in their fertilization needs, and recommendations vary among rosarians. Many fertilizers are available. Stop feeding roses about August 1 to give the tender growth time to harden off before winter. Leaving the flowers on in fall also directs the plant's energy away from new growth. For more on fertilization, pruning, and winter protection, see the individual entries that follow.

'Bonica' Shrub Rose

Rosa 'Bonica'

Height: 4 to 5 ft.
Flowers: Pink
Bloom Period: Summer until frost
Zones: 4, 5, 6
Light Requirement:

The designation shrub rose or landscape rose includes many rugged, carefree roses that can be used as shrubs or groundcovers. Most are so beautiful that they can also be incorporated into perennial beds, borders, and cottage gardens. Shrub roses can add structure, height, beauty, and fragrance to mixed plantings. 'Bonica' has masses of 2½-in. shell pink double flowers in early summer that repeat until frost. It grows up to 4 to 5 ft. tall and is almost 5 ft. wide, sporting dark green glossy foliage. A modern hybrid, 'Bonica' is tough, disease-resistant, and hardy to Zone 4. It needs little or no pruning. Use it for a hedge or as an accent plant. Plant a grouping to soften a deck, edge a walk, or complement a patio. The beauty and appeal of roses are ideal for planting near outside living areas. Few plants can form as beautiful and effective a hedge as shrub roses. Their flowers in mass are spectacular, and they have glossy disease-resistant foliage and ornamental hips that accentuate the point. 'Bonica' and 'Carefree Beauty' are good choices.

When to Plant

Plant bareroot roses as early in the spring as the soil and weather allow. Container-grown plants should be planted in spring or, at the latest, early summer. Avoid container-grown roses that have become potbound.

Where to Plant

Plant shrub roses in soil that is moist, fertile, and well drained. Locate in full sun for best performance. Avoid planting close to mature trees and large shrubs.

How to Plant

Soak the roots of bareroot roses for 12 to 24 hours before planting. Dig a hole 18 to 24 in. deep and at least 18 in. wide. Add well-rotted compost and one tablespoon of superphosphate to the soil, and make a mound in the bottom of the planting hole for bareroot roses only. Prune off any damaged roots as well as any broken or dead canes. Cut back any long canes to about 12 in. Position the bareroot rose on the mound and spread out the roots. If the rose is grafted, it should be placed so the bud union is level with the surrounding soil or, in northern parts of the state, slightly below. Own-root roses should be planted at the same depth they were growing previously. Firm soil gently. Take care not to leave any air gaps underneath the root mass. Fill in about 2/3 of the way with soil and water. Add the remaining soil. For more protection, mound soil around the newly planted bareroot rose about 10 to 12 in. high. After several weeks, when the rose is showing signs of new growth, gently hose off the soil, and apply a 3-in. layer of mulch to conserve moisture and keep the roots cool. Regular watering is important to the establishment of a new rose.

ADVICE FOR CARE

Keep plants watered and mulched. Fertilizer should be applied about 2 weeks after spring pruning and once more about 6 weeks later in the season. Many rose fertilizers are available. Follow directions on the product. Fertilizer applied after August 1 will lead to winter injury. Lightly prune shrub roses in early spring. Remove any dead, broken, or diseased canes. Remove spindly, weak pieces. Some gardeners shorten canes by a few inches to encourage branching. Older large canes should be periodically removed to open up the center and stimulate new growth. Although not essential, light pruning can encourage compact growth and vigorous free-flowering canes. Some gardeners feel that removing dead wood and shortening unusually long canes are the only steps needed.

ADDITIONAL INFORMATION

For a cottage garden effect, plant a sunny part of your garden with 'Bonica', and underplant with the low pale pink hardy geranium *Geranium sanguineum* var. *striatum* for a color echo.

ADDITIONAL SPECIES, CULTIVARS, OR VARIETIES

'Carefree Beauty' (5 to 6 ft.) has rose-pink flowers from summer to fall and has been disease-free in mid-Michigan. Another carefree choice is 'Carefree Wonder' (3 ft). It has sweetheart pink semi-double 4-in. flowers that bloom in early summer and repeat until frost. 'Pink Meidiland' (4 ft.) has 3-in. single pink flowers with a white eye.

'Frau Dagmar Hastrup' Rugosa Rose

Rosa rugosa 'Frau Dagmar Hastrup'

Height: 4 ft.
Flowers: Pink
Bloom Period: Early summer until frost
Zones: 3, 4, 5, 6
Light Requirement:

Hybrid rugosa roses are tough, disease-resistant, and winter hardy in Michigan. Although modest, the flowers are beautiful and fragrant. They bloom all summer, and many have rich fall color and ornamental orange hips the size of large crab-apples. *Rosa rugosa*, a Japanese species rose, has been replaced with hybrids called the hybrid rugosas. 'Frau Dagmar Hastrup' is one of the best. It has silky pink fragrant flowers on thorny compact bushes 4 ft. high. Bloom repeats until frost. Very resistant to diseases including leaf spot and mildew, the textured foliage turns bronze to yellow in the fall, complementing the hips. The compact size and ease of culture make this rose a sure bet for growing with perennials. Try 'Frau Dagmar Hastrup' in masses spaced at 3 ft. with perennials such as Russian sage or 'Hameln' fountain grass. Or plan for late-season color by complementing its autumn beauty with the fiery fall hues of perennials such as bluestar, bowman's root, and flame grass. Rugosas are ideal for use in a perennial herb garden or mixed flower bed. Back them with purple fennel and add thyme, 'Tricolor' sage, dill, chives, and purple basil. Tuck in annuals such as flowering tobacco or petunias for more color. Lamb's ears, cheddar pinks, and star-of-Persia contribute to a cottage garden look. The rose serves as a focal point, an organizing element tying together the jumble of color and texture. Rugosa roses can also be used for hedging, softening a fence, or lining a drive. They are tough, beautiful, and easy to grow. Every sunny Michigan garden should be home to at least one.

WHEN TO PLANT

Plant bareroot roses as early in the spring as the soil and weather allow. Container-grown plants should be planted in spring or, at the latest, early summer.

WHERE TO PLANT

Plant rugosa roses in soil that is moist, fertile, and well drained. Locate in full sun for the best performance.

HOW TO PLANT

Soak the roots of bareroot roses for 12 to 24 hours before planting. Dig a hole 18 to 24 in. deep and at least 18 in. wide. Add well-rotted compost and one tablespoon of superphosphate to the soil, and, for bareroot roses only, make a mound in the bottom of the planting hole. Prune off any damaged roots as well as any broken or dead canes. Position the bareroot rose on the mound and spread out the roots. Look for rugosa roses grown on their own roots. If the rose is grafted, it should be positioned so the bud union is level with the surrounding soil or, in northern parts of the state, slightly below. Firm soil gently. Take care not to leave any air gaps underneath the root mass. Fill in around the rose about 2/3 of the way with soil and water. Add the remaining soil. For added protection for bareroot roses, mound the soil around the newly planted rose about 10 to 12 in. deep. After several weeks, when the rose is showing signs of new growth, gently hose off the mounded soil. At this time, apply a 3-in. layer of mulch to conserve moisture and keep the roots cool.

ADVICE FOR CARE

Keep newly planted roses well watered. Hybrid rugosas are pest- and disease-resistant. Rugosa roses have low fertility requirements; in fact, they are widely naturalized on the rocky and sandy eastern coast of the United States.

ADDITIONAL INFORMATION

Hybrid rugosa roses usually need little pruning. Each plant has its own character, and each gardener develops an individual pruning style. In the spring, remove any dead or damaged canes or any that are out of scale with the plant. Older woody branches may be removed to encourage young vigorous growth.

ADDITIONAL SPECIES, CULTIVARS, OR VARIETIES

The rugosa roses 'Jens Munk' and 'Henry Hudson' are both intro-ductions from the Canadian Explorer series. 'Henry Hudson' is a low-growing rugosa with pink buds opening to white fragrant double flowers. At a height and width of 2 to 3 ft., it is suitable for massing and low hedges. 'Jens Munk', another disease-tolerant and hardy rugosa, has semi-double medium pink flowers with a won-derful fragrance and refined shape. Flowering repeats until frost, followed by red hips. This shrub rose reaches 4 to 5 ft. tall.

'Peace' Hybrid Tea Rose

Rosa 'Peace'

Height: 4 to 6 ft.
Flowers: Cream to yellow
flushed with coral-pink
Bloom Period: Early summer
to frost
Zones: 4, 5, 6 with protection
Light Requirement:

Hybrid teas were bred for perfection of flower, and growing them well usually involves watering, fertilizing, deadheading, and pest and disease controls. Still, many gardeners find a special place—and the extra time and patience—to care for these prima donnas of the summer garden. Most hybrid teas are not reliably hardy in Michigan without some winter protection. Many a garden has winter structure provided by the shape of polystyrene rose cones protecting their fragile beauty. A gardener who wants the full-flowered form of a hybrid tea rose might start with the cultivar 'Peace'. It offers fragrance, disease resistance, hardiness, and history. Introduced in 1945, it was named to commemorate the end of World War II. 'Peace' has blooms that are yellow and suffused with pink or coral.

WHEN TO PLANT

Plant bareroot roses in early spring. Container-grown roses should be planted in early to late spring for the best results. Avoid container-grown roses that have become potbound.

WHERE TO PLANT

Choose locations with full sun and well-drained, fertile soil. A location with good air circulation is preferred. Avoid planting near the competing roots of large trees. Good drainage is critical. Consider planting in a raised bed if the drainage in the area is poor.

HOW TO PLANT

Soak the roots of bareroot roses for 12 to 24 hours before planting. Dig a hole 18 to 24 in. deep and at least 18 in. wide. Add well-rotted compost and one tablespoon of superphosphate to the soil, and, for bareroot roses only, make a mound in the bottom of the planting hole. Prune off any damaged roots as well as any broken or dead canes. Cut back any long canes to about 12 in. Position the barerot rose on the mound and spread out the roots. Plant container-grown roses in the planting hole. If the rose is grafted, it should be positioned so the bud union is level with the surrounding soil or, in northern parts of the state, a few inches below. Firm soil gently. Take care not to leave any air gaps underneath the root mass. Fill in about 2/3 of the hole around the rose with soil and water. Add the remaining soil. For added protection for bareroot plants only, mound soil around the newly planted rose about 10 to 12 in. deep. After several weeks, when the rose is showing signs of new growth, gently hose off the soil. At this time, apply a 3-in. layer of mulch to conserve moisture and keep the roots cool.

ADVICE FOR CARE

Keep plants watered and mulched. Avoid wetting the foliage, which can promote disease. Fertilizer should be applied about 2 weeks after spring pruning and once more about 6 weeks later in the season. Fertilizer applied after August 1 will lead to winter injury. Many rose fertilizers are available. Follow the directions on the product. In spring, cut canes back to live wood, and prune down to about 10 in. at an outward facing bud. Remove dead and damaged canes as well as any canes that cross in the middle of the bush or rub against other canes. This will leave 3 to 5 strong canes and an open framework on which to build new growth.

ADDITIONAL INFORMATION

When deadheading or cutting for arrangements, make the cut directly above a five-leaflet leaf. Hybrid tea roses need winter protection in Michigan. Wait until after several freezes in late fall to mound soil from another part of the garden around the rose to a depth of 12 in. Some gardeners make a collar of folded newspaper, chicken wire, or a bottomless bushel basket to surround the rose, then fill it with soil and leaves. A good snow cover is additional winter protection. The consulting rosarian or county extension agent in your area will have more specific advice on winter protection and on pest- and disease-control for hybrid teas. Make life somewhat easier by planting disease-resistant cultivars.

ADDITIONAL SPECIES, CULTIVARS, OR VARIETIES

Not all hybrid teas are full-figured. 'Dainty Bess', an award winner in 1925, has flat, single soft pink flowers with burgundy stamens. It grows 3 1/2 to 4 ft. tall.

'Sunsprite'
Floribunda Rose

Rosa 'Sunsprite'

Height: 3 to 5 ft.
Flowers: Deep yellow
Bloom Period: Early summer
   until frost
Zones: 4, 5, 6
Light Requirement:

The small flowers of floribunda roses appear in profuse clusters on compact bushes, making them useful for rose gardens, low hedges, or massing, or in perennial beds and flower borders. 'Sunsprite' has large clusters of 4-in. double yellow flowers that are very fragrant. Bloom begins on 2-ft. plants early in the rose season and continues until frost. This low-maintenance floribunda has lush deep green foliage and resists disease. Rosarians have called 'Sunsprite' the best yellow rose for the garden. Plant 'Sunsprite' in the foreground of perennial beds, in mixed plantings, or for a low hedge. Try it with the paler yellow flower of 'Moonbeam' coreopsis, chartreuse lady's mantle, and the deep hue of 'Johnson's Blue' hardy geranium for an early summer combination.

WHEN TO PLANT
Plant bareroot floribunda roses in early spring. Container-grown roses should be planted in spring. Avoid container-grown roses that have become potbound because it will be more difficult for the plants to send roots out into your garden's soil.

WHERE TO PLANT
Plant floribunda roses in soil that is moist, fertile, and well drained. Locate in full sun for best performance. Avoid planting near the competing roots of large trees. Good drainage is critical; consider a raised bed in an area where the drainage is poor. Adequate air circulation will discourage disease.

HOW TO PLANT
Soak the roots of bareroot roses for 12 to 24 hours before planting. Dig a hole 18 to 24 in. deep and at least 18 in. wide. Add well-rotted compost and one tablespoon of superphosphate to the soil, and for bareroot plants only, make a mound in the bottom of the planting

hole. Prune off any damaged roots as well as any broken or dead canes. Cut back any long canes to about 12 in. Position the rose on the mound (container-grown roses do not require a mound) and spread out the roots. If the rose is grafted, it should be positioned so the bud union is level with the surrounding soil or, in northern parts of the state, slightly below. Firm soil gently. Take care not to leave any air gaps underneath the root mass. Fill in about 2/3 of the way with soil and water. Add the remaining soil. For added protection for bareroot roses only, mound soil around the newly planted rose about 10 to 12 in. deep. After several weeks, when the rose is showing signs of new growth, gently hose off the soil. At this time, apply a 3-in. layer of mulch to conserve moisture and keep the roots cool.

ADVICE FOR CARE

Keep plants watered and mulched. Avoid wetting the foliage, which can promote disease. Fertilizer should be applied about 2 weeks after spring pruning and once more about 6 weeks later in the season. Fertilizer applied after August 1 will lead to winter injury. Many rose fertilizers are available. Follow the directions on the package.

ADDITIONAL INFORMATION

Many floribunda roses will need winter protection in Michigan. Wait until after several hard freezes in the late fall, then mound soil from another part of the garden 10 to 12 in. high around the rose. Some gardeners make a collar of folded newspaper, chicken wire, or a bottomless bushel basket and fill it with soil and leaves. A layer of snow is excellent winter protection. The consulting rosarian or county extension agent in your area will have more advice. Although floribunda roses are somewhat more resistant to pests and diseases than hybrid teas, a regular schedule of control is necessary to grow most of them well. Plant disease-resistant cultivars, such as 'Sunsprite', 'Nearly Wild', and 'Betty Prior'.

ADDITIONAL SPECIES, CULTIVARS OR VARIETIES

'Betty Prior' is a single rose with clusters of fragrant medium pink blooms. This long-lived rose reaches 4 to 5 ft. Its bushy full form is suitable for hedging. It is hardy without protection in Zone 5. 'Nearly Wild' is a hardy, low-growing (2 ft.) floribunda rose with single medium pink flowers from early summer until frost. Its name describes the simple five-petaled flowers that resemble a wild rose.

'William Baffin' Climbing Rose

Rosa 'William Baffin'

Height: 9 ft.
Flowers: Deep pink
Bloom Period: Early summer and repeat to frost
Zones: 3, 4, 5, 6
Light Requirement:

Trained on a trellis, pillar, or arbor, climbing roses draw the eye upward. They take just a small amount of space in the garden to make a large romantic impact. These roses don't climb on their own; they have no tendrils or holdfasts as vines do. You must tie the long canes to a support or structure such as a fence, trellis, arbor, or wires. The awkward long canes often have a mind of their own, and the gardener must do his or her best to guide them. Many climbers aren't hardy in Michigan, but the Canadian Explorer series offers new tough, hardy, and disease-resistant climbers that can survive even frigid climates. 'William Baffin' is considered to be the hardiest and heaviest-blooming climbing rose for the North. It has bright strawberry pink semi-double flowers produced in large clusters. Flowering is heavy in early summer and repeats until frost. 'William Baffin' is resistant to the usual rose scourges, blackspot and mildew. It flowers with abandon rather than refined elegance. Use it on a trellis or as a tall hedge.

WHEN TO PLANT
Plant bareroot climbing roses in early spring. Container-grown roses should be planted early to late spring for the best results. Avoid container-grown roses that have become potbound because it will be more difficult for the plants to send roots out into your garden's soil.

WHERE TO PLANT
Plant in fertile well-drained soil and full sun. Climbers like to have the bottom of their canes shaded, so underplant with perennials or annuals. Train climbers on trellises, pergolas, arbors, and fences.

HOW TO PLANT
Soak the roots of bareroot roses for 12 to 24 hours before planting. Dig a hole 18 to 24 in. deep and at least 18 in. wide. Add well-rotted

compost and one tablespoon of superphosphate to the soil, and, for bareroot roses only, make a mound in the bottom of the planting hole. Container-grown plants do not require a mound. Prune off any damaged roots as well as any broken or dead canes. Position the rose on the mound and spread out the roots. Canadian roses should be grown on their own roots (not grafted) to ensure cold hardiness. Own-root roses should be planted at the same depth they were growing previously. If the rose is grafted, it should be positioned so the bud union is level with the surrounding soil or slightly below. Firm the soil gently. Do not leave any air gaps underneath the root mass. Fill in about 2/3 of the way with soil and water. Add the remaining soil. For added protection, mound soil around the newly planted bareroot rose about 10 to 12 in. deep. After several weeks, when the rose is showing signs of new growth, gently hose off the soil, and apply a 3-in. layer of mulch to conserve moisture and keep the roots cool. Regular watering is important to a new rose.

ADVICE FOR CARE

Keep plants watered and mulched. Fertilizer should be applied about 2 weeks after spring pruning and once more about 6 weeks later in the season. Inquire where you purchase the rose about fertilizer recommendations. Fertilizer applied after August 1 will lead to winter injury. In the spring, remove any dead or damaged canes. Loosely tie the canes into the structure with string or fabric strips. In spring and early summer, train the young canes to grow in the direction you desire. A fan-shaped pattern is best for an arbor or trellis. Remove canes heading in the wrong direction. Let the rose grow a few years without pruning. Then in the spring, after the rose has put out a flush of growth, small stems growing from the main cane and long canes can be trimmed to promote vigorous flowering. Make diagonal cuts (on a 45-degree angle) with sharp bypass pruners. After 4 or 5 years, remove old woody canes and tie in new ones.

ADDITIONAL INFORMATION

Clematis and morning glory can be grown in combination with climbing roses. Keep trellises and other supports at least 3 in. away from a wall for air circulation.

ADDITIONAL SPECIES, CULTIVARS, OR VARIETIES

Another Canadian Explorer series climber is 'John Cabot'. It has deep pink, almost red flowers and a long blooming season. Growing to about 8 ft., it can be trained to a trellis or fence or grown as a large arching shrub. 'New Dawn', a sumptuous pearly pink, is one of the most popular climbing roses. It is hardy to Zone 5, but may still need winter protection.

Shrubs

*F*LOWERS AND FRAGRANCES, COLORFUL STEMS AND FRUITS, EXFOLIATING BARK—shrubs offer all these attractions and more. With the right selection, a shrub provides four-season appeal in a relatively compact size.

Shrubs are an important design element in the garden. Trees and shrubs define space, creating a framework in which to fit other plants. They are a backdrop for annuals and perennials during spring, summer, and fall. In winter, when many branches are bare, the strong shapes of trees and shrubs are at their most distinct. They are the landscape's "bones."

There are many shrubs to choose from. This book profiles twenty-nine that offer outstanding attributes and are among the easiest to grow in Michigan gardens.

SELECTING A SHRUB
Shrubs are typically sold in one of three ways: container-grown, bareroot, or balled-and-burlapped.

Container-grown plants have spent most of their lives in pots. These shrubs may be planted at any time during the growing season. There should be signs of new leaves. If roots are growing tightly inside the container, the shrub will have a difficult time making the transition to your garden.

Bareroot shrubs have been grown at a nursery field. They are dug up while dormant, then offered for sale. Open these as soon as you get them and examine the roots for damaged portions. Cut and remove broken or damaged roots back to healthy tissue before planting, which should take place as soon as possible.

Balled-and-burlapped shrubs are also grown in nursery fields. They are dug with a ball of soil left intact around their roots and are usually the largest shrubs available. The rootball is wrapped in burlap or other material to hold it together. Because this takes more labor, these plants are usually the most expensive. They are also heavy, so enlist a friend to help plant your shrub.

Balled-and-burlapped shrubs may be planted in March, April, and May, or in September, October, and November. Spring planting is often preferred because the roots have time to grow before the heat of summer sets in.

When planting shrubs, dig a hole as deep as the rootball or container and three times as wide. Remove the burlap, container, or any other material surrounding the shrub's roots. Hose off the rootball to expose the roots and, if possible, gently loosen the roots with your fingers. With rootbound plants that have built up a large mass of circling roots at the bottom of the ball, score the roots with a utility blade or old kitchen knife. Four or five cuts spaced evenly around the ball will break roots free and encourage their healthy development in the soil.

Position the shrub so it is growing at the same depth it was in the container or field. Replace the soil around the rootball, water well to moisten and to eliminate air pockets, and then check again to see if additional soil is needed. Mound up the soil in a ring around the new plant. The ring creates a retention reservoir that holds water in place so it can slowly percolate into the soil.

After planting, prune out any dead or broken branches. Apply a 2- to 3-inch layer of mulch, such as shredded bark, around the shrub. During the first season, water the shrub during dry periods, continuing until the ground freezes.

Pruning can be used to control shrub size, to promote flowering, and to remove overcrowded growth. It also rejuvenates plants that have lost vigor and need a jump start to get growing again.

Shrubs that bloom on last season's growth, such as lilacs and forsythia, should be pruned after they flower. Those that bloom on the current season's growth, such as *Hydrangea* and *Clethra*, should be pruned in February or March while the plant is dormant.

Anglojap Yew

Taxus × media

Height: Recommended low-spreading forms are under 6 ft.
Foliage: Dark evergreen needles
Zones: 4, 5, 6
Light Requirement:

The yew is a beleaguered plant and in many ways a shrub that Rodney Dangerfield might say "can't get no respect." Overused, hacked, butchered, and vying each year for the unofficial title of "the state shrub of Michigan," yews are caught in an ugly conundrum of versatility versus abuse. While it is certainly true that they are all too frequent in their appearance in Michigan landscapes, they are extremely important shrubs for both landscapers and home owners looking for green relief in the often gray days of winter. The anglojap yew offers several cultivars with a low, spreading habit particularly useful for foundation plantings, evergreen screens, or hedges, or in mass plantings as a backdrop to other colorful trees or shrubs. Yews in general can be kept under control by frequent pruning, which is a balancing act between butchering and styling. The most important factor is not to get too carried away with the shears. Reserved pruning will allow for the natural habit of your selected variety to show through. These are extremely adaptable shrubs that can be planted from full sun to shade in most soil types but will have severe problems in wet conditions, where they become susceptible to root rot. Plant yews to add color where it is most needed in your garden.

WHEN TO PLANT
Plant in the spring or fall. Late fall planting past November is not recommended because plants suffer winter burn.

WHERE TO PLANT
Plant in full sun or shade. Yews make effective hedges or screens, but attention to the ultimate size and spread of the cultivar is critical in the spacing of plants as you plan your hedge. Plants placed too closely will immediately require pruning and will have poor form. Plants placed too far apart will not be effective barriers and will offer welcome entry ways for marauding visitors. The closest distance between 2 points is between 2 shrubs! With their exceptional

dark green needles, yews are indeed colorful winter landscape plants. Planted in combination with other deciduous trees and shrubs, they offer a striking contrast in color and textures. While perfectly hardy in Michigan, the anglojap yew should be planted out of severely exposed windy locations, where needles brown out from water loss.

How to Plant
Plant as a container-grown or balled-and-burlapped shrub.

Advice for Care
Avoid planting in low areas where water accumulates and may cause root rot. When pruning, use hand pruners if time and energy are available. Prune back selected branches to the main body of the shrub, varying the depth of the cuts so that you do not produce a straight line. This results in a more natural effect. Shrubs should be pruned so that they result in wider growth at the bottom versus the top. A large unwieldy top casts shade on the bottom portions of the shrub, limiting growth and perpetuating an imbalanced form. Prune in the winter or early summer. Two pests that sometimes pose a problem with yews are the taxus mealybug and black vine weevil. The mealybug is covered with a white waxy coating and sucks sap from the plant, causing needle drop and loss of vigor. A dormant oil application is the recommended control for mealybug. Black vine weevil feeds on roots, causing needles to yellow. Severe infestations can kill a plant. The adult weevil feeds at night, notching the needles. This is most noticeable on needles in the center of the plant. Orthene™ is the recommended control for the black vine weevil.

Additional Information
Yews with their salt tolerance can be used along walks and driveways where frequent salting is required. Both male and female plants exist in the nursery trade. Female plants have brightly colored fleshy fruit. The fleshy portion of the fruit (the aril) is not poisonous, and birds enjoy it. The inner hard seeds are considered poisonous, however.

Additional Species, Cultivars, or Varieties
'Ward' or 'Wardii' is a low-spreading selection with a flat top and dark green foliage. It is slow-growing with a 20-year-old plant reaching 6 ft. in height and 19 ft. in width. The 'Ward' yew is a female selection. 'Brownii' is a male plant with attractive dark green foliage and a rounded habit, staying below 6 ft. in height and responding well to pruning.

Arborvitae

Thuja occidentalis

Other Name: White Cedar
Height: Dwarf selections to 5 ft.; hedge types to 10 to 20 ft.
Zones: 3, 4, 5, 6
Light Requirement:

Arborvitae grows naturally in the wet cedar swamps in northern Michigan and the sandy dunes that border the Great Lakes. This shrub's adaptability to both wet and dry sites makes it a valuable addition to the landscape where poor soils are a challenge and may limit the plants you can use. Numerous selections are available offering a myriad of shapes and sizes with a tremendous range of evergreen foliage colors, from soft green to intense dark tones. While arborvitaes are often ridiculed for being overused in landscapes, they are extremely versatile, which accounts for their popularity. Perhaps the greatest challenge with the arborvitae is selecting the right one to suit your needs. Choosing the right one for your garden becomes difficult when the variety is overwhelming, but over time a few selections have proven superior for northern climates. If you have a small garden, consider the dwarf selections. 'Globosa', a dwarf rounded shrub, maintains a perfectly round shape with minimal pruning. It is extremely slow-growing, reaching a height of 5 ft. with an equal spread. Although many homeowners are content with the uniform symmetry of evergreen shrubs, others are more adventuresome and prefer something different. 'Smaragd' is an extreme upright form with beautiful bright green foliage. It makes a strong vertical accent in the garden. Use it in mass plantings or as an imposing screen. It is usually found in the local nursery trade as 'Emerald' or 'Emerald Green'. 'Techny', also known as 'Mission', has a large pyramidal form reaching 10 to 15 ft. in height with beautiful dark green foliage throughout the winter months. Large types make effective hedges or screen plantings, adding privacy and seclusion—two valued commodities in the urban jungle.

WHEN TO PLANT

Arborvitae can be planted in spring or fall. When planting in the fall, be sure to water well when natural rainfall is scarce. In extremely windy or exposed sites, a burlap screen is advisable to protect the foliage from winter burn. Keep in mind that when the soil freezes, water becomes limited to the above-ground portions of the plant. Fall watering and winter screening will help new plants make it through the critical first winter season.

WHERE TO PLANT

Dwarf cultivars of arborvitae can be used as foundation plants under windows or as a low-growing hedge. Use columnar or narrow selections to make unusual vertical accents or privacy screens. Arborvitaes are the ultimate evergreen plant for creating hedges because they respond well to shaping and pruning. When choosing from the many cultivars of arborvitae, be sure to determine the shrub's mature size and shape. For instance, 'Globosa' will never respond well to pruning intended to make it into a box. Arborvitaes are weak wooded and easily break under heavy snow loads. Broken branches create unsightly gaps that will require a few seasons of regrowth to overcome. Keep plants away from roof lines, where sliding avalanches may cause heartache for you and disaster for your plants.

HOW TO PLANT

With container-grown plants, be sure to pull apart compacted or circling roots that have built up in the bottom of the pot. Plant high enough so that after watering and settling, the main trunk does not sink below ground level. This is true for both container and balled-and-burlapped plants. Very tall plants may need staking for stability during the first few seasons while they establish their roots.

ADVICE FOR CARE

Despite the fact that arborvitaes grow in sandy soils, they do not tolerate prolonged periods of drought. Water well in dry periods.

ADDITIONAL INFORMATION

Arborvitae leaf miner is an occasional pest that may need control. Leaf miners feed on the inner portion of the foliage, causing it to become translucent or papery in appearance. Light infestations will not seriously threaten the plant. Should heavy infestations occur, spray with an application of Sevin™ following the manufacturer's recommended rates.

ADDITIONAL SPECIES, CULTIVARS, OR VARIETIES

The western arborvitae, *Thuja plicata*, is a pyramidal tree with attractive glossy green foliage and a narrow habit. It needs protection from winter winds to prevent burn. However, 'Euchlora' is a very hardy selection that appears well suited for northern gardens.

Arnold Promise Witchhazel

Hamamelis × intermedia 'Arnold Promise'

Height: 15 to 20 ft.
Flowers: Yellow
Bloom Period: Early spring
Zones: 4, 5, 6
Light Requirement:

Witchhazels are enchanting with their fragrant, spidery spring blooms and beautiful fall color, all combined on a shrub with an architectural branching habit. Once you have one placed in your garden, you will begin to search for more. The witchhazels are a group of North American and Asian species. 'Arnold Promise' is perhaps the showiest of the entire bunch with spectacular early flowers that are both long-lasting and pungently fragrant. The deep yellow flowers are composed of thin strap-like petals that open in the first warm days of March. The petals have a curious habit of unfurling on warm days, only to roll back in again as temperatures decline. This unique antifreeze device will in certain years extend the bloom period for up to 3 weeks. In the W. J. Beal Botanic Garden at Michigan State University, witchhazel in bloom is often accompanied by the flowers of winter aconite, *Eranthis hyemalis*. 'Arnold Promise' is a hybrid shrub resulting from a cross between the Japanese and Chinese witchhazels. It has an upright, vase-shaped open habit reaching 15 ft. or more in height and width. The leaves are gray-green in the summer months, turning a brilliant red in the fall. While it's easy to become enamored with the Asian witchhazels, we can look within our own state borders to find another beautiful witchhazel, *Hamamelis virginiana*. Common in almost all counties of the Lower Peninsula, this tree-sized shrub flowers in October. The yellow petals appear at the same time the witchhazel's yellow fall foliage is peaking. As you pass them in a native woodlot, you sometimes catch a faint fragrance and realize how special this plant is for its late flowering habit. Tim remembers vividly a plant he saw in Ludington one warm and sunny October day. The shrub was nearly 25 ft. tall and reached up a stairway to the second-floor loft of a bed-and-breakfast establishment. Spidery flowers cloaked the spreading branches of this awesome specimen, twisted and gnarled with age.

WHEN TO PLANT

Transplant in the spring or fall as container-grown plants or balled-and-burlapped plants. Protect the first few seasons from rabbits by surrounding the base of the plant with a screening of chicken wire. This will put hungry rabbits at bay and give your new plant a fighting chance.

WHERE TO PLANT

Witchhazels are too large for a foundation planting. Instead, place witchhazels within view of a window or near a well-traveled path. Plant in full sun or partial shade, and you will be rewarded with heavy flowers and good fall color. Avoid planting under eaves where vertical space is limited.

HOW TO PLANT

The 'Arnold Promise' witchhazel is typically a grafted shrub. Be careful when planting so as not to disturb the graft union, a weak point on the plant that can easily be damaged.

ADVICE FOR CARE

Witchhazels are insect- and disease-free. A problem can occur with grafted plants when the understock (the rootstock portion) sprouts below the graft union. If the understock is allowed to develop, it will eventually overtake the top portion of the plant, stealing nutrients and shading out stems. Remove vigorous sprouts as soon as they start to grow. These shoots are normally rank in growth and keep their leaves attached long after the leaves have dropped in autumn. Witchhazels develop a permanent framework that is both strong and attractive and does not require regular pruning. Do not try to shape a witchhazel or reduce it drastically in size. Leave it to develop the wonderful branch structure it is so often admired for.

ADDITIONAL INFORMATION

Witchhazels, despite all their wonderful qualities, are still hard to find at the local garden center. If this is the case in your area, ask them to stock the plant. Its early flowering period is not the normal time of the year when people are out shopping for trees and shrubs; therefore, it is sadly neglected.

ADDITIONAL SPECIES, CULTIVARS, OR VARIETIES

The vernal witchhazel, *Hamamelis vernalis*, is native to the central United States but is fully hardy in Michigan. It blooms before 'Arnold Promise'—sometimes as early as February—with smaller orange to yellow flowers that pack quite a fragrance. This shrub reaches up to 15 ft. in height and width and has beautiful red fall color.

Arrowwood Viburnum

Viburnum dentatum

Height: 15 ft.
Flowers: Creamy white
Bloom Period: June
Zones: 3, 4, 5, 6
Light Requirement:

Viburnums as a group represent some of the most serviceable shrubs for Michigan gardens, and the native North American arrowwood viburnum is no exception. Beautiful in foliage, flower, and fruit, this little-known shrub has seen vast improvement in recent years with new selections adaptable to northern climates. The arrowwood has lustrous dark green leaves that turn to reddish-purple or burgundy in the fall. It's a moderate-sized shrub with delicate branches forming a dense, multistemmed, rounded habit. Size will vary somewhat with cultivar selection but will range from 10 to 15 ft. in height with width of 8 to 12 ft. or more. The flowers appear in June in flat-topped blooms that last for about 2 weeks and are creamy white in color. The fragrance is somewhat of a musty odor that is not noticeable without close inspection. Large crops of blue-black fruits appear in late summer and bring birds to the garden. The twiggy framework of this shrub makes it highly recommended for wildlife plantings because birds find it a very suitable shrub to nest in. The arrowwood is exceptional in its versatility, growing in a variety of soil types and performing well both in full sun and in partial shade.

When to Plant

Plant in the spring or fall.

Where to Plant

Planted in full sun or partial shade, the arrowwood is suitable for a variety of situations—used as a single specimen, planted in mass, used for a hedge or screening, or incorporated into the shrub border. When planting in groups, space at least 12 to 15 ft. apart to prevent individuals from shading each other out. Plants can be placed in moist locations where other plants would struggle. Birds relish the blue-black fruits produced in late August and September and harvest the crop by late fall.

How to Plant
Avoid deep shade when siting.

Advice for Care
Remove older wood periodically to encourage the development of new growth. Shrubs sprout new stems from underground or from the bottom branches. Prune peripheral outside branches that have expanded beyond their boundaries.

Additional Information
Downy mildew is sometimes a problem with the arrowwood viburnum when planted in deep shade and where air circulation is poor in its immediate environment. Leaves become off-colored between the veins and eventually turn brown and fall off. The fungus generally begins by attacking the lower or inner portions of the shrub and then spreads to other areas. Wet weather encourages the development of downy mildew, but the mildew is also favored by sites where there is little air movement. Better air circulation helps keep foliage dry and the disease from proliferating.

Additional Species, Cultivars, or Varieties
The Chicagoland Grows® plant introduction program has released some improved selections of the arrowwood viburnum. 'Chicago Lustre' has thick, dark green glossy foliage, creamy white flowers from mid- to late June, and metallic blue fruits from late August to early October. 'Morton', also known as Northern Burgundy™, has a broad, upright-rounded habit with dark green foliage that turns a beautiful burgundy in the fall. Abundant blue-black fruits are produced in late September through October. The mature size is 10 to 12 ft. in height and spread. 'Ralph Senior', also known as Autumn Jazz™, has an upright graceful habit that is enhanced by its slightly pendulous dark green foliage with colorful red stems. The fall color is a blend of yellow, orange, and red. Attractive creamy white flowers appear in late May and June, eventually producing blue-black fruits from late August through early October.

Bayberry

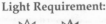

Myrica pensylvanica

Height: 9 to 12 ft.
Flowers: Not showy; waxy gray fruit
Bloom Period: Early spring
Zones: 3, 4, 5, 6
Light Requirement:

Once in a while you come across a plant and cannot fathom why it is not used more often. The common bayberry is in this category. This remarkably adaptable native has a rugged character that admittedly makes it hard to use in more formal landscapes. Attractive glossy green foliage and branches bearing masses of waxy gray berries invite the gardener to use this plant in areas where a more naturalistic look is wanted and birds are encouraged to visit. Bayberry is an upright mounded shrub that is effective in mass planting. On the campus of Michigan State University, it is used extensively along walkways and building entrances that are heavily salted to melt ice for pedestrian traffic. Bayberry is native to the coast of the Atlantic Ocean, where it endures salt spray and high soil salinity. Its salt tolerance, drought resistance, and rugged beauty make it a valuable urban landscape shrub. Bayberry flowers in the early spring. Although the flowers are not showy, a waxy fruit is produced that is light gray in color and lasts well into the winter months. The wax from the fruit is used to produce bayberry candles. Growing at a moderate to fast rate, the bayberry reaches up to 10 ft. in height and slowly colonizes by underground stems.

WHEN TO PLANT
Plant in the spring or fall as a container-grown plant.

WHERE TO PLANT
Plant in full sun or partial shade. Shrubs placed in full sun have more fruits. If you want to keep bayberry growing as a compact foundation shrub, yearly pruning will be necessary. Bayberry is effective on steep hillsides, where you may want to forget about growing grass and instead establish a lush planting. Use the dark green glossy leaves to back up a perennial planting, to set off colorful flowers, or to create an interesting textural contrast. Depending on the exposure, plantings lose most of their semi-evergreen foliage during the winter months in northern areas.

How to Plant

No special requirements are needed for bayberry. It transplants easily and is very drought-tolerant.

Advice for Care

Pruning is recommended if plants have grown too tall or are escaping into other areas and need to be confined. Remove large straggly branches that have grown out of proportion. To reduce the height of mature plantings, cut right back to the ground. New growth will quickly emerge and begin to fill in again. Perform this activity in the spring just before new growth begins.

Additional Information

Male and female flowers appear on separate plants so you must plant both to get fruit. However, the plants sold are not often labeled male or female. The best solution is to buy the plants in the fall when the fruits can be easily seen. Choose at least one plant with fruits and one without. The foliage of bayberry is aromatic, and cut branches work well in flower arrangements. Bayberry is unique in that it can fix its own nitrogen, using special bacteria in association with its roots. This helps the plants survive in low-nutrient, sandy soils. Remarkably, plants also adapt well to heavy clay soils that are frequently waterlogged or wet.

Additional Species, Cultivars, or Varieties

No cultivars exist at this time for bayberry. A dwarf selection would be of great benefit. Male and female selections should be developed because gardeners are often disappointed when the attractive fruits are not produced. Sweetgale, *Myrica gale*, is a dwarf shrubby relative that occurs naturally in the northern half of the Lower Peninsula. It has attractive, aromatic dark green foliage and grows in moist or wet alkaline soils.

Bluebeard

Caryopteris × clandonensis

Other Name: Blue Spirea
Height: 2 to 3 ft.
Flowers: Blue
Bloom Period: Late summer
Zone: 6
Light Requirement:

The bluebeard is a versatile shrub that finds a natural spot in the garden as a stand-alone specimen or in combination with herbaceous perennials. The long arching branches are covered with aromatic silver foliage. Late in the summer, light to dark blue flowers emerge at a time when few other woody plants are in bloom. Because of it size, arching habit, and the textural quality of the foliage, this shrub combines particularly well with ornamental grasses. The foliage and flowers also are attractive with fall-blooming pink and magenta asters or the white blooms of *Boltonia asteroides* 'Snowbank'. Gardeners often consider the bluebeard to be a herbaceous perennial since it is not stem hardy in the North. Each year, the branches die back to the woody center or crown of the plant; however, they quickly grow back with the onset of warmer temperatures. Gardeners often worry about bluebeard in spring. Its new growth is slow to sprout while other plants nearby are well on their way. This is a time for patience. Eventually, the bluebeard will show signs of life. Early spring bare stems can be hidden by surrounding the shrub with spring bulbs such as daffodils or crocus.

When to Plant

Plant in the spring before the beginning of warm summer temperatures. If you decide to plant in the fall, water well and mulch after the ground freezes. This will keep the plant from heaving or lifting out of the ground due to soil temperature fluctuations.

Where to Plant

Placed in the perennial border, the silvery gray foliage is the perfect foil with coral bells, *Heuchera* 'Palace Purple', or other dark-leaved perennials. Plant in full sun for good foliage and flower effect. Plants in shade tend to flop and flower poorly. The bluebeard, with its low stature and wispy branches, does not make a strong hedge plant. Instead, use it where the late summer blooms will add color to a dull spot in your garden, placing the silver foliage and unique flower color to their best advantage.

How to Plant
Plants are mainly available in containers or as small potted plants from perennial mail-order supply firms. The bluebeard has a fibrous root system that responds well to transplanting.

Advice for Care
While reputedly drought-tolerant, the bluebeard will suffer in sharply drained soils during dry periods. Spider mite is occasionally a problem in drought conditions. Water when shrubs start to flag or wilt. Plants normally do not require fertilizer in healthy soils. Rich soils or unnecessary fertilization will cause rank growth that will not produce flowers. Take a wait-and-see attitude with this shrub before fertilizing.

Additional Information
Seedlings will occasionally sprout around the garden and should be removed. They are generally inferior to the mother plant in foliage and flower. Butterflies love this shrub's late-season flowers. Attractive butterfly plantings combine the bluebeard with purple coneflower and the blazing star. Flowering branches make attractive cut flowers.

Additional Species, Cultivars, or Varieties
'Dark Knight' produces striking dark blue flowers from late July to mid-August. 'Blue Mist' has powder blue flowers that combine well with *Sedum* 'Autumn Joy'. 'Worcester Gold' is a newer release with golden foliage and light blue flowers. Time will tell if it is truly stem hardy in the colder regions of our state.

Bottlebrush Buckeye

Aesculus parviflora

Height: 8 to 12 ft.
Flowers: White
Bloom Period: Midsummer
Zones: 4, 5, 6
Light Requirement:

Bottlebrush buckeye is a southeastern native that is perfectly adaptable to Michigan gardens. It has many outstanding features, making it appear as an unusual and exotic plant that is rarely found in our landscapes. The shrub forms a large mound as much as 15 ft. wide, spreading by underground stems to form a dense colony. The leaves are large and divided into 5 parts. Dark green and heavily textured, they hang downward in a lazy fashion. In mid-July to early August, tall spikes appear above the foliage bearing clusters of tiny beautiful white flowers. These upright blooms light up the garden at a time when few woody plants are showing color. The flowers flow over the mounds of foliage in a billowing mass that is particularly impressive in shady areas of the garden. Why this plant is not used more often is a great mystery. The bottlebrush buckeye is well suited to a naturalistic or woodland setting where the underground stems can spread freely to form an untamed mass. The fall season is showtime again as the foliage turns a beautiful yellow before dropping. Although a southern native and rare in the wild, the bottlebrush buckeye is hardy to Zone 4 and is not bothered by frigid Michigan winters. The biggest challenge will be keeping rabbits away from the young succulent new growth, which they munch on like salad greens. Protect young plants by placing chicken wire cages around them as they adjust to their new surroundings.

WHEN TO PLANT

Early spring or fall is the best time to plant buckeyes. The suckering underground stems around the shrub's periphery can be dug as divisions in the spring or fall to add plants to other areas of the garden or to swap with a friend. Be sure to get a large portion of roots with your division to ensure successful establishment in its new site.

WHERE TO PLANT

The bottlebrush buckeye is ideal for the home owner who has a large plot and can plant it out and watch it roam. For smaller landscapes, keep it away from the foundation of your house or it will eventually obscure windows and become a nuisance. Take advantage of its colonizing nature to screen an ugly tool shed or hide utility boxes. Use it to form a privacy barrier that both you and your neighbor will enjoy.

How to Plant

Plants are rarely offered balled and burlapped because of their spreading stems. Container-grown plants often come with suckers ready and willing to spread when you place the plant in its hole. Buckeyes prefer a rich, loamy soil for optimal growth. If your soil is too sandy, work in organic matter (well-rotted manure and peat) to increase nutrients and the moisture-holding capacity of the soil.

Advice for Care

This relatively maintenance-free plant will not ask for much if properly sited. Water well in prolonged periods of drought. Large-sized plants can be cut back to the ground to control their size or to rejuvenate an older specimen.

Additional Information

Demand creates supply. If you can't find this plant at your local nursery, encourage the owners to stock it. Have 10 friends make the same request, and by next season the nursery will offer it—and probably sell all of the stock. There is a reason the bottlebrush buckeye is rarely found in nurseries. The plants produce seeds (the large buckeye nut) only in unusually hot summers and are generally difficult to grow by other means. Divisions from your garden will become a hot commodity with your gardening friends once they see your shrub in bloom or in fall color.

Additional Species, Cultivars, or Varieties

The red buckeye, *Aesculus pavia*, is a medium-sized tree that reaches 10 to 20 ft. in height and produces beautiful red flowers in late June in Michigan.

Carolina Allspice

Calycanthus floridus

Other Name: Sweet Shrub
Height: 6 to 8 ft.
Flowers: Dark maroon
Bloom Period: Late spring to early summer
Zones: 5, 6
Light Requirement:

Common names of plants are sometimes ridiculed in the botanical community because they may be applied to 2 entirely different plants. But common names are often highly descriptive, as is the case with the Carolina allspice, also called sweet shrub. Its bark, branches, flowers, and fruits are highly aromatic. While fragrance abounds both spicy and sweet, the allspice is also a serviceable landscape plant. *Calycanthus* reaches 6 to 8 ft. in height and up to 12 ft. in width. Plants in full sun grow taller. The flowers of the allspice are unusual, with numerous reddish-brown, ribbon-like petals that emit a sweet fragrance. The odor is pervasive on hot sunny days and can vary from strawberry to banana to pineapple. Weather permitting, the flowers can last up to 3 weeks, taking on the scent of cider as they fade. The dark color of the flowers hides them from immediate view, but the smell makes you come closer to discover the mysterious bloom. The foliage is highly ornamental with a glossy dark green sheen produced by a waxy coating. Fall color varies from year to year but can be a beautiful yellow. At times, the display is damaged by freezing temperatures before it has fully developed. Carolina allspice makes an outstanding specimen plant, forming a rounded bush.

WHEN TO PLANT

Plant in spring or fall. Carolina allspice is easy to transplant, whether purchased container grown or balled-and-burlapped.

WHERE TO PLANT

Plant on the windward side of your house to catch the sweet breezes that roll off this shrub as it flowers. Plant in full sun for heavy flowering. In mass plantings, space plants at least 12 ft. apart to allow room to grow. The Carolina allspice spreads from underground stems, which can be dug from the periphery of the bush and planted elsewhere in your garden. Perform division in the spring while the plant is still dormant.

How to Plant

This is an extremely easy shrub to transplant. Water in times of drought.

Advice for Care

Calycanthus is generally disease- and insect-free. It prefers a moist, acid soil and may show signs of chlorosis on high pH soils. The foliage will become a sickly yellow in color, and the output of green healthy leaf tissue will diminish. To lower pH, use fertilizers that contain sulfur or that are known to have an acidic reaction. *Calycanthus* may become straggly after many years in your garden but can easily be rejuvenated by cutting to the ground immediately after flowering. Young shoots will sprout from the base and within a few years produce a dense, full-sized shrub. Prune after flowering to encourage new flowering wood for next spring. Winterkill or dieback of selected branches occurs in very cold years. Remove any dead branches in early spring.

Additional Information

The flowers of this shrub have been used to spice up dresser drawers with their sweet fragrance. The color and scent of the flowers attract beetles as their faithful pollinators. Seed-grown *Calycanthus* in the nursery trade will vary in its flower fragrance; purchase plants that pass your nose test to be sure it's the right one for your garden. The large, dark, urn-shaped fruits are admired by some and disliked by others. Either way, they are unique structures, full of sweet-smelling seeds.

Additional Species, Cultivars, or Varieties

'Edith Wilder' has burgundy flowers that are extremely fragrant and a more open habit that may need pruning to keep it compact and manageable.

'Carol Mackie' Daphne

Daphne × *burkwoodii*

Height: 3 to 4 ft.
Flowers: White
Bloom Period: June
Zones: 5, 6
Light Requirement:

Daphnes are notorious for their challenging culture and their remarkable beauty and fragrance. While most of the species are impractical or nearly impossible to grow in Michigan, the 'Carol Mackie' daphne is a pleasant surprise. This is the perfect plant for a foundation planting or beneath a window where the fragrance from its spring flowers will waft through the air. A dwarf shrub by most standards, it forms a dense, bushy mound 3 to 4 ft. high and wide with small green leaves edged with a gold band. This outstanding foliage makes a wonderful specimen plant that combines well with low groundcovers such as the giant bugleweed, *Ajuga reptans* 'Catlin's Giant'. The variegated foliage is preceded in the early spring by small pink flowers that draw an admiring crowd. Plants grow from a low-branching structure that has very soft wood.

WHEN TO PLANT

Plant in early spring. Avoid fall planting, which will be less successful. Purchase and install container plants with well-established root systems. Balled-and-burlapped plants have problems with transplant shock and are slow to reestablish roots. Daphnes are reputedly very difficult to transplant; when you place the plant in the garden, think of it as a lifelong commitment for both you and your daphne.

WHERE TO PLANT

Plant in full sun for fine foliage and flower display. Place it along a well-traveled walkway where you can enjoy it on a daily basis. Mass plantings actually take away from the splendor of a single specimen. This is truly a unique plant that deserves a prime spot in your garden. Daphne's weak, springy wood makes it an ineffective barrier or hedge plant. A formal planting along the front of a raised deck or among low-growing perennials can be effective. Do not plant near roof lines where snow and ice loads may drop on this fragile shrub.

How to Plant

Be gentle in the planting process to avoid disturbing the root system. When planting from a container, remove the plant carefully, keeping as much of the original root system as possible. Remember that this plant's branches are brittle and break easily if handled too roughly.

Advice for Care

Put mulch around the root zone of the 'Carol Mackie' daphne to help conserve water and prevent weed development. A dark bark mulch makes the variegated foliage stand out. Water in periods of prolonged drought. Prune after flowering in early summer. Do not prune in the fall or winter because you will remove the next spring's flower buds. Daphne can be pruned low when transplanting into its permanent site. Cut back to 1/4 in. above the leaf buds. Low pruning will help build a strong branch structure, creating a dense, full-bodied shrub.

Additional Information

Daphnes may be hard to locate because of their finicky reputation and difficulty in propagation. The daphne's stems, foliage, and fruits are highly poisonous. Be careful if young children play nearby.

Additional Species, Cultivars, or Varieties

'Somerset' is a related selection with a dense round habit, green foliage, and the incredible fragrant flowers that daphnes are known for. The parents of the hybrid 'Carol Mackie' daphne are hardy in Michigan if grown under the right conditions. *Daphne caucasica* is a beautiful small shrub with fragrant pink flowers that bloom from early spring to late fall. The garland flower, *Daphne cneorum*, is a choice plant for the rock garden. A true dwarf topping out at 3 ft. tall, it produces rose-pink fragrant flowers in the spring and often blooms again in the late summer. The garland flower needs a protected spot out of exposed wind and winter sun. All daphnes need well-drained soils to grow well.

Chinese Juniper

Juniperus chinensis

Height: To 12 ft.
Foliage: Blue-green
Zones: 3, 4, 5, 6
Light Requirement:

In Michigan and other colder areas of the country, evergreen shrubs play an integral part of almost any landscape design, adding continuity and color to the long winter season. Junipers represent a large group of utilitarian shrubs that withstand not only bitterly cold but also hot, dry conditions and windy exposed sites. Their salt tolerance makes them particularly valuable around sidewalks and entrances. With their inherent toughness comes their widespread overuse in our landscapes, but their value cannot be underestimated. When selecting a cultivar of the Chinese juniper, think of new ways to use this old standby shrub. Many selections have outstanding foliage with intense coloration ranging from green to blue-green to grayish-green. Several varieties offer beautiful fragrant juniper berries that are found on female selections. When placing junipers in your landscape, pair them with other plants that have winter interest. On the campus of Michigan State University, junipers are often found forming a skirt at the base of heavy fruiting crab apples. The persistent red fruits and dark branches seem even brighter contrasting with the crisp blue-green foliage of the Chinese juniper.

WHEN TO PLANT

Plant in spring or fall.

WHERE TO PLANT

Plant in full sun to avoid leggy, weak growth that develops in shade. Use as a specimen, protective hedge or screen, groundcover, or a foundation plant. Most anywhere you have a difficult site and want evergreen color, the Chinese juniper will have something to offer. When you select a specific juniper, ascertain its ultimate height and spread. The popular Pfitzer juniper is often found hulking outside a first-floor window as a foundation plant. What was once installed as a small shrub has become a menacing giant. Be sure to plant compact, lower-growing selections where space is limited. Junipers prefer full sun and tolerate a wide range of soil conditions with the

exception of excessively dry or wet soils. They make excellent hedge plants because they are very tolerant of pruning and shaping.

How to Plant
Plant as a container-grown plant.

Advice for Care
Junipers are among the toughest groups of landscape shrubs and therefore are frequently planted, often in mass. With large-scale plantings comes the threat of disease when a plant is so frequently used. A fungus called twig blight, *Phomopsis juniperovora*, is a common ailment of junipers that develops in the early spring, particularly in wet weather. The tips of the branches become a reddish brown, eventually turning an ash gray as needles die. Often you can see signs of the disease when the fungus appears as black fruiting bodies at the base of the infected branch. Spores emerge from these structures, attacking young new growth to start the infection process again. To avoid infection, plant in open, dry areas and provide good drainage. Do not use overhead irrigation on your juniper plantings. Overhead watering provides the moist conditions that favor disease development.

Additional Information
Prune the Chinese juniper during the winter months, cutting back branches that have grown out of proportion. Remove long branches with hand pruners back to the main framework of the shrub. Avoid shearing junipers because it creates a rough look. Remove top-heavy growth that shades out the bottom portion of the shrub. Juniper branches and their blue fruits make excellent holiday greens, so many people wait to prune junipers until December.

Additional Species, Cultivars, or Varieties
'Sea Green' has a fountainlike form with dark green foliage. It grows 4 to 6 ft. high and 6 to 8 ft. wide, and it has an upright habit. The sargent juniper, *Juniperus sargentii*, is a low-growing spreading selection with blue-green foliage and long trailing branches. It grows 2 ft. high and up to 10 ft. wide.

Climbing Hydrangea

Hydrangea petiolaris

Height: 75 ft.
Flowers: White
Bloom Period: Late spring to early summer
Zones: 5, 6
Light Requirement:

The climbing hydrangea is an ornamental vine unrivaled for its four-season appeal. A true clinging vine, it has soft green, lustrous leaves and beautiful clusters of large white flowers in late June or July. In the winter months, the rough tan peeling outer bark reveals the orange-tan under bark, which is especially beautiful when affixed to a dark brick surface. This is perhaps why this plant has been described so often as the best clinging vine. The climbing hydrangea's early performance often disappoints gardeners, however. They watch and wait anxiously to see this vine cover a brick wall or cascade over a garden trellis, but nothing much happens for the first few years. This vine is slow to establish, taking 3 to 4 years or more to adjust to its new home. When roots finally become established, it grows vigorously, forming shoots that expand horizontally from the main stems. Large-sized older specimens are majestic in their height and beauty and are truly worth the early years of doubt and worry. Older specimens may reach a height of more than 75 ft.!

WHEN TO PLANT

Plant in the spring or fall.

WHERE TO PLANT

Plants can be placed in full sun or partial shade. Young plants will have a difficult time becoming attached to brick or mortar without encouragement. Use a small wood trellis to train longer stems up and onto the surface you would like it to climb upon. Plants will have a difficult time adhering to aluminum siding and will therefore require a permanent framework, such as a trellis or wooden structure, to grasp onto. Small aerial roots called holdfasts emerge from the undersides of the stems, anchoring the vine, making it upwardly mobile. Periodically check your vine to see that it is in contact with the wall and on its way to developing holdfasts. You can also grow climbing hydrangea on boulders or old tree stumps where the low-spreading branches and flowers produce a beautiful flowering shrublike effect.

HOW TO PLANT
Plant in the spring using container-grown plants. Be careful not to disturb the root system.

ADVICE FOR CARE
The climbing hydrangea requires a rich, moist soil with good drainage, or its roots will suffer. Mulch with an acid base compost to cool the root zone and conserve moisture. Water plants in prolonged periods of drought.

ADDITIONAL INFORMATION
Large-sized plants may become top-heavy over time and can have sections that detach from their growing surfaces. When this situation develops, prune or cut back lengthy sections to lessen the load. In a few cases you may have to tie in with string or wire the sections that have lost their hold.

ADDITIONAL SPECIES, CULTIVARS, OR VARIETIES
The Japanese hydrangea-vine, *Schizophragma hydrangeoides*, is a closely related vine with the same clinging habit but larger, less lustrous leaves and spectacularly large, drooping white flowers. It requires the same conditions for growth as the climbing hydrangea. The Japanese hydrangea-vine 'Moonlight' is a selection featuring silver mottling on each heart-shaped leaf. Flowers are pure white with a lacy, graceful habit. 'Roseum' has rose-colored bracts with lustrous dark green leaves.

'Cornell Pink' Korean Rhododendron

Rhododendron mucronulatum

Height: 6 to 8 ft.
Flowers: Light pink
Bloom Period: Early spring
Zones: 4, 5, 6
Light Requirement:

The rhododendrons are a captivating group of shrubs with numerous species, hybrids, and cultivars available to choose from, but growing azaleas and rhododendrons well is a difficult proposition in Michigan. Heavy clay soils combined with alkalinity (high pH) are two opposing forces working against these beautiful shrubs here. The 'Cornell Pink' Korean rhododendron makes the fight worthwhile. With a little help, it will reward you with years of great beauty in your garden. 'Cornell Pink' has flowers that emerge a lovely light pink before its foliage in late May. The flowers contrast well with the shrub's straw-colored branches. It makes a delightful spring combination with early spring bulbs such as the Siberian squill, *Scilla siberica*, and glory-of-the-snow, *Chionodoxa luciliae*. A moderate-sized shrub reaching 6 to 8 ft. in height, 'Cornell Pink' is a good foundation plant with controlled pruning. The leaves are a pleasing soft green during the growing season but change from yellow to crimson in a marvelous fall color parade.

WHEN TO PLANT
Plant in the spring as a container-grown or balled-and-burlapped plant.

WHERE TO PLANT
The early flowering habit of 'Cornell Pink' sometimes places it in jeopardy as late spring frosts or freezes can kill precocious flower buds. Place your plant in a northern exposure to avoid southern sun, which coaxes an early floral display that endangers the spring show. Plant in partial shade in a well-drained soil. Wet soils will cause root rot and send the plant into decline. 'Cornell Pink' is moderately tolerant of alkaline soils but performs best in slightly acidic conditions. Mulch each year with composted oak leaves and pine needles to help lower the pH of your soil. Shrubs combined with

spring bulbs light up the landscape. Plant 'Cornell Pink' near the buttercup winter hazel, *Corylopsis pauciflora*, for a happy jolt to winter-weary eyes.

How to Plant

Containerized plants may have a buildup of fibrous roots in the bottom of the pot. Break up the root mass, and spread it out in the planting hole. Circling or kinked roots will cause stunted growth and delay establishment. Heavy clay soils may need to be modified to accommodate the drainage needs of this shrub. Aerate or lighten soils by adding well-rotted leaf mold to the backfill soil that was dug from the hole. Avoid planting in low areas that accumulate water runoff from sidewalks or roof eaves.

Advice for Care

'Cornell Pink' is very susceptible to drought and will need watering in the hot, dry times of the year. Deadheading, or removing the faded flowers, is recommended to encourage new flowering wood for the next spring season. Break off spent flowers by hand; pruning shears are not needed. Grasp the old flowers and remove at the base of the flower stalk just before emerging leaf buds. Foliage that becomes yellow and unhealthy in appearance indicates soil alkalinity. Fertilizers that contain sulfur or that are known to have an acidic reaction may bring your plant back to health. Use them according to the manufacturer's instructions. This rhododendron is resistant to two traditional rhododendron problems, black vine weevils and root rot.

Additional Information

Good cultural practices will help keep your rhododendron healthy. These shrubs may occasionally come under attack by lace bugs, however. This tiny insect in abundance causes leaf yellowing. Insects feed on the undersides of the leaves and are difficult to see. The appearance of brown specks on the undersides of leaves is a sign of lace bug. Sunny sites may lead to higher lace bug populations. Orthene™ is a recommended chemical control for lace bug.

Additional Species, Cultivars, or Varieties

The 'Northern Lights' series is recommended for midwestern gardens. The plants are compact and reach a height and spread of 6 to 7 ft. A wide range of colors exists within the series. Some of the more subtle colored flowers are found on 'Orchid Lights' (lilac flowers), 'Golden Lights' (yellow and fragrant), and 'White Lights' (large white, fragrant flowers).

Dwarf Fothergilla

Fothergilla gardenii

Other Name: Witch Alder
Height: 3 ft.
Flowers: White
Bloom Period: Late spring
Zones: 5, 6
Light Requirement:

Dwarf shrubs are at a premium in the horticultural world, and when you find them with the year-round finesse of the fothergilla, you've got to have one. A southeastern native, it performs well under the right conditions in the southern half of Michigan's Lower Peninsula. The unusual short bottle-brush flowers appear in May and June in terminal spikes. Lacking true petals and consisting of cream-colored stamens with yellow anthers, the male parts of the flower make a showy presence. The leathery dark green foliage creates a kaleidoscope of brilliant colors in the fall, turning yellow, orange, and crimson as the season progresses. The dwarf fothergilla has a dense, mounded habit reaching 3 ft. tall and 5 ft. wide. It makes a wonderful foundation plant, fitting easily into small spaces. Used in mass plantings in full sun, the dwarf fothergilla is unrivaled in its fall color display. It also works well combined with a backdrop of straw-colored ornamental grasses, intensifying the fiery hues of the autumn foliage. The branches are of interest in the winter months with light brown zigzag twigs, many sprouting from below ground to form a dense colony.

WHEN TO PLANT
Plant in spring or fall.

WHERE TO PLANT
Place in full sun for best flower and fall color effect. Plants prefer a moist, well-drained acid soil but will tolerate near-alkaline conditions. It has many possible uses as a specimen plant, a mass planting, or combined with herbaceous perennials. An evergreen backdrop is particularly effective at framing the beautiful fall foliage.

HOW TO PLANT
Transplant as a container-grown or balled-and-burlapped plant.

ADVICE FOR CARE

In Michigan, the predominantly alkaline and heavy soils will have
to be modified to encourage optimum growth for fothergilla. When
planting in heavy soils, mix decomposed leaf mold and rotted cow
manure into the planting hole. After planting, mulch with decomposed pine needles and oak leaves to keep the soil slightly acidic.
Chlorosis, or leaf yellowing, will alert you to alkaline conditions
that are detrimental to plant growth. Adding organic matter to the
planting hole in the form of humus, rotted manure and a yearly
top dressing of an acid-based mulch will help keep your plant in a
healthy condition. Be sure to water in times of prolonged drought
or plants will languish and may become susceptible to spider
mite attack.

ADDITIONAL INFORMATION

Pruning is generally not required except to remove dead, diseased,
or dying branches. The dwarf fothergilla suckers from the base,
forming dense colonies. The removal of older stems over time will
rejuvenate your shrub and increase suckering. Prune older branches
right to ground level, being careful not to remove developing young
shoots in the process. Some tip dieback occurs on branches in colder
winters. Remove damaged wood from winter injury. *Fothergilla
gardenii* is a Zone 5 plant that will suffer in Zone 4 in exposed plantings. Flower fragrance is variable among plants, so purchase them in
bloom to ensure that you bring home plants with delightfully sweet,
honey-scented flowers.

ADDITIONAL SPECIES, CULTIVARS, OR VARIETIES

'Blue Mist' has incredible blue-green foliage and grows best in
partial shade. While pleasant in summer, the blue-green foliage is
disappointing in its fall coloring. Grow this selection for its superior
summer foliage color, combining it with pink and lavender annuals
or perennials. It is not as strong a grower as the species. *Fothergilla*
'Mt. Airy' is believed to be a hybrid of *Fothergilla gardenii* and
Fothergilla major, the large fothergilla. It has an upright oval habit
with abundant flowers and an incredible orange-red fall color.

Forsythia

Forsythia × intermedia

Height: 6 to 9 ft.
Flowers: Brilliant yellow
Bloom Period: Early spring
Zones: 5, 6
Light Requirement:

Although often cited as overused in the landscape, this old-fashioned shrub still has modern appeal. Each year, the cheerful early bloom of forsythia is a harbinger of spring. Masses of bell-shaped yellow flowers emerge from arching branches that are a tannish-gray color. While its use as a foundation plant is limited because of its size and habit, it works well in a mass planting and is particularly effective on banks or a raised terrace. Forsythia can reach up to 9 ft. tall with an equal spread. It has an upright stiff habit with branches that arch as they fall from the side of the shrub. In mass, it contrasts well with a dark-green foreground planting of spreading evergreen yews or junipers. In the summer months the dark green foliage provides a pleasant backdrop for a foreground planting of the crimson pygmy barberry, *Berberis thunbergii* 'Atropurpurea'. This shrub is a tough customer that has endured the test of time. It grows in most soil types except those that are consistently wet. Plants are long-lived, some growing for 60 years or more.

WHEN TO PLANT

Plant forsythia in spring or fall.

WHERE TO PLANT

Plant in full sun for best bloom effect. Plants tolerate shade but become leggy and produce fewer flowers. In mass plantings, space at least 12 ft. apart to allow the arching branches to spread. The vibrant yellow flowers show up well with a backdrop of dark nee-dled spruce trees such as the Norway spruce, *Picea abies*.

HOW TO PLANT

Plant as a container-grown or balled-and-burlapped plant.

ADVICE FOR CARE

Over time, mature shrubs will need pruning to rein in their prolific growth. Never try to top prune or make your forsythia into a formal shape. This will ruin the natural arching habit of the shrub and cause flowering wood to develop only on the top portions of the plant. The overall result is very disappointing. To maintain the natural vase-shaped form, selectively remove older branches, cutting back to ground level. New young shoots will form and flower within 3 years. Complete rejuvenation is possible by cutting all the branches right to the ground. Within 3 years, your shrubs will be dense and blooming once again. Plants in shade will respond more slowly to selective and total cut-back pruning. Forsythia flowers on wood formed the previous season, so prune after flowering. Gardeners who wish to increase their stock of forsythia can turn to an old propagator's trick and layer long branches. In the early spring, take a long branch, and bend it down so that it will lie horizontally on the ground. Dig a foot-deep hole. Place 12 in. of the middle of the bent branch in the hole. Pin it down with wire. Cover it with soil, and water the buried branch section during dry periods. Within 2 years, sufficient roots will have formed on the buried stem. Then dig it up, snip off its connection to the parent plant, and plant in another spot in your garden.

ADDITIONAL INFORMATION

You may decide to break the rules and prune in the early spring to get a better look at the naked framework of the plant. Save your cut branches and force them in a vase indoors. The cut stems will brighten up a windowsill or kitchen table and give you a preview of spring's coming attractions.

ADDITIONAL SPECIES, CULTIVARS, OR VARIETIES

Forsythia flower buds are sometimes endangered by frigid temperatures. Two hardy cultivars with superior flower bud hardiness in northern climates are 'Meadowlark' and 'Northern Sun'. The 'Meadowlark' forsythia is a reliable, profuse blooming selection that thrives in tough sites. 'Northern Sun' has spectacular yellow flowers and vigorous growth, reaching 8 to 10 ft. in height. *Forsythia* 'Vermont Sun' has large soft yellow flowers and a distinct erect oval habit that is 8 ft. tall. It's reliably hardy to Zone 4. 'Gold Tide' is a recent introduction from France that is just making the rounds in Michigan but has great promise. An effective groundcover reaching only 20 in. in height with a spread of 4 ft., it flowers prolifically in the spring and has pleasant, soft green summer foliage. The flowers are lemon yellow and are massed along the low-growing stems. Its flower bud hardiness would be challenged in colder areas of Michigan; there, stick with the cold hardy selections.

Fragrant Winter Hazel

Corylopsis glabrescens

Height: 12 ft.
Flowers: Pale yellow
Bloom Period: Spring
Zones: 5, 6
Light Requirement:

Spring is a time of anticipation in Michigan. We wait patiently for the bloom of witchhazel, forsythia, and eventually an assortment of magnolias, ornamental cherries, and crabapples. In the midst of this colorful parade, the fragrant winter hazel blooms soft yellow flowers that hang gracefully from wide-spreading bare branches like tiny bells from a string. This subtle display often goes unnoticed as the more vibrant colors of spring-blooming plants take front and center stage. On close examination, however, the fragrant winter hazel is perhaps unrivaled in its combination of fragrance, grace, and startling beauty. If placed in an open, prominent spot, it becomes a true showstopper. Winter hazel forms a large spreading shrub, reaching 12 ft. high and growing nearly twice as wide. It has a dense oval habit with dark green leaves that turn a clear yellow in the fall. The dense multistemmed habit of this shrub and the zigzag nature of its slender twigs give it a winter artistry that is all its own. Plants are used to best effect if placed in full sun and against an evergreen backdrop, which illuminates their pale yellow flowers and yellow fall color. In late April and early May, the spring bloom combines well with the pale rose-purple blooms of the Korean rhododendron, *Rhododendron mucronulatum*.

WHEN TO PLANT
Plant in the spring or fall.

WHERE TO PLANT
The early spring bloom of *Corylopsis* is at times susceptible to hard freezes, particularly in exposed sites where the warm winter sun causes precocious buds to swell only to succumb to frigid temperatures as winter and spring play a tug-of-war at this time of the year. Avoid a warm southern exposure and sites where strong winter winds and wide temperature fluctuations may occur.

How to Plant

Plant as a container-grown or balled-and-burlapped shrub. *Corylopsis* prefers a moist, well-drained, slightly acidic soil. Add peat and leaf mold to the planting hole to lower the soil pH and increase the moisture-holding capacity of the soil.

Advice for Care

Winter hazel is generally disease- and pest-free. Pruning is not recommended because it might destroy the unique form of this plant. When planting in the vicinity of this shrub, use groundcover plants that will fit below its low-spreading, horizontal branches. A good plant in this role is the Russian arborvitae, *Microbiota decussata*. The purplish-bronze foliage contrasts well with the soft yellow pendant blooms in the spring. The blue windflower, *Anemone blanda*, makes a nice foreground planting in combination with *Corylopsis* and will spread beneath its limbs, creating a most pleasing effect.

Additional Information

Winter hazel can be cut and forced for indoor display. Branches cut in March usually take a couple of weeks to open in a vase placed in a sunny window.

Additional Species, Cultivars, or Varieties

There are other species of the winter hazel for gardeners who live in Zone 6. The word "dainty" most accurately describes the habit and bloom of the buttercup winter hazel, *Corylopsis pauciflora*. It grows to 4 to 6 ft. high with an equal or greater spread. The pale yellow flowers are large and showy on slender twigs. This plant dislikes full sun and prefers some shade to avoid leaf scorch, where leaf margins turn a papery brown in full sun plantings. The buttercup winter hazel makes an excellent foundation plant. If your local climate can support it, by all means grow it!

Gray Dogwood

Cornus racemosa

Height: 15 ft.
Flowers: White
Bloom Period: Late spring to early summer
Zones: 4, 5, 6
Light Requirement:

A real pleasure of the winter season in Michigan is driving along the road and coming upon thickets of gray dogwood in a low ditch or on the border of a marshy wetland. Chestnut-brown stems top the dense gray branches, forming the framework of huge colonies of plants that dominate an entire area. Often they are found cavorting with the Michigan holly, *Ilex verticillata*. This pairing of native Michigan plants is a remarkable combination of beautiful stems and berries, clearly demonstrating why we should use these plants more often in our cultivated landscapes. Gray dogwood is a common native shrub in the Lower Peninsula. Its robust growth and colonizing habit tend to dissuade people from using it. They should take a closer look to see gray dogwood's four-season appeal. The foliage is dark green and takes on purplish coloring in the fall. Flowers are creamy white and are borne on branched stalks in late May to early June. Beautiful white fall fruits are relished by numerous birds. The fruit stalks are an attractive reddish pink and remain on the plant well into the winter season. The combination of old gray stems and brownish new growth terminating with the colorful fruit stalks creates a distinctive winter character of great beauty.

WHEN TO PLANT

Gray dogwood is easy to transplant in spring or fall.

WHERE TO PLANT

Use this shrub in naturalistic plantings, and bring the wild side to your landscape. Gray dogwood is extremely valuable in both wet, swampy and extremely dry sites. Use it on difficult hillsides or eroding banks. A mass planting can create a screen or privacy barrier. Plant in full sun or shade, and be prepared to let gray dogwood run. The shrubs spread by underground stems and should be kept away from confined spaces or areas you wish to remain open. Combine with other winter-interest plants to create fantastic winter vistas.

Plant gray dogwood with the redosier dogwood, *Cornus stolonifera*. The contrast of gray and red twigs creates a colorful winter collage.

How to Plant

Plant as a container-grown or balled-and-burlapped plant.

Advice for Care

Gray dogwood is generally a carefree shrub that adapts well to both poorly drained and dry soils. Occasionally, plants develop leaf spot, a fungal disease that produces dark irregular blotches on the foliage. Leaf spot may be unattractive but is usually not a serious health threat. Plants can easily be rejuvenated by cutting back right to the ground. This will result in vigorous growth and the development of numerous colorful stems.

Additional Information

Ideally suited to low-maintenance landscapes where the goal is a naturalistic look, this is a highly adaptable shrub with year-round appeal. Effective in large-scale plantings and invaluable for use in both poorly drained soils and excessively dry soils, the gray dogwood is truly a versatile shrub.

Additional Species, Cultivars, or Varieties

The silky dogwood, *Cornus amomum*, is a closely related shrub that is not as ornamental in many respects but has beautiful porcelain-blue fruits in the fall. It grows in wet sites, reaching an ultimate height and spread of 6 to 10 ft.

'Green Velvet' Boxwood

Buxus 'Green Velvet'

Height: 3 ft.
Foliage: Dark evergreen
Zones: 5, 6
Light Requirement:

You can't help thinking of the South when garden talk turns to boxwood. It was used there extensively in colonial times, and many old specimens still stand today. Although boxwood has enjoyed southern hospitality for years, its presence in the northern states has been rife with trials and tribulations. The main problems manifest themselves in the winter season as the lush green foliage of the summer becomes a sickly yellowish-brown. The combination of winter sun and drying winds is detrimental to boxwood in its establishment and performance. Nurserymen have tried for years to develop superior selections with tough evergreen foliage and adaptability to northern climates. A hybrid cross of the common box, *Buxus sempervirens*, and hardier Korean box, *Buxus sinica* var. *insularis*, has resulted in a new generation of boxwoods valued for their winter toughness with the added bonus of a dwarf habit. The 'Green Velvet' boxwood is a selection with a compact dense, mounded habit, reaching only 3 ft. with a similar spread. The small dark green leaves are less susceptible to winter burn and sun scald than many boxwoods. 'Green Velvet' makes the ultimate low hedge plant and should be used anywhere you want a touch of formality. The bright green new growth in spring is a sight for sore eyes after a long winter season.

When to Plant

Plant in early spring if possible. Avoid late fall planting because roots may not develop in time to supply the leaves with water to withstand the drying winds of winter.

Where to Plant

Despite its hardier constitution, 'Green Velvet' should be protected from strong westerly winds. Plant on the east side of the house to protect against these winds and to avoid extended periods of winter sun, which heats up the foliage, increasing water loss. Boxwood grows best in full sun or partial shade, but it prefers an exposure that receives some shade in winter. Boxwood can be used to create hedges, define pathways or borders, create artistic topiary, or develop your own medieval knot garden. These shrubs take readily to shearing and are particularly valued for the formal element they give to the garden and landscape.

How to Plant
Plant as a container-grown or balled-and-burlapped plant in spring.

Advice for Care
Boxwood is adaptable to most soil conditions except too wet or dry. Mulching will help conserve moisture and lower root zone temperatures. It will also protect the roots, which are easily damaged by digging or even weeding around the base of the plant. Under certain conditions, 'Green Velvet' may produce a late-summer growth that will become scorched and unsightly in the winter season. Prune out these late flushes in the fall. Boxwood can be pruned to almost any shape you desire, but avoid creating a top-heavy plant that will shade the lower parts of the shrub, limiting growth. Use hedge shears to create a formal look. Hand pruners can be used to cut back leggy stems to the main body of the shrub. Prune in early May. Two pests that can be a problem with boxwoods are spider mite and the boxwood psyllid. Both attack the leaves with piercing and sucking mouth parts. Spider mite is the more serious problem; heavy infestations can cause leaves to drop and weaken the plant. Mite damage is recognizable as whitish or yellowish peppered markings on the foliage. To avoid the conditions that favor mite development, mulch and water during dry times of the year. No matter how favorable the cultural conditions are for boxwood, they inevitably will have boxwood psyllid. This tiny insect damages boxwood by feeding on developing buds, causing cupping of the leaves. The damage is noticeable but generally not life-threatening to the plant. It can be controlled by an early spring spraying program. Orthene™ is a chemical control recommended for treatment of boxwood psyllid.

Additional Information
While boxwoods need some protection in northern climates, they can be rewarding shrubs for their fresh green color and multiple uses in the formal garden in Zones 5 and 6. Gardeners in colder zones should look to other evergreens for winter color.

Additional Species, Cultivars, or Varieties
'Green Mountain' is a pyramidal shrub with more vigorous growth than 'Green Velvet'. It grows 4 ft. wide and just over 3 ft. tall. It has green foliage and a burgundy cast during the winter months. It is also a hybrid selection of the common and Korean boxwoods.

Koreanspice Viburnum

Viburnum carlesii

Height: 10 to 15 ft.
Flowers: White
Bloom Period: Late spring
Zones: 4, 5, 6
Light Requirement:

Viburnums are among the most valuable groups of shrubs for midwestern gardeners. They are winter hardy and offer species and cultivars that serve a multitude of landscape needs. Among the best for bloom and fragrance are the Koreanspice and burkwood viburnums. The clove-scented fragrance of the Koreanspice viburnum is matched by few other woody plants. In late May and early June, pink buds open to form large white clusters composed of many tiny flowers. They emit a wildly intoxicating fragrance. The flowers can last up to 2 weeks, during which time the fragrance causes people to stop in their tracks to take in the heady bouquet. The burkwood viburnum flowers before the Koreanspice, and it, too, has a heavenly aroma. The foliage is a dark, shiny green and superior to the Koreanspice. The dark foliage appears evergreen, although it is not, and gives a formal feeling to the landscape. The Koreanspice viburnum foliage is a pleasant soft green. Both shrubs get up to 10 to 15 ft. tall and 8 ft. wide.

When to Plant

Plant in the spring or fall as container-grown or balled-and-burlapped plants.

Where to Plant

The Koreanspice and burkwood viburnums make excellent single specimens and are effective grouped in mass. Place in full sun or plants will languish and develop flopping branches with poor flower development. Both shrubs command space. When planting in mass, be sure to plant far enough apart to allow room to grow. Plants placed close together will compete and shade each other out, reducing overall growth and flower production. Space at least 10 ft. apart. Plant near a window or a walkway so that you can experience the fragrant blooms that appear as the warm temperatures of summer approach.

How to Plant

Container-grown plants may have circling or congested roots at the bottom of the pot that should be broken apart before placing in the hole.

Advice for Care

Viburnums in general are tough plants but will require water in prolonged periods of drought. As plants become mature, selective pruning is needed to remove old, dead, or dying wood. Removal of older wood allows sunlight into the inner portions of the plant, encouraging new growth. To increase flowering, remove old flower buds as they fade. New flower buds will develop through the remainder of the growing season and will be ready to bloom after a long winter's rest. Plants placed too close together will become bare at the bottom, and foliage and blooms become confined to the upper portions of the plant. If this situation develops, thin out plants nearby to increase the amount of light reaching the lower portions of the plant. Soon, new growth should sprout to fill in bare spots.

Additional Information

Viburnums are generally adaptable to a wide range of soil types with the exception of extremely wet situations. In poorly drained soils, plant the nannyberry, *Viburnum lentago,* or the witherod, *Viburnum cassinoides.* These native shrubs are well adapted to wet conditions. Both have attractive creamy white flowers in spring that later produce an abundance of purple fruits, a real feast for birds. Unfortunately, they lack the fragrance of the Koreanspice and burkwood viburnums but have their own unique appeal.

Additional Species, Cultivars, or Varieties

The cultivar of the Koreanspice viburnum called 'Compactum' will reach up to 8 ft. in height. 'Mohawk' is a wonderful cultivar with deep pink flowers in bud, opening with a spicy fragrance. It is a compact shrub growing to a height and spread of 6 to 8 ft. The doublefile viburnum, *Viburnum plicatum* var. *tomentosum,* and its cultivars are very useful in warmer regions in Michigan. In colder areas, bark splitting occurs, weakening the plants and limiting their performance.

Leatherleaf Viburnum

Viburnum rhytidophyllum

Height: 10 to 15 ft.
Flowers: Yellow-green
Bloom Period: Late spring
Zones: 5, 6
Light Requirement:

Evergreen shrubs in Michigan usually conjure up images of ubiquitous yews or the ever-present junipers. Although these are true evergreen shrubs that have an important place in our landscapes, some semi-evergreen shrubs can be very useful as well. The hardy viburnums commonly referred to as the leatherleaf viburnums offer more or less semi-evergreen foliage in Michigan, depending on where they're planted and how cold minimum low temperatures drop. In certain years, the true leatherleaf viburnum, *Viburnum rhytidophyllum*, has leaves that may persist throughout the winter months. The dark, leathery foliage is heavily textured on its surface, which appears wrinkled or rough. The leaves are large in size, up to 7 in. long and 2½ in. wide. The leatherleaf flowers in May or June with large, flat-top blooms that are a yellowish-green and impressive not by their individual beauty but by their sheer number. The flowers do not carry a pleasant fragrance, but they produce a colorful display of red and black fruits, often devoured by birds by mid-October. A related shrub of hybrid origin is the lantanaphyllum viburnum, *Viburnum × rhytidophylloides*. It is similar in many respects to the leatherleaf but has leaves that are broader and not as heavily textured. The flower buds are tighter in an attractive cluster that is effective through the winter months. The fruits are also quite showy and a favorite for birds. Both shrubs make outstanding plants as screens or as single specimens. Reaching a height of more than 15 ft. with a similar spread, these shrubs need room to develop and are not appropriate for gardens with limited space.

WHEN TO PLANT
Plant in spring or fall.

WHERE TO PLANT
Plant in full sun or partial shade. Plant with protection from winter winds. Plants in microclimate situations retain their leaves longer and are more effective through the winter months. Use in mass as

a screen planting at least 12 ft. apart. Single specimens work well combined with perennials or moderate-sized woody shrubs that offer unique contrasts in foliage. Combine either of these two shrubs with the bluebeard, *Caryopteris* × *clandonensis*. The soft gray wispy branches and powder blue late-summer flowers of the bluebeard are enlightened by the dark, crinkled leaves of the leatherleafs. Plant as a backdrop for the 'Rose Glow' barberry, *Berberis thunbergii* 'Rose Glow'. The mottled red-pink variegated foliage creates a unique color and textural contrast with the leatherleaf viburnums. Landscapers frequently plant these viburnums on the edge of a building, anchoring down a corner and softening an edge.

How to Plant

Plant as a container-grown or balled-and-burlapped shrub.

Advice for Care

In exposed situations, these shrubs will have wind-burned leaves that turn brown and can be unsightly. Fortunately, as new growth emerges in the spring these leaves fall from the plant. Individual flowers within the flat-top clusters will also dry out in exposed situations. Again, plant with wind protection in mind. Rejuvenate older shrubs by selectively removing older wood and allowing young shoots to develop in their place.

Additional Information

The new growth of both shrubs has an attractive feltlike covering on their stems and undersides of the leaves that is interesting to examine on close inspection.

Additional Species, Cultivars, or Varieties

The lantanaphyllum hybrid viburnum has two excellent selections that have proved popular in Michigan landscapes. 'Willowwood' is a shrub with excellent lustrous foliage and an arching habit. 'Alleghany' is a superior form with a dense, rounded habit, reaching a height of 11 ft. at maturity. The fruit is brilliant red in the fall.

Lilac

Syringa vulgaris

Height: 20 ft.
Flowers: Purple, lilac, pink, white
Bloom Period: Spring
Zones: 4, 5, 6
Light Requirement:

It is undeniable that the lilac is an enduring shrub, part of our past and ever popular today. How many of us can recall the sweet smell of a familiar plant at an old homestead or at a friend's or relative's home? With their glorious flowers and sweet fragrance, lilacs are still in demand and offer a multitude of choices with regard to flower size, color, and fragrance. The bloom of lilac is its most important feature, and after the flowers are gone, this shrub fades from the scene with little to offer beyond the large, heart-shaped leaves. Numerous trials and evaluations have helped define what makes a good lilac and how we should grow them to best effect in Michigan. With their popularity and overuse in certain instances, the lilac has been plagued by pest and disease problems that can be overcome by proper selection and planting. Lilacs are large shrubs that are a welcome addition to homes with open areas and plenty of room to plant. They make excellent cut flowers that can be brought into the home where the intoxicating fragrance can be enjoyed. Lilacs can be planted in groupings or as single specimens and are most valuable along pathways or spots where you frequently pass by, so that you can enjoy their remarkable fragrance. They have an upright habit and become leggy and open with age.

WHEN TO PLANT
Plant lilacs in spring or fall.

WHERE TO PLANT
Plant in full sun in a site with good air circulation. This will prevent the development of powdery mildew, a leaf disease that thrives in shady, wind-protected environments. *Syringa* makes an effective privacy screen and, when properly pruned, a nice, informal hedge. Single specimens can obtain tree-sized proportions and are spectacular in bloom.

How to Plant

Plant as a container-grown or balled-and-burlapped shrub.

Advice for Care

The common lilac is not considered a low-maintenance shrub; it requires work to keep it healthy and beautiful. Plants in full sun are less likely to get powdery mildew. The fungus generally appears in late summer, forming white, cottony masses on the foliage. The fungus does little long-term damage to the shrub, and its control is usually not necessary. An insect called the lilac stem borer can be a serious pest of lilacs that are under stress. They cause large-sized branches to die out, requiring their removal. Borers attack branches that are 1 in. or more in diameter, so periodic removal of these older branches will lessen the likelihood of attack. Pruning is an important maintenance item if you decide to plant lilacs. Removing older limbs opens up the shrub to sunlight and air circulation, which discourages powdery mildew and lilac stem borer and increases the production of flowering wood. Vigorous growth of underground stems (suckers) will require their removal each year because they tend to get out of control and crowd the interior of the plant, blocking light and limiting air movement.

Additional Information

Old flowers can be removed to prevent seed development and increase flower production the following spring. Remove at the base of the spent flower clusters with hand pruners.

Additional Species, Cultivars, or Varieties

'Krasavitsa Moskvy' or 'Beauty of Moscow' is a doubled-flower form with lavender-rose buds opening a creamy white with a hint of pale lilac. 'Miss Ellen Willmott' has large flower clusters composed of pure white double flowers and grows 6 to 12 ft. high. 'Edith Cavell' has sulfur yellow buds that open to pure white double flowers. All of these selections are extremely fragrant.

Michigan Holly

Ilex verticillata

Other Name: Winterberry
Height: 6 to 15 ft.
Fruits: Orange, red, or
  yellow; late summer
  to fall
Zones: 4, 5, 6
Light Requirement:

When we think of hollies, we think of the evergreen boughs of the Christmas season that adorn wreaths or doorways with foliage and fruits. In recent years, though, certain native North American deciduous hollies have also come into their own with outstanding fruit displays that persist on naked branches in the winter months. Numerous selections of winterberry or Michigan holly offer a dazzling array of selections with berries that range in color from red to orange to yellow. With so many to choose from, it is important to select cultivars that have proved superior in Michigan landscapes. The winterberry is naturally found throughout Michigan in wet situations bordering marshes, bogs, and lakes. This makes it an excellent candidate for home owners who choose not to drain off their land and would like to add wetland plants to attract and encourage wildlife. The winterberry can take long periods with its roots submerged in water. The flowers of winterberry appear in May or June along dark brown stems. The small white flowers attract the attention of bees searching for nectar. Male and female flowers appear on separate plants so both must be present for fruiting to result. Male and female cultivars have been introduced with overlapping flowering times. When purchasing plants from a nursery, insist that the cultivars will form a fruitful pairing (see the section that follows, "Additional Information"). The foliage of the winterberry is an attractive dark green. In fall color, it sometimes displays purplish tones.

WHEN TO PLANT

Plant in the spring or fall.

WHERE TO PLANT

Plant masses of hollies for an effective winter display. Sizes vary by cultivar selection, but with the species space at least 12 ft. apart and in full sun. These shrubs are thicket-forming plants that will extend their area by producing spreading stems underground. The fruiting display is enhanced by a backdrop of dark-needled evergreen spruces such as the Oriental spruce *Picea orientalis* and Norway spruce, *Picea abies*. Select your planting site so that you may view it from indoors. Create a beautiful winter scene out a bay window combining the winterberry with dark-needled evergreens or the native river birch, *Betula nigra*. The red berries of the hollies stand out against the flaky cinnamon-brown peeling bark of the river birch. The vibrant berries also contrast well against a backdrop of tan ornamental grass foliage in the early winter months.

How to Plant
Plant as a container-grown or balled-and-burlapped shrub.

Advice for Care
While their tolerance for wet soils is well documented, these shrubs have also been promoted for their adaptation to dry soils. In general, they will suffer in long periods of drought and should be watered. Avoid planting too close to brick or cement walls that absorb heat, intensifying drought conditions and creating apt conditions for spider mite, which should be avoided at all costs. New shrub plantings will benefit from a layer of organic mulch that will help conserve moisture, cool the root zone, and discourage weeds.

Additional Information
The early 1980s saw a number of new introductions of the winterberry. Among the best performers so far in Michigan landscapes are 'Afterglow' with thick glossy green leaves and persistent orange-red fruits that can last into February. It makes a multistemmed shrub reaching 10 ft. in height and width and appears to be one of the more drought-tolerant selections. A true dwarf cultivar of exceptional merit is 'Red Sprite' with a mature size of 3 1/2 ft. by 4 ft. wide, fitting nicely into smaller landscapes. The male pollinator for 'Afterglow' and 'Red Sprite' is 'Raritan Chief'. Cut branches make decorative indoor displays and will retain fruits for a longer period of time if not placed in water. Michigan's long-standing Christmas Tree Law prohibits the removal of branches from native stands—all the more reason to grow your own.

Additional Species, Cultivars, or Varieties
There are many. The best for Michigan gardens are presented above.

Miss Kim' Korean Lilac

Syringa patula 'Miss Kim'

> **Height:** 4 to 7 ft. with spread of 4 to 6 ft.
> **Flowers:** Lavender-pink
> **Bloom Period:** Mid- to late spring
> **Zones:** 3, 4, 5, 6
> **Light Requirement:**
>
>

The 'Miss Kim' lilac offers so many outstanding features that it is often difficult to find at your local nursery, where it disappears quickly if witnessed in bloom. Selected in 1954, it is just now gaining the recognition it deserves. This is a diminutive lilac compared with the larger common lilac and related hybrids. It grows very slowly, reaching a height of 4 to 7 ft. with slender, erect branches and abundant lavender-pink flowers in May or June. The flowers appear to hover over the stems in mass and fade to an ice blue. The summer foliage of 'Miss Kim' is dark green that turns a mauve-purple in the fall. This is one of the few lilacs you can count on for good fall color. Take advantage of the compact size of this shrub, and use it as a foundation plant where its slow growth and small stature make it perfect for placement beneath a first-floor window. The spicy fragrance will permeate your house through open windows or doorways, clearing out old winter air.

WHEN TO PLANT

Plant in the spring or fall. Bareroot plants should be planted in spring while dormant.

WHERE TO PLANT

Plant in full sun in an open area with good air circulation. With its small size, 'Miss Kim' makes an excellent rock garden plant. Be sure to plant it close to your house or an outdoor living space to enjoy its fragrant flowers and attractive fall color. 'Miss Kim' works well planted in mass on slightly sloping hillsides, creating a cascade of billowing blooms.

HOW TO PLANT

Plant as a container-grown, balled-and-burlapped, or bareroot plant. When planting, space shrubs at least 6 to 8 ft. apart to allow for air circulation and to prevent overcrowding. Bareroot plants should be planted in spring before leaves emerge.

ADVICE FOR CARE
Plant in a moist, well-drained soil, and avoid areas where drought conditions prevail. Water during dry spells by letting a hose slowly trickle at the base for 15 to 20 minutes, giving your plant a deep-water feed. Do not use overhead water because this may promote the development of the leaf disease powdery mildew. Pruning is generally not needed, but you may decide to remove spent flowers, which eventually move onto seed production reducing the vigor of your plant. Do not prune in the spring, or flower buds will be removed.

ADDITIONAL INFORMATION
Powdery mildew does not afflict 'Miss Kim' as often as it does the common lilac, *Syringa vulgaris*. This leaf disease most commonly occurs in wet seasons, and its likelihood is increased when shrubs are planted in shady locations. White cottony masses develop on the leaf surfaces and can cause leaf loss. Fungicide sprays are available to control the problem, but it is generally not life-threatening. Late-season infestations are not worth spraying since natural year-end leaf fall will soon follow. If you provide the right conditions for healthy growth, your lilac will be less likely to come under attack by powdery mildew. You may find it difficult to locate at your local garden center or nursery, but the 'Miss Kim' lilac is available through mail-order sources as small plants. You will have to wait a few seasons for these plants to fill your garden niche, but they flower at an early age and will reward you with great satisfaction for years to come.

ADDITIONAL SPECIES, CULTIVARS, OR VARIETIES
Syringa meyeri 'Palibin' is another outstanding small lilac similar to the size and spread of 'Miss Kim'. Deep purple buds open to a pink-white to violet color. 'Palibin' is less cold hardy than 'Miss Kim', and its flowers are sometimes susceptible to late frosts. It is hardy to Zone 4.

SHRUBS

317

Panicle Hydrangea

Hydrangea paniculata

Height: 10 to 25 ft.
Flowers: White
Bloom Period: Midsummer
Zones: Panicle Hydrangea
3, 4, 5, 6
Light Requirement:

It's fun to watch some old-fashioned plants undergo a revival. The panicle hydrangea has been criticized as overused along the East Coast, but it is slowly regaining the popularity it once had. Its beautiful pyramidal panicles of pure white flowers appear in July or August and gradually fade to pink. The panicle hydrangea can reach tree size under certain conditions but generally grows to 10 ft. This shrub adapts to most soil types but needs good drainage and dislikes drought situations. Many cultivars are available today that will help keep the panicle hydrangea an enduring part of the cultivated American landscape. The oakleaf hydrangea, *Hydrangea quercifolia*, is similar to the panicle hydrangea in its coarse texture, but that is where the similarities end. This North American native is a real four-season performer with immense 7- to 13-in. conical flowers composed of pure white sterile petals fading to a dusty rose. The broad leaves are deeply lobed, heavily textured, and dark green, turning a fantastic burgundy red in autumn. On older specimens, the bark begins to peel and reveals handsome cinnamon-colored stems that are highly effective during the winter months. The oakleaf hydrangea forms mounds from underground spreading stems. It reaches 6 to 8 ft. tall and rarely grows larger in Michigan. Stem dieback will occur in very cold winters when plants are in exposed situations. A southern native hardy to Zone 5, this shrub requires a protected site that has enough sunlight for development and adequate moisture for growth.

WHEN TO PLANT
Plant in the spring or fall.

WHERE TO PLANT
Plant in full sun for vigorous growth and flowers. These shrubs are excellent planted in a large mass or as a single specimen. The coarse nature of the oakleaf hydrangea makes it hard to use as a single

specimen. Plant in partial shade locations to light up dark areas in your garden with the expansive blooms.

How to Plant

Plant as a container-grown or balled-and-burlapped plant.

Advice for Care

Water well in drought periods, and mulch annually to conserve moisture, cool the root zone, and discourage weeds. Both hydrangeas may need pruning to keep them tidy. The panicle hydrangea should be pruned in winter or early spring because it forms flower buds on the new growth each season. Prune out older wood periodically, cutting it to ground level. Some gardeners prefer to prune the panicle hydrangea each year to prevent straggly old wood from developing. This will work if your soil is fertile enough to support strong new growth each year. Prune the oakleaf hydrangea after flowering as it produces flower buds on growth from the previous season. Underground stems will emerge in great numbers to form a solid framework over time. Remove old, dead, or dying wood as needed.

Additional Information

The large conical flowers of both shrubs can be preserved for dried arrangements by cutting them at their peak. Cut and hang upside down in a dry, cool area.

Additional Species, Cultivars, or Varieties

The panicle hydrangea offers 2 exceptional cultivars. 'Unique' has an upright habit in full sun and large white flowers that turn pink in midsummer. 'Kyushu' has an exceptionally long flowering period, from July through September. Both selections of the panicle hydrangea grow 10 ft. tall and wide. *Hydrangea quercifolia* 'Snow Queen' has been pronounced as "the number one shrub for American gardens" by a popular mail-order nursery catalog. Its numerous upright flowers remain standing even after hard rains. The fall color is an outstanding burgundy red. Mature growth reaches 10 to 12 ft. in size and width.

Redtwig Dogwood

Cornus stolonifera

Other Name: Redosier
Dogwood
Height: 6 to 8 ft.
Flowers: Creamy white
Bloom Period: Late spring to
early summer
Zones: 3, 4, 5, 6
Light Requirement:

Whether developing a large or a small garden, you should plan for year-round interest, and winter is the most neglected season in garden planning. The months between autumn's colorful good-bye and spring's green awakening are the toughest months. But if properly planned and planted for, winter can be a vibrant season of colorful barks, stems, and fruits. The redosier dogwood is the ultimate stoplight shrub. Its light to dark red stems play off the pure white of a newly fallen snow. *Cornus stolonifera* offers a group of cultivars with variations in stem color and summer foliage. Creamy white flowers are borne in May and June on the ends of the stems. The summer foliage ranges from a light to dark green. Fall color is an attractive reddish-purple. Pure white fruits are found in late summer and devoured by birds. The principal ornamental asset of the redosier dogwood is the outstanding stem coloration in its winter habit. The shrub spreads by underground stems and takes on a multistemmed, rounded shape. The colorful stems range from light red, reddish-purple, and dark red to selections with vibrant yellow stems. The branches have a unique characteristic, with stem upon stem breaking opposite each other to form the forked branching habit typical of the dogwood family.

WHEN TO PLANT

Plant in spring or fall. This shrub transplants easily.

WHERE TO PLANT

Plant in full sun for best stem coloration. Its colonizing habit makes it a valuable shrub for steep hillsides or low, wet areas. Place in a spot where the winter sun will shine on the colorful stems and where you can view them from your window. Avoid planting in deep shade and in areas where air movement is limited; planting it this way will deter the development of leaf spot.

How to Plant

Plant as a container-grown or balled-and-burlapped plant.

Advice for Care

Prune in April. To maintain the colorful stems on your shrubs, adopt a regular pruning routine. The most colorful stems are 1 to 3 years in age. On older shrubs, you can approach pruning two ways. The less radical approach is to remove 1/3 of the older stems each year, cutting them to the ground. After a 3-year period your plant will look great, and you will have maintained its rounded natural form throughout the process. The more drastic approach is to cut all the stems back to the ground. Don't worry—new growth will quickly develop and fill the void you've created. The redosier dogwood is occasionally bothered by leaf spot and twig blight. These fungal diseases can be troublesome in wet weather. The leaf spot fungus produces irregular dark blotches on the leaf surfaces. It is generally not life-threatening. The twig blight fungus causes swelling or rough areas called cankers along the stems, causing portions of the stem to die back. Prune out diseased wood by removing the entire stem or branch. Fungicides are available to control both leaf spot and twig blight. Check with your local extension agent on current control recommendations.

Additional Information

One of the most colorful of our native shrubs, the redtwig dogwood combines well with perennials in a mixed border. Plant with the Lenten rose, *Helleborus orientalis*, where the white flowers and ever-green foliage play off the dogwood's dark red stems.

Additional Species, Cultivars, or Varieties

'Silver and Gold' is a newer introduction with yellow winter stems. A memorable combination is the jade-green bark of the moosewood, *Acer pensylvanicum*, surrounded by the yellow stems of 'Silver and Gold'. 'Cardinal' is a red-stemmed selection that looks fantastic placed around the mottled bark of the American sycamore, *Platanus occidentalis*.

Staghorn Sumac

Rhus typhina

Height: 15 to 25 ft.
Foliage: Finely dissected foliage with yellow, orange, and red fall color
Zones: 3, 4, 5, 6
Light Requirement:

Several of our finest native shrubs are sometimes regulated to the "garden thugs" category due to their rampant growth and wild character. Taking a new look at native shrubs, we should reevaluate their perceived negative aspects and instead judiciously use these plants to allow their beauty and utility to come through in our gardens. The native staghorn sumac is often thought of as a coarse, untamed plant with limited garden appeal, but this is simply not true. Sumac has large compound leaves that are composed of many smaller leaflets, bright green in the summer changing to a spectacular array of yellow, orange, and red fall colors. The fall foliage and graceful habit of this colonizing shrub are among its chief ornamental assets, but the sumac also serves as a plant to use in hostile conditions. It is tolerant of drought situations and will prosper in areas where little else will survive or that are difficult to maintain. These include steep banks or hillsides and waste areas with poor soil. The flowers of the sumac are greenish-yellow with male and female flowers appearing on separate plants. While the flowers are subtle but pleasing, female plants produce pyramidal clusters of red fruits that are not the immediate first choice of birds so they persist throughout the winter months in showy style. The stout terminal twigs are covered with a fine brown velvet coating resembling the antler of a male deer. This unique feature softens a rather coarse winter habit.

WHEN TO PLANT
Plant in the spring or fall.

WHERE TO PLANT
Plant in full sun or partial shade, and put in a place where you can let it spread but not get out of control. It makes a wonderful privacy screen when planted in mass. Planted as a single specimen, sumac can be pruned into a tree form, which results in a wide spreading open crown with a picturesque branching habit. Do not use as a

foundation plant, where it will consume your home and become a problem. Avoid planting in deep shade, where plants become straggly and leggy.

How to Plant
Plant as a container-grown or balled-and-burlapped plant.

Advice for Care
The staghorn sumac is a rambunctious plant, so you may occasionally need to temper its vigorous growth habit. To lower or rejuvenate an overgrown plant, cut back to ground level in the early spring. New vigorous growth will quickly result, leading to the reestablishment of its territorial hold. While the staghorn adapts well to dry soils, it is intolerant of extremely wet sites.

Additional Information
Proper siting is important with this shrub that can reach tree-like proportions. Use its growth habits to help you reclaim tough spots in your landscape that you just can't stand to go bare and where you need a tough, resilient plant to fill the bill.

Additional Species, Cultivars, or Varieties
'Dissecta' and 'Laciniata' are two cultivars with finely dissected leaflets, producing an incredible ferny foliage effect. The fall color is outstanding like the species. Both of these selections are female and need a male plant placed nearby to produce fruits. The shining sumac, *Rhus copallina* (20 to 30 ft.), is a large shrub differing from the staghorn with its glossy green leaves and amazing scarlet-red fall color. This, too, is a colonizing plant that needs space and preferably a full sun exposure.

Russian Arborvitae

Microbiota decussata

Height: 1 ft.
Foliage: Soft evergreen foliage
Zones: 3, 4, 5, 6
Light Requirement:

Every year, a few outstanding plants take the horticultural world by storm, creating an almost overnight sensation. That was the case with the Russian arborvitae, a relatively recent discovery from the mountains of Russia. Now the hoopla over this spreading evergreen shrub has waned as many gardeners have tried to grow it and have found that it is not always easy to please. However, if its growing requirements can be met, this is truly a choice and beautiful evergreen groundcover. Sporting bright green foliage with a ferny texture, the horizontal spreading branches curve downward at their tips. A mat-forming plant, it reaches only 1 ft. in height and can spread beyond 10 ft. The Russian arborvitae displays its best virtue after spring rains are over and strong new growth appears. The green new growth lights up a shady corner of the garden and contrasts well with young herbaceous perennials. Use *Microbiota* in areas where its prostrate low growth is an asset, such as a low terrace planting or in areas where taller plants just don't fit the bill. Mass plantings along a steep grade cascade downward in a graceful fashion, stabilizing the soil and providing a cool green splash of color. Use in deep shade areas with drifts of perennials such as hostas and astilbes, which play off the beautiful textural qualities of the Russian arborvitae. The winter color of the foliage has been described as purplish-brown to a russet-copper similar to some junipers. Some gardeners are put off by the coloring, while others see it as an interesting attribute and attempt to emphasize it by planting colorful spring bulbs within its boundaries. The bright flowers of the Siberian squill, *Scilla siberica*, or spring crocus are enhanced by the dark foliage of the Russian arborvitae.

WHEN TO PLANT

Plant in the spring or fall, and water well. Shrubs will benefit from mulching to cool the root zone. Rock mulches that are light in color will deflect sun and lower temperatures, which will help the Russian arborvitae's establishment.

WHERE TO PLANT

Once touted as "a juniper that grows in shade," the Russian arborvitae is indeed shade-tolerant and dislikes full sun. Plants in full sun and dry soil perform poorly and live a miserable life. Use wherever you have cool, moist conditions and need a spreading, low groundcover.

HOW TO PLANT

Plants are generally produced in containers. Remove circling or compacted roots that have accumulated in the bottom of the pot. Spread roots out evenly in the planting hole before backfilling with soil.

ADVICE FOR CARE

Despite its early rave reviews, *Microbiota* has definite cultural needs that must be met. Water well in hot, dry periods, and mulch the root zone to lower soil temperatures and conserve moisture. To keep spreading growth in bounds, remove long wispy branches that are growing beyond their intended home.

ADDITIONAL INFORMATION

While once thought of as a connoisseur's plant, the Russian arborvitae is now readily available. If you have a shady spot that needs a colorful textural component, this plant may be what you are looking for. Cut branches make decorative additions to wreaths.

ADDITIONAL SPECIES, CULTIVARS, OR VARIETIES

None.

Star Magnolia

Magnolia stellata

Height: 5 to 15 ft.
Flowers: White or flushed
  pink to rose or dark red
Bloom Period: Early spring
Zones: 4, 5, 6
Light Requirement:

The star magnolia is a happy wake-up call after a weary winter in Michigan. Among the earliest of magnolias to bloom, its prolific star-shaped petals shine pure and white on an early spring day. The numerous straplike petals radiate out of the center of the flower. The blooms chance late frost each year, emerging in late April or early May, when they emit a fragrant scent and create a cloud of bloom that completely covers the plant before its leaves emerge. The star magnolia is well suited to a foundation planting with its shrubby habit and small stature. Reaching a height of 15 ft. with a more narrow spread, it anchors the corner of a house or works well as an entryway pairing on either side of a door. In winter, the smooth gray bark is exceptionally beautiful, and its fuzzy flower buds are a unique feature both beautiful to look at and useful as they protect the quiescent flowers within. Magnolias, for all their beauty, still have limitations to their performance in Michigan landscapes. Their early blooming habit can get them in trouble. Flowers that push their luck on a warm spring afternoon may get zapped by a hard freeze. Some steps can be taken when siting your star magnolia, increasing the odds that you will be able to enjoy the spectacle of its radiant blooms on a yearly basis.

WHEN TO PLANT

Plant in the spring because magnolias represent some of the more difficult to transplant trees and shrubs. Fall planting is not recommended. If you decide to plant in the fall in Michigan, however, plant before mid-October if at all possible. This will leave some time for roots to become established before the onset of winter.

WHERE TO PLANT

Plant in full sun to promote strong flowering. Magnolias are effective as single specimens or in group plantings. Avoid placement in warm southern exposures. Also, while the star magnolia looks marvelous against a dark wall, it will respond by flowering earlier since

walls absorb and emit heat. Plant in a northern exposure to keep the buds tight and protective until the danger of late frosts has passed. Magnolias suffer under root competition with other plants. Plant in a space where roots can grow unimpeded and without competition. Magnolias create a heartwarming spring scene when underplanted with early spring blooming bulbs such as the grape hyacinth and the Siberian squill.

How to Plant

Preferably plant as a container specimen in the spring. Magnolias are notorious for their thick, fleshy roots that are easily damaged and slow to produce laterals. Do not plant too deeply. Plant at the same soil level found in your container or balled-and-burlapped plant. Magnolias prefer well-drained, slightly acidic, moist soils. Add leaf mold or peat moss to your planting hole to enrich the soil and increase aeration.

Advice for Care

Under the right conditions, your plant will thrive with minimal care. Mulch the root zone, and water in prolonged drought situations. Prune in early summer after flowering. Do not remove the lower branches of the star magnolia if at all possible. Its full pleasing habit is better left alone. Remove vigorous branch shoots that grow straight upward off older limbs. These will deplete the main branches of energy and threaten the natural form of the plant.

Additional Information

The star magnolia is at times susceptible to attack by magnolia scale. The scale appears on branches, stems, twigs, and leaves and causes plants to weaken. Adult magnolia scales look like dark brown, round bumps on twigs. They are often difficult to see but reveal themselves on close inspection. Dormant oil sprays applied before growth begins in the spring will suffocate scales. A crawler stage of the insect can be controlled by Orthene™ applications. Light scale infestations can be removed by hand.

Additional Species, Cultivars, or Varieties

'Royal Star' is pink in bud opening to large white flowers that are 6 in. across with up to 30 petals. It blooms a week later than normal for the species, which gives it some extra protection against late frosts.

Summersweet

Clethra alnifolia

<table>
<tr><td>

Other Name: Sweet Pepper Bush
Height: 9 ft.
Flowers: Soft pink, rose, or white
Bloom Period: Midsummer
Zones: 5, 6
Light Requirement:

</td></tr>
</table>

Native North American shrubs are currently hot items in the horticultural world and deservedly so. While some of these plants are cumbersome or difficult to incorporate into home landscapes with limited room, the summersweet fits right in with outstanding year-round appeal. *Clethra alnifolia* is a moderate-sized shrub reaching up to 9 ft. in height but with many cultivars available at smaller sizes. Dark glossy green summer foliage is topped by intensely fragrant pink, rose, or white flowers that appear in midsummer. The terminal flower spikes form persistent woody seed capsules, which are attractive in the winter months. Fall color is variable in high alkaline (pH) soils. In full sun with slightly acidic conditions it can be an outstanding yellow. The spicy fragrant blooms are the main calling card for this shrub, appearing at a time when most woody plants have already bloomed and are content to ride out the summer heat wave. Summersweet can be planted as a foundation plant or in large-scale mass plantings. In whatever way you decide to use it, take advantage of its beauty by placing it near an outdoor living area or within close proximity to a walkway. Its upright habit makes it useful for narrow areas where few woody shrubs can fit.

WHEN TO PLANT
Plant in spring or fall.

WHERE TO PLANT
Plant in full sun for the most vigorous growth, flowers, and better fall color. Summersweet is tolerant of partial shade and can be used effectively on the edge of a woodland or as an understory shrub to larger-sized trees. This colonizing shrub will eventually spread out, making it a good candidate for massing on a hillside or berm. The smaller selection 'Hummingbird' is perfect for a doorway entrance or beneath a first-floor window. A low-mounded shrub, it reaches 4

ft. and has fragrant white blooms. Its performance in Michigan land-scapes is still under evaluation because it occasionally has stem dieback in severe winters but always comes back strong. *Clethra* is salt-tolerant, so consider it for planting along sidewalks and path-ways that are deiced using salts during the winter months.

HOW TO PLANT

Plant as a container-grown or balled-and-burlapped plant. It toler-ates both dry and wet sites but prefers a moist, slightly acidic soil. Mulch with pine needles or an acidic-based bark mix.

ADVICE FOR CARE

Summersweet will develop leaf yellowing or chlorosis in soils with a pH over 7.5. Fertilizers that contain sulfur or that are known to have an acidic reaction may bring your plant back to health. Use them according to the manufacturer's instructions. Spider mites can sometimes be a problem. Water in periods of prolonged drought to avoid the stressful conditions that predispose plants to spider mite attack.

ADDITIONAL INFORMATION

Rabbits are especially fond of summersweet as a food source in the winter months. Newly planted shrubs should be protected with chicken wire the first few seasons if rabbits are a problem in your area. After a few years, the shrubs will respond to attacks by sprout-ing new underground stems off the root system. Humans may also take part in the pruning process and can rejuvenate an older shrub by selectively removing old wood, allowing young stems to develop and take their place. Winter is an excellent time to prune your plants. Cut back the branches to ground level, being careful not to remove new suckering stems.

ADDITIONAL SPECIES, CULTIVARS, OR VARIETIES

'Paniculata' has large white flowers up to 6 in. long and is known for its strong growth. 'Rosea' has dark pink flower buds that open pink, then fade to light pink. 'Pink Spire' has pink- to rose-colored buds opening to a soft pink flower. These two pink-flowered forms are often confused in the trade; you may think you're getting one but end up with the other. Both are exceptional, regardless of this mix-up.

Weigela

Weigela florida

Height: 9 ft.
Flowers: Red, white, rose, or pink
Bloom Period: Late spring
Zones: 5, 6
Light Requirement:

Some shrubs for one reason or another carry with them a strong feeling of nostalgia. How many of us can remember a favorite plant in a relative's garden as if it were an old friend we recall spending time with? The old-fashioned weigela fits into this category as a plant that was once widely used but has since fallen by the wayside with the introduction of new, more contemporary shrubs. Weigela is no stranger to criticism for its lanky habit and limited seasonal appeal once flowering is over. In the past few years, however, both older and newer selections are bringing the fanfare back to weigela as interest in this old-time shrub has picked up again, slowly but surely putting it back into the mainstream. The brilliant flowers are the drawing card for weigela with long 1- to 1¼-in. trumpet-shaped blossoms that reliably cover the shrub in June. A myriad of flower colors are available, and some selections will bloom again in the late summer. The foliage is a rather dull green with no fall color, but some selections have leaves with darker purplish tones that provide a nice contrast to the flowers. Most selections average 6 to 9 ft. in height and 9 to 12 ft. in width. The overall habit is a tall, open shrub with long, arching branches that bend toward the ground. Compact forms are available that are more suitable for foundation or container plantings.

WHEN TO PLANT

Plant weigela in spring or fall.

WHERE TO PLANT

Plant in full sun in grouped plantings or as a single specimen. Dwarf or smaller selections can be used for foundation plantings. Weigela is adaptable to most soil types except those with poor drainage. This shrub has an extremely coarse winter habit. Place it in an area where it will draw little attention, or obscure it with better winter-interest plants. Once the flowering has past, this shrub needs to blend in with the crowd, so plant in a mixed border with other woody or perennial plants.

How to Plant

Plant as a container-grown or balled-and-burlapped plant. Mulch shrubs after planting to conserve moisture and discourage weeds.

Advice for Care

While weigelas are known for their hardiness, they will need cosmetic pruning every year. Remove branches that have died back or appear damaged. The entire shrub can be rejuvenated by cutting it completely back to the ground or selectively removing older wood over a 3- to 5-year period. Prune after flowering in June or July. Water in prolonged periods of drought. Weigela is generally not bothered by serious insects or diseases.

Additional Information

For country gardens with a lot of open space, a collection of weigelas will light up the landscape and give it that yesteryear appeal so often conjured up by this shrub.

Additional Species, Cultivars, or Varieties

'Java Red' has purplish-green foliage, pink flowers, and a compact form, growing to a height of 4 ft. with an equal or greater spread. 'Polka' has been proclaimed as "the best pink weigela" by many nursery catalogs. Developed in Canada, it has an extremely long bloom period from June to September. Soft pink flowers appear on this shrub that reaches 5 to 6 ft. in height with a greater spread. 'White Knight' produces pure white flowers that bloom throughout the summer. It grows 5 to 6 ft. in height and has an equal or greater spread.

CHAPTER NINE

Trees

*T*REES ARE A LIVING LINK BETWEEN THE PAST AND THE
FUTURE. One of life's most satisfying and humbling experiences is to plant a sapling and see it grow in 20 or 30 years into a
fine, mature tree. Yet these days, many people demand instant
results, including—and perhaps especially—in their gardens. So
why plant trees?

First, trees are beautiful all year. They intensify our awareness
of the changing seasons, from their first pale green leaves in spring
through their lush summer foliage. The splashy autumn reds,
oranges, and golds of Michigan trees draw visitors from all over
the country. When winter arrives, deciduous trees are dramatic and
sculptural, and evergreens become more conspicuous, bringing
cheer to the otherwise stark landscape.

Trees shade us in summer, cooling our houses by blocking the hot
sun. Bare of leaves in winter, they allow sunlight and warmth to
reach us when we need them most. Trees remove carbon dioxide
and furnish oxygen to the air we breathe. They provide a sense of
emotional comfort and stability for people as well as habitats for
birds and other wildlife.

SELECTING YOUR TREE

Trees may be purchased with the rootballs wrapped in burlap.
These balled-and-burlapped trees are grown in fields, dug, and then
wrapped with burlap and sometimes wire baskets. Remove at least
the top third of the burlap and wire at planting. New synthetic
burlap wraps will not decompose and must be removed entirely
after placing the tree in the planting hole. Balled-and-burlapped
trees may be planted March to May and September to November.

Bareroot trees are grown in a field, then dug when dormant, in
very early spring or late fall. Once dug, these trees must be planted

immediately so the roots don't dry out. They may require staking after planting.

Trees that have been grown in containers are also available. Look for signs of healthy new growth on a container-grown tree. If roots have grown into a dense, encircled ball, they should be teased or even cut at planting to encourage lateral growth. Container-grown trees may be planted at any time during the growing season, but spring and fall are preferred. Take the tree out of the container before planting.

Planting Your Tree

A soil test will tell you what nutrients, if any, should be added before you plant the tree. If you have matched the tree to the site, you should not have to add many or any amendments to the soil. On heavy clay soils, however, you may add organic matter in the form of leaf mold, well-rotted compost, or mushroom compost. This will help aerate the soil, improving drainage and encouraging root development.

Dig the planting hole as deep as the container or rootball and three times as wide. Fill the hole with water, and let it stand for an hour. If water remains, drainage is poor and you will need to plant the tree higher than the existing soil level. Put some of the soil back in the planting hole, creating a mound that will elevate the top one-third (or 3 to 4 inches) of the rootball above grade. Mound up the soil around the base of the trunk so the tree is at the same depth it was in the container or field. Gently slope the sides of the mound back toward the ground.

The most critical factor for tree growth the first two years after planting is water. Fertilizer is usually not needed for the first year or so. If the tree has poor stem or leaf development, you may choose to fertilize. The best time to fertilize trees is in late fall.

American Smoketree

Cotinus obovatus

Height: 30 ft.
Flowers: Large hazy plumes of green flowers fading to pink with seed development
Bloom Period: Summer
Zones: 4, 5, 6
Light Requirement:

The American smoketree has been called one of our most spectacular fall-color plants, and this is no exaggeration. Few trees can match both the flowers and the foliage of this handsome native tree. In fact, every season puts forth an exciting feature on this plant that is too rarely seen in our modern landscapes. Spring begins with bronze new growth that develops into attractive summer foliage that is a dark blue-green. Early summer flowers erupt from the terminals of the tree in a distinctive plume consisting of many small green flowers that create a smoky or hazy effect. As the blooms progress into seed formation, they take on a rosy color that is magnificent in contrast to the blue-green foliage. The seeds have tiny hairs attached to them that turn a rosy color and catch the early morning dew. The show continues after flowering as the summer foliage goes through a fall color parade of yellow to orange to reds and purples. Fantastic! The winter aspect of this plant is striking, and the bark, with its scaly gray-brown plates, is quite attractive on bare trees. The American smoketree is the perfect choice for small landscapes, forming an upright dense rounded crown reaching a maximum height of 30 ft. Trees make great specimens when placed against a wall or evergreen background, where their flowers and fall foliage really come alive.

WHEN TO PLANT
Plant in spring or fall.

WHERE TO PLANT
Plant in full sun to partial shade. The smoketree adapts well to high pH soils and is very drought-tolerant after a few years of establishment. It also tolerates compacted soils and is a good choice for high-traffic areas. Smoketree will not tolerate wet soils for any length of time, so avoid low, poorly drained locations.

HOW TO PLANT

The planting hole should be at least 2 to 3 times as wide as the root-ball. For balled-and-burlapped trees, after placing in the hole, remove any twine, rope, or wire that is wrapped around the root-ball. This is important for the top 1/3 of the rootball, where feeder roots will develop. Be sure the top of the rootball or container root system is planted level with the surrounding grade. In heavy or poor soils, plant the top of the root system 3 to 4 in. above the surrounding grade. Some sinking or settling of the rootball can be expected in these situations. Mulch after planting with 2 to 3 in. of organic material.

ADVICE FOR CARE

The smoketree is slow growing and will take time to get established. The wood of the tree is fragile and susceptible to ice and storm damage. Trees are also susceptible to *Verticillium* wilt, a fungus that is found in the soil and enters the plant through its roots. The fungus moves into the tissues that conduct water and food, disrupting their function and normally causing portions of the tree to wilt. Branches of the tree slowly die out as the fungus spreads. Remove all infected branches, and burn them. Encourage healthy growth by watering during droughts and fertilizing in the late fall.

ADDITIONAL INFORMATION

The American smoketree has been exploited in its native habitat for its wood, which produces a yellow-orange dye. Trees are becoming rare in their native habitats.

ADDITIONAL SPECIES CULTIVARS, OR VARIETIES

Cotinus coggygria, the common smoketree or smokebush, is a large shrub with similar but smaller leaves and flowers with the same distinctive smoky effect. Many cultivars are available, including several purple-leaf forms that are spectacular in combination with herbaceous perennials in a mixed shrub border.

Amur Chokecherry

Prunus maackii

Height: 35 to 45 ft.
Flowers: White
Bloom Period: Late spring
Bark: Shiny rich cinnamon-
brown, often peeling
Zones: 3, 4, 5, 6
Light Requirement:

The remarkable blooms of ornamental cherries awaken us from our winter doldrums with beautiful white to pink flowers, but the amur chokecherry offers more than spring blooms. It has outstanding winter bark that is a shiny cinnamon-brown and peels away in strips. This is an extremely hardy tree of moderate size that becomes a prime time plant each winter season when some other cherry species show little to no winter interest. While the winter season brings out the best in the amur chokecherry, it also has a pleasant spring display of flowers. Usually blooming in late May and early June, the flowers are white and borne in profusion. From these flowers black fruits ripen and are carried away by birds. Plant in a prominent position where the handsome bark and twigs can be frequently viewed along a walkway or out a window. The tree has a dense, rounded form and reaches 35 to 45 ft. in height. The shiny brown bark looks spectacular when surrounded by a planting of the purple beautyberry, *Callicarpa dichotoma*. The violet fruits of the beautyberry play off the ornamental bark of the amur chokecherry in dynamic fashion.

WHEN TO PLANT
Plant in the spring of the year. Fall transplanting will yield less success.

WHERE TO PLANT
Plant in full sun in a well-drained soil. It does not tolerate hot, dry conditions, so keep away from hot concrete and dry sites where plants will suffer.

HOW TO PLANT
The planting hole for the amur chokecherry should be at least 2 to 3 times as wide as the rootball. For balled-and-burlapped trees, after placing in the hole, remove any twine, rope, or metal wire that is

wrapped around the rootball. This is important for the top 1/3 of the rootball, where feeder roots will develop. Be sure the top of the root-ball or container root system is planted level with the surrounding grade. In heavy or poor soils, plant the top of the root system 3 to 4 in. above the surrounding grade. Some sinking or settling of the rootball can be expected in these situations. After planting, apply a 2- to 3-in. layer of organic mulch.

ADVICE FOR CARE

This is one of the few ornamental cherries that bloom on wood set from the previous season's growth. In general you should avoid pruning your tree if possible. Tree wounds will take away from the winter beauty of this tree, so only prune to remove dead, diseased, or broken branches. Prune after flowering. Most cherries are extremely shallow-rooted, so avoid planting groundcovers or shrubs in the immediate vicinity of your tree. This will help prevent compe-tition for water and nutrients and limit possible damage to the roots from cultivation of the soil. Mulching around the root zone will encourage a healthy root system.

ADDITIONAL INFORMATION

Demand creates supply. If you can't find this plant at your local nurseries, encourage them to stock it. Several small mail-order nurs-eries carry a nice selection of ornamental cherries. See the source guide.

ADDITIONAL SPECIES, CULTIVARS, OR VARIETIES

Prunus serrula is a small tree with a rich mahogany-colored bark that glistens in the sun and is very effective in the winter months. It reaches a height of 20 to 30 ft. and is hardy to Zones 5 and 6.

Baldcypress

Taxodium distichum

Height: 50 to 70 ft. or more
Spread: 30 to 40 ft.
Foliage: Soft green needles turning reddish-brown in fall; deciduous
Zones: 4, 5, 6
Light Requirement:

Imagine a swamp in the southeastern United States and you'll probably picture tall cypress trees covered with Spanish moss, with alligators and other critters ready to pounce nearby. The tall cypress tree *Taxodium* represents a symbol of the South that is perfectly hardy in Michigan. More commonly known as the baldcypress, this tree grows naturally into southern Illinois, where it reaches the northernmost point of its natural range. But it is useful in the southern half of the Lower Peninsula as well. Brought out of the swamp and placed in our landscapes, the baldcypress makes an outstanding year-round tree of great beauty. The baldcypress begins the season with a flush of bright-green growth on slender twigs. The growth is late to appear in the spring. The narrow needles darken in the summer and create a fine, soft-textured tree. While it is definitely a cone-bearing tree (a conifer), it is not evergreen. Instead, the needles turn a distinctive copper-brown in the fall and then drop, along with the soft outer twigs. The winter habit is dense and twiggy with the main trunk an attractive reddish-orange. *Taxodium* is valued for its four-season appeal. It tolerates both extremely wet soils and poor dry soils. In northern areas it can reach a height of 50 to 70 ft. but has a narrow pyramidal habit that makes it a good choice for street tree plantings. For wet areas it is effective in group plantings along a pond or stream side where standing water presents no problem for the growth of this tree.

When to Plant
Spring planting is recommended for the baldcypress.

Where to Plant
Plant in full sun for stronger growth and better fall color. Trees are particularly effective as textural contrasts with other woody plants and perennials. The fall fruit crop of the Michigan holly, *Ilex verticillata*, sparkles against the copper-brown needles of the baldcypress. *Taxodium* is a great plant for providing summer shade for your

house and with its annual needle drop allows winter light and
warmth to come through when you most need them.

How to Plant

The planting hole for the baldcypress should be at least 2 to 3 times
as wide as the rootball. For balled-and-burlapped trees, after placing
in the hole, remove any twine, rope, or metal wire that is wrapped
around the rootball. This is important for the top $1/3$ of the rootball,
where the feeder roots will develop. Be sure the top of the rootball
or container root system is planted level with the surrounding
grade. In heavy or poor soils, plant the top of the root system 3
to 4 in. above the surrounding grade. Some sinking or settling of
the rootball can be expected in these situations. After planting,
apply 2 to 3 in. of organic mulch.

Advice for Care

A relatively carefree tree, the baldcypress should be watered as
needed during the early years of its establishment. If chlorosis or
leaf yellowing develops as a result of high soil pH, fertilize using
mixes that contain sulfur or that are known to have an acidic reaction. Use them according to the manufacturer's instructions. Mulch
every year with composted oak leaves and pine needles to lower
the pH of your soil. The baldcypress has a natural "church spire"
habit that should not be altered by pruning. Remove only dead,
diseased, or dying limbs, being careful not to alter the main central
trunk or leader.

Additional Information

Lower limbs will diminish over time as the tree grows tall, exposing
its flared trunk as it meets the ground. With its strong central leader
and slender branches and twigs, the baldcypress is perfect for
exposed, windy situations.

Additional Species, Cultivars, or Varieties

'Shawnee Brave' is a very narrow, upright form of the baldcypress
that is particularly useful in street tree plantings or for specimen use
where space is limited.

Black Gum

Nyssa sylvatica

Other Name: Tupelo
Height: 30 to 50 ft. or more
Foliage: Fall color yellow-
orange to scarlet-red
Zones: 3, 4, 5, 6
Light Requirement:

Our North American native trees are the envy of the world when it comes to autumn color. Among the finest of trees for fall color is the black gum or tupelo, *Nyssa sylvatica*. Found naturally in Michigan in moist bottom lands and wet areas, it develops into a large tree, reaching 50 ft. or more in height. It has a pyramidal habit when young and grows slowly to form a flat-topped crown. The foliage of the black gum is outstanding for its lustrous shiny green appearance in the summer and incredible yellow-orange to scarlet colors in the fall. After the foliage has dropped, the smooth silver bark and distinct horizontal branching habit of the tupelo enliven the winter with its architectural beauty. The pewter bark darkens as the tree matures and forms rectangular blocks or ridges that resemble an alligator's hide. The black gum is perfect for wet sites or sites where you want to establish a naturalistic planting. It makes an exceptional specimen tree that casts light shade, allowing turf to develop beneath its wide-spreading branches. Black gum has been used to some success in street tree plantings but is generally not tolerant of pollution in urban areas. Black gum is particularly effective with an evergreen backdrop to illuminate its amazing fall color.

WHEN TO PLANT
Plant in the spring only; fall-transplanted trees are notorious for failure.

WHERE TO PLANT
Plant in full sun to partial shade. *Nyssa* is tolerant of shade, but it does not promote the full-spreading form that is so admirable in this tree. Black gum prefers moist, slightly acidic conditions and will develop leaf yellowing or chlorosis in alkaline (high pH) situations.

How to Plant

For best results, plant smaller trees. Avoid transplanting trees larger than 3^1/$_2$ in. diameter. Black gum's taproot makes transplanting at larger sizes difficult. Small containerized trees are preferable if you can find them. The planting hole should be at least 2 to 3 times as wide as the rootball. The addition of organic matter to the planting hole in the form of humus or rotted manure and a yearly topdressing of an acid-based mulch will help keep your plant in a healthy condition. For balled-and-burlapped trees, after placing in the hole, remove any twine, rope, or metal wire that is wrapped around the rootball. This is important for the top ^{1}/$_3$ of the rootball. Be sure the top of the rootball or container root system is planted level with the surrounding grade. In heavy or poor soils, plant the top of the root system 3 to 4 in. above the surrounding grade. Some sinking or settling of the rootball can be expected in these situations.

Advice for Care

Chlorosis or leaf yellowing will alert you to alkaline conditions that are detrimental to plant growth. Fertilizers that contain sulfur or that are known to have an acidic reaction may bring your plant back to health. Do not prune or disrupt the main trunk or stem that forms the central leader of the tree. This will damage the natural form of this plant. Cankers may develop on stems and branches, causing portions of the tree to die back. Remove infected branches.

Additional Information

While the flowers of black gum are barely noticeable to humans, they provide sweet nectar to bees; tupelo honey is a popular commodity in southern states. This tree has a remarkable native range, growing all the way into Mexico. Michigan populations are some of the northernmost in its natural distribution.

Additional Species, Cultivars, or Varieties

None.

Corneliancherry

Cornus mas

Height: 20 to 25 ft.
Flowers: Yellow
Bloom Period: Spring
Zones: 4, 5, 6
Light Requirement:

Each spring as we wait for the appearance of spring bulbs and the disappearance of the last remnants of winter snow, a surprisingly early-blooming dogwood bursts into flower on leafless branches. The corneliancherry's bright yellow flowers cover the tree in mass, making it quite noticeable even from a distance. When you approach the tree, you can see that it also has flaky attractive bark ranging from a warm gray to rich brown color. The summer months offer fine lustrous green foliage, and by August red, cherry-like fruits appear partially obscured by the foliage. The fall color is a reddish-purple when trees are planted in full sun. The corneliancherry is the perfect small landscape tree. With a round, dense shrub-like habit, it reaches 20 to 25 ft. high and grows 15 ft. wide. On the campus of Michigan State University, it is often found at the corner of a building or in an open area as a small specimen tree. The corneliancherry has many uses and is particularly valuable for small landscapes. Plant it as a single specimen small tree at the corner of a house, or use a grouping as a privacy screen or windbreak. This early-blooming dogwood is stunning placed against a backdrop of dark-needled evergreens.

WHEN TO PLANT
Spring transplanting is recommended. Fall planting yields less success.

WHERE TO PLANT
Plant in full sun for best growth and flower production. This a one of the easiest-to-please dogwood trees you will come across. It is highly adaptable to most soil types except those that are too wet or dry, and it is virtually disease- and insect-free.

How to Plant

When planting in groups, space the trees at least 20 ft. apart to allow room enough to spread. The planting hole should be at least 2 to 3 times as wide as the rootball. For balled-and-burlapped trees, after placing in the hole, remove any twine, rope, or metal wire that is wrapped around the rootball. This is important for the top $1/3$ of the rootball. Be sure the top of the rootball or container root system is planted level with the surrounding grade. In heavy or poor soils, plant the top of the root system 3 to 4 in. above the surrounding grade. Some sinking or settling of the rootball can be expected in these situations. Mulch after planting with 2 to 3 in. of organic mulch.

Advice for Care

The corneliancherry will generally not require pruning except to remove dead, diseased, or dying branches. You may have to occasionally prune older specimens where growth has become too crowded. Nursery plants are available in single stem trees or as multistemmed shrubs. Tree forms are good if you want a raised canopy, but shrub forms have better winter interest with numerous branches showing the flaky bark.

Additional Information

Cut branches are great to force into bloom; simply place in a vase on a warm windowsill. The fruits can be made into jams and syrup. If you don't eat them, the birds will!

Additional Species, Cultivars, or Varieties

'Golden Glory' is an amazing upright form with an incredible flower display. It is perfect as a paired planting on either side of a doorway. The Japanese cornel dogwood, *Cornus officinalis*, is a closely related tree that is similar in most respects but has a showier bark with rich brown to orange tones and pops its flowers open a few days earlier than *Cornus mas*.

Dawn Redwood

Metasequoia glyptostroboides

Height: 70 to 100 ft.
Foliage: Soft, feathery bright green needles
Zones: 4, 5, 6
Light Requirement:

Every plant has a story, and the dawn redwood's story is fascinating. This ancient tree was first discovered as a fossil in the early 1940s; then a few years later it was found alive and well in central China. This large cone-bearing tree drops its needles each year, which clearly sets it apart from the average conifer. Its size and width make it unsuitable for smaller landscapes, but it's a great addition to large landscapes, adding beauty and a touch of rarity and intrigue to the garden. A tall pyramidal tree that can grow more than 70 ft. tall and 25 ft. wide, the dawn redwood commands a lot of space and should not be shoved into a corner. The soft bright green needles have a feathery texture and turn a beautiful russet or orange-brown color in the fall before dropping. Use the dawn redwood to great effect in a grove planting. Its unique winter habit and twiggy growth are impressive when planted in mass. The bark of the tree exposes its wonderful qualities in the winter months with warm red-brown colors and a hint of gray. The stout base of the trunk flares outward as it meets the ground and may have a fluted or ridged appearance. The dawn redwood is known for its impressive annual growth; some trees have been measured as growing 50 ft. over 15 to 20 years. Dawn redwoods are perfect for energy-conscious gardeners who plant them for shade in the summer and then have full sun available in the winter after the needles drop.

When to Plant
Plant in the spring or the fall.

Where to Plant
Plant in full sun in a slightly acidic, well-drained soil. The dawn redwood likes moisture but does not tolerate excessively wet soils. Avoid planting in low areas because this exposes the tree to a greater likelihood of frost damage. Also avoid planting close to sidewalks. The dawn redwood's aggressive roots can lift and crack concrete.

How to Plant

The planting hole should be at least 2 to 3 times as wide as the root-ball. For balled-and-burlapped trees, after placing in the hole, remove any twine, rope, or wire that is wrapped around the root-ball. This is important for the top 1/3 of the rootball, where feeder roots will develop. Be sure the top of the rootball or container root system is planted level with the surrounding grade. In heavy or poor soils, plant the top of the root system 3 to 4 in. above the surrounding grade. Some sinking or settling of the rootball can be expected in these situations. Mulch after planting with 2 to 3 in. of organic material.

Advice for Care

Dawn redwood seldom needs pruning. The central trunk or leader should be left to develop the distinct pyramidal habit the tree is noted for. If the main leader becomes damaged on the tree, a new vigorous shoot normally takes its place. Trees usually do not require fertilization. They often grow continuously into the fall and have tip dieback with the first hard frosts of autumn. This is noticeable on trees that have a curled branch at the very top of the tree. This is nothing to be concerned about, but you should avoid fertilizing trees after midsummer. Late fertilization would encourage vigorous growth well into the fall season.

Additional Information

The dawn redwood once grew widely across western North America, the Arctic, Europe, and Asia 15 million to 90 million years ago. In the nursery trade, dawn redwood is often confused with the baldcypress, *Taxodium distichum*, a close relative. To help distinguish between the two, remember that the dawn redwood has opposite needles or leaves. The baldcypress has alternate needles or leaves.

Additional Species, Cultivars, or Varieties

The selections 'National' and 'Sheridan Spire' are narrower with more upright branches compared to the species.

Flowering Crabapples
'Prairifire' and 'Professor Sprenger'
Malus 'Prairifire' and *Malus* 'Professor Sprenger'

Height: To 20 ft.
Flowers: 'Prairifire', reddish-purple; 'Professor Sprenger', white
Bloom Period: May
Zones: 4, 5, 6
Light Requirement:

Flowering crabapples represent some of the most popular trees in the nursery trade. Their cheerful, often fragrant blossoms light up the spring landscape and are followed by impressive fruit crops that can last deep into the winter months. Not all crabapples were created equal and certain cultivars are superior in performance when compared to others. The principal diseases associated with crabapples are particularly destructive to their ornamental display in Michigan landscapes. The foliage diseases—powdery mildew, apple scab, and cedar apple rust—wreak havoc on the foliage and fruit quality of trees. The more serious bacterial disease, fire blight, can completely kill a plant. Two of the top-performing crabapples are 'Professor Sprenger' and 'Prairifire'. Both cultivars offer the perfect balance of superior characteristics in crabapples—attractive form, clean foliage, beautiful flowers, persistent fruit, and disease resistance. 'Prairifire' flowers in May with crimson buds opening to deep red-purple single flowers. The foliage is a handsome deep green with purple tones. The fruit is nearly 1/2 in. wide and persists some years into February. The reddish-brown bark is covered with cross-hatchings called lenticels that give this crabapple distinctive winter interest. 'Professor Sprenger' is an upright tree reaching 20 ft. in height and width. It has pure white fragrant flowers that emerge from deep rose-pink buds. The fruit changes from a yellow-orange to orange-red and persists well into the winter months. Underplant with daffodils to create a colorful spring display. All the cultivars recommended here have shown good disease resistance and flower every year. Some crabapples flower and fruit every other year, so in some years are disappointing in their display.

WHEN TO PLANT
Plant in spring or fall. Crabapples are easy to transplant.

WHERE TO PLANT

Plant in full sun in an exposed location. Crabapples will tolerate most soil conditions except those that are not well drained. Space group plantings at least 20 to 25 ft. apart to avoid overcrowding. Plants should not be placed in stagnant or wind-protected areas because these conditions favor the development of leaf diseases.

HOW TO PLANT

The planting hole should be at least 2 to 3 times as wide as the rootball. For balled-and-burlapped trees, after placing in the hole, remove any twine, rope, or metal wire that is wrapped around the rootball. This is important for the top 1/3 of the rootball, where feeder roots will develop. Be sure the top of the rootball or container root system is planted level with the surrounding grade. In heavy or poor soils, plant the top of the root system 3 to 4 in. above the surrounding grade. Some sinking or settling of the rootball can be expected in these situations. Bareroot whips can be planted while dormant. Remove any damaged roots before planting. Spread the roots out radially in a wide hole, and backfill with the original soil. Stake for one season with a thick bamboo cane for support. Mulch after planting with 2 to 3 in. of an organic mulch.

ADVICE FOR CARE

Almost all crabapple selections are grafted (attached) to a vigorous understock or rootstock that sometimes sprouts growth off the base of the trunk. Remove these sprouts as soon as they develop, or they will quickly overtake your tree. The leaf size and shape of the rootstock are different enough in appearance that you will recognize it.

ADDITIONAL INFORMATION

Crabapples will generally not require fertilizer on a regular basis. Prune to remove rootstock sprouts and stems that are too closely spaced or are growing back into the center of the tree. Prune during the winter months to work the bare branches of the tree. Disinfect your pruners after each cut with isopropyl alcohol. Doing this will prevent the spread of fire blight, which overwinters on the bark and twigs of crabapples and other rose family members that may live in your garden.

ADDITIONAL SPECIES, CULTIVARS, OR VARIETIES

'Sugar Tyme' is an exceptional crabapple, forming an upright oval tree 18 ft. high and 15 ft. wide. The flowers are pale pink in bud, opening to single white fragrant flowers. It was selected at Michigan State University by former landscape architect Milton Baron.

Ginkgo

Ginkgo biloba

Other Name: Maidenhair Tree
Height: 50 to 80 ft.
Foliage: Unique fan-shaped
leaves with a golden
yellow fall color
Zones: 3, 4, 5, 6
Light Requirement:

Every fall, youngsters around Michigan capture the falling leaves of majestic trees to take home and press between sheets of waxed paper. Their leaf collections display oak and maple leaves, which are impressive for their sheer size and earthy colors. But the most prized specimen may be the fan-shaped golden leaf of the ginkgo. A remarkable curiosity, the gingko is known as a living fossil. Its ancestors are represented in the fossil record as far back as 225 million years ago. The unusually shaped leaves have been described as looking like fishtails. They have parallel veins stretching vertically across the leaf. In the summer months, they are an attractive emerald green. When fall arrives, they turn a spectacular golden yellow for about a week, and then all at once trees drop their leaves almost overnight, creating a carpet of gold around the base. Gingko is a large tree that demands a lot of space and may not be suited to smaller landscapes unless an upright form is selected. It grows 50 to 80 ft. with a pyramidal habit when young to an open spreading habit as it matures. It has a coarse winter habit that takes some getting used to, but its performance and beauty in the summer and fall make it all worthwhile.

WHEN TO PLANT

Plant in spring or fall.

WHERE TO PLANT

The ginkgo prefers a well-drained, deep sandy soil but will grow in heavy clay soils as long as they are not waterlogged. The tree is generally slow growing and is frequently used as a street tree because it tolerates urban conditions. Plant in full sun.

HOW TO PLANT

The planting hole should be at least 2 to 3 times as wide as the rootball. For balled-and-burlapped trees, after placing in the hole, remove any twine, rope, or metal wire that is wrapped around the rootball. This is important for the top $1/3$ of the rootball. Be sure the top of the rootball or container root system is planted level with the surrounding grade. In heavy or poor soils, plant the top of the root system 3 to 4 in. above the surrounding grade. Some sinking or settling of the rootball can be expected in these situations. Mulch after planting with 2 to 3 in. of organic mulch.

ADVICE FOR CARE

The ginkgo is virtually disease- and pest-free. The tree has a main trunk or central leader that provides the framework for the large horizontal branches, giving it a spreading habit at maturity. Do not remove the central leader. This would cause a new branch to grow vertically in its place, ruining the form and creating a weak point where the two branches meet. In general remove only dead, diseased, or damaged branches.

ADDITIONAL INFORMATION

The fruit (naked seed) of the ginkgo is reviled for the horrible smell of its orange pulpy covering. It is truly one of nature's funkiest offerings. The seeds within the pulp are treasured as a delicacy in Asia where they are called "silver apricots." Fortunately for those who want to pass on the fruit instead of pass out, male trees are available in the nursery trade. Herbal remedies abound for various parts of the ginkgo tree, adding to its mystery and allure. Extracts from the foliage are used to make blood thinners and circulatory medicines, and some claim they improve memory.

ADDITIONAL SPECIES, CULTIVARS, OR VARIETIES

'Autumn Gold' is a male selection with excellent fall color. 'Fastigiata' is an upright tree well suited for street tree plantings. When purchasing plants, insist that the trees are males, and preferably buy a named selection to be sure. Seed-grown trees do not produce fruits until 20 or more years of age.

Hop-Hornbeam

Ostrya virginiana

Height: 25 to 40 ft.
Bark: Attractive peeling or shredding bark
Zones: 3, 4, 5, 6
Light Requirement:

Some of our finest native trees in Michigan go unnoticed or underappreciated because they seem to blend in with the crowd. They are not particularly vibrant in flower or bold in their architecture, so they remain reclusive or hidden from our view. The American hop-hornbeam is a "blend-in" plant, a tree with the kind of beauty that becomes apparent on closer inspection. The first thing you notice about this tree is the gray-brown bark that hangs loosely in longitudinal strips unattached at either end. This shredding or peeling bark has afforded the tree another common name, the cat scratch tree. Hop-hornbeam is a medium-sized tree reaching a height of 25 to 40 ft. with handsome foliage that is bright green and soft to touch. The leaves have a prominent narrow ending and a distinct jagged edge and turn a pleasant yellow in the fall. The male flowers (catkins) are quite noticeable on the tree in the winter months, usually appearing in threes as short brown buds before they open in early spring. The female flowers are more difficult to see but produce distinctive papery pods resembling the fruit of the hop vine. These appear in the early summer in greenish clusters that hang from the tree and contain small nutlets that are a favorite of turkeys and other wildlife. The hop-hornbeam is useful for naturalistic plantings or as a lawn specimen. It has been used extensively as a street tree in Lansing. With the lower branches removed, its small size makes it suitable for a narrow street lawn. Be aware that although it is used in street tree plantings, it is highly sensitive to salt.

When to Plant
Plant in the spring. Fall planting generally is less successful.

WHERE TO PLANT
Plant in full sun or partial shade. It will do quite well on the edge of a woodlot or planted as an understory tree. It prefers a moist, well-drained soil that is slightly acidic.

HOW TO PLANT
For best results, plant small-sized trees. Avoid transplanting trees larger than $3^1/_2$ in. in diameter. The hop-hornbeam's taproot makes transplanting at larger sizes difficult. Small containerized trees are preferable if you can find them. The planting hole should be at least 2 to 3 times as wide as the rootball. The addition of organic matter to the planting hole in the form of humus, rotted manure, and a yearly topdressing of an acid-based mulch will help keep your plant in a healthy condition. For balled-and-burlapped trees, after placing in the hole, remove any twine, rope, or metal wire that is wrapped around the rootball. This is important for the top $1/_3$ of the rootball, where feeder roots will form. The top of the rootball or container root system should be level with the surrounding grade. In heavy or poor soils, plant the top of the root system 3 to 4 in. above the surrounding grade. Some sinking or settling of the root-ball can be expected in these situations.

ADVICE FOR CARE
Newly transplanted trees are slow to establish. Trees under stress are sometimes attacked by the two-lined chestnut borer. The larvae of the borer tunnel within the bark of the trees, causing branch dieback that is usually first noticed at the top of the tree. Contact your local extension agent for current recommendations on the control of wood-boring insects. Keeping your trees well watered and vigorous will protect them from attack.

ADDITIONAL INFORMATION
This tree is often in limited supply and may need to be ordered through small mail-order nurseries.

ADDITIONAL SPECIES, CULTIVARS, OR VARIETIES
None.

Katsuratree

Cercidiphyllum japonicum

Height: 40 to 60 ft. or more
Foliage: Blue-green
Zones: 4, 5, 6
Light Requirement:

The katsuratree has exotic written all over it. Almost every aspect of the tree seems strangely beautiful. Particularly captivating is the blue-green foliage that flickers in the wind. This large shade tree reaches well over 100 ft. in its native Japan and China but will grow to a lesser size in Michigan gardens. Katsuratree typically has multiple stems. Its shape is pyramidal when young, but it develops a broad-spreading crown at maturity. It is a rapid grower, normally putting on 2 ft. of growth per year under optimum conditions. The bark of the tree appears smooth when young and becomes somewhat shaggy with age. The foliage is its most remarkable asset. It emerges reddish-purple in the spring, then develops a blue-green color in the summer months. Fall is a special time for this tree as the foliage goes to a fine yellow with hints of apricot and brown. An additional bonus to the color is the delightful scent of the foliage, which has been compared to brown sugar or toffee. Use this tree as a large specimen or a street tree if you can find it as a single-stem form. All in all, not many trees can compare to the katsura in grace, habit, and year-round beauty.

WHEN TO PLANT

The katsura can be finicky in its transplant requirements. Plant in the early spring for best results. Fall transplanting generally yields less success.

WHERE TO PLANT

Plant in full sun or partial shade. The katsura should receive morning sun if possible. It prefers a moist, slightly acidic soil. Trees grow quickly, so they should be grown only where adequate space is available. The habit of the tree becomes wide spreading over time, and multistemmed trees can become susceptible to breakage with age.

How to Plant

Plant as a balled-and-burlapped or container-grown plant in the early spring. The planting hole should be at least 2 to 3 times as wide as the rootball. For balled-and-burlapped trees, after placing in the hole, remove any twine, rope, or metal wire that is wrapped around the rootball. This is important for the top $1/3$ of the rootball, where feeder roots will develop. The top of the rootball or container root system should be planted level with the surrounding grade. In heavy or poor soils, plant the top of the root system 3 to 4 in. above the surrounding grade. Some sinking or settling of the rootball can be expected in these situations. Mulch after planting with 2 to 3 in. of organic mulch.

Advice for Care

The katsuratree will need to be watered over the first few years as it gets established. It has very few insect and disease problems but is sometimes susceptible to bark splitting.

Additional Information

Katsura has both long and short branches. The short branches are quite noticeable with distinct short spurs. Male and female flowers appear on separate trees. The females produce clusters of tiny banana-shaped fruits that split open and contain numerous seeds. The seeds are easy to germinate and grow. Collect the small fruits in October, and store dry in a paper bag or plastic bowl with a tight-fitting cover in the refrigerator until March. Then plant the seeds just under the surface in a sterile soil mix and place on a warm windowsill. You will be amazed at the number of trees that sprout.

Additional Species, Cultivars, or Varieties

'Pendula' is a weeping form of the katsura that produces a cascading waterfall effect of blue-green foliage that is spectacular! It is choice and very expensive.

Kentucky Coffeetree

Gymnocladus dioicus

Height: 60 to 75 ft.
Habit: Unique coarse winter habit with architectural branching and scaly bark and twigs
Zones: 3, 4, 5, 6
Light Requirement:

Some trees are just misunderstood. The Kentucky coffeetree is one of them. Unique in so many ways, it is still an outcast in our landscapes and gardens due to its rare qualities that both perplex and please people. Tim once heard it referred to as the "Dr. Seuss tree." With its stark winter habit, knobby branches, and scaly gray bark, it defines the word "coarse" and takes it to a new level.

With all its curious features and individuality, the coffeetree remains an undeniable beauty and a high-value shade tree. It remains bare for nearly 6 months of the year; it leafs out late and drops its leaves early in the fall. The time in between is remarkable as new growth emerges with pink tones and changes over time to a dark bluish-green and finally, as fall approaches, turns an attractive yellow. The leaves are immense and are composed of numerous smaller leaflets that cast a light shade, enabling turfgrass to grow beneath its canopy. It has a slow growth rate, eventually reaching 60 to 75 ft. in height and form-ing a narrow crown. The coffeetree's flowers appear separately on male and female plants. They are not very noticeable, appearing as new foliage is just emerging. The female flowers are borne in pyrami-dal blooms that are greenish-white and fragrant. Female trees produce large 5 to 10 in. leathery seedpods that hang from the tree throughout the winter season. The fruits contain hard black seeds that were once used as a coffee substitute by the early settlers. The seeds are toxic if eaten raw.

WHEN TO PLANT
Plant in spring or fall.

WHERE TO PLANT
Plant in full sun. Be aware that the coffeetree may have slow growth, but it reaches a large size and needs adequate room to develop. It is adaptable to a wide range of soil conditions from moist areas to drought situations. Tolerant of alkaline soils and

valuable as a street tree, it withstands urban conditions and should be used more often than it currently is. The coffeetree has branches that are easily broken, so place it away from high-traffic areas. The fruits on female trees and large leaf stalks that support the many leaflets drop in mass and require periodic cleanup throughout the year.

How to Plant

The planting hole should be at least 2 to 3 times as wide as the rootball. For balled-and-burlapped trees, after placing in the hole, remove any twine, rope, or metal wire that is wrapped around the rootball. This is important for the top $1/3$ of the rootball, where feeder roots will develop. Be sure the top of the rootball or container root system is planted level with the surrounding grade. In heavy or poor soils, plant the top of the root system 3 to 4 in. above the surrounding grade. Some sinking or settling of the rootball can be expected in these situations. Mulch after planting with 2 to 3 in. of an organic mulch.

Advice for Care

The coffeetree has few insect pests or diseases. Prune only to remove dead, diseased, or broken limbs. Prune in the dormant season; trees will bleed sap at other times of the year. Remove suckers that emerge at the base of the tree or close to the trunk.

Additional Information

The coffeetree is rare throughout its natural range with a patchy distribution. In Michigan it reaches the northern limit in its natural distribution.

Additional Species, Cultivars, or Varieties

Work continues on the production of male varieties that do not have messy fruit. A designated male variety is currently not widely available in the trade.

Littleleaf Linden

Tilia cordata

Height: 60 to 70 ft.
Flowers: Fragrant, yellow
Bloom Period: Midsummer
Zones: 3, 4, 5, 6
Light Requirement:

Some trees we see commonly planted along our city streets are remarkable for their resilience and beauty. A lovely tree often planted is the littleleaf linden. Small, dark green heart-shaped leaves grace this rather uniform pyramidal tree, making it an elegant charmer in the urban jungle. Fragrant flowers appear in midsummer visually hidden by the foliage but easy to find with the nose. The pendulous yellow flowers hang from the tree, perfuming the air and drawing throngs of bees to their nectar. In the fall, clusters of tiny pea-shaped fruits hang delicately from a papery bract, adding another form of ornamentation. The littleleaf linden is the perfect street, lawn or specimen tree with many cultivars available that easily fit into the small landscape. Reaching a height of 60 to 70 ft., it thrives in difficult sites where few trees can. While its primary use is as a specimen or street tree, it is often planted in large cement containers outside malls or shopping plazas. It can be pruned and trained into a remarkable tall hedge for screening or privacy purposes. Its twiggy dense branches and solid pyramidal form make it a distinctive winter landscape tree.

WHEN TO PLANT

Plant in the spring or fall.

WHERE TO PLANT

Plant in full sun for best growth and development. This linden is very adaptable to high pH soils but prefers a moist, well-drained soil and will not tolerate excessively wet conditions.

HOW TO PLANT

The planting hole should be at least 2 to 3 times as wide as the rootball. For balled-and-burlapped trees, after placing in the hole, remove any twine, rope, or metal wire that is wrapped around the rootball. This is important for the top 1/3 of the rootball, where feeder roots will develop. The top of the rootball or container root system should be planted level with the surrounding grade. In heavy or poor soils, plant the top of the root system 3 to 4 in. above the surrounding grade. Some sinking or settling of the rootball can be expected in these situations. Mulch after planting with 2 to 3 in. of organic mulch.

ADVICE FOR CARE
Littleleaf linden is generally trouble-free with few insects or diseases. Water in drought periods because spider mite can become a problem on stressed trees. Linden aphid is also a troublesome pest but rarely causes enough damage to warrant control.

ADDITIONAL INFORMATION
The fragrant flowers of some linden species are narcotic to bees.

ADDITIONAL SPECIES, CULTIVARS, OR VARIETIES
'Greenspire' is the most popular selection with a uniform straight trunk and excellent branching habit. *Tilia × flavescens* 'Glenleven' is a fast-growing selection with a more open habit reaching 40 ft. in height and 30 ft. in width. Both selections of the littleleaf linden are extremely tough trees that are highly recommended for street tree plantings. *Tilia tomentosa*, the silver linden, is a spectacular shade tree with large heart-shaped leaves that are two-toned, dark green on top and silvery white on the bottom. It is a much larger tree than the littleleaf linden, reaching 80 ft. or more in height and producing a mass of fragrant flowers in June. 'Sterling' is a broadly pyramidal tree with dark green leaves that are reputedly not bothered by Japanese beetle. It reaches 45 ft. in height and 35 ft. in width. The silver linden is hardy in Zones 4, 5, and 6.

Norway Spruce

Picea abies

Height: 40 to 60 ft.
Foliage: Dark evergreen
needles
Zones: 3, 4, 5, 6
Light Requirement:

The Norway spruce was once a popular windbreak tree for new homesteads and farmhouses, where there was a need for a fast-growing tree that would develop into a tough windbreak and privacy screen. Among the finest of evergreen trees for winter color, in more recent years the blue spruce has become the evergreen tree of choice, and the Norway spruce is used less often. This is unfortunate because the Norway spruce offers grace and beauty beyond that of the metallic blue spruces. Norway spruce is a large, majestic tree, reaching 60 ft. or more in height and with a pyramidal habit. In youth, the dark green needles are borne on stiff, flat branches. As the tree matures, the needles hang gracefully down off long, arching branches that come off the main trunk in ski slope fashion. The Norway spruce with its large size and spreading branches makes the ultimate windbreak tree and an interesting backdrop for smaller trees and shrubs with colorful bark, winter stems, or early spring flowers. Use as a backdrop for the 'Arnold Promise' witchhazel or the fragrant winter hazel, *Corylopsis glabrescens*. The colorful twigs of the redtwig dogwood or the fruits of the deciduous Michigan holly are beautifully luminous against the dark evergreen needles of the Norway spruce.

WHEN TO PLANT

Plant in spring or fall.

WHERE TO PLANT

Plant in full sun, and allow enough room for this large tree to grow. Norway spruce prefers a moist, slightly acidic soil and will suffer in poor drainage conditions. An effective windbreak can be established by placing trees 18 to 20 ft. apart. The long, sloping branches will intertwine to create a miniforest, blocking wind and ensuring privacy. Avoid planting near sidewalks or along roads. This tree is not tolerant of salt and is easily burned.

How to Plant

The planting hole should be at least 2 to 3 times as wide as the root-ball. For balled-and-burlapped trees, after placing in the hole, remove any twine, rope, or wire that is wrapped around the root-ball. This is important for the top 1/3 of the rootball, where feeder roots will develop. Be sure the top of the rootball or container root system is planted level with the surrounding grade. In heavy or poor soils, plant the top of the root system 3 to 4 in. above the surrounding grade. Some sinking or settling of the rootball can be expected in these situations. Mulch after planting with 2 to 3 in. of organic material.

Advice for Care

Water to help new trees become established, especially before the onset of winter. A well-watered tree in the fall will help provide moisture for the needles in the winter when bitter winds can have a freeze-dried effect on exposed evergreen plantings.

Additional Information

The Norway spruce makes wonderful cut greens for holiday wreaths. The spruce gall aphid is an occasional pest of Norway spruce. Their feeding causes a cone-shaped gall or woody, cone-shaped growth to form on the branches of the tree. They are generally not life-threatening, but serious infestations will reduce the aesthetic appeal of trees. Consult a local arborist for a spray control program if necessary. The fungus *Cytospera* causes the browning and death of branches. It usually appears on the lower branches and works its way up. Remove infected branches by cutting them back to the main trunk. Help prevent infections of this canker by keeping the lower portions of your plant free of tall grass and weeds, which limit air movement. Mulch around newly planted trees to discourage grass and weed growth.

Additional Species, Cultivars, or Varieties

Picea omorika, the Serbian spruce, is a beautiful alternative to the Norway spruce with a slender trunk supporting short, drooping branches with glossy dark green needles. It reaches a height of 50 to 60 ft. The Oriental spruce, *Picea orientalis*, has the shortest needles of the spruces, forming a dense, narrow tree with very dark green foliage. It is similar in size to the Norway and Serbian spruce but is better suited to smaller landscapes with its dense and compact growth habit.

TREES

Pagoda Dogwood

Cornus alternifolia

Height: 16 to 25 ft.
Flowers: Yellow-white
Bloom Period: Late spring
Zones: 3, 4, 5, 6
Light Requirement:

A remarkable tree for its abundance of bloom and picturesque branching habit, the pagoda dogwood is a neglected native that unfortunately plays second fiddle to its close relative, the flowering dogwood, *Cornus florida*. With a recent upsurge and interest in native plants and naturalistic gardens, the pagoda dogwood is quickly gaining a devoted following with its four-season appeal. The most remarkable feature of this Michigan woodland native is its delicate but sophisticated branching habit that reveals itself in the winter season. The horizontal branches have a tiered or storied effect. They appear in a sequence of vertical layers, each stretching outward and upward toward the tips of the branches. This is an amazing sight to see after Michigan ice storms. The flowers may not be as showy or bright as the flowering dogwood but are attractive nonetheless. Large flat-topped blooms appear in the late spring on the upturned ends of branches. The flowers are a creamy white and have a frothy quality to them. By October they produce many bluish fruits on red stalks and are a favorite of birds. The fall color is a deep wine-red. The pagoda dogwood is particularly effective when combined with vertical elements in the garden such as columnar evergreens or upright deciduous trees. It also helps break the starkness of a tall wall or brick surface. Use this dogwood for planting in a shady woodland setting where it finds itself right at home.

WHEN TO PLANT

Spring planting is best for the pagoda dogwood. Fall planting in general yields less success.

WHERE TO PLANT

Plant in partial to full shade; this plant will languish in full sun and drought conditions. It prefers a well-drained, moist soil and will not tolerate standing water for long periods of time. Plant where your tree will receive morning sun and afternoon shade. Mulch to cool the root zone and conserve moisture. Avoid planting in narrow or confined spaces where its horizontal growth would be restricted.

How to Plant

The planting hole should be at least 2 to 3 times as wide as the rootball. For balled-and-burlapped trees, after placing in the hole, remove any twine, rope, or metal wire that is wrapped around the rootball. This is important for the top $1/3$ of the rootball. Be sure the top of the rootball or container root system is planted level with the surrounding grade. In heavy or poor soils, plant the top of the root system 3 to 4 in. above the surrounding grade. Some sinking or settling of the rootball can be expected in these situations. Mulch after planting with 2 to 3 in. of organic mulch.

Advice for Care

The pagoda dogwood will not tolerate drought and hot conditions. A canker disease can cause stem and branch dieback. Remove infected branches if they appear.

Additional Information

Unlike most other dogwoods, the pagoda dogwood has alternate (not opposite) leaves.

Additional Species, Cultivars, or Varieties

Cornus controversa, the giant dogwood, is a larger-sized version of the pagoda dogwood. It reaches 30 to 45 ft. with the same picturesque horizontal branching habit, large white flat-topped flowers, and bluish late-summer fruits. It does well in full sun but reportedly is susceptible to bark splitting.

Paperbark Maple

Acer griseum

Height: 20 to 30 ft.
Bark: Cinnamon-brown, exfoliating
Zones: 4, 5, 6
Light Requirement:

Not every garden needs rare plants to make it complete, but their incorporation into the landscape adds an extra spark. A small tree of immeasurable beauty is the paperbark maple. Its main claim to fame is expressed in its common name. Paper-thin sheets of bark peel off the tree, revealing cinnamon-orange colors that create unrivaled winter display. The peeling bark is especially appreciated on multistemmed trees that create a fantastic garden focal point with year-round appeal. Three-part dark green leaves are attractive in the summer months and turn bright orange-red in the fall. Reaching a height of 20 to 30 ft., paperbark maple is especially valuable for use on a patio or in a small courtyard. The tree's small size and slow growth are ideal for landscapes where limited planting space is available and where four-season appeal is desired. One of the most memorable trees Tim has come across is in East Lansing and is underplanted with the Alleghany pachysandra, *Pachysandra procumbens*. *Acer griseum* is difficult to produce in plant nurseries because it rarely produces viable seed and is difficult to grow by other means. Because of this and the fact that it grows so slowly, it is usually expensive. But paperbark maple is a first-rate plant that will provide years of enjoyment and will make you the envy of your neighbors.

When to Plant
Plant in the spring. Fall planting in general yields less success.

Where to Plant
Plant in full sun to partial shade but protect from hot afternoon sun. It prefers a well-drained soil and will not tolerate compacted or hard ground beneath its canopy.

HOW TO PLANT

The planting hole should be at least 2 to 3 times as wide as the root-ball or container. For balled-and-burlapped trees, after placing in the hole, remove any twine, rope, or metal wire that is wrapped around the rootball. This is important for the top $1/3$ of the rootball. Be sure the top of the rootball or container root system is planted level with the surrounding grade. In heavy or poor soils, plant the top of the root system 3 to 4 in. above the surrounding grade. Some sinking or settling of the rootball can be expected in these situations. Mulch after planting with 2 to 3 in. of organic mulch.

ADVICE FOR CARE

Water in drought periods, and mulch around the base of the tree to conserve moisture and protect its shallow root system.

ADDITIONAL INFORMATION

This sought-after rarity is available from small mail-order nurseries. (See the source guide.)

ADDITIONAL SPECIES, CULTIVARS, OR VARIETIES

Acer triflorum, the three-flowered maple, is a close cousin of the paperbark maple with excellent cinnamon-red bark that peels away in vertical strips. The fall foliage show is outstanding with orange to carmine-red coloring. The three-flowered maple (for Zones 5 and 6) is easier to transplant than the paperbark maple, but, unfortunately, it is just as rare in commerce. It has a more moderate growth rate, reaching 24 ft. at maturity. It will also need protection from afternoon sun. The nikko maple, *Acer nikoense*, rounds out the "big three" of trifoliate or three-leaf maples. This small tree with a vase-shaped habit and attractive summer foliage turns a brilliant scarlet-red in the fall. Reaching a mature height of 20 to 30 ft., this rare tree is perfect for a small garden.

Pawpaw

Asimina triloba

Other Name: Michigan
  Banana
Height: 15 to 25 ft.
Fruit: Delicious custard-like
  fruit in the fall
Zones: 5, 6
Light Requirement:

Michigan's most exotic tree thrives in the deep, rich bottomland river basins of the Lower Peninsula. The pawpaw, *Asimina triloba*, is one of our most unusual native North American trees. A pawpaw tree is amazing to see in the wild with lush, tropical-looking foliage nearly 10 in. long hanging downward in a peculiar fashion. The curious flowers appear in May with 6 reddish-maroon petals nodding like bells from the branches. They are difficult to see in a shaded woodland but are worth examining up close. The petals and nectaries of the flowers have a fetid or rotted smell that is not noticeable unless you put your nose to them. While the smell does not exactly attract humans, it does attract flies and beetles, which are the principal pollinators. For more than 100 years, many people have sought to domesticate pawpaw for its most famous feature, its large, delicious custard-like fruit. The fruit is an acquired taste for some and immediately delectable to others. Whether you take to it or not, the fruit is not the only reason to grow this tree. It has many wonderful features that make it an exceptional tree for large or small landscapes. In full sun, the pawpaw grows into a distinct pyramidal habit reaching up to 25 ft. tall. The lush green leaves turn a beautiful butter yellow in the fall. Trees can be used as specimens or planted in an orchard setting. The natural habit of the tree is to produce sprouts off its roots that form large thickets that are commonly referred to as pawpaw patches. These patches make for a marvelous naturalistic planting for larger landscapes where a privacy barrier or screening is desired. In the fall, a colorful thicket of pawpaw trees is an incredible sight to behold.

WHEN TO PLANT
Plant in the spring. Fall planting generally yields poor results.

WHERE TO PLANT
Young trees in the sapling stage need protection from sun, or their leaves will get sunburned. Plant in partial shade, or provide full sun

plantings with a shade screen for the first 2 or more years of development. A burlap screen placed on the west side of the tree will shade it as it gets started. Pawpaws like moist, slightly acidic soils and will need plenty of moisture to get established. Water deeply to help establish the long taproot that will later serve the plant well in times of drought. Pawpaw trees like to keep good company, so plant more than one to increase the chances for cross-pollination and fruit set. Lone trees rarely produce fruit, but a named variety called 'Sunflower' reportedly is self-fertile. In Michigan, the fruit of 'Sunflower' is sometimes spoiled by frosts since ripening normally occurs during the first week of October. If you don't have room for more than one pawpaw tree, buy two anyway and present one as a gift to your neighbor.

How to Plant

You will likely have to acquire your pawpaw through mail-order sources. Local nurseries do not generally carry them and do not grow field trees for sale. The deep, fleshy taproot makes field-grown pawpaw a risky venture because they generally transplant unsuccessfully. Mail-order trees should be planted while dormant and provided shade and adequate water as they get established.

Advice for Care

There are few pests and diseases of pawpaw, in part due to their amazing ability to ward off attack through natural chemical compounds found in the stems and foliage of the tree. These natural plant toxins are being studied for their use as possible natural pesticides for use on vegetable and fruit crops.

Additional Information

Pawpaw is enjoying new popularity in recent years. There is interest in anticancer compounds that have been found in pawpaw and show great promise in antitumor treatments. Corwin Davis from Bellevue, Michigan, is a noted national pawpaw expert who has worked with the tree for more than 30 years, naming new cultivars and promoting its virtues.

Additional Species, Cultivars, or Varieties

'Taylor' and 'Taytoo' are cultivated varieties collected in the wild from Eaton Rapids, Michigan. These two cultivars have light green skin and tasty yellow flesh. Their names honor J. Lee Taylor, professor emeritus of the Michigan State University Horticulture Department, and his wife, Jane. 'Sunflower' is a self-fertile clone with large fruit with butter-colored flesh and is reportedly quite tasty.

Redbud

Cercis canadensis

Other Name: Eastern Redbud
Height: 20 to 30 ft.
Flowers: Rose-pink
Bloom Period: Spring
Zones: 5, 6
Light Requirement:

The redbud is one of our most beautiful spring-flowering trees. Several features make it valuable to use as a single specimen tree or along the edge of a woodland understory. In May, after the shadblow has bloomed, the small rose-pink flowers of the redbud open into a cloud of pink that shines brightly against the tree's dark, leafless branches. The redbud has a unique feature called cauliflory, which is the ability to produce flower buds on older wood. This is how even old gnarled stems of the tree can produce small reddish-purple buds each spring. The foliage is elegant and emerges with reddish tones, gradually becoming green with a distinct heart-shaped outline. The leaves have variable fall color that at times can be a decent yellow. The redbud is a small tree with a short trunk and wide-spreading lower branches that, with age, may even rest on the ground. It reaches a height of 20 to 30 ft. with a slightly greater spread. Trees produce papery 2- to 3-in. brown pods that can be a nuisance to clean up on a patio or in an outdoor living area.

WHEN TO PLANT
Plant in the spring or fall.

WHERE TO PLANT
The redbud is naturally found as a woodland understory plant, so it tolerates shady areas and sites that receive a half day of full sun. Plants in full sun grow with more vigor and produce more flowers. Avoid planting in areas near salted walks or driveways because the redbud is highly sensitive to salt. The redbud is pH adaptable but is not tolerant of poorly drained or heavy soils.

HOW TO PLANT
The planting hole should be at least 2 to 3 times as wide as the rootball. For balled-and-burlapped trees, after placing in the hole, remove any twine, rope, or wire that is wrapped around the root-

ball. This is important for the top $^1/_3$ of the rootball, where feeder roots will develop. Be sure the top of the rootball or container root system is planted level with the surrounding grade. In heavy or poor soils, plant the top of the root system 3 to 4 in. above the surrounding grade. Some sinking or settling of the rootball can be expected in these situations. Mulch after planting with 2 to 3 in. of organic material.

ADVICE FOR CARE

The redbud grows vigorously as a young tree but slows down with age; its typical life span is 30 to 50 years. Older trees become susceptible to canker that kills larger limbs. Remove infected limbs if they appear. *Verticillium* wilt is a soil-borne fungus that gets in the water transport portions of the tree and causes them to clog. This results in branch dieback and, eventually, in the tree's death. There is no guaranteed method of control for the fungus at this time.

ADDITIONAL INFORMATION

The flowers of the redbud are edible and can be used in salads as a garnish.

ADDITIONAL SPECIES, CULTIVARS, OR VARIETIES

Many cultivated varieties are available but not all are adaptable to Michigan's climate. When choosing a tree at a nursery, be sure to ask about the seed source or region where the tree originated. Plants from Georgia or Tennessee will suffer in our climate. A cultivar called 'Royal White' has large white flowers. It was selected from a wild population in Illinois and is hardy to the southern half of Michigan's Lower Peninsula.

River Birch

Betula nigra

Height: 40 to 70 ft.
Bark: Flaky whitish-brown
to cinnamon-brown
exfoliating bark
Zones: 4, 5, 6
Light Requirement:

In the midst of a Michigan winter, the gardener's eye moves upward from the snow-covered plants at ground level to the remarkable architectural beauty of trees that have exceptional form, bark, and structure. The river birch, *Betula nigra*, found along streams and in wet areas in the wild, has a flaky whitish-brown to cinnamon-brown exfoliating bark. It is very showy during the winter months. At maturity, this tree can reach 30 to 50 ft. in height, forming a rounded crown. Multistemmed specimens are particularly effective because you get "more bang for your buck"—that is, more trunks and stems with an attractive winter habit. River birch foliage is dark green in the summer mouths, sometimes followed by a short-lived yellow fall color. It can be planted in low, wet areas of the garden and is generally adaptable to most soil types except those that are alkaline with a pH over 7.0. Use it as a prominent specimen plant in a prime spot in the winter garden where its warm bark colors will take the winter chill away. Plant in full sun for best growth but also to enjoy the early morning and late afternoon glow on the bark and stems. Combine it with the colorful red stems of the redosier dogwood, *Cornus stolonifera*, which also likes moist soils. The river birch comes to life in the winter months when planted against the dark evergreen needles of the Norway spruce, *Picea abies*. While many trees need adequate space to develop without competition, the river birch is used to dramatic effect in naturalistic grove plantings, where single-stem trees are spaced 20 ft. or less apart and the canopies intertwine. The lower limbs can be removed to allow foot traffic if necessary.

WHEN TO PLANT
Plant in spring or fall.

WHERE TO PLANT
Plant in full sun for best performance and winter light effects. Plants make a nice enclosure when planted as a group on a raised berm.

Single or group plantings combine attractively with the red persistent fruit of the Michigan holly, *Ilex verticillata*, or surrounded by the spreading juniper, *Juniperus horizontalis*.

How to Plant

The planting hole should be at least 2 to 3 times as wide as the rootball. For balled-and-burlapped trees, after placing in the hole, remove any twine, rope, or metal wire that is wrapped around the rootball. This is important for the top 1/3 of the rootball, where the feeder roots will develop. The top of the rootball or container root system should be planted level with the surrounding grade. In heavy or poor soils, plant the top of the root system 3 to 4 in. above the surrounding grade. Some sinking or settling of the rootball can be expected in these situations. After planting, apply a 2- to 3-in. layer of organic mulch.

Advice for Care

Plants may experience leaf yellowing or chlorosis in alkaline soils of 7.0 pH or higher. Birch leaf miner is occasionally a pest of the river birch. The adult females lay eggs in the leaves that hatch small larvae (worms) that eat the tissue between the upper and lower leaf surfaces. This mining activity causes the leaf surface to turn brown. Orthene™ is the recommended chemical control for leaf miner. Apply in mid-May as the larvae begin feeding. Use according to the manufacturer's recommended rates.

Additional Information

In addition to its attractive bark, the river birch has slender twigs topped by the male flowers (catkins) that are dark brown and highly ornamental upon close inspection. Because the degree of exfoliating bark varies from tree to tree, it is best to purchase trees that already exhibit showy bark.

Additional Species, Cultivars, or Varieties

Heritage™ is an exceptional tree with handsome peeling bark and dark green glossy foliage, which, at times, turns to an impressive yellow in the fall.

Saucer Magnolia

Magnolia × soulangiana

Height: 20 to 30 ft.
Flowers: White to rose-pink
Bloom Period: Spring
Zones: 4, 5, 6
Light Requirement:

Magnolias are the aristocrats of spring-blooming trees. The large saucer-shaped flowers appear from fuzzy gray buds and seem to float on the upturned branches of the tree like water lilies on the surface of a pond. The large flowers can be 5 to 10 in. wide and appear white suffused with pink or rose colors. The saucer magnolia has a multistemmed habit that forms a broad, rounded tree reaching 20 to 30 ft. in height. The smooth gray bark is highly ornamental in the winter months as are the fuzzy buds that terminate the branches. Plant it as a specimen tree or in mass to create an unrivaled spring blooming display. Magnolias are particularly striking when placed against a dark evergreen background such as the oriental spruce, *Picea orientalis*, or the Norway spruce, *Picea abies*. Magnolias, for all their beauty, at times have a limited performance in Michigan landscapes. Their early-blooming habit gets them in trouble as late frosts can wreak havoc on the flowers of exposed specimens. See the section below on "Where to Plant" magnolias to increase the odds that you'll be able to enjoy the spectacle of their radiant blooms.

WHEN TO PLANT

Plant in the spring; magnolias are among the more difficult to transplant trees and shrubs. Fall planting should be avoided. If you decide to plant in the fall in Michigan, however, plant before mid-October so roots have some time to become established before the onset of winter.

WHERE TO PLANT

Plant in full sun to promote strong flowering. Magnolias are effective as a single specimen or in group plantings. Avoid placing the trees in warm southern exposures. Also, while the saucer magnolia looks marvelous against a dark wall, it will respond by flowering earlier since walls absorb and emit heat. Plant in a northern exposure to keep the buds tight and protective until the danger of late frosts has past. Magnolia roots will not compete well with other plants. Locate your tree where its roots can grow unimpeded.

HOW TO PLANT

Plant container-grown plants if available from your nursery. They will generally have a well-developed root system and will transplant more easily than balled-and-burlapped trees. The planting hole should be at least 2 to 3 times as wide as the rootball or container. For balled-and-burlapped trees, after placing in the hole, remove any twine, rope, or metal wire that is wrapped around the rootball. This is important for the top $1/3$ of the rootball. Be sure the top of the rootball or container root system is planted level with the surrounding grade. In heavy or poor soils, plant the top of the root system 3 to 4 in. above the surrounding grade. Some sinking or settling of the rootball can be expected in these situations. Mulch after planting with 2 to 3 in. of organic mulch.

ADVICE FOR CARE

Magnolias under the right conditions will thrive with minimal care. Mulch the root zone, and water in prolonged droughts. Prune in early summer after flowering. Do not remove the lower branches of the saucer magnolia if at all possible. Its full pleasing habit is better left alone. Remove vigorous branch shoots that grow straight up off older limbs. These will deplete the main branches of energy and threaten the natural form of the plant.

ADDITIONAL INFORMATION

The saucer magnolia is sometimes susceptible to attack by magnolia scale. The scale appears on branches and has a waxy covering over a hard shell-like body. The scale is often difficult to see but reveals itself on close inspection. Dormant oil sprays applied before growth begins in the spring will suffocate scales. A crawler stage of the insect can be controlled by Orthene™ applications. The crawlers are difficult to see, so spray dormant oils preferably or remove light infestations by hand.

ADDITIONAL SPECIES, CULTIVARS, OR VARIETIES

'Alexandrina' has deep red-purple blossoms that open later in spring, giving them additional protection against late frost.

Shadblow

Amelanchier canadensis

Other Names: Serviceberry
Height: 20 ft.
Flowers: White
Bloom Period: Early spring
Zones: 3, 4, 5, 6
Light Requirement:

Among our native trees, few can match the four-season appeal of the shadblow. It often occurs as an understory plant in woodlands, where its delicate white flowers appear on the naked gray branches well before spring truly kicks into gear. The early flowers produce purplish-black fruits in June that are treasured by birds and humans alike. The fall is remarkable for the myriad of leaf colors ranging from yellow to orange-red. The winter months expose the smooth gray reflective bark that is spectacular on specimens with a multistemmed habit. The small size of *Amelanchier* makes it perfect for smaller properties and for use in patio plantings and as a foundation plant. Group plantings work well in mass in naturalized landscape plantings where the clumping or suckering habits of the tree and bountiful fruits draw wildlife to the garden. The fleeting white delicate flowers of the shadblow are enhanced against a backdrop of dark evergreens, which bring the clear white blossoms into focus. An underplanting of dark spreading yews is very effective in contrast to the smooth gray bark.

When to Plant

Plant in spring or fall.

Where to Plant

Plant in full sun to deep shade. The shadblow is adaptable to different light exposures. Trees planted in full sun will in general have more blooms and a better fall color. Soils should be well drained, slightly acidic, and not too wet. Provide protection from rabbits the first few years after planting. Surround small plants with chicken wire screening supported by bamboo canes.

How to Plant

The planting hole should be at least 2 to 3 times as wide as the rootball. For balled-and-burlapped trees, after placing in the hole, remove any twine, rope, or wire that is wrapped around the rootball. This is important for the top ¹/₃ of the rootball, where feeder roots will develop. Be sure the top of the rootball or container root system is planted level with the surrounding grade. In heavy or poor soils, plant the top of the root system 3 to 4 in. above the surrounding grade. Some sinking or settling of the rootball can be expected in these situations. Mulch after planting with 2 to 3 in. of organic material.

ADVICE FOR CARE

The shadblow sometimes experiences problems with the bacteria called fire blight. Shoots or branches of the tree die back in the summer months and look as if they have been scorched by fire. They form a characteristic "shepherd's crook" or curved terminal stem that alerts you to the infection. There is no guaranteed cure for this disease, but you should remove infected branches. Disinfect your pruners after each cut with isopropyl alcohol. This will prevent the spread of fire blight, which overwinters on the bark and twigs of serviceberry and other rose family members. Avoid fertilizing because excess nitrogen will produce soft new growth, which is more susceptible to the spread of the bacteria.

ADDITIONAL INFORMATION

Common names are interesting because they tell us a lot about the interactions of humans and plants. One source describes how the serviceberry got its name. The pioneers would wait for the bloom of the serviceberry to signify the end of winter season and the time to bury those in the community who had died during the winter months. By the time that flowers began to open, the ground had thawed enough that burials could proceed. Of course, this could take place only after a proper funeral service was performed—hence the name "serviceberry." The common name "shadblow" comes from the belief that when the tree blooms, the shad are running in the river to spawn.

ADDITIONAL SPECIES, CULTIVARS, OR VARIETIES

Amelanchier arborea is a larger tree-sized serviceberry with the same delightful characteristics but generally does not develop the thicket-type growth that *Amelanchier canadensis* does. It reaches more than 30 ft. in height.

Sweetgum

Liquidambar styraciflua

Height: 60 to 75 ft. **Foliage:** Lustrous green foliage with excellent fall color **Zones:** 5, 6 **Light Requirement:**

The American sweetgum is a tree with many positive virtues, yet it is uncommon in Michigan landscapes and should be used far more frequently than it is. For foliage quality alone, this large shade tree rates as one of our most outstanding North American trees. The leaves are star-shaped and resemble the maple, for which it is often mistaken. The surface of the leaves is heavily waxed, giving them a glossy sheen. The fall color is a blend of yellow to purple to red colors and can be quite spectacular in open, full-sun plantings. The distinct winter habit of this tree makes it easy to identify with its symmetrical outline and uniform pyramidal shape. The stems often have corky ridges or wings that aid in their identification and winter interest. Most obvious are the fruits—rounded woody seed capsules with short spines or projections from the surface. Sweetgum has been described as one of the few trees that comes with its own Christmas ornaments. Many people enjoy the fruits for their decorative effect, but eventually, the fruits are shed over the winter months and because of their woody nature do not decompose readily once they are on the ground. Here they become a prickly nuisance for the barefoot crowd and can jam lawn mowers. Because of its large size and its "love-it-or-hate-it" fruit, you should plant the sweetgum in an open area where you can provide a large mulch ring and let the fruits collect on your wood chips instead of on your lawn or patio. Young children love the look of the spiny fruits and can paint them to make real ornaments for decorative use.

WHEN TO PLANT
Plant in the spring. Fall planting generally yields less success.

WHERE TO PLANT
Sweetgum prefers full sun and a deep, moist, acidic soil. Plant in an open area because this tree will suffer in a confined space for root development. The roots of older trees will eventually rise to the surface and should be covered with mulch to protect them from lawn mowers.

How to Plant

The coarse, thick, fleshy roots of the sweetgum make it a challenge
to transplant successfully. Plant smaller trees that have been root-
pruned in the nursery or are grown in a container. The planting hole
should be at least 2 to 3 times as wide as the rootball. For balled-
and-burlapped trees, after placing in the hole, remove any twine,
rope, or wire that is wrapped around the rootball. This is important
for the top 1/3 of the rootball, where feeder roots will develop. Be
sure the top of the rootball or container root system is planted level
with the surrounding grade. In heavy or poor soils, plant the top
of the root system 3 to 4 in. above the surrounding grade. Some
sinking or settling of the rootball can be expected in these situations. Mulch after planting with 2 to 3 in. of organic material.

Advice for Care

Its strong central leader maintains the symmetrical form of this tree.
Do not prune or alter the central leader, or the pyramidal habit may
be lost. If chlorosis or leaf yellowing develops as a result of high soil
pH, fertilize using mixes that contain sulfur or that are known to
have an acidic reaction. Use them according to the manufacturer's
instructions. Mulch every year with composted oak leaves and pine
needles to lower the soil pH.

Additional Information

The common name comes from the resin obtained from the tree that
was used as chewing gum and for medicinal purposes.

Additional Species, Cultivars, or Varieties

The sweetgum has many cultivated varieties available but not all are
adaptable to Michigan's climate. When choosing a tree at a nursery,
be sure to ask about the seed source or region of origin of the tree.
'Moraine' is a northern selection hardy to Zone 5 with an upright
oval habit and brilliant red-yellow fall color.

Tuliptree

Liriodendron tulipifera

Height: 70 to 90 ft.
Flowers: Yellow petals splashed with orange at the base
Bloom Period: Late spring
Zones: 4, 5, 6
Light Requirement:

The tuliptree is among the largest of the eastern North American trees and grows naturally in the southern half of the Lower Peninsula. In moist forests, the tuliptree has an impressive straight trunk with thick bark that is dark gray and deeply furrowed. Few have witnessed the unique foliage and flowers of this tree because they are simply too high in the canopy for easy viewing. A great debate exists as to whether the tree gets its common name from the resemblance of the flowers or the foliage to the tulip. The flowers appear in early summer on upturned branches with a distinctly tulip shape with 6 yellow petals flushed bright orange at the base. They are beautiful but not often seen due to the fast growth of this tree and the tendency for it to shed its lower branches. Homeowners who have the room should allow the sweeping lower branches of the tree to remain for as long as possible. This way, you can view the incredible flower display at eye level. The foliage of the tuliptree is another asset, resembling, as one astute plantsman commented, "a mitten with two thumbs." While it is somewhat tulip-shaped in outline, its bright green in the summer and spectacular golden yellow fall color make it a first-rate shade tree for those who can handle its eventual size of 70 to 90 ft. Homeowners can use the tuliptree as a lone specimen in a large open lawn or plant many together to create a tall canopy and a woodland effect. The reward will be a fantastic four-season display with the distinctive foliage, flowers, fruits, and winter habit that make this one of our finest native North American trees.

When to Plant
Plant in the spring. Fall planting generally yields less success.

Where to Plant
Plant in full sun in deep, rich, well-drained soil, and place well away from the house because large limbs are susceptible to breakage from ice storms, wind, and lightning. The root system of this tree is very aggressive, so plant it well away from the foundation of your house.

How to Plant

The tuliptree is generally difficult to transplant, which accounts for its rarity in the nursery trade. Plant smaller trees that have been root-pruned in the nursery or are grown in a container. The fleshy taproot of this tree makes it tough to move at larger sizes. When planting, retain as much of the root system as possible. The planting hole should be at least 2 to 3 times as wide as the rootball. For balled-and-burlapped trees, after placing in the hole, remove any twine, rope, or wire that is wrapped around the rootball. This is important for the top 1/3 of the rootball, where feeder roots will develop. Be sure the top of the rootball or container root system is planted level with the surrounding grade. In heavy or poor soils, plant the top of the root system 3 to 4 in. above the surrounding grade. Some sinking or settling of the rootball can be expected in these situations. Mulch after planting with 2 to 3 in. of organic material.

Advice for Care

The tuliptree will suffer in hot, dry periods; water well during establishment, and mulch the root zone. Young plants are particularly susceptible to sunscald, so wrap the trunk during the winter with a paper tree wrap. Start at the bottom, overlapping the paper so that it covers all the exposed trunk up to the large side branches. Trees are also susceptible to *Verticillium* wilt, a fungus that is found in the soil and enters the plant through its roots. The fungus moves into the water- and food-conducting tissues of the plant, disrupting their function and causing parts of the tree to wilt. Branches slowly die out as the fungus spreads. Remove all infected branches, and burn them. Although you may not be able to save your infected tree, you can encourage its health by watering in drought periods and fertilizing in the late fall to give it a nutrient boost.

Additional Information

Aphid insects are not uncommon on tuliptree foliage. They excrete the sugars in a substance called honeydew, a clear sticky substance that attracts ants. Honeydew also is the growing substrate for sooty mold, a fungus that causes the twigs or leaves to turn black. This is generally not life-threatening for the tree, but the honeydew will drip on cars and other items immediately beneath its leaves and it can be difficult to remove. Aphids can be controlled by chemical sprays, but spraying is not normally necessary. Aphids have many natural predators that keep their population levels under control.

Additional Species, Cultivars, or Varieties

None.

377

White Ash

Fraxinus americana

Height: 50 to 60 ft.
Foliage: Deep green summer foliage, yellow to purple and maroon fall color
Zones: 3, 4, 5, 6
Light Requirement:

In Michigan's magnificent hardwood forests, it's easy to become mesmerized by the incredible size and strength of our native trees. The white ash is easily recognizable among these giants by its straight trunk with conspicuous diamond-shaped furrows and forked ridges. While content to develop into a massive shade tree in a mixed native canopy, the white ash also has value as a solitary specimen in gardens or along city streets. Its attractive compound leaves provide valued shade and subtle fall colors of yellow to purple and maroon, which last for up to 3 weeks depending on fall weather conditions. The white ash is a large tree more suited for use in open lawns or homes that have enough space to accommodate its height of 50 to 60 ft. and open, spreading branches. The foliage of the white ash is unique with a dark green lustrous top side and a pale white lower surface. Ash has some basic requirements for growth that must be met for it to remain insect- and disease-free in the landscape. Trees require full sun for growth and, at the very least, average soils that are neither too wet nor too dry. This large shade tree has many cultivars that are reduced in size and are seedless. The winged seeds of the ash hang in bunches persisting through the winter season and then tumble down to the ground. This creates quite a mess and adds to the yearly spring cleaning of the garden.

WHEN TO PLANT
Plant in spring or fall.

WHERE TO PLANT
Plant in full sun and far away from buildings or they may interfere with the spread of this large tree. The white ash is adaptable to a wide range of soils but prefers good drainage and may require watering in periods of prolonged drought. Some outstanding selections are available for street tree plantings in residential areas where narrow sidewalk plantings require a tough shade tree that is tolerant of salt.

How to Plant

The planting hole should be at least 2 to 3 times as wide as the root-ball. For balled-and-burlapped trees, after placing in the hole, remove any twine, rope, or metal wire that is wrapped around the rootball. This is important for the top of the rootball. Be sure the top of the rootball or container root system is planted level with the surrounding grade. In heavy or poor soils, plant the top of the root system 3 to 4 in. above the surrounding grade. Some sinking or settling of the rootball can be expected in these situations. Mulch after planting with 2 to 3 in. of organic material.

Advice for Care

While the white ash is a favorite for its outstanding ornamental characteristics, it will suffer serious ailments if its growth requirements are not met. Vigorous trees that are sited correctly are normally not bothered by pests and diseases, but trees under stress are susceptible to attack. The ash-lilac borer can be a serious pest of the white ash, particularly if trees are allowed to come under drought stress or are not properly sited. The insect appears in two stages, an adult stage that deposits eggs into the tree and a larval stage, which tunnels through the wood and causes damage. It is important to control both stages of this insect as they appear. Pheromone traps are available that attract and capture the adult clear-winged moth borer. Monitoring population levels will alert you to when it is time to take control measures. Consult your local extension service for current control recommendations.

Additional Information

The white ash is one of the last of our native trees to leaf out in May and one of the earliest to color up and drop its leaves in the fall.

Additional Species, Cultivars, or Varieties

'Autumn Purple' is the most popular and therefore the most used selection of the white ash. It has superior, long-lasting fall color that is reddish-purple. The summer foliage is a glossy green produced on a tree that reaches 45 to 60 ft. in height. 'Chicago Regal' is the perfect choice for narrow street tree plantings with its upright narrow growth habit and purple fall color.

White Fir

Abies concolor

Other Name: Concolor Fir
Height: 30 to 50 ft.
Foliage: Attractive bluish-green evergreen needles
Zones: 3, 4, 5, 6
Light Requirement:

Evergreen trees are valuable to the winter landscape, both for the color they offer and for the protection they give from harsh winter winds. An outstanding but underutilized evergreen tree is the white fir, *Abies concolor*. Found in arboreta and botanical gardens, it still has limited availability in the nursery trade. It forms a large tree, reaching 30 to 50 ft. or more with a narrow, pyramidal habit. A large tree is stunning on a winter day. The bluish-green needles are very colorful and have a unique habit of curving upward off the stem as if reaching for the sky. The waxy needles are extremely tough and rarely experience yellowing or winter burn. The branches of this stately conifer are whorled and cast a dense shade. As the tree matures, the ash gray bark becomes deeply furrowed. Trees are appropriate for larger landscapes and are effective as a screen or privacy planting. Use them as a backdrop for deciduous hollies or the colorful stems of the redosier or gray dogwood. They also combine well with spring-blooming shrubs such as forsythia and the 'Arnold Promise' witchhazel. The orange-red fall color of *Fothergilla major* is beautifully framed by the bluish-green needles of the white fir. It can also be used as a tall hedge, but this requires continual pruning and the maintenance may not be worth it.

WHEN TO PLANT

Plant in the spring. Avoid late fall planting, which may not leave enough time for root development before winter.

WHERE TO PLANT

Plant in full sun in a rich, moist, well-drained soil. Heavy clay soils with poor drainage and high alkalinity (pH) will not work for this tree. In windy exposed situations you may want to erect a burlap screen on the windward side of the plant to prevent windburn. This will be needed only the first few years as the tree becomes established.

HOW TO PLANT

Plant smaller-sized trees to ensure better success. Larger balled-and-burlapped trees are difficult to transplant successfully. The planting hole should be at least 2 to 3 times as wide as the rootball. For balled-and-burlapped trees, after placing in the hole, remove any twine, rope, or metal wire that is wrapped around the rootball. This is important for the top 1/3 the rootball. Be sure the top of the rootball or container root system is planted level with the surrounding grade. In heavy or poor soils, plant the top of the root system 3 to 4 in. above the surrounding grade. Some sinking or settling of the rootball can be expected in these situations. Mulch after planting with 2 to 3 in. of organic mulch.

ADVICE FOR CARE

Although this tree is known for its tolerance of hot, dry conditions, it will need help the first few years of establishment. Water in prolonged periods of drought and in the fall before the soil freezes. Pruning is generally not required. The main stem or leader of the plant should never be cut or topped, or the pyramidal form of the tree will be lost. Look for plants in the nursery that have a single or main trunk and a low branching habit already well established.

ADDITIONAL INFORMATION

Abies concolor is considered the best fir for the Midwest. It will grow up to 1¹/₂ ft. per year if properly sited. The cones are quite beautiful but rarely seen because they are produced on the uppermost branches and readily disintegrate over winter. Trees are at times available as "live Christmas trees," balled and burlapped to decorate for the holidays and then ready to plant in the ground.

ADDITIONAL SPECIES, CULTIVARS, OR VARIETIES

The nordmann fir, *Abies nordmanniana*, is an exceptional dark-needled fir that has performed well on the campus of Michigan State University. It reaches 40 to 60 ft. with a narrow, pyramidal habit. It is available through mail-order nurseries.

White Oak, Red Oak

Quercus alba and *Quercus rubra*

Height: White Oak, 50 to 80 ft. or more; Red Oak, 60 to 75 ft. or more
Zones: White Oak, 3, 4, 5, 6; Red Oak, 4, 5, 6
Light Requirement:

The oaks are recognized in history and lore as symbols of strength and durability. These impressive giants are unparalleled in their architectural beauty and majesty. A large oak tree connects us to our past and future as many trees grow to be more than 500 years old. The white oak, *Quercus alba*, is a native tree common throughout the Lower Peninsula. It is particularly notable for its tremendous girth and stout, wide-spreading horizontal branches that reach far off the main trunk and are twisted and gnarled in form. Spring is a special time to witness the new emerging leaves and flowers as they appear together in soft pink and pastel colors. The fall color of the leaves ushers in the cooler temperatures with various shades of crimson. Once the leaves have fallen, the tree's winter beauty becomes evident. The bark on older trees becomes light gray with blocky patches. The red oak, *Quercus rubra*, is also a native Michigan tree but grows at a faster rate and generally occupies moister sites. In hardwood forests, the tree's strong trunk is quite conspicuous with long, vertical smooth plates on the bark that accentuate the sheer height and reach of the branches. The large leaves with their distinct pointed lobes are cool green in summer, turning a beautiful red in the fall. Gardeners with a small residential lot may not be able to accommodate the large size of an oak, but others who have open land can plant grand, majestic trees—and will be doing future generations a great favor.

WHEN TO PLANT

Plant in the spring. Oaks are somewhat difficult to transplant because of their thick, fleshy taproots. Plant trees that are 3 in. in diameter or smaller to lessen the likelihood of transplant shock and to help ensure successful reestablishment in their new homes.

WHERE TO PLANT

Plant in full sun, and allow enough room for these trees to develop. Keep them away from a house or other building that would eventually become engulfed by trees planted close by. Trees placed in open areas will develop into large specimens that may someday provide shade for family gatherings at picnic tables or a contemplative spot for a solitary individual.

How to Plant

Plant small-sized trees in the spring. The planting hole should be at least 2 to 3 times as wide as the rootball or container. For balled-and-burlapped trees, after placing in the hole, remove any twine, rope, or metal wire that is wrapped around the rootball. This is important for the top $1/3$ of the rootball. Be sure the top of the rootball or container root system is planted level with the surrounding grade. In heavy or poor soils, plant the top of the root system 3 to 4 in. above the surrounding grade. Some sinking or settling of the rootball can be expected in these situations. Mulch after planting with 2 to 3 in. of organic mulch.

Advice for Care

The white oak is more drought-tolerant than the red oak, but both will need water as they become established. Gypsy moth prefers oak leaves over most other hardwood trees and therefore represents a threat when repeated defoliation occurs. A certified arborist may be contracted to spray your trees if significant damage warrants control. Municipalities are now experimenting with several new biological controls that may someday prove effective in curbing the voracious feeding of this imported pest. Oak wilt, a fungus, may be a problem, especially on red oaks. Symptoms include wilting leaves that turn brown. Prune oaks only while dormant because fresh pruning cuts during the growing season attract the bark beetles that spread this disease.

Additional Information

The acorns of oaks are easy to grow if you have patience. Collect seeds just as they begin to drop from the trees. Plant them in the spot you would like them to grow, but cover with a 6-by-6-in. square of wire screening. This will prevent squirrels from digging them up. Remove the screen in the spring as new growth emerges.

Additional Species, Cultivars, or Varieties

Quercus muhlenbergii, the chinkapin oak, is one of the few native oaks that is tolerant of alkaline soils. The leaves have beautiful wavy leaf margins with a lightish underside. Like the white and red oaks, the chinkapin grows tall and wide.

383

TREES

White Pine

Pinus strobus

Height: 50 to 80 ft. or more
Foliage: Aromatic blue-green needles
Zones: 3, 4, 5, 6
Light Requirement:

To catch a glimpse of Michigan's past, travel to Hartwick Pines State Park near Grayling. You'll see amazing stands of the state tree of Michigan, the white pine. Once a dominant tree in northern Michigan, the white pine was the major species of lumber harvested between 1850 and 1900. In northern parts of the state, large white pines are still a common sight. Their distinctive silhouette of graceful horizontal branches is displayed in a layered fashion on tall, majestic trees. The needles are grouped in bunches of 5 and are soft to touch. The aromatic blue-green needles have a slightly nodding habit, which gives the tree a weeping effect. Watch the large whorled branches rock back and forth in the wind. White pines planted in the landscape grow quite quickly, displaying a habit and form that make them valuable as a single specimen tree or as an effective windbreak.

WHEN TO PLANT
Transplant in the spring or early fall.

WHERE TO PLANT
The white pine is a fast-growing, long-lived tree that can be used in landscapes with enough open space so that it can develop properly. Plant it as a single specimen or in naturalistic groupings to form a screen. Trees spaced 25 to 30 ft. apart will form a dense privacy barrier when young and then, as the wide-spreading branches meet in the upper canopy, will develop into a small pine plantation. Plant in full sun and in well-drained soil away from exposure to salt. Wind-blown salt in the form of tiny droplets of water blown off the street can stick to needles and cause burning.

HOW TO PLANT
The planting hole should be at least 2 to 3 times as wide as the root-ball or container. For balled-and-burlapped trees, after placing in the hole, remove any twine, rope, or metal wire that is wrapped around

the rootball. This is important for the top $1/3$ of the root, where feeder roots will develop. Plant so the top of the rootball or container root system is level with the surrounding grade. In heavy or poor soils, plant the top of the root system 3 to 4 in. above the surrounding grade. Some sinking or settling of the rootball can be expected in these situations. Mulch after planting with 2 to 3 in. of organic material.

ADVICE FOR CARE

Keeping your pine trees healthy will discourage the development of pests and diseases. Some problems to look out for, however, are white pine weevil and blister rust. The larvae (worms) of the white pine weevil attack the terminal branches of white pine, causing death or distortion of the branches. The symptoms are white drops of a sticky resin on the branches. The adult form of the weevil emerges in late summer, but by this time the shoot is dead. Homeowners should prune out the infected branches by midsummer and burn them to disrupt the life cycle of this insect. White pine blister rust is a serious disease that causes a canker that will kill individual branches or whole trees if the main trunk becomes infected. The disease develops through a complex alternate host life cycle with the currant, *Ribes* sp. Currant plants carry part of the fungal life cycle on their leaves, releasing spores that infect the white pine. The spore infection can develop into serious canker problems. You should check with local county extension agents to see if white pine blister rust is a common problem in your area.

ADDITIONAL INFORMATION

The white pine is the tallest eastern North American tree.

ADDITIONAL SPECIES, CULTIVARS, OR VARIETIES

'Fastigiata' is a unique form of the white pine with limbs that angle upward instead of horizontally. This prevents ice and snow from accumulating and makes this selection less vulnerable to breakage. 'White Mountain' has a light variegated foliage with a frosted effect. It is available through small mail-order nurseries.

Yellowwood

Cladrastis kentukea synonymous with
Cladrastis lutea

Height: 30 to 50 ft.
Flowers: White
Bloom Period: Early summer
Zones: 4, 5, 6
Light Requirement:

When you come upon the American yellowwood in full bloom in the summer or view the artistry of its smooth gray bark in the depths of winter, you can truly begin to appreciate its spectacular beauty. The fall season is also a prime time for this plant when the foliage turns a clear yellow. The yellowwood is a moderate-sized shade tree, reaching a height of 30 to 50 ft. and a spread of 40 ft. or more. In early summer, fragrant white flowers hang gracefully from the branches in long chains very similar to the flowering wisteria vine. The tree's graceful stature continues through the summer with large compound leaves composed of many smaller leaves that bow or arch out and have a weeping effect. The leaves become a radiant golden yellow in the fall and contrast beautifully with the smooth, reflective gray bark that resembles the native beech. The upright spreading branches of this tree come off a short trunk creating an unforgettable winter interest scene. The bark sometimes becomes covered with gray-green lichens, which add a pleasing mosaic effect and do not harm the tree. The American yellowwood makes a fine specimen tree for properties with enough room for it to grow. Place it where you can enjoy its smooth gray bark in the winter months and ts fragrant blooms in early summer.

WHEN TO PLANT
Plant in the spring. Fall planting generally yields less success.

WHERE TO PLANT
Plant in full sun to partial shade in well-drained soil. Trees suffer in poorly drained, wet soils, so avoid low areas or spots where water accumulates for any length of time.

How to Plant

The planting hole should be at least 2 to 3 times as wide as the rootball. For balled-and-burlapped trees, after placing in the hole, remove any twine, rope, or wire that is wrapped around the rootball. This is important for the top 1/3 of the rootball, where feeder roots develop. Be sure the top of the rootball or container root system is planted level with the surrounding grade. In heavy or poor soils, plant the top of the root system 3 to 4 in. above the surrounding grade. Some sinking or settling of the rootball can be expected in these situations. Mulch after planting with 2 to 3 in. of organic material.

Advice for Care

The yellowwood, with its distinctive vase-shaped habit, tends to develop narrow crotches that are susceptible to breakage over time. This occurs when two branches fork off in opposite directions, forming a weak point as they grow into each other at their point of attachment. Eventually, a weak crotch develops, and the trunk splits. When the tree is in its formative stages, prevent narrow crotch angles from developing through selective pruning. Remove the weaker or smaller of two branches that are beginning to compete with each other. Prune in the late fall because spring pruning results in excessive sap flow or bleeding. The scientific name *Cladrastis* translates into "brittle branch," alluding to the weak wood of this tree that is highly susceptible to wind, ice, and storm damage.

Additional Information

Protect the trunk from lawn mowers, which may damage the bark. Wounds create entry points for fungus, which attacks the wood and causes rot and decay.

Additional Species, Cultivars, or Varieties

'Rosea' is a pink-flowered form that has not been adequately tested for its cold hardiness in Michigan and is difficult to find. It is available from small mail-order nurseries.

TREES

387

Woodland Flowers and Ferns

*I*N SPRINGTIME, THE WOODS OF MICHIGAN ARE A SPECTACLE OF NATURAL BEAUTY. Although the tall trees are still bare, signs of life begin to appear as strengthening sunlight filters toward the earth, warming the soil. Soon trillium, cranesbill, and columbine push up through the thick mat of leaves and open their pristine flowers toward the sun.

We share the responsibility for preserving and protecting Michigan's native plants, so admire the woodland flowers where they grow but never disturb them. When buying plants for a woodland garden, purchase only nursery-propagated plants or plants that have been rescued with the landowner's permission from sites slated for development.

Cultivating a woodland garden encourages flowers and ferns that may once have grown in the region. You will have pleasure in seeing these plants in your own backyard, a small but satisfying reflection of Michigan's biodiversity. A woodland garden doesn't have to be large. Even a tiny spot under a shade tree can be effective.

The goal of a woodland garden is not to pack it with continuous or overwhelming bloom, but to set a stage for and enjoy a naturalistic drama.

BUYING PLANTS FOR YOUR WOODLAND GARDEN

A good source for native plants is a responsible wildflower rescue operation, such as the one at Cranbrook House and Gardens Auxiliary in Bloomfield Hills in May. Otherwise, buy only plants that have been propagated in a nursery, and refuse to buy plants that were dug from the wild. The New England Wildflower Society offers a booklet listing sources of propagated plants and wildflowers. For information, write to the society at Garden in the Woods, 180 Hemenway Road, Framingham, MA 01701-2699.

Digging plants on public land is illegal, and anyone collecting plants for his or her own use on private land must have the owner's permission. In addition, the large-flowered white trillium, the Michigan lily, native orchids, and some other plants are protected by the state's Christmas Greens Act.

BEGINNING YOUR WOODLAND GARDEN

A successful woodland garden mimics the conditions the plants prefer in nature where they grow amid decaying leaves. These plants prefer a rich soil high in organic material such as leaf mold or well-rotted compost. This soil retains moisture but drains well and allows air and water to penetrate easily. Nutrients are returned to the soil as the organic material breaks down.

After setting the plants into the ground, firm the soil and water well. A mulch of pine needles, shredded leaves, or shredded bark will conserve moisture and discourage weeds from growing while the wildflowers and ferns get established. Continue to water during dry periods. In a humus-rich soil, most woodland plants will not require additional fertilizer.

Bulbs such as daffodils, snowdrops, winter aconite, and windflower are often planted in a woodland garden. These colorful flowers precede or complement the delicate pinks, blues, and whites of many native spring blooms. Add further interest to the woodland garden by creating winding paths with natural materials such as pine needles or wood chips. A curving walk draws visitors into the scene and invites them to enjoy a closer look at the flowers, many of which are small.

Most woodland plants are low growing and look most natural under tall trees. You may, however, design an island bed in a shady area or tuck a few in the shade near the house, combining them with hostas, astilbes, goat's beard, and other perennials.

Bloodroot

Sanguinaria canadensis

Height: 4 to 6 in.
Flowers: White
Bloom Period: Early to mid-spring
Zones: 3, 4, 5, 6
Light Requirement:

A spring triumph, the delicate white flowers of bloodroot push up through the brown and desiccated leaves of winter to shine against the leaf litter. The simple white flowers with a yellow center have a pure radiant beauty that is unmatched by exotic spring bulbs. Breathtaking flowers aside, bloodroot has other endearing characteristics. The protective blue-green leaves arise folded, hugging the flowering stem, and expand to form unusual lobed leaves with a wavy margin. Also, the flowers remain closed in the early morning and open in the brighter light of midday. The sap prevalent in the root and other parts of the plant is a bright orange-red, hence the common name. Break a stem while weeding and it will stain your fingers. Native Americans used bloodroot for fabric dye, face paint, and medicine. In April and early May, bloodroot is widespread in Michigan, blooming on 6-in. stems in rich deciduous woods and floodplain forests. The 8-petaled flowers are short-lived but appear over a 2-week period. Although its fragile flowers would lead you to believe otherwise, this native wildflower is an easy-going garden resident, thriving in native woodland gardens and also any shady border or bed. Bloodroot prefers moist, humus-rich soil and the spring sun and filtered light found beneath deciduous trees. It is tolerant of average garden conditions, however. In ideal locations bloodroot will spread to form colonies. The blue-gray lobed foliage may disappear in August; ample moisture prolongs its stay. Plant bloodroot where you will notice its early bloom. Just as you look forward to the first snowdrop, you will anticipate the opening of its gleaming white flowers. Try a combination of bloodroot, blue-violet windflower with the deep purple-green foliage, and dainty flowers of the Labrador violet, *Viola labradorica*. Add maidenhair fern to fill in during the summer.

WHEN TO PLANT
Plant bloodroot in early spring or September.

WHERE TO PLANT

Choose garden locations with partial shade, preferably with spring sun and summer shade. Bloodroot will tolerate considerable sun if provided with ample moisture. Moist, humus-rich soil is preferred; avoid dry sites. Use it in woodland gardens in drifts with ferns and foamflowers, but also consider bloodroot for shaded locations near doorways, combined with spring bulbs.

HOW TO PLANT

Plant bloodroot in the garden 6 to 10 in. apart. The double form will not bloom if planted too deeply. Water thoroughly. Mulch such as shredded leaves or finely shredded bark will help the plants stay moist.

ADVICE FOR CARE

Extra water during dry spells is beneficial and will help to prolong the foliage display. Special fertilization won't be needed in good garden conditions. The rhizomes can be easily divided for propagation. Do this when the foliage dies back in late summer. Dig and cut the rhizomes into pieces, and plant them 3/4 to 1 in. deep. Keep the divisions well-watered. Despite standard advice, bloodroot can be also be divided in the spring after flowering and even when in flower. Dig carefully, disturbing the roots as little as possible, cut apart, and replant. Mulch yearly with chopped leaves.

ADDITIONAL INFORMATION

The sap of bloodroot, although widely attributed with a range of medicinal properties from eliminating warts to treating cancer, is considered poisonous. Never ingest any part of the plant, and wear gloves when handling the roots. Purchase only nursery-grown plants, and never collect plants from the wild.

ADDITIONAL SPECIES, CULTIVARS, OR VARIETIES

A choice form called 'Multiplex' has fully double flowers. What the flowers lack in simplicity they make up for with beauty and staying power, lasting almost twice as long in the garden. The first double-flowered form was discovered in 1907 near Whitmore Lake. The double-flowered bloodroot is sterile.

WOODLAND WILDFLOWERS & FERNS

Foamflower

Tiarella cordifolia

Height: 6 to 12 in.
Flowers: White
Bloom Period: Mid- to late spring
Zones: 3, 4, 5, 6
Light Requirement:

Our native foamflower grows so enthusiastically it could be included in the groundcover section. The overlapping bright green, maple-shaped leaves create a patterned carpet throughout the season. Fluffy white flowers appear in mid-spring, obscuring the foliage in a foamy mass. One of the easiest woodland plants to grow, foamflower spreads by runners (stolons), creating lovely drifts. Foamflower occurs in the northern and eastern part of Michigan's Lower Peninsula, often forming extensive mats in deciduous and mixed woods and wet forests. The starry white flowers, sometimes tinged with pink, are produced on 6- to 8-in. spikes. Grow foamflower in partial shade and moist, rich woodland soil. The foamflower foliage is as appealing as its flowers. The hairy, coarsely toothed leaves are evergreen and a perfect foil for trillium, wild blue phlox, bloodroot, and other natives. The leaves are persistent and add interest to the woodland floor when the majority of spring-bloomers and bulbs have disappeared. Some plants have foliage marked or mottled with burgundy, and many new cultivars in the trade offer this feature. Use foamflower generously in flowing drifts. Combine its patterned foliage with other wildflowers for a tapestry of color and texture. The cool blue flowers of wild blue phlox are a natural complement. In shaded beds, contrast foamflower foliage with the bold texture of hostas and the fine textures of ferns or astilbe.

WHEN TO PLANT
Plant foamflower in the spring.

WHERE TO PLANT
Foamflower prefers partial to full shade and cool, moist, humus-rich soil. It is not a plant for dry soils. Too much sun is a detriment, causing the foliage to fade and scorch. Soil should be rich in organic matter for the best results. Foamflower is unsurpassed among natives for use as a groundcover in shade. Plant it in natural areas under trees and shrubs, and as a carpet for the woodland garden.

How to Plant

Plant foamflower in the garden 8 to 12 in. apart or more; plants will spread. Dig a hole and position the plant so that the soil level is the same as it was in the pot. If the plant has runners, cover them lightly with soil. Water thoroughly. Apply mulch such as shredded leaves or finely shredded bark to conserve moisture.

Advice for Care

Divide clumps in the spring to propagate or to control spread. Foamflower produces small plantlets on the ends of runners, much like a strawberry. Once these have formed roots, you can easily sever them from the mother plant to transplant in another location. In woodland conditions, no extra fertilization is necessary. Mulch annually with shredded leaves.

Additional Information

Foamflower has an innate ability to weave together plants in the shade. Try foamflower with the crested woodland iris (*Iris cristata*), fringed bleeding heart (*Dicentra eximia*) and Christmas fern for a spring combination of flowers followed by an interesting design of foliage color and texture in the summer season.

Additional Species, Cultivars, or Varieties

A wide range of selections with unique foliage variations is now on the market. Some of these may look unnatural massed in a native woodland garden, but they will bring interest to shade gardens and a mosaic of shade-loving groundcovers. *Tiarella cordifolia* 'Running Tapestry' (12 to 15 in.) has prominent wine-red centers and a vigorous spreading habit. 'Brandywine' (10 in.) has maple-like leaves with red centers and pink flowers. Many more cultivars are available from perennial nurseries. *Tiarella wherryi*, native to the Southeast, is very similar to *T. cordifolia* but does not have a spreading habit. It is marginally hardy in Zone 5. For gardeners with a collector's bent, hybrids between foamflower and coral bells, *Heuchera*, have been made and are called × *Heucherella*. They have the foliage of foamflower and the flowering habit of coral bells. × *Heucherella* 'Bridget Bloom' is an attractive pink-flowered selection. Give this plant the same growing conditions as foamflower.

WOODLAND WILDFLOWERS & FERNS

Large-Flowered White Trillium

Trillium grandiflorum

Height: 12 to 24 in.
Flowers: White
Bloom Period: Spring
Zones: 3, 4, 5, 6
Light Requirement:

White trilliums are abundant in woodlands across Michigan in May, when the elegant white flowers open as the sun warms the soil under still-leafless trees. *Trillium grandiflorum* is probably the best-known native wildflower in the state. It is easy to recognize with its 3 showy white petals, each 2 to 3 in. long, which fade to pale pink as they mature. The bloom includes 3 shorter green sepals under the petals. Some white trilliums have green markings on the petals that are caused by a type of infection. Each trillium has 3 large leaves, about 6 in. long with prominent veins. The spread of the trillium plant is 12 to 18 in., and they typically form clumps with age and vigor. In the garden, trilliums are easy to grow and long-lived once established. Their distinctive flowers add a pure, artistic beauty to a woodland setting. While trilliums remain common in undisturbed woodlands, they are disappearing in other areas of Michigan as development erodes their natural habitat. Michigan's trilliums are protected by what is commonly called the Christmas Greens Act, which prohibits people from taking plants from public or private land without permission or a bill of sale. In addition, several other native trilliums are listed as threatened or endangered. Commercial growers have tried to propagate trillium by tissue culture and from seed, but so far it has proved too time-consuming and expensive. Plants may be purchased from responsible wildflower rescue operations, which have the landowner's permission to dig plants at sites slated for development. Otherwise, refuse to buy trillium collected from the wild. Plants labeled "nursery grown" may have been dug illegally and then potted and held in a nursery for a season or two. In the woods, help educate children and others who admire trillium to look, but not to touch. The large-flowered white trillium is native to each of Michigan's 83 counties as well as much of eastern North America. Once established, it is easy to grow and makes a spectacular plant with ferns, wild geranium, and bloodroot. Two leading authorities on trillium are Frederick and Roberta Case of Saginaw. For more on this fascinating plant, refer to their book *Trilliums*, published by Timber Press. The book includes identification keys for the more than 40 species of trillium and color plates. According to Fred Case, the worst natural enemy of trillium at present is the burgeoning deer population, which has wiped out trillium in some parts of Michigan and other states. He protects those in his garden with an electric fence.

WHEN TO PLANT
Plant trilliums in fall, if available, or spring.

WHERE TO PLANT
The best spot is in the woodland garden, where the trillium will get sun before the trees leaf out. Trillium favors moist, well-drained soil that is rich in organic material. Enrich the site if necessary with leaf mold, well-rotted compost, or other amendments.

HOW TO PLANT
Plant trillium so the rhizome is about 4 to 5 in. deep, and space plants 12 to 18 in. apart, or cluster in groups of 3.

ADVICE FOR CARE
Trillium is easy to grow once established. It has no serious diseases or pests other than deer. It will self-sow.

ADDITIONAL INFORMATION
Native Americans used the root of trillium for labor pains, which accounts for one of its common names, "birthroot."

ADDITIONAL SPECIES, CULTIVARS OR VARIETIES
Trillium grandiflorum var. *roseum* has vibrant salmon-pink flowers, a much livelier shade than the pink of the aging trillium blooms. 'Polymerum' has double flowers. The odor of *Trillium erectum*, or stinking Benjamin, is sometimes compared to that of a wet dog. Despite its fragrance, stinking Benjamin has lovely flowers in a velvety maroon color, a striking contrast against its green foliage. All trilliums are protected in Michigan. It is illegal to dig them from public or private property without the landowner's written permission or a bill of sale. Some trilliums are also listed as endangered or threatened species.

Native Ferns

Adiantum pedatum, Polystichum acrostichoides, Dryopteris marginalis

Height: 10 in. to 2 ft.
Flowers: None
Zones: 3, 4, 5, 6
Light Requirement:

Ferns bring the cool, lush feeling of Michigan's north woods to your garden. Grown for their delicate texture and verdant splendor, ferns are often overlooked because they lack flowers. For all their delicacy, ferns are easy to grow given the partial shade and rich, moist soil they require. Hundreds of millions of years ago, they dominated the world's flora. Give them some territory to rule in your garden. Our native ferns are supremely at home in woodland gardens, but you should also consider ferns for the shady side of your house, for edging a walk, or for waterside plantings. A difficult and shady spot in your garden where little else grows could be the perfect place for these carefree plants. Ferns are the perfect complement to spring wildflowers and bulbs. Their curled fiddleheads are a curious spring sight. Later, when the spring ephemerals and bulbs die back, the ferns unfurl to fill in. Under deciduous trees, ferns cover the ground and look elegant alongside native wildflowers such as foamflower, trillium, and woodland phlox, but also hold their own with hostas and every resident of the shaded garden. There are a wide range of ferns, and some are better suited to garden culture than others. Most need moist, well-drained soil that is high in organic matter, but some are tolerant of wetter sites. The unique fan-shaped fronds of maidenhair fern, *Adiantum pedatum* (10 to 18 in.), native to moist, well-drained woods, are a favorite. In shady, moist conditions, maidenhair fern will spread to form large airy clumps. Christmas fern, *Polystichum acrostichoides* (18 to 20 in.), has dark green leathery evergreen fronds that were used in holiday decoration. A wonderful complement to spring wildflowers and bulbs like snowdrop, this fern is easy to grow in partial shade and moist, well-drained soil. The marginal shield fern *Dryopteris marginalis* (18 to 24 in.) is also suited to culture in a woodland garden. It has slow-growing clumps and shiny evergreen fronds.

WHEN TO PLANT

Plant in early spring or late September through early October.

WHERE TO PLANT

Soils should be moist and high in organic matter. Good drainage is critical for some; others will grow in wet situations. Grow ferns in partial shade, preferably the dappled light under deciduous trees. Ferns are also adaptable to shady beds and foundation plantings.

HOW TO PLANT

Plant ferns in the garden 1 to 3 ft. apart, depending on the mature size of the fern selected. With container-grown ferns, gently loosen the rootball if it is potbound. Also remove any excess soilless mix that may be hard to moisten. Dig a hole and position the plant so that the soil level is the same as it was in the pot. Don't bury the rhizomes; planting too deeply may kill ferns. Water well and frequently until plants have established. Mulch with chopped leaves to conserve moisture and to add organic matter to the site.

ADVICE FOR CARE

Ferns benefit from an annual mulching with chopped leaves. In rich moist soil, no fertilizer is necessary. Established plantings will need water only in drought conditions. Ferns can be divided in early spring to propagate or to control spreaders. To avoid breakage, do this before the fiddleheads begin to unfurl. Sever the rhizome cleanly with a sharp knife, and replant at the same depth. Disturb the roots as little as possible. Mulch and keep watered.

ADDITIONAL INFORMATION

During your spring garden cleanup, be careful of the emerging shoots called fiddleheads. Don't clean out beds with a metal rake or you'll risk damage. Always buy nursery-grown plants.

ADDITIONAL SPECIES, CULTIVARS, OR VARIETIES

The following ferns are large. Both need plenty of room and moisture to reach their dramatic potential. The ostrich fern, *Matteuccia struthiopteris* (3 to 5 ft.), is native to swampy, wet woods. Where moisture is abundant, it creates a bold architectural presence. It spreads, sometimes aggressively, from a running rhizome. Keep it in check by removing unwanted offshoots in the spring. Cinnamon fern, *Osmunda cinnamomea* (3 to 4 ft.), another denizen of swampy, wet areas, has attractive sienna-colored fertile fronds resembling cinnamon sticks in the center of the clump. A vase-shaped beauty, it forms slowly spreading clumps and is best for cool, moist garden sites, especially near streams or ponds. If it has wet feet, cinnamon fern will grow in full sun.

WOODLAND WILDFLOWERS & FERNS

Solomon's Seal

Polygonatum biflorum

Height: 2 to 3 ft.
Flowers: Creamy white
Bloom Period: Mid- to late spring
Zones: 3, 4, 5, 6
Light Requirement:

A glade of Solomon's seal is the epitome of refinement. It doesn't need flashy flowers to do what it does best—add a note of woodland grace to the garden. Long statuesque stems arch over, each carrying two rows of 4-in.-long leaves above pairs of creamy white tubular flowers. The almost horizontal nature of the stems and the upward angle of the leaves allow the flowers to dangle freely. After spreading by way of creeping rhizomes, a mature colony produces a forest of arching stems. The heavily veined leaves create an almost tropical texture. And unlike the spring ephemerals, it isn't here today and gone tomorrow. Solomon's seal remains in the garden all season, adding architectural interest. Later the flowers give way to round blue-black berries, and in autumn the foliage turns to a warm straw brown. Solomon's seal, *Polygonatum biflorum*, is native to the southern half of the Lower Peninsula, where it grows in woods, wet forests, and woodland edges. It has adapted itself to moist roadside borders, and you may see occasional stands emerging from the forest along roads in southeastern Michigan. Like most woodland plants, it favors partial shade and cool, moist, humus-rich soil. It will tolerate some sun if the soil is damp and fertile. The height of Solomon's seal varies from 2 to 3 ft. where conditions are ideal, providing a vertical accent in the garden above ground-hugging wildflowers. Even larger forms, up to 5 ft., are available. Use Solomon's seal in the woodland garden, but also in shady beds, near outdoor seating areas, and under trees and shrubs. As a focal point, its distinctive form and texture are unmistakable. Large colonies of this stately native are suited for use as a groundcover under deciduous trees. Combine Solomon's seal with Virginia bluebells and bloodroot, flowers that disappear by midsummer, or use it to complement lungwort, hosta, astilbe, fern, and wild oats in a mixed shady garden.

WHEN TO PLANT
Plant Solomon's seal in early spring or early fall.

Where to Plant

Choose partial shade and cool, moist soil rich in organic matter for best results. Solomon's seal will tolerate some sun with adequate moisture and will also perform well in dry shade once established. Let it form large colonies in naturalized areas, or use it as an architectural plant in shady borders. Place it by ponds, shady porches, and patios where you'll appreciate its graceful form.

How to Plant

Plant Solomon's seal in the garden 18 to 20 in. apart. Dig a hole and position the plant so that the soil level is the same as it was in the pot. Water thoroughly. Mulch will help it stay moist.

Advice for Care

Water new plantings during drought. If provided with the humus-rich soil they require, extra fertilization won't be necessary. Apply an organic mulch, preferably shredded leaves, every year. The fleshy rhizomes are easy to dig and divide. Do this in spring, when the rhizomes are still dormant, for best results. Cut the rhizome into sections with a sharp knife. Each piece should contain at least one bud, or growing point. Plant rhizomes 1 to 2 in. deep with the bud facing upward and in the direction you want the plant to grow. Keep new divisions moist until established.

Additional Information

Solomon's seal is a nice addition to flower arrangements. Also, like hosta, it makes an elegant choice for a large container in a shady site. Use Solomon's seal as an accent, rising above other ground-covering plants. Don't collect Solomon's seal from the wild. Buy it from nurseries that propagate their own.

Additional Species, Cultivars, or Varieties

The great Solomon's seal, *Polygonatum commutatum*, sometimes listed as a variety of the above species, is very impressive, growing to 5 ft. Use it where you have room to let it dominate. Variegated Solomon's seal, *P. odoratum* 'Variegatum' (18 to 24 in.), a selection of a plant native to Europe and Asia, has leaves edged in cream. It gives a lift to shaded areas.

Virginia Bluebell

Mertensia virginica

Height: 12 to 24 in.
Flowers: Blue
Bloom Period: Spring
Zones: 3, 4, 5, 6
Light Requirement:

If you've never seen Virginia bluebells before, one glimpse of these sturdy native beauties will turn you into a permanent admirer. Their sweet blue blooms nod on tall stems in the woodland or woodland garden in May. The leaves of Virginia bluebell spring up suddenly from the forest floor in early spring. They start out purplish or green, the basal leaves growing quite large. They eventually advance to about 8 in. long and 2 to 4 in. wide, forming a 1-ft. clump. Then Virginia bluebell sends up a stem bearing smaller leaves and ending with a drooping cluster of pink buds opening to porcelain blue. The bell- or trumpet-shaped corollas of the flowers, which open in April and May, are 1 in. long and crinkled, the texture of a sheet of paper that has been finely folded accordion-style and then smoothed out again. The flowers remain attractive for several weeks, taking on a more pronounced pink blush as they fade. Plant Virginia bluebell under tall deciduous trees where it will receive sun at the beginning of the season and shade after the trees leaf out. Virginia bluebell may be planted effectively in mass or used in combinations with other woodland plants such as bloodroot, bellwort, and fringed bleeding heart. Or team it with daffodils, whose clear yellow makes a beautiful contrast. Virginia bluebell goes dormant after it flowers. It is best located where other plants such as foamflower, hostas, and ferns will hide the ripening foliage and quickly fill in the empty spot left where Virginia bluebell bloomed in spring. As with many other woodland plants, Virginia bluebell requires a shady site with well-drained but moist and fertile soil—the kind it finds amid decaying leaves and other organic material in Michigan woods, where it grows naturally. With those conditions, Virginia bluebell will spread quickly, frequently self-sowing. It returns for many springs as a testament to your foresight in introducing this beautiful plant into your garden.

WHEN TO PLANT

Container-grown plants are best set out in spring, before the Virginia bluebell goes dormant. Planting later will be an act of faith on your part; the foliage and flowers will be gone by early summer.

Where to Plant

Woodland gardens, under deciduous trees, in shady borders, and along streams are ideal spots for *Mertensia*. It prefers areas that are moist (especially in the spring), but if planted in part to full shade, a well-drained spot is the best choice. The soil should be rich with organic material. If this does not describe your garden, amend the soil with well-rotted compost or leaf mold. Combine Virginia bluebell with other spring-blooming woodland plants, such as bloodroot, large-flowered white trillium, and foamflower. The soft blue color is stunning with the bold yellows of 'King Alfred' daffodils, or the more delicate cream-and-orange blooms of poet's narcissus.

How to Plant

Plant Virginia bluebell at the depth it was growing in the containers, and space the plants about 18 in. apart. A mulch of shredded leaves or shredded bark will conserve moisture and discourage weeds.

Advice for Care

Virginia bluebell needs adequate moisture. Fertilizer should not be necessary as long as the site is rich in organic material. Planting may be left undisturbed for years. The best time to divide is as the foliage dies back. Mulch with chopped leaves, which will break down, releasing nutrients and mimicking Virginia bluebell's native habitat. These hardy plants have no serious diseases or pests, although they are a particular favorite of some rabbits.

Additional Information

The large leaves of Virginia bluebell must stay on the plant after flowering, turning yellow and then brown. During this period the plant is making nutrients. If you are planting Virginia bluebell where it will be highly visible, such as along a frequently traveled path or in an often-visited perennial bed, place it near hostas and ferns, which grow quickly in mid- to late spring and will disguise the ripening bluebell foliage. *Mertensia virginica* has had a number of colorful common names used in different parts of the country, including Virginia cowslip, gentleman's breeches, old-ladies'-bonnets, and puccoon. It was also known as lungwort because botanists classified *Mertensia* as a type of *Pulmonaria* or lungwort.

Additional Species, Cultivars, or Varieties

Mertensia paniculata is also native to Michigan, occurring in the Upper Peninsula near Lake Superior. This species has smaller flowers than Virginia bluebells and is covered with fine hairs.

WOODLAND WILDFLOWERS & FERNS

Wild Blue Phlox

Phlox divaricata

Height: 12 to 15 in.
Flowers: Blue, white
Bloom Period: Mid- to late
  spring
Zones: 3, 4, 5, 6
Light Requirement:

Large drifts of wild blue phlox are a remarkable sight in mid-spring. Widespread in the rich deciduous woodlands of the Lower Peninsula, this agreeable native wildflower is easy to grow in a partly sunny or shady garden. Wild blue phlox, sometimes called wild sweet William because of its light fragrance, forms loose clusters of five-petaled 1½-in., soft blue flowers on stems that are 12 in. high and wiry. White-flowered forms are also available. The narrow dark green leaves on prostrate stems root at the leaf joints to form a spreading clump. It prefers the filtered sun of deciduous woods—sun in May before the leaves have fully expanded and shade later in the summer. Grow *Phlox divaricata* in moist soil with plenty of organic matter. Well-suited to a native woodland garden, wild blue phlox mingles naturally with trillium, foamflower, and ferns. This adaptable native is equally at home in a shade garden, wooded suburban lot, or partially shaded perennial bed. Its spreading nature makes it suitable for use as a groundcover in the woodland garden or under shrubs. Plant it in drifts for a sea of blue combined with the fine-textured fringed bleeding heart, *Dicentra eximia*. In a moist, shady area, grow wild blue phlox with European ginger, hostas, and the spotted foliage of Bethlehem sage. The muted blue flowers blend softly with all the colors of the spring garden. Wild blue phlox even makes a refined companion for a confetti-colored mix of tulips.

WHEN TO PLANT

Plant wild blue phlox in the spring or in September so roots can develop during cooler temperatures.

WHERE TO PLANT

Wild blue phlox prefers early spring sun followed by partial to full shade in summer. Moist, rich soil high in organic matter is ideal. Often seen at woodland edges, wild blue phlox will tolerate summer sun but only if moisture is plentiful. Plant this delicate native in woodland gardens, in shade plantings, and as a groundcover with other native woodland wildflowers and ferns. Use it to edge a woodland walk.

How to Plant

Plant wild blue phlox in the garden 12 to 14 in. apart. Dig holes and position the plant so that the soil level is the same as it was in the pot. Water thoroughly. Apply a mulch, such as shredded leaves or finely shredded bark, to help the plants stay moist.

Advice for Care

Water plants during drought. If provided with the humus-rich soil they require, additional fertilization won't be necessary. To control their spread or to propagate, divide plants in spring or late summer. Gently pull apart sections and plant at the same level, or dig sections from around the edge of the planting. Get a significant portion of roots on each division. Firm pieces into the soil, then water and mulch with shredded leaves or finely shredded bark.

Additional Information

Shear back plants after blooming to encourage new foliage. Wild blue phlox combines beautifully with the dangling orange-red and yellow flowers of wild columbine. In a shady corner, plant blue or white phlox as a companion to a specimen bleeding heart, *Dicentra spectabilis*. Always buy nursery-grown plants. Never collect plants from the wild.

Additional Species, Cultivars, or Varieties

Although a white-flowered form of wild blue phlox is available, it is scrawny compared to the selection called 'Fuller's White' (8 to 12 in.). This isn't as delicate as the species, but it is showy, staying covered with large white flowers for close to a month. Use it in the shade garden with pulmonarias or *Lamium*, or in a more formal display with tulips. Var. *laphamii* or 'Laphamii' (12 to 14 in.) is a deeper, almost periwinkle, blue and is more vigorous. 'Dirigo Ice' has pale lavender flowers with darker centers. Creeping phlox, *Phlox stolonifera* (6 to 8 in.), is another ground-covering woodland phlox. Native to the southeastern U.S., it is lower growing and very shade tolerant. Cultivars are available in blue, pink, white, and lavender.

Wild Columbine

Aquilegia canadensis

Height: 12 to 24 in.
Flowers: Orange-red and yellow
Bloom Period: Late spring to early summer
Zones: 4, 5, 6
Light Requirement:

Dainty and curious, the spurred flowers of columbine are among the most intriguing of the garden and appear in May and June. Attached to each petal is a long hollow spur of red-orange, sticking out backward and ending in a knob. From the side, the flower looks something like a whimsical jester's hat. The long spurs hold its sweet nectar, making wild columbine a hummingbird's delight. Its leaves, which are green with a hint of blue, are rounded, deeply lobed into three leaflets, and remain close to the ground. Slender, branching stems hold the flowers aloft. From leaf to stem to flower, the effect columbine presents is airy and sprightly. This is an easy-to-grow plant for a well-drained spot in sun to partial sun. Possibilities include the rock garden, perennial border, or the edge of a shady woodland planting. Wild columbine self-sows and will establish large stands. Flowers persist best where protected from afternoon sun. Although wild columbine is native to Michigan, many gardeners will be more familiar with columbine hybrids. These are available in different colors—white, blue, pink, red, yellow, purple—and sometimes with double flowers, which are lovely when cut and displayed in a vase.

WHEN TO PLANT

Plant container-grown wild columbine in spring or September. The small jet-black seeds may be collected and scattered while still fresh. Seed-grown plants usually flower the following year.

WHERE TO PLANT

The best soil for columbine is well drained, light, and high in organic material. It also grows in sandy or rocky spots. Before planting columbine where the soil is heavy, work in leaf mold, well-rotted compost, or aged manure. Good drainage is a critical factor to growing columbine successfully. If planted in heavy clay or where the soil stays wet in winter, the plant will suffer. Growing it in raised beds is one way to promote good drainage where the soil is not appropriate. Sun to partial sun is preferred, such as at the edge of a woodland planting. Columbine may also be added to a rock garden or perennial bed. Try combining it with coral bells, wild ginger, Solomon's seal, and woodland phlox.

How to Plant

Place container-grown columbine at the same depth in the garden as the plant was growing in its pot. Space columbines 12 in. apart. Mulch after planting to conserve moisture, keep the root zone cool, and discourage weeds from germinating.

Advice for Care

Established in well-drained soil with sufficient organic material, wild columbine should grow without additional care. Individual columbine plants are short-lived. Trying to revive them through division, a tactic that works well with many other perennials, is a waste of time with columbine. Because wild columbine self-sows so readily, however, it will keep the population increasing with new plants. Hybrid columbine should be dug up and discarded after several years when the plants lose their vigor. Leaf miners are the most serious pests affecting columbines, although wild columbine is less affected than the hybrids. The tiny larvae hatch from eggs laid on the undersides of the leaves and start chewing nonstop, leaving irregular trails or tunnels on the leaves. The leaf miners are active for about 3 weeks in spring. The damage is unattractive but does not hurt the plants. As soon as you notice leaf miner damage, cut back the foliage. The plant should then send out new, healthy leaves.

Additional Information

Native American bachelors crushed columbine seeds and used it as a perfume. It was also used as a medicine, and seeds were valued commodities and often traded.

Additional Species, Cultivars, or Varieties

A selection of wild columbine called 'Corbett' (18 in.) has light yellow flowers. The alpine columbine, *Aquilegia alpina*, has blue flowers and is suited to rock gardens as well as perennial beds. *Aquilegia caerulea* (24 in.) is Rocky Mountain columbine and grows up to 3 ft. with large flowers. There are many columbine hybrids. The 'Biedermeier' columbines are 12 in. tall with short-spurred flowers. 'McKana' hybrids have pastel flowers and grow to 30 in. Columbines in the 'Music' or 'Musik' series are 18 to 20 in. with large flowers. 'Song Bird' series columbines are vigorous, and flowers are plentiful; they were good performers at the Michigan State University Horticultural Gardens.

Wild Geranium

Geranium maculatum

Height: 12 to 20 in.
Flowers: Rose-purple, white
Bloom Period: Late spring
Zones: 5, 6
Light Requirement:

Wild geranium grows throughout much of the Lower and some of the Upper Peninsula, especially near ponds and swamps and along streams. This is a different plant from the red, salmon, or pink garden pot plants *Pelargonium*, which are commonly called geranium. (Sometimes it seems that botanists do these things with plant names to drive the rest of us crazy!) You'll find the geranium with a lowercase "g" in the chapter on annuals. *Geranium* is the hardy geranium. In addition to the wild geranium, other hardy geraniums appear in the chapters on groundcovers and perennials. The leaves of wild geranium are deeply lobed or palmate, like fingers on a hand, and both the leaves and the stems are covered with fine hairs. The slender stems end in 1-in. flowers, which have 5 wide petals that are usually rose-purple to nearly white. The petals often have veins of a darker color. "Geranium" comes from the Greek word for crane, a reference to the long beaklike capsule or seedpod. When ripe, the pointed pod bursts open, flinging its single seed. Wild geranium is sometimes called spotted cranesbill. It is an open, branching wildflower that can turn sprawling if unsupported, so it is best for the informal garden, where there will be no objections to its relaxed habits. Wild geranium is suited to borders and the edges of woodland gardens with rich and somewhat moist soil, or on top of a stone wall or ledge, where it may cascade over the edges, putting its natural floppy tendency to good effect. This is one of the few woodland wildflowers that performs well in summer sun. It spreads rapidly.

WHEN TO PLANT
Plant container-grown wild geraniums in spring or September. Sow seed in spring.

WHERE TO PLANT
Wild geranium does best in well-drained soil and sun, or partial sun to partial shade. Flowering will be reduced in deeper shade. Try combining wild geranium with other woodland plants and wild-

flowers, such as wild blue phlox (*Phlox divaricata*), Solomon's seal, Siberian bugloss, and ferns. Trillium and bloodroot are other excellent companions.

HOW TO PLANT

Place wild geraniums 10 to 12 in. apart in the garden, and take care not to plant them too deeply. After planting, apply a mulch of shredded bark or leaf mold to conserve moisture, keep the root zone cool, and discourage weeds from germinating.

ADVICE FOR CARE

Wild geranium requires no special care and is trouble-free. It may be cut back to encourage more compact growth.

ADDITIONAL INFORMATION

Geranium maculatum is found in many counties south of Traverse City and less commonly in the central and western Upper Peninsula. It self-sows.

ADDITIONAL SPECIES, CULTIVARS, OR VARIETIES

Geranium maculatum 'Album' is hard to find but very pretty. The geranium called 'Johnson's Blue' has a longer flowering season and grows to 24 in., featuring blue flowers with a darker vein. Bigroot geranium (*Geranium macrorrhizum*) has evergreen and aromatic foliage. Its vibrant pink flowers appear in late spring to early summer. At just 12 to 18 in. tall, this plant grows into a dense clump. Bigroot geranium is hardy to Zone 3. For more information on bigroot geranium, see its profile in the groundcover chapter.

RESOURCES

Public Gardens

*M*ICHIGAN HAS MANY EXCELLENT GARDENS AND ARBORETA. This list offers a selection of them. Before visiting, call to check the current hours, admission costs, and special displays.

Ann Arbor

The University of Michigan's Matthaei Botanical Gardens covers 350 acres and has an indoor conservatory with more than 1,000 plant varieties. It is a teaching and research facility that is open for public tours. Outdoor attractions include the Gateway Garden of New World plants, walking trails, a woodland wildflower garden and prairie, rose and perennial gardens, an herb knot garden, a shade garden, and a reconstructed wetland. Matthaei Botanical Gardens also sponsors the Ann Arbor Flower and Garden Show every spring. 1-313-998-7060.

Nichols Arboretum, near the University of Michigan's central campus, was founded in 1907. Landscape architect O. C. Simonds incorporated many native plants in the original design for the rolling terrain. Since then, the Arb, as it is known, has grown to 123 acres. It is a favorite spot for students and area residents as well as a teaching laboratory. Recent work has restored the original peony garden and a prairie. 1-313-763-4033.

Battle Creek

The Leila Arboretum is a 72-acre park and botanical garden planted 75 years ago. It features many mature trees and a large planting of conifers. The arboretum also maintains the W. K. Kellogg Community Garden in downtown Battle Creek with seasonal displays. 1-616-969-0270.

Berrien Springs

The 1,600-acre campus of Andrews University is considered an arboretum. A brochure describing a self-guided walking tour is available. More than 500 trees are labeled. 1-616-471-3344.

Bloomfield Hills

The 40 acres around Cranbrook House include spring bulb displays, perennials, roses, a bog garden, an herb garden, wildflowers,

408

RESOURCES

Public Gardens

an Oriental garden, statues, and reflecting pools. The home was built in 1908 for George and Ellen Booth, who founded Cranbrook. The Cranbrook House and Gardens Auxiliary maintains the grounds. 1-810-645-3149.

BURTON

The For-Mar Nature Preserve and Arboretum, part of the Genesee County parks system, is located on 380 acres and includes a 120-acre arboretum. A visitors' center, which opened in 1996, is named for Forbes and Martha Merkley, who gave the land for the preserve in 1968. There are collections of conifers and of flowering trees including crab apples, lilacs, viburnums, and North American native species. 1-810-789-8568.

DEARBORN

Arjay Miller Michigan Arboretum of the Ford Motor Company is on 14 acres next to the automaker's world headquarters. Special attractions include more than 1,000 trees and shrubs. 1-313-322-3000.

The 70-acre Henry Ford-Fair Lane estate, built by Henry and Clara Ford, is considered a significant example of Jens Jensen's landscape work in the prairie style. Fair Lane, now part of the University of Michigan's Dearborn campus, includes gardens and renovated vistas, a greenhouse, and Clara Ford's potting shed. 1-313-593-5590.

DETROIT

The Anna Scripps Whitcomb Conservatory and Gardens are operated by the City of Detroit on Belle Isle. The Victorian-style conservatory includes a palm house, orchids, and ferns; there are seasonal displays such as the annual poinsettia show. The conservatory is nearly 100 years old, and the surrounding grounds are popular sites for weddings. 1-313-852-4065.

The Detroit Garden Center in the historic Moross House features a garden designed by the Garden Club of Michigan. Volunteers maintain it. The Garden Center also offers a library of gardening and horticulture books and classes. 1-313-259-6363.

409

RESOURCES

Public Gardens

EAST LANSING

Michigan State University has several sites of particular interest to gardeners:

The W. J. Beal Botanical Garden is among the oldest continuously operated botanical gardens in the United States. The Beal Garden was established in 1873. Its displays include woody plants, annuals, perennials, and a special section on Michigan's threatened and endangered plants. 1-517-355-9582.

The Horticultural Demonstration Gardens, which opened in 1993, cover 7 1/2 acres of perennial gardens, rose beds, and an extensive display of annuals. It is a test site for the All-America Selections. 1-517-355-0348.

Part of the Horticultural Demonstration Gardens is the Michigan 4-H Children's Garden, designed with suggestions from youngsters around the state. Visitors can touch, pinch, and smell plants as they wish. Features include an Alice in Wonderland maze, an alphabet of plants, and a science discovery garden. 1-517-355-0348.

The Clarence E. Lewis Landscape Arboretum is a 6-acre teaching laboratory and demonstration site for landscape plants, shrubs, groundcovers, and perennials. A popular attraction with visitors is the Mawby Fruit Collection of fruit plants grown in Michigan. 1-517-355-0348.

FLINT

Guided tours of Applewood, built for Charles Stewart Mott in 1916 as a gentleman's farm, are available to educational groups and garden clubs; tours must be arranged in advance. The landscape of the estate's 18 acres has been renovated during the last two decades. It features a formal perennial garden and collections of lilacs, rhododendrons, azaleas, daylilies, hostas, wildflowers, roses, and annuals. The apple orchard includes 25 heritage varieties that Mott planted. 1-810-233-3031.

GRAND RAPIDS

The Frederik Meijer Gardens, which opened in 1995, includes more than 70 acres and a 15,000-sq.-ft. conservatory. James van Sweden designed an area in the front in the style of the New

Public Gardens

American garden. There are also an English perennial and bulb garden, a sculpture collection, a woodland garden, a nature trail, a boardwalk, and a tram. 1-616-957-1580.

GROSSE POINTE SHORES
The Edsel and Eleanor Ford House, completed in 1929, is surrounded by 63 acres, most of which is now open for public viewing. The Fords hired Jens Jensen, the Chicago landscape architect who specialized in naturalistic designs and native plants, to plan the grounds. They include a rose garden and a reflecting pool. The Ford House also offers programs related to its grounds, such as spring wildflower tours. 1-313-884-4222.

HILLSDALE
The 40-acre Slayton Arboretum at Hillsdale College has more than 1,100 plant species as well as wildlife, walking paths, and gazebos. 1-517-437-7341.

LANSING
Frances Park is part of the Lansing parks system, a 58-acre facility with more than 150 varieties of roses and an overlook view of the Grand River, themed displays of annual plants, a woodland garden, rhododendrons, azaleas, and hostas. 1-517-483-4277.

The City of Lansing has renovated Cooley Gardens in downtown Lansing, a 1.4-acre perennial garden just a few blocks from Michigan's Capitol. 1-517-483-4277.

MIDLAND
Dow Gardens is the former estate of Herbert Dow, who founded Dow Chemical Company. The 100-acre facility includes displays of bulbs, annuals, perennials, wildflowers, roses, and crab apples. A collection of woody plants and a sensory trail are added features. Dow Gardens is a display garden for the All-America Selections. 1-800-362-4874.

NILES
Fernwood Botanic Garden's fern conservatory contains 100 species. This conservatory is just one feature of these 105 acres,

Public Gardens

which include more than 3,000 types of plants. Fernwood also has a nature center, 3 miles of wilderness trails, and a 6-acre tall grass prairie. 1-616-695-6491.

ROCHESTER

Landscaping on the 25 acres surrounding Meadow Brook Hall, an estate completed in 1929 for Matilda Dodge Wilson and Alfred Wilson, includes a cutting garden, a rose garden, a children's garden, and many ornamental displays. Meadow Brook Hall is on the campus of Oakland University. 1-810-370-3140.

ROYAL OAK

In its early days, the 125-acre Detroit Zoological Institute was known for its magnificent landscapes and plantings. Recent renovations are restoring these noteworthy vistas. In addition, volunteers plant and maintain "adopt-a-gardens" on the property. 1-810-398-0900.

SAGINAW

Roses and perennials are the star attractions at the Lucille E. Andersen Memorial Garden, which is administered by the City of Saginaw's central parks system. A Marshall Fredericks statue, *The Flying Geese*, is also featured. The garden is adjacent to the Andersen Enrichment Center, a conference and event facility. 1-517-759-1362.

TIPTON

Hidden Lake Gardens, operated by Michigan State University, is a nearly 800-acre preserve with both natural and landscaped areas. It includes the Harper Collection of dwarf and rare conifers as well as a large selection of hostas, wildflowers, ornamental trees and shrubs, an All-America display garden, a conservatory, and 6 miles of paved drive through the property. 1-517-431-2060.

WHITE CLOUD

Loda Lake Wildflower Sanctuary, part of the Manistee National Forest, is 6.8 miles north of White Cloud. There is a guide to identifying wildflowers along the 1 1/2-mile hiking trail. A picnic area is also available. 1-616-745-4631.

Mail-order Sources

*M*ANY SEEDS AND PLANTS ARE AVAILABLE AT LOCAL GARDEN CENTERS. Others may be purchased through the mail from specialty nurseries, some of which appear below. Browsing through catalogs is an essential winter gardening activity. *Gardening By Mail*, a reference book by Barbara Barton (Houghton Mifflin Co., 1994), includes names and addresses of additional sources.

Arborvillage Farm Nursery
P.O. Box 227
Holt, MO 64048
Trees, shrubs

Arrowhead Alpines
P.O. Box 857
Fowlerville, MI 48836
Trees, shrubs, perennials

Badger Hill Farms
1178 62nd St.
Fennville, MI 49408
Trees, shrubs

B & D Lilies
P.O. Box 2007
Port Townsend, WA 98368
Lilies

Kurt Bluemel, Inc.
2740 Greene Lane
Baldwin, MD 21013-9523
Ornamental grasses, perennials

Bluestone Perennials
7211 Middle Ridge Rd.
Madison, OH 44057-3096
Perennials, shrubs

W. Atlee Burpee & Co.
Warminster, PA 18974
Seeds, flowering plants

Carroll Gardens
444 E. Main St.
Westminster, MD 21157
Perennials, roses, shrubs, trees

Chiltern Seeds
Bortree Stile
Ulverston
Cumbria LA12 7PB, England
Seeds

The Daffodil Mart
7463 Heath Trail
Gloucester, VA 23601
Bulbs

Eastern Plant Specialties
P.O. Box 226
Georgetown, ME 04548
Trees, shrubs, perennials

Ferry-Morse Seeds
P.O. Box 488
Fulton, KY 42041-0488
Seeds, plants, bulbs

Forestfarm
990 Tetherow Rd.
Williams, OR 97544-9599
Trees, shrubs, perennials

Mail-order Sources

Jackson & Perkins
1 Rose Lane
Medford, OR 97501-0702
Roses

Klehm Nursery
4210 N. Duncan Rd.
Champaign, IL 61821
Perennials, shrubs

McClure & Zimmerman
108 W. Winnebago St.
P.O. Box 368
Friesland, WI 53935
Bulbs

Milaeger's Gardens
4838 Douglas Ave.
Racine, WI 53402-2498
Perennials

Oikos Tree Crops
P.O. Box 19425
Kalamazoo, MI 49019-0425
Trees, shrubs

Old House Gardens
536 Third St.
Ann Arbor, MI 48103
Heirloom bulbs

George W. Park Seed Co.
Greenwood, SC 29647-0001
Seeds, bulbs, plants

Prairie Nursery
P.O. Box 306
Westfield, WI 53964
Native wildflowers, native grasses

John Scheepers Inc.
23 Tulip Dr.
Bantam, CT 06750
Bulbs

Seed Savers Exchange
3076 North Winn Rd.
Decorah, IA 52101
Vegetable and flower seeds

Seeds of Change
P.O. Box 15700
Santa Fe, NM 87506-5700
Organically grown vegetable and flower seeds

Select Seeds
180 Stickney Rd.
Union, CT 06076-4617
Heirloom flower seeds

Thompson & Morgan Inc.
P.O. Box 1308
Jackson, NJ 08527-0308
Seeds, plants, bulbs

Wayside Gardens
Hodges, SC 29695-0001
Perennials, shrubs, roses, bulbs

We-Du Nurseries
Route 5, Box 724
Marion, NC 28752-9338
Perennials, wildflowers

White Flower Farm
P.O. Box 50
Litchfield, CT 06759-0050
Perennials, shrubs, roses, bulbs

RESOURCES

Bibliography

Armitage, Allan. *Herbaceous Perennial Plants*. Varsity Press, 1989.

Art, Henry W. *A Garden of Wildflowers: 101 Native Species and How to Grow Them*. Garden Way Publishing, 1986.

Bailey, Liberty Hyde. *The Standard Cyclopedia of Horticulture* (three volumes). Macmillan Publishing Co., 1963.

Ball, Jeff and Liz Ball. *Rodale's Flower Garden Problem Solver*. Rodale Press, 1990.

Barnes, Burton and Warren H. Wagner Jr. *Michigan Trees*. University of Michigan Press, 1992.

Bales, Suzanne Frutig. *Roses*. Burpee American Gardening Series. Prentice-Hall, 1994.

Bennett, Jennifer and Turid Forsyth. *The Harrowsmith Annual Garden*. Camden House, 1990.

Bird, Richard. *Growing and Propagating Showy Native Woody Plants*. University of North Carolina Press, 1992.

Brennan, Georgeanne and Mimi Luebbermann. *Beautiful Bulbs*. Chronicle Books, 1993.

Brooklyn Botanic Garden handbooks: *Butterfly Gardens*, 1995; *Natural Insect Control: The Ecological Gardener's Guide to Foiling Pests*, 1994; *Perennials*, 1991; *Shrubs: The New Glamour Plants*, 1994; *Trees: A Gardener's Guide*, 1992. For information on these and other titles, call 1-718-622-4433 ext. 274.

Brown, George E. *The Pruning of Trees, Shrubs and Conifers*. Faber and Faber, Ltd., 1972.

Bryan, John E. *John E. Bryan on Bulbs*. Burpee Expert Gardener Series. Macmillan, Inc. 1994.

Burrell, C. Colston and Elizabeth Stell. *Landscaping with Perennials*. Rodale Press, 1995.

Callaway, Dorothy. *The World of Magnolias*. Timber Press, 1994.

Clausen, Ruth Rodgers and Nicolas Ekstrom. *Perennials for American Gardens*. Random House, 1989.

Coffey, Timothy. *The History and Folklore of North American Wildflowers*. Houghton Mifflin Co., 1993.

Crockett, James Underwood. *Annuals*. Time-Life Books, 1979.

Crockett, James Underwood. *Crockett's Flower Garden*. Little, Brown and Co., 1981.

RESOURCES

Bibliography

Crockett, James Underwood. *Crockett's Victory Garden*. Little, Brown and Co., 1977.

Darke, Rick. *Ornamental Grasses at Longwood Gardens*. Longwood Gardens, 1993.

Dirr, Michael. *Manual of Woody Landscape Plants*. Stipes Publishing Co., 1990.

Everett, T.H., editor. *New Illustrated Enclyopedia of Gardening*. Greystone Press, 1960.

Faust, Joan Lee. *The New York Times Book of Annuals and Perennials*. Times Books, 1980.

Ferreniea, Viki. *Gardening with Wildflowers*. Random House, 1993.

Fiala, Fr. John. *The Flowering Crabapples*. Timber Press, 1994.

Frankel, Edward. *Ferns: A Natural History*. The Stephen Greene Press, 1981.

Frederick Jr., William H. *The Exuberant Garden and the Controlling Hand: Plant Combinations for North American Gardens*. Little, Brown and Co., 1992.

Garden Club of America. *Plants that Merit Attention, Volume I—Trees* (1984) and *Volume II—Shrubs* (1996). Timber Press.

Greenlee, John. *The Encyclopedia of Ornamental Grasses*. Michael Friedman Publishing Group, 1992.

Griffiths, Mark. *Index of Garden Plants: The New Royal Horticulture Society Dictionary*. Timber Press, 1994.

Harper, Pamela. *Designing with Perennials*. Macmillan Publishing Co., 1991.

Harper, Pamela and Frederick McGourty. *Perennials: How to Select, Grow and Enjoy*. HP Books, 1985.

Heath, Brent and Becky Heath. *Daffodils for American Gardens*. Elliott and Clark, 1995.

Hensel, Margaret. *English Cottage Gardening for American Gardeners*. W.W. Norton and Co., 1992.

Hill, Lewis and Nancy Hill. *Bulbs: Four Seasons of Beautiful Blooms*. Storey Communications, 1994.

Hole, Lois. *Lois Hole's Bedding Plant Favorites*. Lone Pine Publishing, 1994.

Hollingsworth, Buckner. *Her Garden Was Her Delight*. Macmillan Co., 1962.

Jelitto, Leo and Wilhelm Schacht. *Hardy Herbaceous Perennials*. Timber Press, 1990.

RESOURCES

Bibliography

Jimmerman, Douglas, editor. *Better Homes and Gardens Bulbs for All Seasons.* Meredith Corp., 1994.

Knox, Gerald, editor. *Better Homes and Gardens Step-By-Step Successful Gardening.* Meredith Corp., 1987.

Kowalchik, Claire and Willim Hylton, editors. *Rodale's Illustrated Encyclopedia of Herbs.* Rodale Press, 1987.

Lacy, Allen. *Gardening with Groundcovers and Vines.* HarperCollins Publishers Inc., 1993.

Loewer, Peter. *The Annual Garden: Flowers, Foliage, Fruits and Grasses for One Summer Season.* Rodale Press, 1988.

Lyon-Jeness, C. *They Hoed the Corn.* Michigan History Magazine, July-August, 1994.

MacKenzie, David. *Complete Manual of Perennial Ground Covers.* Prentice Hall, 1989.

Mathew, Brian and Philip Swindells. *The Complete Book of Bulbs.* Reader's Digest Association. Reed International Books Ltd., 1994.

Mathew, Brian. *The Year-Round Bulb Garden.* Souvenir Press, 1986.

Osborne, Robert. *Hardy Roses.* Garden Way Publishing, 1991.

Ottesen, Carole. *Ornamental Grasses.* McGraw Hill Publishing Co., 1989.

Phillips, Ellen and C. Colston Burrell. *Rodale's Illustrated Encyclopedia of Perennials.* Rodale Press, 1993.

Reilly, Ann. *Parks's Success with Seeds.* Geo. W. Park Seed Co., Inc., 1978.

Roth, Susan. *Better Homes and Gardens Complete Guide to Flower Gardening.* Meredith Books, 1995.

Rutz, Miriam. *Genevieve Gillette: From Thrift Garden to National Parks.* From a book to be published by Sagapress.

Rutz, Miriam. *Public Gardens in Michigan.* 1996.

Safe and Easy Lawn Care. Taylor's Weekend Gardening Guides. Houghton Mifflin Co., 1997.

Selecting and Planting Trees. Gary Watson, editor. The Morton Arboretum, Lisle, Ill.

Smith, Helen V. *Michigan Wildflowers.* Cranbrook Institute of Science, 1979.

Sommers, L. K. *Innocent Recreations.* Michigan History Magazine, July-August, 1994.

Sperka, Marie. *Growing Wildflowers.* Scribner's, 1973.

RESOURCES

Bibliography

Spongberg, Stephen A. *A Reunion of Trees*. Harvard University Press, 1990.

Springer, Lauren. *The Undaunted Gardener*. Fulcrum Publishing, 1994.

Sternberg, Guy and Jim Wilson. *Landscaping with Native Trees*. Chapters Publishing, Ltd., 1995.

Still, Steven. *Manual of Herbaceous Ornamental Plants*. Stipes Publishing Co., 1994.

Stuart, David and James Sutherland. *Plants from the Past*. Penguin Books, 1989.

Sunset Lawns and Ground Covers. Sunset Publishing Co., 1994.

Taylor's Guide to Annuals. Houghton Mifflin Co., 1986.

Taylor's Guide to Perennials. Houghton Mifflin Co., 1986.

Taylor's Guide to Roses. Houghton Mifflin Co., 1995.

Taylor's Guide to Shade Gardening. Houghton Mifflin Co., 1994.

Taylor's Master Guide to Gardening. Houghton Mifflin Co., 1994.

The Hillier Manual of Trees and Shrubs. David and Charles Publishers, 1993.

Thomas, Graham Stuart. *Ornamental Shrubs, Climbers and Bamboos*. Timber Press, 1992.

Thomas, Graham Stuart. *Perennial Garden Plants, or, The Modern Florilegium*, third edition. J.M. Dent, Ltd., 1990.

Tripp, Kim and J.C. Raulston. *The Year in Trees*. Timber Press, 1995.

Voss, Edward G. *Botanical Beachcombers and Explorers*. University of Michigan Herbarium, 1978.

Voss, Edward G. *Michigan Flora* (in three parts). Cranbrook Institute of Science and University of Michigan Herbarium; 1972, 1985, 1996.

Wilson, Jim. *Landscaping with Container Plants*. Houghton Mifflin Co., 1990.

Wilson, Jim. *Landscaping with Wildflowers*. Houghton Mifflin Co., 1992.

Winterrowd, Wayne. *Annuals for Connoisseurs*. Prentice Hall, 1992.

Wister, Gertrude S. *Hardy Garden Bulbs*. E.P. Dutton and Co., Inc., 1964.

Woods, Christopher. *Encyclopedia of Perennials*. Facts on File, 1992.

Wyman, Donald. *Ground Cover Plants*. Macmillan Co., 1966.

Wyman, Donald. *Wyman's Gardening Encyclopedia*. Macmillan Publishing Co., 1986.

Yeo, Peter. *Hardy Geraniums*. Timber Press, 1985.

INDEX

Index

Index

Index

ABOUT THE AUTHORS

TIMOTHY M. BOLAND is the nursery manager/ plant propagator at Beaumont Nursery for the Grounds Maintenance Department at Michigan State University. He was born in Grand Rapids and has a bachelor's degree in horticulture and a master's degree in botany from MSU. He has worked at some of the finest public gardens, including a year at the Royal Horticultural Society's garden, Wisley in England. A plantsman with an interest in plant conservation and Michigan native plants, Tim and his wife, horticulturist Laura E. Coit, garden with their two children in Lansing.

LAURA E. COIT is a horticulturist, perennial garden designer and illustrator. She is the former horticulturist at the MSU Horticultural Demonstration Gardens, where she designed, planted and maintained the DeLapa Perennial Garden. Coit worked as a gardener at the Royal Horticultural Society's garden, Wisley in England. Coit has a degree in horticulture from Cornell University and was a Fellow in the Longwood Graduate Program in Public Horticultural Administration. She lives in Lansing with her husband, Timothy M. Boland, and their two children.

MARTY HAIR is the garden writer for the *Detroit Free Press*, where she has been a news and feature reporter and editor for 19 years. Before that, she was a writer for the Associated Press. She has a bachelor's degree in English and master's degree in journalism from the University of Michigan. She has lived in Michigan and has been interested in plants and gardening for most of her life. She earned the advanced certification from the Michigan Master Gardener program. She lives in the Detroit area with her husband, Darrell Amlin, and their daughter.

MICHIGAN GARDENING
ONLINE

www.coolspringspress.com

Now available, exclusively for Michigan gardeners!

Wanting to serve the needs of today's gardeners, Cool Springs Press
has created one of the most advanced home pages in America
devoted exclusively to gardening. It offers expert advice on how to
make Michigan gardening more enjoyable and the results more
beautiful.

Consult the Cool Springs Press home page for monthly information
from the *Michigan Gardener's Guide.* Keep up to date with
Michigan gardening on the internet.

– LOCALIZED GARDENING CALENDAR FOR THE MONTH

– SELECTED "PLANT OF THE MONTH"

– DISCUSSION ROOM FOR CONVERSATION AND ADVICE, JUST FOR
  MICHIGAN GARDENERS

www.coolspringspress.com

424